ABOUT THE AUTHOR

Simon Klapish was born in Manchester, U.K. in 1957, and came to Australia after university (Applied Biology – Plymouth Polytechnic) in 1979 on a 12-month working visa, and then emigrated to Melbourne in 1982. He has worked in the telecommunications industry in business development and marketing roles (12 years), and after completing a Master of Business – Marketing degree, at RMIT, he joined the power industry just before the Victorian privatization era, working in marketing, business development, and corporate social responsibility roles over 23 years. He also spent 12 years in the Australian Army Reserve (Royal Australian Infantry), retiring as a captain in 1993. Apart from consultancy work on renewable energy projects, he is semi-retired, lives on the Sunshine Coast in Queensland, is married with a daughter, and loves to travel, having 'ticked off' 86 countries so far.

He is the author of seven novels, of which *'Ripples of Revenge'* just missed making it onto the 'long short list' of 24 titles in the Angus and Robertson Fiction Prize in 1998, but which nevertheless spurred it on to eventual publication.

ALSO BY SIMON KLAPISH

Adult Fiction

Ripples of Revenge

Chasing Margaret

Rubbish (Co-authored with Chris Barfoot)

Removal (A God-Dilemma Chronicle)

Revelation (A God-Dilemma Chronicle)

Children/young adult fiction

Dancing for an Angel

Scarlet's Secret

REVELATION

(A God-Dilemma Chronicle)

SIMON KLAPISH

Published in Australia in 2024 by Community Connect CSR Pty Ltd
ABN: 45 918 859 880
Tewantin, Queensland, Australia

First published in Australia 2024
Copyright © Simon Klapish, 2024

Cover design by: Snir Alayof
Typesetting by: Community Connect CSR Pty Ltd

The right of Simon Klapish to be identified as the Author of the Work has been asserted by him in accordance with the Copyright, Designs and Patents Act 1988.

This book is a work of fiction. Names, characters, places, organisations, and incidents either are products of the author's imagination or are used fictitiously. Any resemblance to actual events, organisations, or persons living or dead, is entirely coincidental.

All rights reserved. No part of this publication may be reproduced, stored in a retrieval system, or transmitted, in any form or by any means without the prior written permission of the author (enquiries should be made to the author at www.SimonKlapishAuthor.com), nor be otherwise circulated in any form of binding or cover other than that in which it is published and without a similar condition being imposed on the subsequent purchaser.

National Library of Australia Cataloguing-in Publication entry: Klapish, Simon, 1957 - Revelation
Paperback edition - ISBN: 978 1 7637477 6 0
eBook edition – ISBN: 978 1 7637477 7 7
Typeset in Calibri 10Pt/12Pt

Foreword

When I created Removal, it was the geopolitical intricacies that interested me. There was no hidden agenda in choosing one religion over another, only how the storyline could best be delivered. After reviews from my inner team of critical readers, they had concerns. Not about the story itself, or how any religious group was portrayed, but some felt that political correctness, and radical fringe elements might take exception. One reader critic, a very devout Muslim, and a beautiful, calm and intelligent man, said, "This isn't an anti-Muslim book in any way". I agreed. But he then said, "Nevertheless this could get you into trouble from those that object just to the premise, will never read the book, but still take offence." He wasn't suggesting I'd be treated like Salman Rushdie – these books are purely fictional with no agenda other than entertainment and stimulation for my readers.

Consequently, and years later, but pre-publication of Removal, I considered its opposite proposition, which is why 'Revelation' was written. Removal and Revelation are separate works, can be read in any order, or just the one that interests readers the most. I defy anyone enjoying either book, not to immediately start to read its alternative. So, I have released Removal and Revelation together, each as 'A God-Dilemma Chronicle'.

I have a genuine respect for anyone that has the faith to follow any religion or belief system, especially if they do not attempt to convert others. If any reader is upset by any elements of these stories, I apologise. No religion is intended to be denigrated, but characters might state their views, in the same way that people do in daily discussions, and due to world events. I would like to think that elements of these stories stimulate thoughtful debate, as well as a newfound respect for those of different beliefs. I wish everyone a peaceful future.

PRINCIPAL CHARACTERS

UK

The Ahmed family, Riaz and Mina, and their children, Charlie, Michael and Salina.
Mustafa Harry, an elderly neighbour of the Ahmeds.
Jeffery Buliya, newly appointed Imam of Manchester
Freddy, maintenance engineer at a London hospital
Phillip Abuja, Head of maintenance, Crumpsall Hospital, Manchester
Sitting Members of Parliament of Muslim faith in the British Government:
Tasmeena Hikaka, Mark Catchpole, Peter Sati, Jonas Mehmood, Julian Karra, Yasmin Hussein, and Naz Javed
Yusuf Bertrand, French Ambassador to the UK

USA

Paul Habbib, new President of the USA, previous Chief of Staff to President Andrew Kendall
Badiah Malaki, journalist/reporter within the White House
Imran Malouf, U.S. Secretary of State
Amelia Sanchez, White House media advisor, and Population Liaison officer
George Saba, Chief of Staff
Major John Cummins, U.S. Marine Corps (a Muslim convert)

INDIA, PAKISTAN

Lieutenant General Sabal Kalil, highest ranking Indian General after Revelation Day, then President of India
Colonel Ashraf Kumar, Indian Army, Chief of Staff to General Kalil
Ghulam Asif, Prime Minister of Pakistan
Admiral Muhammed Pereira, Commander of the Pakindesh fleet

GREATER SOMALIA

Abdellahi Artan Dhulbahante - President of Greater Somalia
Artan Marehan - Chief Minister to the President

REVELATION

CHARLIE

The wind had howled through the night, adding to the intermittent heavy rain, shaking windows, and threatening to damage roof tiles. The water poured from drainpipes and flooded culverts, and with no moon visible there was an added intensity to the darkness. Charlie had huddled beneath the sheets and quilt, listening to the anger of the weather. At one point he'd gone to the window to look at the storm, and there wasn't a light to be seen in the street of semi-detached 1950's houses. No cars braving the weather either. In the early hours of the morning the tempest fizzled out, but by then he was fast asleep.

'God, it feels so early; what's the time?' Looking across at the bedside clock, 'Bugger! Quarter to six!' Why's it so quiet? It feels like a new snowfall day, no sound of cars or birds. Not likely to have been snowing though, not in April. May as well get dressed, now that I'm wide-awake.' He dressed quickly, peeked out of the window, saw no obvious storm damage, and no moving cars about, often the way this early, and he made his way quietly downstairs for breakfast.

Halfway through a bowl of Coco-Pops, the silence hit him again. The Donaldson's dog wasn't barking. That's odd; nice though. Stupid dog usually barked every morning, until it had run around the garden like a mad thing when it was let out around six. He opened the back door and looked out. No noises at all, not traffic, dogs or people. Not that it was a noisy place, but it felt wrong. He walked across the lawn to the side fence and looked over. No dog and no kitchen lights on either. Strange. Billy Donaldson was an early riser, and they usually walked to school together, and Billy was often the first up next door to let their crazy dog out.

'Something's up'. He went out to the back garden, hopped over the fence, and went to the Donaldson's back door, always unlocked, and walked in. 'Billy, it's Charlie. You up yet?'

No answer. No breakfast stuff on the table. Mr Donaldson's jacket on the back of his chair. No greeting from the Jack Russell, Wolverine, either. He went to the hallway, listened for movement and when there wasn't a sound to be heard, he tiptoed quietly upstairs, so as not to wake the parents, nor Billy's sister Janice. Should I peek into her room, and see if she's asleep too? Could just look at her adorable face. Better not, I suppose. I've heard her call me Billy's Paki mate. Accept it, Charlie, she's two years older and not interested in you.

Pushing his friend's door open, and seeing him asleep, he calls out, 'You lazy bugger, you're going to be late for school if you don't make a move, Billy.'

No answer or movement. Talk about dead to the world. Time to give his friend a fright, so he jumped on him, 'What time d'yer call this, eh?' he said as he ruffled Billy's head, but then immediately stopped and backed away, standing up quickly, the colour draining from his face. 'Billy? Holy shit! Billy! Wake up!'

He ran to the bedroom next door and pushed the door open without knocking, 'Mrs Donaldson, something's up with Bil...' He stopped dead. There was no response from the Donaldsons. They just lay there in bed, still, pale, and...

'Janice!' he screamed out as he ran to the next room and through the door, already dreading what he'd find, then seeing it, her, a face he loved as much as his other wannabe girlfriend, her blond hair on the pillow, her face immobile. He slowly approached her and put out his hand and placed it on her cheek. She was cold. The whole family was dead; he knew it. Tears began to stream down his cheeks. He ran to the phone and dialled 999 for emergency. It just rang and rang, unanswered. He dropped the phone and ran home, rousing his parents and siblings, screaming about the Donaldson's being dead in their beds.

His father, Riaz, quickly threw some clothes on, told his wife to call 999, and went next door with Charlie, who led him upstairs, but slowly, the tears now dried on his face. Riaz went to the parent's room, and Charlie went again to look forlornly at Janice Donaldson. Within a few minutes, Riaz confirmed that they were all dead, taken quietly in their beds. He came back down the stairs towards the kitchen, but Charlie was standing at the bottom of the steps and pointed to the lounge room. Riaz looked in and there was the little dog, also dead. He and Charlie returned home.

Charlie's mum, Mina, was shaking her head and shaking. 'There's no answer from 999, or from the local police station either. What's going on, Riaz?'

His father didn't answer but went to his mobile phone and called his office number. Even though still early there was always someone either monitoring the main line, at the security desk or patched through to the customer service person on call. The call went unanswered and after more than a minute, Riaz ended it.

'Charlie? We need to check the neighbours. Something's very wrong. I think maybe the Donaldson's have been poisoned by a gas leak. Come with me. Mina? Stay here with Michael and Salina. We'll be back soon.' Riaz left with Charlie following behind, his wife and other children looking worried.

They walked past the Donaldson's house and into the gate of the next neighbour, Mr Freeman, a widower, and keen gardener, about 70 years of age. Riaz knocked on the front door but didn't wait long and walked around to the back, hoping that the rear door would be unlocked. It was and they walked into the kitchen and called his name. Walking swiftly through the house to the stairs and almost jogging up to the first floor, Riaz was already certain of what he'd find, albeit inconceivable. Mr Freeman was dead too. His face was cold, and his eyes closed. Riaz sniffed the air. There was no smell of gas, but it might have dissipated already, although that seemed odd. 'Come on, Charlie, next house.'

'Dad, what's going on?'

'I don't know yet, but I think it's a major gas leak or something. Are you OK with this?'

'I think so, Dad.'

'Good lad. Let's go.' At the next house, they repeated the performance but had to smash the back-door windowpane to unlock the door and get inside. The Phillips family, parents and 3 girls under ten were in the same state, cold, calm, and gone.

Charlie was never going to forget the next hour and a half. He saw over a hundred bodies, as well as their dogs and cats.
The Riaz family were the only ones left alive in the entire street.

SAUDI ARABIA

The khamsin came out of the desert from an unusual direction, the sand on the dunes playing and whirling in clockwise spirals, hundreds of them atop the features. Ali watched, screwing his face up and narrowing his eyes to keep the sand out of them, unconsciously lifting a hand to wrap his keffiyeh tighter. The noise intensified. There was an odd sound to it, screech like. He turned and ran down the dune slope to the camels tethered below him and checked their leg hobbles, then assisted them to lie down, their heads facing into the centre of the group of eight. He checked the ties on the tents again and went inside. His father was frail but awake. His mother slept fitfully, making the odd sound. All the younger children were asleep around her. Wind was nothing new. It blew all night, but then abruptly at daybreak it stopped, not slowing to insignificance over time, just stopping. Ali came out of the tent, stretched, coughed, hawked some spittle into the ground, and looked around. The camels were standing again, at peace.

At mid-morning, he and his next youngest brother took two camels into the outskirts of the city. His brother would mind the animals whilst Ali bought provisions. The city was not large, but it served as the nearest place for the foreign workers to live; those that toiled at the strange place full of steel pipes and cylinders that attracted the infidels and foreigners to his country. The atmosphere in the streets was odd, and many people were crying and looking to the heavens, kneeling on prayer mats, beseeching Allah, thanking him, asking for signs. However, their actions were not in fear but thankfulness. What was going on?

'What is happening?' Ali asked an old man nearby who was smiling but also had tears running freely down his face.

'Allah has delivered us. The infidels are all dead. He took them away during the khamsin. All of them died in their sleep,' he said, wonder clear in his voice.

'Are you sure? All of them?'

'Yes, the army and police have checked. Every infidel in this land has been taken by Allah; maybe all over the world too.'

Ali stared at the man, looked around at the scenes of joy, and wondered if the people were crazy.

CHARLIE   TWO MONTHS LATER

'Charlie! It's getting cold. Come on, now!' His father was calling.

'Coming!' he shouted back, sighed and then started down the stairs to his parents and siblings. He glanced around the table. His mother was sitting at one end, his father at the other, the head of the table, as usual. Michael and Salina sat opposite him, which left him feeling alone or at least without an ally, also as usual. Although the eldest, at seventeen, he still felt inferior to the fourteen-year-old twins at times.

'I thought about what you said, Dad,' he said quietly, his head down as he ate his pasta, making sure not to make eye contact with anyone. 'But I don't want to do it, I'm sorry. I'm not changing my name. I like being Charlie, or Charles.'

His father looked up and banged the table with his fist. 'Now; now after all these years, when you used to ask why we named you Charles, and told us you hated to be teased at school for it? Now, when there is sound reason to give thanks to Allah and take on an Islamic name that befits the new world, you decide to be stubborn? I will not allow this disrespect. You will become Muhammed, as should have been my decision when you were born in the first place. It's decided.'

'Not by me it isn't, and I won't answer to it,' Charlie said with a slightly raised yet still respectful voice. 'Anyway, there's too many Muhammeds. How the hell will anyone know who's talkin' to who? It's madness, Dad.'

'He does have a point,' his mother agreed, in rare support for her eldest child, thinking back wistfully to when they named him. 'Riaz, remember when we made the decision, in the hospital, not to go with tradition, but to take on a name from our adopted country, to fit in and give our son a better chance in life?'

'That is no longer of any importance, praise be to Allah. It might even be detrimental now,' her husband suggested.

'Riaz, we have discussed this, and Charles is correct. If he was to change his name now to Muhammed, he might be accused of not being sincere, apart from the fact that every third male is seemingly now the same. It's not sensible. I respect your position on this, but it is not practical. What purpose would it serve other than to confirm him as the first-born male?

'So, I am to be disobeyed within my own house, is that it?'

At this point, Mina knew she had won. Riaz had not raised his voice, nor banged his fist down again, which had not been within character anyway. 'The new world needs diversity of opinion, Riaz, perhaps more now than ever. Charles can be one of those voices, God willing, as can Michael and Salina. Let's eat,' she concluded, and the discussion was over.

MINA

Later, in bed, after she had given her husband sex and allowed him to be a little more forceful than usual, in part to rebuild his ego, they discussed events as they would have done before the changes.

'Riaz, my love, the kids are frightened, you know that. They are hardly alone. The talk of the faithful, or should I say the self-righteous, does not help. We need to keep calm but also keep vigilant. The last thing I want for the UK now is to become another Iran after the Ayatollah stole their revolution. You didn't come here to experience democracy, only to have it disappear again.'

'Mina, that's the reason why we need to blend in, not stand out, don't you see?'

'I understand, but your logic is flawed. Being accused of false devotion is a bigger risk. It's the road to being unmasked as a false believer. The fact that we're alive is our best defence against any accusation of that kind. There are bigger trials to come, I think. Let's keep the kids on side and close to us. They are going to need our help more than ever. This so-called glorious new world is fragile. I fear it. Don't you?'

Riaz sighed and nodded his head, tears starting to mist his eyes. 'Yes,' he whimpered, 'yes I do.' Then he nestled his head in his wife's shoulder and wept.

CHARLIE

Taking a notebook out from under his mattress, Charlie clicked the top of a biro. He hadn't expected to win the argument with his father and was thrilled when his mum supported him. Without her he couldn't have remained strong. He knew his dad was only trying to make them all safer, but the argument was crazy; surely, he should have seen that for himself?

Manchester had changed. But going from one of a sizeable minority at school, to being just another member of the only survivors was just plain weird, and the scary part was that it left him more frightened now than at any time in his life. Not that he had particularly felt threatened in his life. Well, maybe once or twice when there was a bit of bullying going on, but really that was minor compared to all of this. More than anything, he hated the ridiculous joy that the extremists displayed every day. But he feared it more than hated it, coz if they knew what he thought then he'd really be in for it. That meant playing a role every day now and he wasn't sure he could keep it up.

He started to cry, thinking of Sarah, gone, like all the rest of them. The first girl he'd ever kissed, loved in fact. He was surer of that now than ever. He'd told her but wondered if it was really love or lust. He wished they'd made love. Not because he wished that he'd experienced it, but because in some odd way it might have made a difference. If whatever power had done all of this had been able to understand his feelings for Sarah, maybe, just a faint maybe, she might have survived. He stopped his silent sobbing and pulled himself together. He had to remain strong; if not for himself then for the twins. He worried about them a lot. They weren't yet old enough to be careful. He just hoped that his mum could do what was necessary, and for his dad too.

He folded back the first page of the exercise book and wondered how to start. Other thoughts were uppermost in his mind, apart from telling his story or creating a diary. Was this dangerous? Depending on who might read it uninvited, could it get him or his family into trouble? Then again was he just being daft? It was just his thoughts and writing about the world as it changed. Something for his own kids to read in the future maybe. Why did he feel like this? Why was he so angry? Be honest with yourself, Chuck. Why can't you just say it out loud, what so many others must be thinking too? Allah, what have you done to the world? Or are you a myth too and it all has to do with something completely different. He threw the book at the wall and started to hyperventilate but managed to get his breathing in order after a few minutes of concentration.

What should I call this? Something safe, or something honest? No, if I can't be honest in my own diary then why bother. Am I that weak? Tell the truth. Be a real journalist if that's what you want to be; don't cop out now. Right, OK then. Let's start this, he decided, picking the book back up from the floor, and writing.

When it all started, it was surreal. That's a word that I've heard a lot of lately. I didn't really know what it meant so I looked it up and then I liked it; surreal. It fits. Sort of means unreal, like out of the ordinary, unbelievable, except that it happened so from then on it becomes the new reality. Yet in the back of everyone's minds it's still unreal or surreal. If this was a movie, you'd know that there's some answer going to be revealed, but in my case, or the world's case, I'm not so sure. Maybe we'll never know, and maybe that's the scariest part, not knowing. Everyone wants to know the answer to a puzzle or a trick or a mystery, don't they? It's only natural. But for me that's not the worst. The worst is that I hate it, and I hate that the majority out there don't. They like this new world. At least they say they do. I wonder if that's true in their own minds or if they're just as scared as me. Scared that... what? What is it that scares me the most? It's like an annoying thing that's just out of reach of your memory, on the tip of your tongue. I know what this fear is. I think I always knew but was frightened to admit. I'm scared that I'm an imposter. That I've survived by default, by some quirk of fate and name and family connection. Coz I'm from the Ahmed family, and that my dad's originally from Iran, although his dad was a Paki, so we're just a bunch of mongrels really, without any true lineage. So here we are, survivors of The Revelation, or Infidel's End, as some stupidly call it. That day when every non-Muslim in the whole world died in their sleep and the world woke up to having only one point seven billion people left alive, and all of them Islamic. The day when I became one of the chosen people, even though I've never believed in any of this God or Allah stuff, hardly ever set foot in a mosque and realised that I was a living imposter, just like the rest of our family.

    I can remember the day of course. Who wouldn't be able to, something that life changing? But it was the second day that really made me feel ill. Seems so bizarre that we went off to school like normal – habits die hard I suppose. There were hundreds of people in the street, singing and dancing and crying and laughing and doing weird stuff. I didn't think about it until later that they were all Paki's, Indians, Arabs, whatever, but no whites. It hadn't hit me yet that this was a Muslim city now, in a Muslim country. Why would it? Didn't take long though before the weird stuff started to filter through and the crazy talk, as I thought it then. Stories of how all the Christians were dead and Allah had saved the Muslims and the faithful alone. I got scared and I wanted out, away from these lunatics. Hadn't they had Anglo friends like me too? Didn't they cry over their lost friends, or girlfriends? How could they be that horrible?

    I ran all the way to school; not waiting for the bus – wouldn't have been one anyway. I ran 2 miles to the gates and rushed in. There were hardly any kids there at first, then bit by bit they started to arrive. I couldn't have told an Indian Hindu from a Paki Muslim most of the time, but it was clear that there were no white kids around, nor any Asians either and presumably no Hindu's. Within an hour or so we knew it was true. But there was still doubt. We decided, me and a few mates, to check it out more. Maybe we shouldn't have but you don't know what it was like. We had to make sure. Even though dad and I had checked every house on our street the day before.

We went across the road, to the first house, and broke a windowpane in the backdoor to get inside. There was no breakfast laid out in the kitchen. One of the lads shouted 'Upstairs,' and we took the stairs two at a time, panting by the time we got to the top, then we split up. I went into a bedroom on the left. There was a girl in bed, about eight I thought. Just looked asleep. I went over and called out to her, trying to wake her up. I've never wanted anything so bad in my life before. I wanted her to wake up and scream at me and just be alive and make all this a stupid mistake. But she didn't. I went up to her. Her eyes were closed, fast asleep. I slowly put my hand on her face and neck. It was cold, unnaturally cold. I tried to find a pulse in her neck, where I'd often felt my own. There was nothing. Just then Joe came in and said that the parents were stone dead, his words. Then the other lad confirmed that the brother was dead too in the other room. All of them just dead in their beds. I started to cry then. That girl was lovely, just a little kid really. The others just stayed quiet. I was glad of that. We left a bit later.

Seemed like others had done similar. Stories were all over the school, or at least from the fifty or so kids there that day. Every non-Muslim person was dead. Must have been about a week later that the bodies disappeared, sort of. They sort of dissolved, into dust really. Not that I saw a lot of that, just a bit. Our next-door neighbour, Mr Kinsella, an old Irish bloke that I sometimes played chess with, he was dead in his chair in front of the tellie when we went into his place on that first day. We left him there. He looked peaceful. A week later there was just a pile of stuff there that looked like a mixture of salt and pepper and flour. No smell, no flies, nothing, just minerals.

It wasn't just the non-Muslims that were dead; I refuse to use the word Infidels. A bit of me has died too.

HABBIB

Washington DC was hot; the summer was worse than usual it seemed, partly because the use of air conditioning was sporadic at best, relying on diesel generator sets for power. President Paul Habbib had received only one phone call, through a direct landline phone link from the prior American Ambassador in New Delhi, who happened to be of the Muslim faith, and had been the only staff member left alive there, or anywhere else in the world, as far as he knew. That one call had provided Habbib with an update about world affairs, to a degree. But, Habbib had not heard anything from his ambassador for a month now, so the news was very stale, which vastly irritated, and worried him.

He was now being interviewed, which seemed ridiculous. He brought his mind back to the present and answered the reporter's question. 'To be honest, I'm still numb about it all,' he stated in a monotone, devoid of facial emotion, his eyes glazed over. He swivelled around a little in his chair, away from his interviewer, and looked out across the lawn of the Oval Office, clearly reminiscing, then came back around, embarrassed.

Badiah Malaki looked at him and faltered a little before her next question, 'Mr President, do you think that the United States is now… insignificant, given its small population I mean, and the clear dominance of the Middle East in future world affairs?'

Habbib smiled, without mirth. 'I'm sure that is the current view from Riyadh, Tehran, and Cairo. Perhaps less so in Jakarta and Kuala Lumpur and Islamabad and Delhi, who probably see themselves as the future dominant powers. It's only been a matter of months since the non-Muslim population died and disappeared. Their removal has seemingly not yet led to enlightenment and a glorious future, no matter what the new Caliph of Mecca apparently stated, has it?'

'No, I suppose not,' she replied with a degree of discomfort.

'Look, Badiah, if I may call you by your first name?' She nodded. 'From what we know, or can assume, Saudi Arabia has about 26 million people, maybe more now with so many migrants heading to Mecca and Medina, but that was the number before what they have called Infidel's End… God, I hate that term! Anyway, with only about three and a half million Americans left alive, we can no longer claim any world power status, clearly. However, this country still represents a higher level of freedom and individuality and innovation than the rest of the world, and that must be protected and nurtured. It was the reason that many of us, or our parents and grandparents, fled our original homelands to come here. It was to escape tyranny and poverty and inequality. I don't see the Caliphate of Mecca enhancing the opportunities that we take for granted here in the U.S., do you?'

'Well, perhaps not, Mr President, but then again, it's early days. I mean it has been less than six months, and the world is still coming to terms with Islam being the chosen religion. I'm sure that when things calm down the future will be glorious.'

Habbib laughed. 'Miss Malaki, I admire your faith... in the future I mean, not in the Prophet... that's taken for granted. Maybe my previous role as Chief of Staff to President Kendall makes me more sceptical, even critical of my fellow world leaders. I too wish for this brighter future that the world now expects to be delivered. Time will tell.'

'Is it true that you plan to move the capital to New York, Mr President?'

'No, not now. I was originally of the view that we should have the seat of government where there was the largest remaining population, and either New York or Chicago made sense, and New York has better infrastructure and access to institutions and people skills. But it seems that our population likes some diversity, and that makes sense too. It didn't take long for New York, Washington, and San Francisco to be the places where everybody made for. Chicago was obviously not liked enough; no one stayed there very long. As far as we know there's about a million or more in New York and perhaps close to a million in San Francisco and Washington has grown to half a million or so, as far as we can estimate, and that's probably how it will be for the future, apart from a smattering of smaller population centres. We don't have the diversity of skills to spread out further, and there's enough infrastructure back online now to possibly keep these three cities viable.'

'How will the country flourish in the future, Sir?'

Habbib shrugged, 'Possibly by immigration, like it did historically. That's our only course now. But while those countries with the ability to run things and build on skills and move the world forward are likely to be found more in India and Indonesia for instance, their people have far less desire or need to come here for a better life. Perhaps our challenge is to offer them something worth the move. In the meantime, we need to make our three key cities vibrant again, and that's not going to be easy. Although I am heartened to learn that we retained a sustainable level of high-end software industry skills. It seems that Muslims were well represented in Silicon Valley. That is why San Francisco became the preferred city to L.A. What are you going to do with this interview, Badiah?'

She smiled weakly, and shrugged, 'I'm not sure Mr President. It's not like the old days where it would have been on the news within hours. I'll just store it for later when the communications networks get back up again.'

'I never thought that I'd miss the media,' Habbib laughed.

After the reporter had left, Habbib stood and paced for a while. It was a new habit he'd developed, and one he despised yet couldn't break, although he tried to only pace when alone. 'Thank the Prophet that you're not here to see this new world order, Andrew. But I'll continue to channel your thoughts, because God knows the U.S. is going to need help to keep its dreams alive in this now barren country.'

An hour later he sat in front of a small group of people that he still did not know well, nor fully trust for that reason, yet who nevertheless represented his Cabinet. Whilst one of the staff was delivering coffees around the table to this new elite, he evaluated them, without making it obvious. His new Secretary of State, Imran Malouf, was probably the most competent, having served in the previous administration as a low-level advisor on Islamic Affairs, and having degrees in commerce and political administration from UCLA. At 30 he had more experience than most of the others, and his knowledge of the world was clearly superior to most of his new colleagues.

On his left sat Amelia Sanchez, 28, a product of a Lebanese mother and a father, now deceased, from Costa Rica. Tall and fair-haired, her Middle Eastern heritage was not obvious, apart from her fluent Arabic, which along with Spanish, English and French had seen her progress well as a foreign correspondent at CNN. Her face was well known from hotspots around the world but her change of career direction and entrance into the previous White House staff as media advisor had surprised her journalist colleagues the most. Now she was playing the part of Population Liaison Officer, with the difficult task of communicating with key people in the other population centres, and hopefully around the world, one day, when possible.

By agreement, the group was sharing responsibilities and planning, except for the positions of the President, Secretary of State, and some redundant treasury officials. George Saba, 42, had been given the role of Chief of Staff. This was very different from the days when the position meant something for a population of over 345 million Americans. Now it meant the guy to get things done, the go-to person, and George's background as a Senate lobbyist had given him insights into political processes, as well as skills in how to influence people and win their votes. But in his new role he had never been even close to dealing with the difficulties that he now faced. Influence in a world of extremes, from excessive wealth to lower socio-economic poverty was a long way from the new world order, where everything you would have wanted in your previous life was now there for the taking. Want a penthouse apartment overlooking Central Park? Just take it if you have the electricity available to get the elevator to work. No power, or at least very intermittent supply at best, altered the desirability of those apartments and so the new need was power, in the form of electrons that used to be taken for granted in the first world. The power grid had been George's first task. Without it there was no first world lifestyle, nor modern communications. Long range radio transmissions were being received, seemingly dominated by commentary in poor English from the Saudi Caliphate, with a few other ad hoc musings from India, Indonesia, and Malaysia, none of which could be verified. George was still a long way from achieving his mission, and this remained the usual first, and now unspecified, question of the day, as always.

'George?' Habbib asked.

'Ok, Sir, well first off, the town hall meetings are hitting the mark. Yesterday's session pulled in about three thousand people, so the decision to move them to the stadium worked well. I put the question to the crowd about what we still needed most in the way of people that could run the power system, and we got six guys come forward who had a background in the industry. To cut a long story short, the road we're going down, concentrating on a gas-fired peaking power station that can run initially on diesel makes sense. They said that if it was possible to isolate any supply to as small an area of electricity transmission as possible, then that would be easier to manage. Problem is, none of these guys have the intimate knowledge we need to solve the problem, but they think that together they might be able to work it out, and especially if I can find others to help. So, I've had the posters printed and they've gone up around the key areas.'

The President ignored the slight snort of derision that came from Amelia Sanchez. 'Thanks, George. Still seems a long way off though. The current diesel generators are doing their job, but we need a system with more failsafe in it. Amelia? Seems you wanted to say something?'

'It's OK Mr President, just my irritation with the issue of these posters we're using around the city. Surely, we can come up with a better way to communicate than billboards?'

'Well, that's your area of expertise, Amelia, so what do you suggest?' George countered.

'If you get the power system up to the stage where we can broadcast something, I'll be able to get confidence back up again.'

'Seems like a "hole in my bucket, Catch-22" debate, children,' Imran Malouf stated, smiling. 'I suggest you stop sniping at each other. Your two problems, I mean our two problems, in relation to power and communications are intimately linked. Whether we like it or not, in this once proud country we are reduced to a position of communicating by ancient means. Forget the past, and mobile phones and internet. For the time being those days are a long way from being revisited. Billboards advertising meeting places and needed skills are working. We have no other easy options.'

'I apologise, Mr President.'

'Forget it, Amelia. Ending up back in the 1800's is frustrating and well out of the norm for all of us. Next on the agenda is food security. Where are we at with that analysis, George?'

'Well, Sir, this is a case of two extremes as well in some ways. From the perspective of real food security, as in shortfalls, we're fine, as expected. There are thousands of warehouses full of non-perishable food all over the country. If we have the means to fill trucks with diesel then we can move those goods around for a hundred years, in theory. But it's the perishable and fresh food that needs our attention. No-one is going to starve, clearly. And even in relation to fresh fruit and vegetables we're hardly in danger of getting scurvy like the old seafarers, because there's enough tinned fruit and vegetables for everyone. But to rely on this is a sort of failure of planning for the future. Whilst it removes the imperative, we should still be seeking to get back to primary production. But quite frankly, none of us were in those jobs. There weren't many Muslim farmers in

America. None of us survivors raised cows and milked them. We didn't grow crops. We didn't do manual labour, build things, or keep them going; at least not many of us. Therefore, finding and nurturing those skills is something we need to consider. But, for now, that's a secondary objective. All my efforts are focussed on the power problem.'

'Water supply?' Malouf asked.

'OK for now as well. Like I said regarding supermarket stores, there's billions of litres of bottled water, and we can catch rainfall and treat it,' Saba said.

'Sewage system?'

'Getting there, Imran. When the power runs, we can run the pumps for sewage, at least in those areas we've isolated, but that's still less than ten percent of the population covered at present. For the time being people are just using random toilets where there's one last flush of the cistern left. But it's going to get ugly one day,' Saba suggested.

'OK then, let's get on with what we can,' President Habib said, and as he stood up the rest of his cabinet made their farewells and went back to their primary tasks.

CHARLIE

What I wrote yesterday happened months ago. I thought I'd jump forward now, partly because I can't remember what happened in what order and because it doesn't really matter and it's easier to just bring this story up to date. I'm still not sure if this is all a waste of time, but I hope not.

The first month was awful, but not because of what you might think. Nothing to do with the bodies and stuff – they evaporated within a week. No, it was the lack of all the normal things. Things you might not appreciate; or I didn't. There was no TV, no newspapers, nor Internet–just stuff that was saved on iPads, until the batteries ran down. There were no mobile phones working. There were no aircraft in the sky. We didn't have radio stations broadcasting for at least two months, I think, apart from some odd stuff coming from the Middle East. But the weirdest was having almost no cars on the road, and no trucks at all.

Because, whilst all the devout Muslims were in the streets cheering that Allah had proven that we're the chosen people, and not the Jews at all, nor the Christians, Hindus nor anyone else, it wasn't long before the cracks started to appear.

First question was why's the tellie not working, we need to find out what's going on in the world and is this something that's only happened in the UK or Europe or what? Trouble was, as we now know, the UK population was down to about 4 or 5 million people, 450,000 of them around London. So how many of them ran things, like TV or radio stations, trains, airports, the electricity, gas, water, and sewage systems? Er, how about none? That's right. The UK Muslim population didn't do that sort of thing, or at least not to the extent that was needed to run this stuff. So, we were in the dark, literally, coz the power went off within a day or so, as fuel and back-up systems failed.

After a week passed with limited connections to water, gas and power there was a mini revolution in the streets. Sadly, it was the Mosque leaders, the Imams and their supporters that wanted to show that they were now in charge of everything, even though they clearly weren't. Mind you, there was so much stuff around to start with that the urgency didn't seem to be uppermost in the minds of these new leaders. For instance, the fridges went off coz there was no power. But some supermarkets had automatic back up diesel power, for a while. So, for about a fortnight we didn't run out of milk or other perishable food. Then we began to. Lack of fresh bread was noticeable in our house. I love toast in the morning. Well, forget that. I haven't seen much bread now for months. There are a few bakeries now, but not many. And before you ask if the limited bread supply means that it's expensive, I need to tell you about money.

We all became instant millionaires, well sort of. There were quite a few people that went to shops, broke in and nicked the cash. Idiots! What use is money when no-one is making things and there's no modern economy left standing? No-one was working unless they wanted to make stuff that was really needed, like to get the TV and radio stations back on the air, or to get the electricity and gas back on. That was the priority. Took no time at all for everyone to figure that out. But they weren't doing it for the money, they were doing it to get society back together. Money was useless now. If you needed anything you just took it from shops. And if it wasn't readily available then no amount of money made any difference. Want a flash car? Nick one. All easy until the petrol runs out, coz there was no power for the petrol stations to pump any more out. That's why there's still so many abandoned cars everywhere. And let me tell you there's loads of kids driving them and crashing them all over the place.

Anyway, there was this old geezer up the street who must have been in his eighties I reckon. He was one of those blokes that played around with the ancient radio sets. They were called ham radio enthusiasts in the old days, I've learnt now. So, he found out what was happening, or bits of it anyway, by connecting with other old blokes in other countries and around the UK. He became the early main sort of news. He said his name was Harry, or at least that was his Anglo name. Real name was originally Mustafa, I think. He came from Bahrain and arrived here after the Second World War as a young kid, but his dad was a radio lover and he learned it all off him. Without Harry we'd have been in the dark a lot longer. Mind you the Imams didn't like what they heard, not all of it anyway.

Mustafa-Harry, as he gets called now, found out that it was true, that it seemed that all the non- Islamic population really were dead. Most people had come to that conclusion anyway. But he told us that there was apparently a power struggle going on in the Middle East and in Indonesia to be the new superpower, because the Americans were gone, apart from maybe 4 million left over there, so like here in the UK, but more spread out. There was next to no-one left in South America, and Europe was like here, struggling to get stuff up and running again.

But there was conflict in the Middle East – so what else is new, eh? Took no time at all for there to be arguments between the Sunnis and the Shiites again. But I had to laugh when Mustafa-Harry said the biggest problem for the Arabs was finding people to do any work now that the foreign workers had died. Most of them had never done the physical work and now had no clue what to do. Well, many of them anyway. More so in Saudi than other places he said. That's why it seems that Indonesia and India and Pakistan are vying for superpower leadership status. Also seemed to be some conflict between Pakistan and India and Bangladesh. I reckon it's going to be a long time before the world's a working place again, the way we all liked it, or at least those of us that weren't caught up in all the religion stuff. I wonder what's happening in other places too. Considering that I hardly watched the TV news before, it's the one thing I really want back. That and football.

KALIL

Lieutenant General Sabal Kalil took a deep breath of the moist hot air and surveyed the city from his vantage point on the roof of the main building of Jami Masjid, the great mosque of Old Delhi. He had always loved it here, more so for the architecture of the seventeenth century buildings than its religious significance. He was in uniform and wondering about how long to remain that way, rather than adopt civilian attire. The people increasingly accepted him now as the President of India, rather than the previous commander of India's Western Command, and the hastily assembled Mechanised Infantry Division that he cobbled together from the surviving troops, which quelled the initial looting and irrational behaviour following Infidel's End. Kalil assessed quickly what had happened. The hundreds of millions of dead, none of them Muslim, told him the result, if not the cause, of the tragedy. Never slow to action, after speedy appreciation of the situation, he assembled a force capable of taking control and he drove them to New Delhi as fast as was possible. It had not been necessary to kill many looters, very few really. Control was in place within three hours of his men arriving in Delhi, which was only 2 days after Infidel's End.

Indians of all castes had always admired strength, and the speed at which he took control of the initial mayhem was spoken of with appreciation. More important though was his continuing ability to create order out of chaos and re-establish government functionality.

India was well positioned by having a significant surviving population of over 204 million people that were represented across all walks of life, rich and poor, skilled and unskilled, and geographically dispersed through cities and rural areas. It therefore retained a high level of functionality. What was now more urgently required was to secure its territory and maintain its superior capabilities than its equally populated neighbours in Pakistan and Bangladesh. Pakistan was already encroaching into Indian territory and Kalil had to stop that, or he would become irrelevant. But his army was no match for the Pakistani's now.

Bangladesh was no longer a problem. Its entire cabinet and almost all the 300 elected officials has died in a massive explosion, a week after Revelation Day. It was thought to have been planned by radicals opposed to the award-winning building, rather than against the members of parliament. A brief message was received at the same time as parliament was sitting to debate the future of the country. It stated that the building was cursed by Allah, due to its architect having been an American, Louis Kahn, who had also designed churches. The fact that Kahn had died in 1974, before seeing his masterpiece completed, led to the threat being ignored. The explosions, via suicide bombers, and subsequent fires, coupled with blocked fire exits, were responsible for the exceptionally high death rate. Kalil had been approached soon after the event and asked to take interim control of the country, which he did speedily and efficiently. He did not relish being the latest President of India, and Bangladesh, if his reign was destined to be the shortest. His personal security from that time on remained tight.

'You called for me, Sir?'

Kalil looked around, not having heard his right-hand man, Colonel Ashraf Kumar, approach.

'Yes, Ashraf. What news from your sources?'

'The Pakistani incursions seem to have slowed, Sir. Border units report that there seems to be less random activity, and more control applied by the Pakistani officials. Your communication with their Prime Minister must have worked.'

'Maybe. I am not convinced yet. Could just be a weighing up of options. What would you do in the Pakistani's place?'

'Pretend to comply, use some diplomacy, plan for a major assault, and then take us over in a lightening attack on all fronts, capturing key installations and consolidating within a week,' Kumar said.

'Yes, me too. Obvious really. Then what?'

'Get you to comply as an ally of Pakistan, becoming a puppet leader, and become absorbed into their new empire. If you disagreed, they'd kill you and find someone else to bribe into that role.'

Kalil laughed aloud. 'That's what I love about you, Ashraf; no bullshit.'

Kumar laughed too and shrugged. 'What is it that the American's used to say? It's a no brainer.'

The General sighed. 'Exactly, Ashraf, a no brainer. So how are we going to stop our Islamic brothers next door from taking us over?'

'Appeal to common sense, Sir. There is absolutely no imperative for them to take too much territory from us. There is plenty of land, housing, everything to go around. You could offer them a buffer zone. That would buy time at least.'

'Under normal circumstances, with access to the full suite of secure telecommunications, or aircraft to get us both to a neutral location for bi-lateral talks, that would be a good idea and eminently sensible, my friend. However, with the loss of email networks, when we are relying on the passing of sealed dispatches with a thousand kilometres between our capitals, the nuances of diplomacy are lost, or at least we are not used to the new rules. So, the problem is still buying time. As dangerous as it might be, I need to arrange a face-to-face meeting with the Pakistani leadership.'

CHARLIE

Waking up after a fitful night, he heard the wind outside and looked out of his window. 'Pissin' down again! Shit! I'm not goin' out in that.'

His parents and siblings were at the breakfast table when he came down the stairs. The gas camping stove was fired up and Michael was eating baked beans, Salina some breakfast cereal with warm water and honey poured over it. His parents were drinking black tea, not eating.

'Still no milk then?' he stated.

Michael looked up, 'What happened to all the cows d'ya reckon?'

'Nuthin,' Salina replied. 'Just no-one to milk them, that's all.'

'But wouldn't they die if no-one milked them?' Charlie asked.

Michael looked confused, 'Why would they?'

Salina answered, 'Coz their udders would burst I think, or they'd get mastitis or somethin', unless there were calves to drink it.'

'Maybe we should check. You know, go into the countryside and see what's happening on the farms, see if there's animals that need help,' Charlie suggested.

'Are you daft?' Michael laughed. 'What the hell do any of us know about looking after farm animals?'

'We could learn.'

'Why?' Salina asked.

'To become sustainable, and not rely on robbing supermarkets for a start. I'd prefer not to live like a thief for a change,' Charlie said with some passion.

His father suddenly took an interest. 'Charlie, it's not theft, not really. There's plenty of food around, praise be to Allah. He has provided for us all.'

'But, dad, don't you feel… I don't know…'

'Unfulfilled, Charlie?' His dad replied, his face saddened. 'Yes, I do, and I don't like the fact that we can't talk about it without being treated as ungrateful.'

'I'm scared, dad,' Salina volunteered.

Mina looked worried too, 'We have to be careful now. All of us,' she said. 'It's OK to talk like this with each other, but not outside, not in public. You also need to be careful with your friends because we don't know which of them might report what you say to the Imams.'

'Why would they do that?' Michael asked.

Riaz said, 'That's the way it works, I'm afraid. I've seen it before when we were in Iran. The religious police there took a very hard line with those that they believed weren't being sufficiently devout. These are strange times and it's going to take a while before everything settles down.' He looked at his children's faces and saw the new concern. 'It's good that we can talk like this together, but we do all need to be careful. Don't say or do anything that can be criticised by your friends or strangers.'

Charlie nodded his head. 'Maybe we should move to a farm, somewhere a bit isolated where we can be self-sufficient then.'

'We know nothing about farming, Charlie,' Riaz replied.

'We can learn. Growing food can't be that hard. We could get vegetable seeds from a garden centre. We don't have to be good at it straight away, there's plenty of stuff still around. But if we found a farm then we could be protected a bit too, away from everyone?'

'There's hardly anyone left alive, and you want to move away from those that are?' Salina scoffed.

Riaz put up his hand, 'It's not a silly suggestion, but let's just wait and see, just for another few weeks. But I see nothing wrong in scouting out the countryside nearby as well. Maybe take a few long rides on your bikes if the weather's good, Charlie?'

The kids all nodded their agreement.

A few days later they took provisions in back packs, pumped up the tires on their bikes and rode off. It was at least ten miles to the outskirts of their suburb and then they were in green fields and more sporadic housing and small farms. Charlie was happier. 'It's lovely out here,' he said. Salina nodded.

Michael looked less sure. 'It's eerie. Too quiet. I don't like it. We haven't seen anyone for maybe the last half hour.'

'Nice spot though,' Charlie countered. 'What about that place over there?' he pointed. 'House is big. Let's see.' They rode towards it. The doors were unlocked, and they went inside. The kitchen had some food scattered on the table, but there were mice droppings around it, and flies buzzing around. 'No smell. Let's look around,' he ordered. They each explored separately, calling to each other with commentary as they went.

'Good bathroom.'

'Three bedrooms and an office up here.'

'Nice lounge room, big TV in it.'

'Walk in pantry that's full of food. Potatoes have gone to seed though, and the carrots are rubbery, and the lettuce is rotten.'

After further investigation, they regrouped in the kitchen.

Charlie took control. 'Know what I like about it as well?' he asked, but then continued, 'it's defendable. You can see anyone coming up the driveway for ages. Upstairs rooms give good vantage points too. And there's solar panels on the roof as well, and two water storage tanks in the back, plus a tractor and what looked like a few jerries of diesel near it.'

'Plenty of tools in the shed as well,' Michael added.

'Better'n our place,' Salina agreed.

'Did you see the dog dishes?' Michael asked, continuing as his siblings nodded, 'what happened to all the dogs and cats in the world do you think?'

'I've never really thought about it,' Salina said. 'That is weird. I saw some kids walking a dog the other day though. So only the pets of non-Muslims died. Why?'

'So that they didn't starve to death I reckon,' Michael suggested. 'It's Allah's way of not being cruel to them. They were innocent bystanders, so they were taken at the same time, so they didn't suffer.'

'Maybe,' Charlie accepted. 'Better than pining for their owners and slowly starving I suppose. Never thought about that really.'

'Were you there the other day when that bloke in the square was going on about Sharia now being the only way forward in seeking justice?' Salina asked.

'Yeah. Sounded a bit scary to me,' Michael said. 'I mean there's no crime goin' on now anyway so why get all bothered about stuff like that. Let's face it there's no shortage of stuff, so there's no need to steal, least not in the way it would have been thought of before. No racism either, less pub fights too now,' he laughed.

Charlie started to laugh too. 'Yeah, hardly likely to be a bunch of Muslim pissheads on a Saturday night getting tanked up and starting a brawl, eh?'

Salina was giggling too, 'And no-one having a go at a girl for wearing a Hijab either.'

Charlie suddenly went serious, 'But they're not, are they, Salina? The girls aren't wearing Hijabs now, are they?'

She thought about it for a while, 'No, now that you mention it, they're not. Even though I never wore one, a few of the other girls in school used to and now they're not. That's weird.'

'Do you think dad's right,' Michael asked, 'that it'll get crazy like he saw in Iran, with the really religious ones making us all do the same things?'

'I hope not, but I think it's more likely to go that way,' Charlie suggested, the happy mood suddenly ending.

Salina changed the subject, 'There's no animals in the fields.'

Charlie nodded, 'Might not have been a dairy farm.'

'No sheep or chickens neither,' Michael added.

BADIAH

Badiah Malaki grabbed a vase and threw it against the wall, smashing it to pieces, and followed that with a heavy ashtray into a wall mirror, then pushed over a small side table, spilling some trinkets and a book to the floor, before collapsing onto her couch and sobbing uncontrollably into a cushion. She cried for at least ten minutes.

'Fuck you, Allah, fuck you, do you hear me!' she screamed. 'Strike me down if you want, you bastard! Why? Why did you do this?' She screamed at the top of her lungs then, an ear-piercing high-pitched wail, then continued to cry. A few minutes later she ran into the kitchen of her apartment and threw open a high cupboard door, pushing aside bottles until she found what she was looking for. She unscrewed the cap of the Johnny Walker Black Label scotch and poured a healthy measure into the nearest water glass. She started to gulp it down, soon coughing and choking as it burned her throat.

'See that, you false prophet? Alcohol. You drove me to this, you prick. What did you think? That us survivors would thank you? That we'd be grateful that you killed off all our friends, ruined our lives, destroyed families?' She gulped more whisky. 'Is this what you expected; or did you think we'd suddenly become more devout?'

'What have you done?' she asked, quietly this time, flopping down again on the nearest chair. 'We weren't your enemy. Why couldn't you have killed me too? What have you left for me here? No boyfriend, no career, no future... nothing. Just this,' she said, waving the whisky bottle around. This, that you don't allow even,' she laughed, hysterically.

'Maybe I should just get wasted and go out and let some power mad man fuck me to death, eh? Just continue the downward spiral of despair. Or do you have plans for me? As if! All your mysterious ways, I suppose. Had good reasons to murder most of the world, eh?' She drained the glass, went for the bottle again, missed grabbing it, fell sideways and crashed to the floor.

It was dark when she woke up, her head throbbing, her mouth furry and dry. She got to her knees, then quickly jumped up and ran into the kitchen where she retched into the sink, moaning. Over the next five minutes she guessed that she'd vomited up all the whisky and anything else that had been in her stomach.

She walked into the bathroom, took off her clothes and walked into the shower, turning the taps on, slipping down to the floor as the water cascaded over her head. She cried again, sobbing loudly and long. She didn't move again until the water started to go cold, thankful for the solar hot water system, although it rarely lasted long. She switched the water off, exited the cubicle and wrapped herself in a large fluffy towel, lay down on the rug, curled up and fell into a sleep. When she woke again, her head was a little clearer. There was a faint light now, dawn approaching. She dressed in jeans and a sweater and went to make coffee.

Sitting at the small kitchen table, watching the sun rise over a dead city without traffic or noise, her tears ran again, but silently this time. For a micro-second she contemplated making amends, praying to Allah for forgiveness, then pushed that thought away. She was still angry with Him, and she felt justified.

ASIF

Ghulam Asif, the Prime Minister of Pakistan, opened the sealed letter from his Indian counterpart in private. He perused the envelope and satisfied himself that the correct markings were on it. Yes, the Indian General had been astute in providing details on this aspect of security for their correspondence. He frowned, cursing himself for missing the American technology, making life so difficult now, even though he used to wish for it to fail and leave the Americans in the dark. Now it was the whole world that was too often in the dark. He spread the letter on his desk, admiring the handwriting.

My Dear Prime Minister Asif,
It was with gratitude that I learned of your orders to the Army of Pakistan to put a halt to the incursions of your population into the territory of India. I admire your control of your countrymen and your foresight in avoiding conflict between our two great nations.

I think we agree that there is nothing to be gained by squabbling over land when between us we have so many advantages over the rest of the new Islamic world. In your case, you have the amazing advantages, praise be to Allah, of a population virtually untouched by the removal of the Infidels. This leaves Pakistan as one of the few countries where the infrastructure is totally intact, with the people skills to keep it that way, and with no threat to its security or culture from outside forces. I congratulate you on your good fortune.

We too have many advantages - a healthy and thriving population, with skills in so many critical areas of modern life, nuclear power plants that remain viable, a thriving agricultural base, significant renewable energy sources, skills in Information Technology, and a navy to explore the new world.

But these are less important than the common future that we could share. With Pakistan and India's combined human capital we can take over the Unites States of America and get it back to superpower status. They do not have the population or the skills to do this without help, and without an influx of people, their natural wealth of resources will be wasted. It is only a matter of time before Indonesia or Malaysia, or the Arabs, come to the same conclusion. But they do not have the skills that we share.

We must meet and talk about this as soon as possible. I see a time in the very near future where Indian and Pakistani aircraft will fly to the US and inherit our destiny.

I would like to meet with you, in ten days, to discuss our joint future, my friend. Let us meet halfway between our two great cities, in Amritsar at the Golden Temple, which we plan to re-dedicate to the glory of Allah. I will bring a core group of senior people with me, no more than 10, but feel free to bring more of your cabinet and advisors if you wish.

Until then, may Allah smile upon you.

Sabal Kalil
President of India

Clever bastard, Asif chuckled. Well, you write a good letter, General, no doubt about that. Not overly subtle, with talk of nuclear power and your navy. But that's OK. But more to the point, this crazy idea of taking over the world, for that's what it would amount to. Is it just a ploy to gain time, or deflect me? Or is it a real suggestion? Your points are valid. Why not? If we don't do it someone else will. Why squabble over Indian dirt and housing for my people when we could take over the now barren cities of America?

Yes, Kalil, I will meet with you. But on my terms.

RIAZ

'Where the hell have you been, Michael?' Riaz asked as the rest of the family were eating breakfast.

'Had to go as far as number 31 this time.'

Riaz looked momentarily confused.

Michael provided the facial expression that to all of them meant "get with the program, dad," but still had to elaborate, 'To find a clean loo.'

'Why not just go to one of the neighbour's houses closer by?'

'Dad! They're... horrible. They stink and they're getting full, coz they don't flush. If you go as far as number 31 there's still a last flush left in them.'

'Just hold your breath and be quick and go somewhere closer, Michael,' Charlie suggested, 'you can't keep going further and further from home, that's ridiculous.'

'Well, if the bloody authorities got the sewers working again, I wouldn't have to, would I? All this about the chosen people and Allah smiling down on us and we don't even have flushing toilets anymore. It's crazy.'

'That's enough, Michael! I don't want to hear you speak that way of the Prophet again. It's dangerous. Do you understand? We need to be vigilant. There are people that will take offence, even though I know you didn't mean it that way, but from now on I don't want to hear talk like this. We need to be careful at home too, so that when we're out in public we don't say the wrong thing. Understand?'

Everyone nodded their agreement, but Charlie couldn't leave it like that. 'Dad, someone has to take a stand and agitate for things to get back to working order again. It's ridiculous!'

Riaz sighed, 'And just what do you suggest, Charlie?'

'Go and see the new head man at the town hall or something. Suggest that he sets up technical groups that can get the essential stuff working again. I don't know why that hasn't happened yet. I'll come with you if you like. Or maybe we should all go.'

'And what if the Senior Imam of Manchester accuses me of impatience with God or something, what then?'

'You're cleverer than that, dad. You know how to talk to these people. You've been through something like this before, in Iran, like you said. You know what to do, and if you tell them you're an electrician that might make them listen. Surely, they all want the power on again, like us?'

'Maybe Charlie is right, Riaz,' Mina agreed, 'maybe they just need technical people to come forward. Their posters around the streets have been asking for professionals to assist this new Central Council of Imams. Why not go?' 'Sometimes it is better to keep your head down, believe me.'

Charlie shook his head, 'Not this time, dad. I think you're forgetting the bigger picture. This isn't like the Iranian revolution you went through. This is different. Everybody left alive on Earth has been chosen, by Allah himself, haven't they? So, who are the Imams to contradict that? Surely everyone left is divine, and anyone that tries to harm them is going against the will of Allah. That'd be my argument anyway.'

Riaz looked at his eldest son with wonder. Where did the new wisdom in his fifteen-year-old suddenly come from? And how had his own courage deserted him. He decided. 'OK then, we'll go today as soon as we've eaten.'

An hour later it was clear than the planning was easier than the execution. It took longer than expected to find a working car. It wasn't just the need to find a car that had fuel in it, but they also had to find the keys in the previous owner's house. The first few times they'd done this it had been easy, and the keys had been either on a table in the hallway, or on a hook in the kitchen or in a handbag. This time it was not as easy. It took until the third house to find the keys to a vehicle that had fuel. Thirty minutes later they were in Manchester city centre. Travel time was short with so little traffic on the roads. They saw a few vehicles. Riaz parked the car right outside the Greater Manchester Town Hall. They approached the main doors with determination, Riaz having rehearsed his speech in the car on the way.

There was no-one guarding the entry. They walked in, saw a woman in a Hijab at the main desk, writing on something in front of her. She looked up at the sudden noise, but appeared relieved to have something to break the monotony, and smiled, 'Can I help you?'

'Yes, Madam. I am Riaz Ahmed, and this is my family,' he began, 'my wife Mina, my sons Charles and Michael, and my daughter Salina. I would like to offer my services to the Imam. I am an electrician and I thought that as there are clearly many problems with the power and water systems, I could perhaps be of service in this area.'

'You know how to get the power and water working again?' she asked, her eyes widening in hope.

'Not by myself, but I think if we get the right team together, we can perhaps make it happen, God willing,' Riaz offered.

'Wait here,' she said and quickly left her desk and almost ran through the adjoining door to another office. Less than a minute later she came back, just popped her head around the door and called, 'Please, come through here, Mr Ahmed; and all of you.'

The Imam didn't waste any time on pleasantries. As soon as the family entered his office he began, 'Can you get the power back on?'

'Well, Mr., er... your Excellency...' Riaz stammered.
'Just call me Jeff,'
'Jeff?' Riaz asked in disbelief.

'My name's Jeffery Buliya. My father was the local Imam, but he died in the week following the deaths and I was pressed into taking on his role. I know what's required, from the religious aspect, but I was an accountant beforehand, and I did the books for the Mosque. No-one else wanted the role. They were afraid of the responsibility in this new world order, so I took it on. However, the time for niceties is long gone. We need to get things working again. I suppose you saw our posters. Is that why you've come?'

'Posters?' Riaz asked.

'Yes, calling for professional and technical people to come forward and help to get society working again.'

'Oh. Well not really. I mean, I have seen some, but this was my son Charlie's idea. He said I might be able to help, and it was long overdue to get the power and water working again, so I thought I'd offer myself, as an electrician. But I don't know what the problems are exactly, so I don't know if I can help. Aren't there other professional people for the power and water companies left around?'

'Doesn't seem to be. We did have a man call around who used to work for a power company, but he was only in their billing area, not from an actual power station. Then there was finally a power station worker who'd retired ten years ago. But he worked on an old coal-fired plant in the midlands, and we need to get one of the peaking gas power stations up and running and we haven't been able to do that.' The Imam shrugged his shoulders.

'Why not?'

'It's a 'chicken and egg' problem I'm afraid. We need the power to get the gas compression units working so that enough gas will flow through to the burners, or that's what I've managed to learn from books. But there's no emergency back-up systems left operating to do that. I'm not technical, so this might be rubbish and there might be a better solution. I don't know.'

Riaz sat in the empty chair across from the Imam's desk. 'Hmm, that does sound feasible, the problem I mean. So apart from the two people you mentioned, there's been no-one else come forward to help?'

'No, unfortunately. The problem we have, as I'm sure you've probably learned yourself, is that most of the Islamic population in the UK was working in other fields. Sure, we probably had people working in a host of semi-technical jobs, but not enough to know how things worked from start to finish. So, for instance, we might have had a TV camera operator, and journalists, and writers and designers. But no-one that knows exactly how a TV signal gets transmitted from the studio to the public, assuming the power is working in the first place. It's like being a top-class chef, but now having to cook over a wood fire. We have experts in many fields that are all now totally redundant,' the Imam said with a mixture of grief and comedy.

Charlie laughed, 'Sounds like The Hitchhikers Guide to the Galaxy.'

'What do you mean?' the Imam asked.

'The Douglas Adams books. There was this planet where they wanted to get rid of the useless third of their population, so they tricked them into believing they were going to all go and colonise a new planet. But the first of the three groups to be sent off was all the telephone sanitisers, hairdressers, advertising account executives and other useless people. Now that's us.'

'Don't be disrespectful, Charlie. The Prophet would not have brought us into enlightenment without a plan. It is for us to prove ourselves worthy of him, and this is clearly a test,' Riaz suggested.

'Possibly,' the Imam conceded. 'But in a way your son's anecdote is correct. Whatever Allah has in store for us will be revealed in due course, praise be to Him. But it still leaves us with numerous problems to solve.'

'So, what has been done so far to improve the situation?'

'We've been collecting all the bottled gas we can find, from petrol stations, bulk suppliers, factories etcetera. We've also been collecting diesel generator sets. I've asked for an audit with details for the population of Greater Manchester, and the Imams in other major cities are doing the same. The problem is that the speed of collection is so slow, without Internet or computer-based systems. Luckily there are more than enough vehicles with fuel in them to make the trips. On the first Wednesday of each month 2 representatives from the five Islamic Councils of the UK meet in Birmingham. The five councils are London, Birmingham, Manchester, Leeds-Bradford and Glasgow. We've set up technical lead-house areas of research, so that we can split up the necessary tasks to get the country back to normality again.

'London has responsibility for internet and computer technology, and air transport. Birmingham is power and water infrastructure, Manchester is food production and distribution, Leeds-Bradford is hospitals and medical support, and Glasgow is maritime transport and commerce.'

'That's impressive,' Riaz said. 'So, progress is good, and we'll soon get things back up and running again?'

'Hmm, well, I wish I could say that was the case but really it's proving to be immensely challenging. Communication is one key area of need. It takes forever to get messages back and forth, and people are very frustrated at getting no news or television. Unfortunately, the idea of getting all the key technical people related to a specific task to move to the same city and work together on solving each problem area is still a work in progress. It's very slow going.'

'Have you made any progress at all?' Michael asked, suddenly taking an interest.

'Some,' the Imam replied. 'But nowhere near what I'd hoped for.'

Mina put up her hand, like she was in school, then saw the inappropriateness of the act and pulled it down, looking embarrassed.

'Yes, Mrs. Ahmed?'

'I... well, you don't seem like a traditional Imam, Sir... I, sort of wondered...'

'Please speak freely. I won't bite, I promise,' the Imam smiled. 'Call me Jeff if that helps. I miss being addressed that way at times.'

Mina smiled at that. 'Well, Jeff... my husband is worried that this new world will bring back some of the worst aspects of radical belief, like he experienced in Iran in 1979. What do you see happening, and what is Allah's message to us all now?'

'You ask very difficult questions, Mrs. Ahmed...'

'Mina.'

'Mina, then. As for the Prophet's intentions, I am not worthy to hazard a guess. Clearly, He has spoken in a way that is unambiguous, and as such has shown us that Islam is the only true path to God. The non-believers have been removed; there is no other way to interpret that fact. But this has left us with the challenges we've been discussing. Challenges are a test of fortitude, faith, and resourcefulness, are they not? Allah wishes us to rise to the occasion and prove our worth and our love, without resorting to despair or feeling sorry for ourselves. That is my belief anyway. We must prove ourselves worthy of His great trust in us and in the fact that we are the chosen people. This is our current task. As for the fear you might have about religious fanaticism, I do not see this occurring, because all of us have been chosen, so there can be no doubt of our worthiness in the eyes of Allah, naturally.'

'That is what Charlie said, about us all being chosen by God,' Mina said.

The Imam looked across at Charlie and nodded, 'Very wise, young man.'

Charlie didn't smile. 'That doesn't mean we won't see the loonies doing the wrong thing and misinterpreting Islam and stoning women for not covering up and stuff though,' he suggested.

'Charlie, that's enough!' Riaz admonished his son, fear showing his face.

'No, that's okay, Riaz. It's understandable for your son, for all of you, to have these concerns. It would be naïve of me to suggest that there won't be issues like these raised in the future. But in my opinion, we need to resist any narrow interpretation of the Quran. If we have been chosen by Allah, then we need to keep that in mind and counter any actions that cause harm to the community. This isn't a revolution from the ground up like we saw in Iran, those of us old enough to remember it. This is the rebirth of the world, and it will be a glorious world from now on, without want, without poverty, without injustice, without prejudice. That is my hope and my belief, thanks be to God.'

Riaz looked a little overawed again and quickly changed the subject, 'So is there anything I can do to assist in getting things back to normal?'

'Perhaps. We've moved all the medical staff we've been able to find to Crumpsall Hospital in Cheetham Hill, as that was the largest public hospital close to a large Islamic population. But we're having some issue getting the back-up power supplies running smoothly. If you know anything about diesel generation and could help over there that would be most useful,' the Imam suggested.

'I can try. Do I need anything from you to give me the authority?' Riaz asked.

The Imam smiled, 'Not really, but if it makes you feel more comfortable, I'll write a note for you. The new hospital maintenance head is Phillip Abuja, originally from Nigeria. I think you'll like him; very practical fellow,' he said as he started to write a note of introduction. 'Here, take this with you. Good luck and please come and see me anytime.' He stood and shook hands with each member of the family, and they left, a little more confident than when they'd arrived.

Once outside, Mina hugged her husband. 'Well?' she said, looking at each of them in turn.

'It's a start I suppose,' Charlie answered first. Michael nodded, as did Salina.

'It would be good to be needed again, to have something concrete to do,' Riaz added. Yes, he thought, this is good. I can make a difference, I hope.

CHARLIE

There was a faint sound of crying coming from Salina's room that made Charlie automatically walk in unannounced.

'You okay, Salsa?' he asked, using his sister's nickname.

She tried to stop her sobbing but was finding it hard to catch her breath.

'Take it easy, no hurry. Catch your breath and tell me what's up. I'm here for you, you know that.'

She nodded and wiped her sleeve across her eyes. 'Ed's dead too. I can't believe that I didn't realise that until now,' Salina said, followed by more increased sobbing.

'Ed who?'

'Ed Sheeran! He'll never write another song. It was only last year that I saw him at Wembley, and he was so good, such a great bloke, everyone said so, everyone loved him, and now he's gone. It's like there's no music left, just a gap in the world. How can Allah be so cruel? Ed was lovely. He didn't deserve to die, Charlie.'

'I know he didn't. I don't reckon that most of the world deserved to be taken away, Salsa. But I don't think anyone suffered if that's any relief at all?'

'No, it's not. Why Charlie? Why?'

'Buggered if anyone really knows, kiddo. Probably we'll never know. I know that makes it hard. I feel the same as you do. Mates gone; good people taken from us. We've just got to make the most of it. For their sake, we must make the world a better place, I think. Maybe that's the test, to prove ourselves worthy, and if we don't then maybe we'll be taken away too and maybe another group brought back. Who knows?'

Salina looked up, her eyes clearing, 'Do you think so, that we might be taken away too?'

'Anything's possible but don't worry about something like that. There's nothing we can do about it.'

'No but do you mean that if we're not judged worthy then maybe the rest of the world will return? If that's the case then maybe we should be bad too, to bring the others back. I'd sacrifice myself to make that happen, wouldn't you, Charlie?'

'Now wait a minute, Sis, I didn't mean that. Don't go doing something crazy. It won't work like that.'

'How do you know? Maybe it will. Maybe if we show that we're no better than those that were taken away then Allah will realise he's made a mistake and bring the others back but this time it would be a warning to all to be good. Maybe that's His plan?' she suggested.

Charlie took a deep breath and didn't answer straight away. He watched Salina pull herself together. 'No. It won't work that way. There's no way that something this big can be turned around by doing stupid things, Salina. You must promise me that you won't do something crazy. Please, Salina, don't go nuts on me or try to top yourself, okay. I couldn't go on without you by my side. I need you; we all do. Please promise me that you'll always be here for me, please?'

She looked at him and smiled, put her hand out and stroked his cheek. 'It's okay, I won't kill myself. I wasn't thinking that, honest. I just miss the old world so much, and my friends and all the things we had. I just never realised how much we had, that's all. Will it ever get back to normal do you think?'

'Well, not normal, no, how can it. Normal is gone for ever. But the future can be good, better maybe, once we get back to the twenty first century again. That will happen, it must. Think about the positives, like… a cleaner environment, no wars, plenty of food for everyone, no poverty, the world's fish stocks coming back again, millions of whales in the seas again one day, more rhinos and all the animals that our overpopulation had impacted, the end of global warming, lots of stuff.'

'Charlie, you're bloody weird, you know that. Trust you to think of more fish in the sea instead of not being able to fly to Spain for a holiday,' Salina laughed.

He was glad of her laugh again. 'We just need to stick together, Salsa, and Michael too of course. We need to keep an eye on dad as well, make sure he doesn't get carried away by any new loonies.'

'He seemed happier about having something to do again. I couldn't believe how much he was chatting about his day at the hospital getting the generators working better.'

'Yeah, that was good. A bit like the old days. Where's Michael?'

'Playing football. He's started a league with the lads in the next few streets.'

'Really? He never said.'

'Yeah, well, he didn't want you to take it over, but his plan was to ask you to play once they've got a few teams going. He wants to surprise you, so act it, okay?'

'Of course. Sounds good. Thanks, Salina. I'm off out, just for a walk, but you can come if you like?'

'No, it's okay, I'll be right. Thanks, Charlie.'

'Okay, see ya.'

KALIL

The heat in Amritsar was oppressive, but that wasn't what made him sweat. It was the thought of whether his Pakistani counterpart, President Ghulam Asif, would be true to his word and come to this meeting with just a small contingent of advisers and not see this as an opportunity to remove a rival. In his place he'd have considered an ambush and removal of a neighbouring President, although perhaps in this new world he needed to change his way of thinking, be less suspicious and more conciliatory? Time would tell.

An hour later, as Asif was sitting in front of him with three advisers by his side, he decided that good will and a certain level of curiosity had perhaps made his counterpart more open than ever before. The pleasantries and introductions aside, the two Presidents smiled at each other.

As India's President, as he was now referring to himself more often, he was on home ground in Amritsar, but the city was still close to the border and if things did not go well, and if President Asif had a contingency plan up his sleeve, then he could be in trouble.

'President Kalil…'

'Please, President Asif, call me Sabal. We need to become allies and friends if you wish?'

'Thank you, Sabal, I do wish it, and please call me Ghulam,' Asif offered. 'Do you know what made me the most intrigued by your letter and the reason why I chose to come as invited rather than play politics or… do something uncharitable?'

'Presumably the idea of taking over the USA?' Kalil suggested.

'Exactly! From what we can determine, the whole new world's focus has been on the Middle East, and the importance of Mecca and Medina and the role of the new Caliphate in guiding the world. All eyes are on Mecca and the interpretations of the Quran now that we are free of infidels, and contemplation about the wishes of Allah, praise be to Him. Yet your first thought, or one of them, Sabal, was to invade the USA, rather than worry about my intentions. Why?'

Kalil nodded his head and waited a few seconds before answering. 'Ghulam, we have several ways that we can move forward. In short these include thinking in the old ways, or adapting to the new world, and for the latter, that provides two distinctly different paths. But first, let me expand, if you'll indulge me,' he paused and waited for his guest to nod his interest.

'Let me say from the start that none of us can second guess the future intended for us by Allah, praise be His name, naturally. But I do not accept that we should await the proclamations of the Caliph of Mecca. Since when do we bow to the interests of the Saudi's, or any Arabs? How long is it that the Saudi's have mistreated our countrymen that have gone there to work, yet be looked down upon, paid poorly, imprisoned for minor offences, treated as anything other than devout Muslims should be? This doesn't need an answer as we both know what I mean by this. Just because we now live in a totally Islamic world does not mean that those that control Mecca and Medina and Jerusalem have the right to dictate the direction of the world to those of us that have experienced true democracy. We have all been chosen by Allah for this new world. It is for us to show our appreciation and to make the most of what is on offer. If Allah intended for us all to be ruled on Earth by the Saudi's, then this would have been made plain to us, or so I believe.

'Now, there are certain countries that are in a prominent position to be major powers. This includes countries that were largely left intact, such as Pakistan, Indonesia and those of the Middle East and North Africa and the various 'Stans' to our north. Then there's India, which with 204 million people is also a 'going concern' as the west would have termed it. After that there are a series of non-viable underpopulated nations in Europe and further afield. These can be either ignored, encouraged to migrate their populations to places that will thrive, or become outlying villages of faith, of no real consequence to us.

'So, where and how is the new world going to thrive? In only one of two ways. First, it will be ruled or dominated by the functioning democratic powerhouses. That means your country, mine, and Indonesia, mainly. If it is to be dominated by Pakistan and India then that should be achieved together, not in conflict or competition, but I will come back to this issue. The second option is to think outside of the square. Before Infidel's End, the new growth nations that would have increased their dominance in the latter half of this century were China, India, Indonesia and Brazil, with the US remaining as the key superpower, because I think Russia would have eventually faltered and the despotic Putin removed eventually. What held India back was its caste system and population, both a benefit and a curse. What held Pakistan back, in my humble opinion, was its fixation on Islam under threat and your internal problems with the northern tribes and fundamentalists that held the country back from necessary reforms. So, to change our destiny means to escape our historic bounds whilst we can. We need to take over the USA and utilise its modern infrastructure and resources before anyone else does this. How? By exporting our key people and sending 10 million of our people there this year and another 50 million next year, and for the years following.'

'Impossible! How can we do that?'

Kalil smiled internally at Asif's use of 'we', rather than ask how India would do this. 'I have a functioning blue water navy. You have the most highly trained military ground forces left in the world. We have between us 130 long-haul wide-bodied aircraft that can make the trip to the US east coast. We send my ships with your army to secure Manhattan, and then we fly the first wave of groups of 32,000 migrants to the new United States of Indiastan, with another group following every few weeks.'

'My God, you've really thought this through, haven't you? This is no idle chat about cross border incursions is it, Sabal? You want to be the new President of the USA!' Asif stated, incredulous.

HABBIB

The President walked into the Oval Office after visiting the bathroom and nodded to his three colleagues already sat there, who rose formally and then took their seats again. Imran Malouf was sat in the second most important chair, he noticed, but didn't begrudge the Secretary of State staking his claim, as he was most definitely doing the lion's share of the work. Across from him was George Saba, who he was developing a close relationship with, much like his own in the days of President Kendall. Amelia Sanchez was looking a little depressed, which was unusual. She had managed to stay upbeat in the middle of significant challenges so far, but at times he wondered how much of a toll the changes had wrought on her, with half of her family dying on Revelation Day. He preferred this new term that had recently been coined by someone, rather than Infidel's End. It seemed less antagonistic, or more charitable. Perhaps he just chose to believe that Allah the merciful would be treating the non-Islamic dead kindly.

'I hear you have some good news, Amelia, so why don't you start?' he offered.

She smiled, clearly somewhat surprised. 'Thank you, Mr President. Yes, I suppose I have had some good news, or progress. We've finally made electronic contact with the west coast. Some bright individuals in Silicon Valley have got a live link set up again, sort of like Skype used to be, but within a narrow group of PCs. In effect, it's an email and video link set up between San Francisco, New York and Washington with ten PC terminals on it.'

'How?' Malouf asked.

'I really have no idea, Imran. They tried to explain it to me, but it was in geek language and really, I don't care. I'm just so thrilled to finally have something electronic working again that allows us to talk in real time. The next phase is to get some form of cell phone connection between a small number of base stations in the three cities, but this might take another few weeks to pull off.'

'Holy crap, that's great!' Saba shouted, punching the air in triumph. 'Yeah, baby, America back on the air!'

Habbib couldn't help but laugh in appreciation of his Chief of Staff's enthusiasm. 'Well, it's nice to have something to celebrate. Good work, Amelia.'

'I wish I could take credit, Sir, but it was the geeks that did it,' she smiled.

Malouf smiled too, 'Who cares. Like you said, George, American ingenuity has us back in the game. Any other progress, like with international comms?'

'Not yet,' Amelia admitted, 'but close. The few ham radio enthusiasts we've got on the books are providing reports of a sort. The problem is that they're often, or almost always, individuals without a link to their own country's leadership. So, their own knowledge of what's going on in their own back yards is quite limited. But we're trying to get them to find the answers to a common group of questions; that's the next stage.'

'Like what?' Saba asked.

'Like, what have their countries or cities managed to get working again, do they have regular power supply, what's the food situation like, what are their key areas of need, is it safe there, are there demonstrations in the streets, are the schools up and running again, what is happening with their transport networks, stuff like that.'

'Any main threads coming through?' Habbib asked.

Sanchez looked at her notes, 'Well, yes there's a few that seem common...'

'Wait a minute. Who are we talking about here, which countries are these people in?' Saba interrupted.

Sanchez looked at her notebook, 'Well we have contacts now in the UK, France, Germany, India, Indonesia, Iran and Morocco.'

'So, what's the consensus?' Habbib asked.

'Well, Indonesia, Iran and Morocco seem to be continuing as usual, apart from the general loss of international communications, trade, tourism and air traffic. But their economies and systems are intact. From a social perspective, there's general positive feelings and we haven't been told about any negative issues so far. India seems to be coping, albeit with far fewer people but enough to be across all areas of technical need. As for the Europeans, it's chaotic, with limited services and facilities, much as like here. There's also more dismay at the change to life.'

'Nothing that we couldn't have guessed by ourselves then?' Saba scoffed.

'True, but we'll get more now that we've asked specific questions, hopefully,' Sanchez answered.

'Anything else, Amelia?' Habbib asked.

'Yes, Mr President. I've found you a military officer, a Major John Cummins. He's waiting outside.'

Habbib looked startled, 'What? Well for God's sake, bring him in.'

'Yes, Sir, I was just waiting until the end of normal business,' she said, as she rose and went to the door and called out.

A man in uniform, some six feet 4 inches tall, strolled in, saluted the President, and stood at attention. 'Major John Cummins, Mr President, US Marine Corp.'

'A pleasure to meet you, Major. Please, sit down,' Habbib offered. 'Tell me about yourself.'

Cummins took a noticeable deep breath and a surreptitious glance around the room, clearly awed. 'Well, Mr President, I've been in the Marine Corp for twenty years, last posted to Fort Bragg as a liaison officer to General Steve Marshall. I spent time in Afghanistan and Iraq, two tours of each theatre. Had some other interesting postings too, I suppose. But now I find myself largely alone. Waking up at Bragg on the morning after Revelation Day was not something I'd ever imagined. It was like… well it was like the aftermath of a nuclear war but without the physical damage. Quite frankly, Sir, I wasn't sure why I was the only one alive.'

'Cummins isn't exactly an Islamic surname,' Malouf stated.

'No, I converted, late in life. My wife was from Iran. We met when I was posted to Germany, where her family had lived for many years. I became interested in Islam after about a year and liked many aspects of the religion. Sadly, she died a few years ago… breast cancer. In many ways, I see my adherence to Islam as honouring her memory now. But I must say, that being the sole survivor, and losing all my friends and colleagues… well, I wonder about all of this, and I don't understand the Prophet's motives at all. I miss the world we had, even with all of its problems.'

'I don't think you're alone in that, Major,' Habbib said. 'Tell me more after you found yourself isolated at Fort Bragg.'

'Well, I checked everywhere. Every building, every square inch of the place, praying for survivors… you can imagine, I'm sure. I thought I'd gone mad at one stage, succumbed to mental illness maybe. Then I assumed that we'd been gas attacked and that I was just lucky to survive by some freak of nature. I took a vehicle and went into the town. Same story everywhere, just thousands of dead, men, women, children. I'm not ashamed to say that I cried for a long time. I waited in the town for a day and then went back to the base and took what I needed from the stores and loaded up a vehicle and started driving. At first, I had no idea where I was going, but I headed north. About a week later I realised there were no more bodies. Weirdly that made me feel even more alone. I ended up in Michigan, maybe because I had family there. Stupidly I thought my sister and her family would be alive. It still hadn't dawned on me that I was saved by my religion, not by chance. Her house was empty, but I could see where they'd been, the dust of their minerals left on the beds. I just hoped it had been painless and that the kids hadn't been afraid or aware of it all.' He put his head in his hands and tried to compose himself.

'We all went through it, Major, but I think your experience was worse than most of ours,' Habbib consoled him, 'at least we had some people around us to ease the mental anguish.'

Cummins nodded, 'It was rough, Sir, very hard. I found a mosque in one of the suburbs of Detroit and my first contact with other people. God that felt so good. I stayed with them for a month. Everyone decided to move to New York, on the basis that there had to be a bigger Muslim population there. But I still felt that I needed to report to someone. I know that sounds stupid, but it nagged at me. So, after living in New York City for the past few months I decided to head to Washington and see if there was anyone at the Pentagon. There wasn't. So, I came here and met Ms Sanchez.' He looked across at her and she smiled.

Habbib sighed. 'Major, you might be the only military man left alive, although I'd have thought that we'd at least have a few thousand military personnel within the faith, but maybe they're so scattered that we'll never get them together, at least not for a long time.'

'I suppose we're not needed now anyway, Mr President. I mean there's not likely to be warfare breaking out in a totally Islamic world with adequate resources for all,' Cummins suggested.

'I don't share that optimism, Major,' Saba replied.

'What do you mean, Sir?'

'Think about it. The Islamic world was hardly a place of peace and love within the Middle East. Shia versus Sunni versus Islamic State versus Assad, and the Syrian conflict. Iran versus Saudi Arabia via proxy conflicts through terrorist organisations and their support of the Houthis in Yemen. Turkey against the Kurds. The Taliban resurgence. The list goes on,' Saba outlined.

Cummins nodded in partial agreement, 'Sure, but there was plenty of fuel for those fires from the west's meddling in the Middle East, in areas of conflict that were complex to say the least.'

'Agreed, but even if we leave aside the Sunni and Shia issues, which are largely a problem in the Middle East rather than elsewhere, I don't see there being an instant era of brotherly love taking place, at least not in the longer term. Whilst we don't really know what's going on in any detail, there will come a time when the power brokers seek to exploit their strengths or hold on to power. Human nature isn't likely to undergo a transformation just because there are adequate resources for all,' Saba opined. 'Don't you agree, Mr President?'

'Sadly, I do, although I also hope that this new world will rapidly adjust to having been chosen by Allah and that therefore we will be judged harshly if we fail to make the most of it. However, in the meantime I imagine that those countries left largely intact will flex their muscles to become the new superpowers. Places like Pakistan, India, and Indonesia in particular.'

'I suppose so, Mr President. That does make sense,' Cummins acceded, 'but we have different challenges here. We don't need to concern ourselves with distant power plays. We need to get the US back up and running first.'

'That's right, Major. I'd like you to stick around if you will. It would be useful to have a military expert on staff. Are you OK with that?'

'I'd be honoured, Sir, although I'm no expert.'

'You're the closest we have to a Military expert now and given your experience I think you're being a little modest,' Habbib said. 'Amelia, find the major an office and give him a rundown on things as they now stand.' He stood up and proffered his hand, which the Major shook, then saluted again and Amelia took him out of the Oval Office and down the hall.

'Could be useful,' Saba said, once he'd left.

'In a way, I hope you're wrong and that we don't need him,' Habbib replied. 'Because if we do need military assistance then it means we have bigger problems coming than I want to even contemplate, George.'

CHARLIE

He knocked on the door of the run-down semi-detached house with the messy garden that was occupied by Mustafa-Harry.

'The door's unlocked, come on in, whoever you are!'

He pushed on the door, and it swung open with a creak. The hallway smelled musty and was dark. He knew from experience that Harry would be in the kitchen or the lounge room, which doubled as his ham radio den. He walked down the passage and looked along the way at the other two rooms he passed. Old and in need of renovation he thought. Then he smelled burnt toast coming from the kitchen and it made him hungry. The site that met him was not what he'd expected, automatically going back in time to the joys of an automatic toaster. Harry was sitting with a toasting stick over a little bundle of wood burning in a small square cast iron barbecue stove. He had just added a fresh piece of bread to a metal pronged fork.

'Bloody hell, where did you get the bread from Harry?'

'Everly Avenue, 3 streets over from here. Bloke called Muhammed. What a surprise, another bloody Muhammed, eh? Anyhow, he's got himself a pizza oven in the back yard and has managed to bake bread in it. Bloody marvellous I reckon. Would be better if we had some butter mind you. Still, I have a jar of marmalade here. Would you like some, young Charlie?'

'Would I ever? Thanks, Harry.'

'Sit yourself down then, lad, and you can fill me in on the news whilst I get this piece browned.'

Charlie sat mesmerised, his mouth watering at the anticipation of toast and marmalade, even though he preferred strawberry jam. 'Did you hear that dad got a job working at Crumpsall Hospital helping them to fix up the generators and stuff?'

'I did. Michael told me. He was here last week.'

'Was he? He never said.'

'I asked him not to, Charlie.'

'Why?'

'Coz, I want real visitors, not toast desperadoes. If people visit me of their own accord, with genuine friendship, then I'll feed them and have a natter. But I'm not giving good bread away to any Tom, Dick and Charlie that comes beggin', if you get me drift?'

He nodded, 'Sure, sounds reasonable. I'm with you on that.'

'Are you just?' Harry said with a twinkle in his eye. 'So, what brings you here then?'

'I wanted to hear what you've found out on your radio lately. Like, what's goin' on around the world? Have other people got electricity and TV and stuff or they all still in the dark like us?'

'Well, I had a bit of a problem, young man. I ran out of power too, so I was off the air for a week until I managed to acquire a little petrol generator and so I got my batteries charged again. But in answer to your question, I'd say that the world seems to be split into two groups. The haves and the have-nots. The haves are those where their populations are large and pretty much untouched, like the Paki's and Indians and in the Middle East, plus Indonesia, and Malaysia. The others are like us, the Europeans, Yanks and those countries left with a decimated population compared to pre-Revelation Day. I think the French are a bit better off, coz there was plenty of North African Muslims in Paris, so it's coping better than London, I think. Maybe we should move there, eh?'

'Really? Do you think that would be better, Harry?'

'Why not, the weather's better too, which will be a real bugger here come winter if we don't get the friggin' power back on before then.'

'Has Paris got power then?'

'Actually, I don't think they have. Same issues as for us, not enough technically capable people that worked essential services. How's your dad doin' at Crumpsall then? Has he made progress with the generators?'

'I think so, but they're just diesel gensets he says, so they aren't going to help us much with the big stuff on the grid.'

'Hmm, no s'pose not. The way I see it we're going to have to conglomerate into a single suburb with a larger generator and direct current being wired around it maybe.'

'Why don't you come over for tea tonight and talk to him about that. He'd love to talk techo stuff with you I'm sure, as well as learning what you've found out on your radio. Will ya?'

'Another mouth to feed for your mum, that. Better ask her first.'

'No, it'll be fine, honest. Just come over at five, please?'

'OK then, I'll be there. I'll bring some bread too, but don't tell your mum in advance.'

'Great! I won't, I promise. See you later, Harry,' he beamed and then ran home to tell his mum about their dinner guest.

When Harry arrived later, bearing the gift of bread, everyone was thrilled to see him. Riaz arrived home after Harry but was also happy to have a guest. After the meal, the discussion turned to world affairs.

'So, what's happening elsewhere, Harry? What does your radio tell you?' Riaz asked.

'Well, much the same as here in places with only a few people left, but like I was telling Charlie here, seems a bit better in Paris, but still largely strugglin' with the same stuff, like lack of power. But I did pick up some weirdness from a bloke that calls himself Saul84 in Saudi Arabia. He was very cagey, sounded a bit hesitant really, but then given what that place is like I wasn't too surprised. His English wasn't great but good enough. Seems that the Caliph of Mecca, the bloke that took over from the King as the leader, is calling for the whole world to accept Arabic as the global language, but it's being resisted outside of the Middle East and North Africa.'

'Huh, I'm not surprised. Can you imagine it, trying to get the rest of us to learn Arabic?' Riaz exclaimed. 'That's just daft.'

'Not to them it ain't,' Harry said. 'Would make perfect sense to an Arab and seein' as how they can now state that Mecca's the centre of the world, I can understand the push for it.'

'Humph, well I can't see that happening here. Too many other problems to sort out anyway,' Riaz added. 'What happened to the royal family in Saudi then? How come there's this new Caliph bloke on top?'

'No idea. I couldn't get much sense out of him on that. Don't know whether they were overthrown or killed by the masses or are just now under the control of this Caliph.'

'What else, Harry?' Charlie asked.

'Loads of people have started migrating to Mecca and Medina it seems, and the local population are struggling to feed them all. Sounded like the military were trying to keep them out. Saul wasn't too sure whether there was any violence, just that there was a bit of an anti-foreigner campaign goin' on.'

'This guy's in Mecca then?' Riaz asked.

'No, in Riyadh. Took me ages to get him to confirm that though. He's not exactly unsuspicious of authority listening in. Probably being wise, there.'

'Who else do you talk to?' Salina asked.

'Well, I did once get a contact in Jakarta, Indonesia, but it was full of static, and he wouldn't give his name either. Overall, they seemed to be living as usual, with no real change to their way of life apart from a lack of foreign visitors. Met a few enthusiasts in India though. They seem very happy. Lots of food, houses for the taking and no discrimination anymore. It's still sad for me though. Before Revelation Day there were over two million amateur radio enthusiasts in the world, about 850,000 in the US. I had a network of maybe 50 people I'd talk to regularly. Not one of them is still on the air. All dead now I suppose. Wasn't really a hobby that many Muslims were into, or at least not that I came across. But I think there'll be more. Trouble is you still need power for it. Not that it's too hard. I mean I got mine up and running again on batteries and then with my petrol generator. That'll last ages now. Maybe there's too few people out there that know how to tinker about with their kits to keep them in working order.'

'Maybe they've got other priorities, Harry,' Riaz suggested.

'No way. Once a ham enthusiast, always one, and especially now when there's such a need for information. Now's the time when they should be flooding the airwaves, just like used to happen after natural disasters. I mean, after Hurricane Katrina in the US it was the ham radio community that provided most of the information to emergency services. This has always been the case, so now's no different. We're living in the middle of an emergency, aren't we?'

'Not an emergency, Harry, just a test, sent to us by the Prophet, blessed be His name,' Riaz stated.

'Give over, Riaz. You don't believe that stuff do you, about a test of faith I mean? Bloody hell, if this is a test, I can't imagine how the heck I've passed it. I haven't set foot in a mosque for twenty years at least. How did I qualify for saving?' Harry laughed.

Riaz shrugged, clearly contemplating what to say and then seemed to come to a decision. 'You're right actually. We're much the same, not regulars at any mosque and not really all that familiar with the Quran. I mean I was when I was young, in Iran, and then it lost its importance for me. Maybe that was partly because of what I experienced there, with the religious police after the revolution. That put me off completely. Life here was easier. But now I'm worried about that. What if the fanatics take over?'

Harry scratched his head, a worried look on his face, 'Yes, well, there might already be some of that. I didn't want to spoil the atmosphere after such a lovely evening, but I also picked up on some weird stuff from Saul too.'

'Like what?' Charlie asked.

'Well, he said that there was rumours goin' around out there and some things that I wasn't sure if he'd seen himself or just heard about. Wasn't too clear. He said that there was a planned stoning of an adulterous woman in the town square. A mass of people had turned up to stone her. Her husband had accused her apparently. Anyway, Saul said that when the crowd picked up the stones ready to throw at her there was this huge groan and then the whole lot of them dropped dead in the act of throwing them, and the Imam that was watching it being carried out, he died as well. Since then, there's been no Sharia pronouncements, his words not mine.'

'So, what happened?'

'No idea. He seemed to think it was a message from Allah of course.'

'About what? Violence against women?' Mina suggested.

'Be a good thing if so, wouldn't it?' Harry replied.

'What happened to the poor woman?' Mina asked.

'He said she was let off and was an offering from Allah but that her husband was one of those that died too and so it was assumed that she was innocent, and divine intervention was the proof to the people.'

'Lucky for her,' Salina said.

'Makes you wonder though,' Riaz contemplated.

HABBIB

'Good morning, John,' President Habbib called out as he met the Major making coffee in one of the kitchenettes of the White House.

The Major jumped like a kid caught with his hand in the cookie jar, spilt some of his coffee and looked embarrassed and not sure what to say, 'Er, Mr President, Sir, sorry, I...'

'Relax, Major. You're going to have to get used to more informality than you clearly expected around here. I'm sure in different circumstances, like in my predecessor's day, this bumping into each other whilst I want to make my own coffee would never have happened. But as you've no doubt noticed, there's only twenty staff working here, and probably ten of them are under employed. I'm OK with you using whatever level of protocol you're comfortable with but we need to be practical. We now live in a country of four million people, only 3 real cities inhabited, no military, no clear threats, limited infrastructure, and a hell of a lot of practical problems to overcome. Being informal is the only way forward, don't you agree?'

'I guess so, Mr President,' Cummins answered as he simultaneously mopped up the bench top. 'Can I make you a coffee, Sir?'

'No thanks, I'll do that for myself. Whilst I do, you can tell me whether you've given any thought to the potential for military threats to the United States?'

'Yes, Sir, I have. Quite a lot. I must admit that I was a little taken aback by this, but I now see what perhaps you were getting at.'

'Well, that's kind of you, Major, but I'm not so sure that I had any clear thoughts in my head, rather than putting a good military mind back to work. Anyway, what are your conclusions?'

Cummins' expression suddenly changed, 'Can I be extremely crude and blunt, Sir?'

Habbib laughed, 'Go ahead, Major, say what's on your mind.'

'Under any threat scenario at all, Sir, the US is fucked!'

'Hell, Major! I wasn't expecting quite that level of bluntness, but I did ask for it. Go on, tell me why.'

'Well, we have the biggest military in the world in terms of assets; ships, planes, tanks, and facilities… with no men at all to use them, or maybe a hundred personnel if we can find them. I'm a good shot with a rifle, Sir, but holding off even a minor invasion is impossible, unless I go out and arm the whole of New York and train them, ready for something that might never happen. Which takes me to the threat analysis.'

'Keep going,' Habbib encouraged.

'OK, so who would come here and why? My first thought was that nobody would want or need to invade the US. We are no threat, we aren't back up and running, and we provide no tangible benefit to anyone, or so I thought. I can only assume that the Islamic world remains largely intact, with sizable populations and thriving economies, even if somewhat isolated now from what was world trade beforehand. So, I thought, let's take Indonesia as the world's largest Islamic state and analyse that. They'd have lost very few people, and mainly Buddhists and a few Hindus perhaps, maybe some Christians, and their Chinese community, but all up not a lot in population percentage terms. Their country is green and fertile, they have adequate resources and if they needed minerals they'd expand into Australia, presumably now an uninhabited country, pretty much.

'So, then I went wider and looked at the Middle East. There's no way that the Arab world is going to leave the area that spawned Muhammed. It wouldn't abandon Mecca and Medina and Jerusalem, not now. If anything, I expect thousands, or even millions of new migrants are flocking there to be closer to the Prophet's birthplace and upbringing. North Africa? Similar story, or, if they wanted an easier life, of sorts, then they'd expand north into Europe.

'OK, so what about India and Pakistan and Bangladesh? Are they any different? Not really. Plenty of space for them to spread out now that over a billion Hindus, and Sikhs, have gone. It's a new land of plenty; fertile, a good going concern. OK, so what if I'm misreading the ambitions of these players? What if they would come here, some of them, just to be the new superpower, to take our military assets to strengthen themselves? That led me to a different conclusion. The new power brokers will probably be the Indian subcontinental trio, versus Indonesia and Malaysia, versus the Middle East, maybe with Iran isolated. That led me to consider Iran as the only strong and dominant Shiite country. I don't believe that Revelation Day will have brought peace across the Islamic world. Sadly, human nature overrides logic and I still think that Sunni versus Shiite conflict will be there or start again in the future. If that's my view, then I can bet Iran will come to a similar conclusion. So, what would I do if I was the Iranian government? I'd get the hell out of there and move a sizeable portion of my population over here so that the Shiite world can spread itself throughout the Americas unhindered by the Sunnis. In short, I think Iran is one potential threat, Mr President, but there will be others.'

KALIL

Ghulam Asif had readily extended his stay in Amritsar after the revelations he'd heard from the mouth of Sabal Kalil. He adjusted his clothing as he made ready for their second evening meal together. By agreement they had stayed together in a local palace that allowed them to walk to the Golden Temple each morning for further discussions. Neither was concerned about using the previous Sikh holy site for their meetings. The location was just too good to ignore and neither man was superstitious about it.

It was a very pleasant evening, with a cool breeze and delightful smells of spices from somewhere nearby. Kalil waited for his counterpart to be seated before speaking. 'Ghulam, I've taken the liberty of pre-ordering a feast with local delicacies, which I hope you'll enjoy.' His guest bowed his head in acknowledgment, allowing the opening remarks to be continued. 'Earlier you posed a very good question…'

'What's to be gained from this strategy?' Ghulam interrupted

'Yes, exactly. I didn't wish to answer straight way, although clearly, I have thought long and hard about this. But your question made me re-evaluate my own logic and try to consider it from different angles. Maybe I just wanted to use the military appreciation process again and test my own preconceptions a little more critically; always a valuable exercise I've found.'

'And your conclusions?'

'Patience my friend,' Kalil laughed, 'allow me some theatre in all of this. It is not often that I get the chance these days to play to an audience of equal intellect.'

'Now I am worried,' Ghulam laughed. 'Is this a dinner or a seduction?'

Kalil smiled. 'So, allow me some build up here, as that will test my thinking process again. Firstly, what does the US have that we need? We don't need land, or their food, their goods, their cars, their material possessions. And their winter weather makes life more difficult without adequate and secure power systems, which I would imagine are proving a problem to their small remaining population now. But they do have a lot of military hardware, and especially their navy. If we think of the world now as being like the pre-industrial age, then it is naval capability which drove the times of plenty for the great European explorers and colonisers. Whilst clearly there was no alternative then, no flying of course, it is still shipping that drives our world trade, or did. And it is naval power that will determine the new superpowers. So, from a military strength perspective we have the biggest capability. We either enhance it or potentially lose it to another player.'

'Who?'

'Indonesia, in alliance with Malaysia,' Kalil suggested.

'Yes, I can see that makes sense.'

'Then I considered other factors, like the new Caliphate of Mecca. Whilst I fully understand the importance of the holy sites and Allah's clear message to us, the faithful that have been chosen, it does not mean that the new world should concentrate on Mecca. It cannot anyway, we can't all go there to live, it's in the desert. Take a pilgrimage, certainly, and I look forward to doing that at the earliest opportunity, but the Middle East will not become the new superpower, clearly.'

Asif looked inquisitively at his new colleague and slowly shook his head. 'No, there is something else. Whilst your logic seems sound, there must be more. I don't disagree with your analysis of naval capability and trade, but the alternative is to leave the US as it is, insignificant, and make our region the new centre of the world. What else is driving this ambition, Sabal?'

'Have you ever been to America, Ghulam?'

'Once, briefly. Just New York and Washington for four days.'

'What did you think of it?'

'Brash, confident, enormously wealthy but with little appreciation of it. But also, a little naïve. Certainly friendly, but… I'm not sure how to describe it, but I think I'd say childlike in their enthusiasm and outlook.'

Kalil considered that last comment, then nodded, 'Yes, that's a good interpretation, I think. Childlike, but in a good way. The Americans certainly enjoyed life, but they also had an odd and inaccurate sense of their own place in the world. They did not see the disparity between rich and poor or the vast differences in real opportunity. They truly believed that hard work could bring riches, when that happened to relatively few, and those at the bottom of the pile tended to stay there, for generations. Yet this never diminished their patriotism. It was like a place with lots of promise and high ideals but that had failed miserably to look after its own people sufficiently.

'But, for all of that it was still an amazing accomplishment, Ghulam. The wealth was everywhere, in buildings, bridges, infrastructure, railways, and industrial might, albeit much in need of maintenance. I was also on a military exchange in Canada for three months, as well as a shorter visit to West Point. On weekends, I visited as many places as possible. One thing stood out for me above all else, and that was the beauty of the environment, the mountains, rivers, national parks, coastal areas, forests, and vast farmlands. That is the wealth, Ghulam, and it's there for the taking. Yes, you are right when you say that this region of ours can be the centre of this new world now, but whoever controls the American continent will be the eventual winner. It's not just the US, Ghulam, it's also the access to South America too. Brazil for instance, or Mexico. Christopher Columbus and the other explorers might have found a new continent to exploit, but we have the technical expertise within our populations to capitalise on known existing riches beyond count.'

'I get the impression that you already have an invasion plan in your mind in quite astounding detail?'

Kalil laughed, 'Yes, I do. And I'm happy to share it with you and get your input.'

'Later. First, tell me how you see your own personal position in all of this?'

'I see you as the first President of Pakindesh, my name for the new country that incorporates Pakistan, India and Bangladesh. I will be the new President of the Americas,' Kalil said confidently.

'The Americas in total?'

'Yes, from Alaska to Argentina.'

'My God, I thought I was ambitious, but your vision for yourself is boundless.'

'Not for myself, Ghulam, for our people, yours and mine. Pakindesh has over six hundred million people now. Indonesia has two hundred and forty million. There are maybe twenty-two million in Malaysia. The western world is ours for the taking. We start with New York and Washington, then the west coast. We send thirty thousand people across every two weeks, expanding that number after six months. Within a year, we should be able to transport a million of our people there. It needs to begin with technical experts in industrial fields, and especially power system and transport engineers, pilots, train drivers, ship and dock workers, doctors, nurses, teachers...'

'Wait a minute, Sabal, you can't expect to deplete the population here by taking the best away to America.'

'We can afford it; we have sufficient human capital to pull from. Within ten years we need to have migrated at least two hundred million to the Americas. So, the question is, are you with me or not?'

RIAZ

'We're moving,' Riaz told his family over dinner. The responses were immediate.

'What? Where to... why?' Salina stammered.

'What for?' Michael echoed.

'I like it here, Dad,' argued Charlie.

'Hear me out, please!' Riaz replied, holding up his hand for some silence from his children. 'The council of Imams has decided that it makes more sense for the population of the UK to all move to London and the home counties. There is power connected there now. One of the gas-fired power stations is up and running and London has reliable power at last, although it still has some issues, but they've also made progress with the water and sewage systems, so it makes sense to consolidate the population where things are working. And there's plenty of accommodation. We can find somewhere nicer to live and just take it. But the better houses will go fast, so the sooner we move the better. I've been given a job working with one of the hospitals on their back-up power systems. It's all good. We'll get back to normal life again, or close to it anyway. You should all be happy. There's even going to be TV on air again soon.'

The family remained stony-faced. Mina captured the mood, 'I know you will miss it here, because of our memories, but your father is right, and if everyone is being encouraged to go to London it would be silly to stay here. Things can only improve if we all stick together. I don't mean just the family but the whole population. You'll see. It will be good. Imagine a type of normality again once we're in a working city.'

'Can we take our own things?' Charlie asked.

'Of course, or at least what we can get in a car or small van. There's no need to take anything other than personal possessions. We don't need furniture or household things, they'll be in the new houses anyway,' Riaz stated.

Salina wasn't convinced. 'It'll be weird. I mean, we'll be taking over someone else's memories. There'll be stuff there from a dead family, won't there?'

'We'll soon make it ours, Salina,' Mina replied.

'It won't feel right, mum,' she countered.

Charlie could see that the decision was made, and he knew that it made sense, although he shared his sibling's views, as well as their fears. 'It'll be OK I suppose. Can we take Harry with us?'

'Well, maybe he... I mean...' Riaz began.

'He's alone, dad,' Charlie said. 'And I like him. Plus, he has skills with his radio stuff. He'll need to bring that along too. Can I ask him?'

Riaz looked across at Mina, who made a slight nod. 'OK then, you can ask him. But he might not want to come, Charlie.'

'He will, I know it. It'll just need a good argument for him first. I'll ask him in the morning.'

'There's no hurry but we should aim to get there within a week if we can. I'll look for a bigger car with petrol in it tomorrow, or maybe a minibus. Do you want to help me with that, Michael?'

'Sure, I can do that, Dad' Michael answered, brightening up.

'Salina and I will decide what personal things we need to take with us,' Mina added, and noticed her daughter nod her agreement, although with limited enthusiasm.

Within four days they were ready to leave. Harry had agreed to accompany them, not willing to stay behind alone. He took the minimal amount of equipment with him to get back on the air and had contacted another enthusiast in London that promised some spare equipment and advice. Michael had sourced a Toyota Tarago with a tow bar, and a trailer was discovered in a nearby driveway. Salina had helped her mother to box up their most precious possessions. They took no household items, assuming these would be plentiful or easy to find in London.

Before they left, they walked around the house and made their separate farewells, each in a different and somewhat private way, exorcising their private ghosts and fears.

On the way south they noticed a few fires raging, seemingly just houses burning, maybe a few dozen in total. They speculated that it was the previous owners that wanted to deny their own memories to another family that might take possession.

'Where are we heading for, dad?' Charlie asked.

'My first choice is Number Ten Chesterfield Street, not far from the parks.'

'What kind of place is it?' Salina asked.

'Should be lovely. It used to be the house for the High Commission of the Government of the Bahamas. So, I thought it was hopefully not occupied by anyone else just yet and is close to the parklands around Buckingham Palace and Kensington Palace and Green Park. If someone's already taken it, I'm sure we can find something else suitable nearby. It's also near enough for an easy bike ride to St. Thomas' Hospital where I'm going to be helping with their electrical systems. Fingers crossed that it's uninhabited,' Riaz said, smiling.

'How the heck did you come across this place, Dad,' Michael asked.

'I once met a bloke that was going to the Bahamas for a job, as a teacher, and he had to go to the High Commission to get his visa stamped and I went with him, and we stayed in London for a weekend at a backpacker's hostel in Bayswater. That was a dump, but the Bahamas joint was just beautiful I thought. Never forgot it. Was always jealous of the way that those people lived.'

'If you think we're going to start calling you Mr Ambassador, you've got another think coming, Riaz,' Mina laughed.

'Hey, they should have some good comms equipment there though,' Harry suggested. 'Sounds like a great choice, Riaz. Thank you for making me a part of your extended family.'

Riaz coughed in embarrassment, 'No problems, Harry, you're welcome.'

The journey was uneventful, although finding the address a little more difficult than envisaged – he really missed Google Maps and satellite navigation. But four hours after they'd left Manchester, they were finally there. The building was impressive, and a little imposing, almost antagonistic in its silence. The doors were locked but Charlie and Michael broke a small window nearest the main door, cleared away the glass as best they could and crept in. It took a little time to get the main door open, but once they did the family walked in, with some trepidation and then in awe of their surroundings. There was an eerie feeling about it. No-one wanted to walk anywhere alone, and they wandered about the house, exploring each room together. After an hour, they'd each laid claim to a bedroom, and started to unpack the car and bring in their personal possessions.

Mina and Salina went to work in the kitchen, clearing away the spoiled food and getting rid of some of the worst smells. Once they'd disposed of the dairy and meat products, sprayed an air freshener around the room to neutralise the bad odours, and then opened all the windows to get some fresh air into the house, it felt much better.

Harry found what might have been the communications office for the High Commission and started setting up his radio equipment, with Charlie's assistance. 'I wonder when we'll get back to normal and be able to communicate across the world again, young Charlie?'

'Won't that happen once the power's back on?'

'Ha! I wish that were so, but I doubt it. Once you have major blackouts it's no easy matter to get back up and running again. Takes more than electrons flowing. It needs a lot of knowledge and not a little bit of luck. Someone needs to get into the BBC offices and see if they can get us back into the twenty-first century. Still, first things first, eh? Let's get my kit up again and I'll see what I can find out.'

'Charlie!' Riaz called out, 'I'm going to the hospital with Michael and we're going to look for a cycle shop on the way and get some bikes. Come with us.'

'What, now, dad?' Charlie argued.

'Yes, before it gets dark. Come on, I need help.'

'Sorry, Harry, I have to go; see you later,' Charlie apologised, running down the stairs to the ground floor from the third storey office.

They took the Tarago and its trailer and drove into Knightsbridge, aiming for Selfridges department store, the nearest place that Riaz suggested would have bikes, unless they came across a cycle shop along the way. They were lucky and found a bike shop called Cycledelik along the way that seemed intact. The door was locked, as expected, but they broke in and looked around. Within ten minutes they'd selected two top of the range mountain bikes from Diamond Back, a Raleigh All Terrain 30 Women's Sport and a Raleigh All Terrain 10 Men's version. The retail value was 5,850 pounds and they all high-fived their good fortune and had huge smiles on their faces. They took some helmets, water bottles, and a host of other accessories and carefully loaded them into the car and the trailer.

Next stop was the hospital, across the Thames. There was at least a few hundred people there, mainly medical staff but with a few dozen technical staff too. Riaz found someone that seemed to be in charge and approached him.

'Excuse me, can you help me, sir?' Riaz asked and was met with a surprised look in return.

'I'll try, what problem do you have?'

'Nothing medical, doctor,' Riaz began. 'I've been allocated this hospital by the council of Imams to see if I can help you to get the electrical power systems back up and running or maintained or whatever. I wondered if there's a maintenance manager I should report to?'

'Oh, that's great. I thought you were a patient or needed medical help. As you can see, we've got the lights on now and they stay on most of the time, but there's a man that seems to oversee all of that. Let me call him for you. Come along if you like?' he said and made his way to a reception desk, leapt over the counter, surprising them all, and picked up a type of microphone, pressed a button and spoke into it. The hospital PA system boomed into life as he said, 'Freddy, please come to reception, I have another electrical engineer for you here,' then put down the mike and smiled. 'Freddy is great. He managed to coordinate the back-up generators a few weeks ago, but now that there's baseload power on again for London, we rarely need it. But there's still a lot to do to get the operating theatres back to a state of being usable and we desperately need people with practical skills so I'm sure you'll be valuable. My name's Doctor Hamdid, Rashid Hamdid, welcome aboard.'

Riaz shook hands and introduced Michael and Charlie.

'I'm afraid I must go, patients to see. But wait here for Freddy, Riaz. He's a very tall guy so you won't miss him. I'll see you around. Good luck,' he called over his shoulder as he walked off at a rapid pace. They watched him leave and then were amazed to see a man aged in his early twenties, with red hair running up to them. He had to be six foot five inches tall and was broad shouldered and muscular, wearing jeans and a T-shirt that advertised Singha Beer. The latter was what struck Charlie the most, espousing beer within a religion that was anti-alcohol. For that alone he instantly liked him.

'Who's the sparky then?' Freddy called out, looking correctly at Riaz.

'That'd be me; Riaz Ahmed. How do you do,' he said, putting out his hand.

Freddy ignored the proffered hand and embraced Riaz warmly. 'You are an electrician I take it?'

'Yes, definitely.'

'Allah be praised, I've been needing a partner here for months. Mind you, things are pretty much OK now. As soon as they got that power station back on-line it was like winning the lottery, let me tell you,' he said, beaming, his cockney accent further confusing the image of a Muslim with Indian features but red hair.

'What's your background?' Charlie asked, less intimidated than his father.

'Don't beat about the bush do you kid?' Freddy laughed. 'No harm in that. Life's too short, eh? Too much to do. Born and bred here in London, as you can probably tell by the accent I s'pose. My dad came from Mumbai, mum from Madras, if that's what you mean?'

'Who'd you support before all of this?' Charlie asked, referring to football.

'Tottenham, the mighty Spurs. You?'

'Man United,' Charlie said, sadly.

'Yep, I share your pain, brother. I really miss the game too. Saturdays at White Hart Lane were some of my best memories. Course, yours were better, being a Man U fan, lucky bugger,' Freddy suggested, which brought a smile from Charlie.

Riaz immediately liked this giant of a man. Freddy looked at him and said, 'Want to see the engine room of this place?' Riaz nodded and he took off with the Ahmed family in tow. Keeping up with his pace and enthusiasm was a challenge. By the time they reached the basement and had walked through several passageways they were starting to tire.

'Here she is my friend, the diesel heartland of this building. Five megawatts of back-up,' Freddy announced, pointing to the generators.

'Five megawatts!' Riaz exclaimed.

'Yep, did nothin' by halves in this place. Let me give you a run down,' he said and then got into technical detail as Michael and Charlie followed their father around.

'So how did the power come back on, Freddy?' Charlie asked.

'I heard that they eventually managed to find some clever techo people that had worked in the industry, and between them they got the plant going. Mind you it wasn't easy. All sorts of issues to solve first, but once that was up and they made the gas supply safe, it wasn't long then before the water supply and sewage systems were working again. I think that was why they decided to get everyone that was willing to come to London. Makes sense to have us all together and get back to a working city again, eh? Less lonely too, don't you think?' Freddy suggested.

'S'pose so,' Charlie admitted. 'I still miss the old days though. Don't you?'

Freddy looked at Charlie and each of the Ahmeds in turn, and then looked over his shoulder to make sure there was no-one else around. 'It's OK to think that, and I understand, but don't go saying it, not to anyone you don't know. It can be heresy, you understand. There are people around that want to introduce the strictest interpretation of Islam, sayin' that this is Allah's will and that there's goin' to be another cleansing, that's the word that's used. They reckon the undevout ones will also be judged. So be careful, that's all.'

Riaz nodded, 'I understand, thank you Freddy.'

'That's OK, Riaz, just be aware that not everyone is your friend. Things are still being sorted out, and there's always ambitious people that will take advantage of chaos, and there's still a hell of a lot of chaos about.'

CHARLIE

Sorry, Diary, I've not exactly been good at writing things down lately. Too much has gone on, and I've not been clear in my own mind what I feel lately. We moved to London a few weeks ago. That was OK I suppose and we're living in a great house that used to belong to the chief of the Bahamas or something. It's close to huge parks and not far from Buckingham Palace too. I wonder who lives there now, some big shot I suppose. Anyway, dad is much happier. He's working at a hospital that's got loads of regular staff now, doctors, nurses, maintenance people, everything. Every day now we see thousands of people coming into London, more cars on the move than I've seen since Revelation Day. Seems like everyone had similar ideas in taking the good houses in the best spots. We've got neighbours now. But there's loads of good places to go around so there's been no arguments or fights from what I can tell.

The big news is that we've got news, on TV. There are regular broadcasts now on a single channel that used to be the BBC, or at least it comes from there. Radio too. Problem is there's only news on it, no regular stuff like films or comedy or anything. Mind you I suppose that's what people want now, considering we've had none since it all happened.

Know what I love most though, and it'll sound weird – flushing toilets! Honest, it's wonderful. Who'd have thought it? And the fridges work too. Still no milk available or yoghurt or cheese or anything like that, but soon will be we're told. I can't wait for that.

Bad side, for me anyway, is a constant load of stuff from the Caliph of Mecca, telling us all how to behave and what it all means and how the Prophet wants us to live. But there's others out there that are arguing against that stuff too and that seeing as how we all survived then the way that we lived before can't have been bad. Mustafa Harry is still living with us, and that's good too because we get other news from his radio, and he says that there's trouble about and that the Caliph isn't getting all his own way. Seems to be fighting going on in places too. Mainly between Iran and Saudi Arabia. Harry said there was more rumours about people dying that were trying to punish people under Sharia, and that the Caliph has become less harsh lately and talks a bit more about Allah being merciful.

Only bad thing on the horizon now is that the schools are reopening, and we have been ordered to go back next week, to a big secondary school near here. I can get there on my bike OK. Salsa and Michael are happier to go back than me. I think they just want to make some new friends. I'm worried about it though. Not sure what the teachers are going to be like – not mad clerics, I hope.

KALIL

'So how do you like New Delhi, Ghulam?'

'Just between you and I, Sabal, I prefer it to Islamabad in some ways, and in others not so much. But I agree that it makes sense to have the combined capital here or in Mumbai.'

'Yes, Mumbai would work too, given the port access and the higher population, but Delhi can work well now with less than two million inhabitants. The city has much to offer. Of course, there are more people moving here every day to take advantage of it. Ultimately, you can choose the seat of Government, in time. For now, I am pleased that the population has accepted the concept we presented of a triumvirate for our two countries and Bangladesh,' Kalil said.

'How do the preparations go for the fleet, Sabal?'

'All is ready. We will leave with our two aircraft carriers, 10 destroyers, 14 frigates, 4 fleet tankers, and fifty merchant ships. Our naval defence capability here will remain strong, with one nuclear-powered attack submarine, 14 conventionally powered attack submarines, 26 corvettes, 7 mine countermeasure vessels, and 10 large offshore patrol vessels, apart from about 100 patrol boats, as well as those from your naval fleet. Pakistan's 10 frigates, 3 mine hunters, 12 fast attack craft, plus your auxiliaries, 17 coastal patrol boats, and 12 hovercrafts, need not move out of their normal patrol waters, unless we see any unusual activity from Indonesia, which I very much doubt.'

'This will be the biggest naval deployment since D-Day,' Asif said with pride.

'Possibly. It was easier than I expected to recruit the new pilgrims,' Kalil laughed. 'I think many see this as their ticket to immense wealth. That might not be the case, but we will have two hundred thousand new migrants for the US on the merchant ships, and once we have secured our new territory, we will start the air deployment.'

'You still wish to airlift 30,000 people every two weeks?'

'I do, but not until we secure JFK as the refuel airport. As for the west coast, it is the aircraft migrants that will mainly populate California, because we don't know if the Panama Canal is still operable for ships to navigate. The commercial aircraft will then return westwards from LA or San Francisco,' Kalil stated confidently.

'When will you move on Washington DC?'

'Within the first month is the plan.'

'So, your dream of being the new President of the United States will be achieved before the end of the year, Sabal; congratulations.'

'Thank you, but your new empire will have more power, Ghulam.'

'Perhaps so, but it will need more careful management too,' Asif reflected. 'I remain a little worried by the lack of naval power we will have here when you are gone. When do you see the main naval capacity returning to Pakindesh?'

Kalil smiled at the easy way that Asif used the new three-nation federation name. 'I will send much of the fleet back as soon as we've secured the country and assessed any external threats. We will also have enough personnel to commandeer a large number of US

Navy assets, to bring some back here and to patrol the US coast and deter incursions from others, like Indonesia.'

'And if the Indonesians happen to have the same plan?'

'They don't, Ghulam. Our envoys and spies have reported that Indonesia remains interested in expansion into Indochina and China. I think China's fifty million survivors will welcome them. But, discussions with Indonesia over how China and Southeast Asia should be split up is taking all of their energy,' Kalil explained.

'But surely they must have thought about the America's too?'

'We had a phrase in the military when you had superiority and knew it. The options available we called a target rich environment. We find ourselves now in that world. So many options, so little time. China is a big piece of meat to chew on. Swallowing it takes time, and all of Indonesia's planning and thinking looks north. America is ours for the taking, for now at least.'

RIAZ

'What's new, Harry?' Riaz asked as he wandered into the Ham radio room. There were dozens of 'blue-tacked' notes plastered on the wall in front of the radio set, seemingly with call-sign names and frequency information and locations scribbled on them.

'Summat pretty weird actually, Riaz,' Harry said as he scratched at his unshaven face. 'Yep, pretty bloody weird indeed, I'd say.'

'Tell me.'

'Well, there's this bloke I've had many conversations with over the past month or so; he's located in Lebanon somewhere; Beirut I assume. Anyway, he says that there's no such thing as Islamic State no more, nor Hezbollah or Hamas. He reckons they didn't survive Revelation Day. Says that he tried to discover if this was true and the only way he can prove it is that there's absolutely no mention of them anywhere. They aren't referred to by the Caliph of Mecca, there's no further refugee movements at all, like there was before Rev-Day, and more to the point there's nothing coming direct from them, which is clearly out of character, assuming they survived. He's sure they all died, and he says that makes sense coz they were bad people and distorted the Quran.'

'Well, he's right there, isn't he? Let's face it they were a bunch of savage lunatics, just crazy murderers really. Just a pity that they corrupted so many to join them.'

'Hmm,' Harry scratched his head, clearly not convinced.

'What?' Riaz prompted.

'Well… whilst they were lunatics, I agree, but they were, at least in their own crazy way, trying to expand Islamic influence, weren't they, or murder Jews, or Americans of course?' Harry suggested.

'So what? They corrupted the Quran, and they murdered thousands of innocent people, most of them fellow Muslims.'

'I know, but let's say you were Allah, and you had a choice of saving non-practicing Muslims, like you and me, people that rarely went to a mosque or prayed, versus extremist lunatics, who, whilst misguided, were driven by their adherence to Islam. Who would you save?'

'Us. No question. By saving us, we'll come back to the religion and become more devout. But the extremists are killers and have gone against the meaning of the Quran, so they deserve to die and go to hell. They would be a threat to a peaceful Islamic world,' Riaz stated with conviction.

'You reckon? I mean, about you becoming more devout now?'

'Of course!' Riaz said.

'Really, Riaz? When did you last go to a mosque? Even now, after Rev-Day, how often do you pray?'

'You don't either!'

'I know, and I don't care. I'm not changing my ways now. I was saved, maybe because my heart is pure, even if I don't go to the mosque. I believe that Allah sees me for what I am and He's happy with that. If He wasn't, He'd have taken me away too. Allah is all seeing, so pretending to be something that you're not, isn't going to please Him, is it? Just be careful, Riaz. Be true to yourself and you'll be OK. That's the message of the death of the extremists, I reckon. Just my thought for the day. Take it as you will, my friend,' Harry stated as he put his headphones on again and turned back to his equipment.

Riaz walked away in contemplation. He walked into Salina's room. She was reading an old encyclopaedia. 'Where did you get that?' he asked.

'The British Library. You should see all the books there, Dad. We're allowed to borrow them, if we return them within a week. It's amazing what's there. Just like the internet but harder to find stuff.'

Riaz laughed. 'I know. That's how we had to find out things in my school days. It was all in books. But it had advantages.'

'Like what?'

'Like no rubbish being in print. To get into a book meant that the information was checked beforehand. People couldn't just put up lies or silly stuff and have it published. If it was in print it was real and you could trust it,' Riaz explained.

'But it's so hard to find things though. Not like a Google search. God, I miss that,' Salina said with genuine grief in her voice.

'Yes, well I suppose I do too, in a way. I do understand, Salina, really. Don't worry, things will get back to that, I promise. It will just take time that's all. Are you happy though? Do you like it in London now?'

She nodded, un-smiling. 'Yes, in a way. I mean the house and school and where we are is nice. And it's good to be with kids that are all the same and without any prejudice now; not that we had much before. I still miss my friends though, and shopping, and music, and... well, normal things, Dad. You know?'

'I do. It'll get better again. Just be patient, Salina,' he said, then patted her head, bent down, and kissed her cheek and walked away, his eyes misting.

AMELIA

Amelia Sanchez was warming towards Major John Cummins. He'd made dinner for her twice, proving to be a decent cook. She hadn't gone to bed with him yet and was loath to do so for now. At 38, he was ten years older than her, more than acceptable to her mother as a future potential match, attractive and interesting. Her reporting experience and interest in foreign affairs matched his on the ground experience, so the early getting to know each other conversations were relaxed. He was a little reserved, but that tallied with his experience and profession. She'd met several front-line officers who were loath to discuss their combat days. Nevertheless, they had resulted in some of her better relationships, not that she was overly promiscuous. If all went well this evening, she might allow him to make love to her. She knew that he wanted to, but it needed to be played delicately. There was no hurry though. If tonight wasn't right, there would be other opportunities. Each of them was working in a very small group of people, and the world had changed so much that there was an element of wartime fervour about it. George Saba had been about to make a play for her, she was sure. But it didn't happen, and now she was glad. If he had made a move, she'd probably have gone along with it in the early days as she was so very lonely, and sex as a comforter worked for her. Even now, with a growing conservative attitude and greater observance of Islam, there was still a lot of short-term relationships occurring, or so it seemed.

Her daydreaming ended abruptly as Paul Habbib entered her office, 'Amelia?'

'Oh, yes, Mr President?'

'Now that we have some access to news reports, can we rely on these or are they to be treated with some caution?'

'Well, Sir, I was a little sceptical of the last ones coming out of the Middle East, but really it's hard to determine as we don't have very many ways to check their validity,' she replied.

'But these are official government to government interviews that we've managed to tune into recently, aren't they?'

'Yes, they are. Since we restored some power, we are accessing occasional broadcast satellite TV. Those countries that lost the least people remain pretty much as they were pre-Revelation Day, so much of their broadcast capabilities are intact. The issue is whether we believe them or not...'

'Meaning, can we trust them more now that the geopolitical regime has changed so much, you mean?'

'Yes, Sir, exactly. I mean that Iranian commentary a few days ago about everlasting peace now being sanctioned by Allah between the Shiite and Sunni sects was obviously for propaganda purposes.'

'Aimed at the new Caliph of Mecca?'

'Exactly, Sir. From what we've managed to pick up from unauthorised transmissions, I don't think it's all peace and love out there, sadly. It should be. Clearly Allah has sent us the clearest message possible, that we are all chosen, irrespective of which sect of Islam we have followed. All are valid paths to Him. It would be crazy to still be fighting each other over narrow interpretations,' she said passionately.

'I agree, but human nature is sadly flawed, and the hatreds go way back for them to be forgotten overnight. Is this all being analysed by the new team down the hall?'

'Yes, Mr President. I've got five people monitoring the broadcasts now. I never thought I'd miss the never-ending news services, but I really do.'

'I know how you feel,' Habbib began, but then noticed a few tears running down Amelia's cheeks, 'Amelia, are you OK?'

She quickly caught her breath, 'Sorry, Sir... I... I just miss everything the way it was,' she sobbed, 'and I know I should be grateful to Allah for saving us all, or choosing us, but I just miss so many friends, and they didn't do anything wrong.'

Habbib put his arm around her, and she sobbed into his shoulder for a minute, then pulled herself together, stood up again and wiped her eyes, 'I'm sorry, Mr President,' she sighed.

'Don't be. I feel the same way. You have no idea how much I wish that Andrew Kendall was chewing me out in the Oval Office again, rather than me sitting in that chair instead, managing this underpopulated and newly insignificant country.'

'It's not, Sir! Insignificant I mean. The United States still stands for something. We might be fewer now, but we're American, and our constitution is still to be admired and protected,' she said passionately.

'I don't disagree with that sentiment, Amelia, but protecting it might be the most difficult challenge we face. Where's Major Cummins, by the way?'

'He'll be back in an hour, Sir; he went over to the Pentagon.'

'What the hell for, to walk the hallways alone and try to ignore the ghosts?'

'He said he needed to check some statistics, Sir, and that having no internet access was driving him crazy, so he went to look for some reports.'

'Any news on that score from the boffins in Silicon Valley yet?'

'Some. They think we might be able to gain some limited access within another few months.'

'What's the holdup now that we have power back on?'

'Apparently, it's to do with isolating some of the circuits to cut down on power consumption, Sir. They said that the power used by the net was enormous and the world doesn't have that kind of capacity available anymore. So, when access is resumed it's not going to be like it was before, at least not here in the US.'

'Shit! The things we took for granted. Sorry, not your fault, Amelia, just venting my frustration. I shouldn't be so critical. Compared to a month or more ago we're doing OK again. Then again, everything's relative, isn't it?'

'I guess so, Sir.' She said, as he nodded and left her office, his attention moving to other things.

She opened her desk drawer and took out a photo of her parents, rubbed her father's face gently and whispered, 'I love you and miss you, Dad, and I'll never forget you.' Her tears started to flow freely again.

HABBIB

Habbib caught up with John Cummins an hour later when he returned to the White House. 'Any new thoughts, Major, or is your previous analysis of Iran being the most likely threat to us still valid?'

'Yes, Mr President, lots of revised thinking, and different conclusions now.'

'That doesn't surprise me at all. They probably match my own. Care to speculate? No holds barred, Major, you can say whatever you want. I'm not going to critique it, just add my thoughts where appropriate. I have a gut feeling that we're going to have come to similar conclusions anyway, so go ahead.'

'OK, Sir. Well, I suppose I looked at the situation again through several other scenarios, and some might be less than charitable, and I'd be cautious in front of an Imam, to say the least,' he began.

'Forget that. I'd be the same, perhaps. Give it to me straight.'

'OK. Forgive any repetition from our last discussions on this, Sir, but let me take it from the top again. Scenario one is the charitable and therefore easy view. In this I see an amazingly peaceful world of Islamic benevolence, all sects living and working together, and sharing in the new world's bounty. It's now a world of plenty, after all. So, there's no need for greed or power plays to distort the new paradise, as no doubt offered to us by Allah Himself.

'Then there's scenario two, one where the old enmity between Sunni and Shia adherents continues to be fought out, as well as enmity against the minor sects, like the Druze, Kurds and others. Whilst that doesn't concern us here as much, it plays havoc within the Middle East in particular, but mainly in the power plays between Iran and Saudi Arabia. It's potentially going to be a blood bath, at some stage.'

'So, who wins it?' Habbib interrupted.

'The easy answer is no-one, we all lose from this level of stupidity. But strategically and militarily it's not so clear cut. Within the immediate area of the Middle East, Iran is the strongest, in numbers, and military capability at the individual level. The Saudi's have the hardware upper hand, significantly, and clearly enough to overwhelm Iran, especially in air power. On the ground the Iranians would do better. They have more experience, and frankly the Saudi Army is lazy, incompetent, and unskilled, despite their intelligence at an individual level and their superior equipment. But they are used to an era of entitlement and don't like to do the hard work. However, if their country was invaded that would make a difference compared to going on the offensive. If it was a case of protecting Mecca, for instance, that might fire them up, assuming they agree with the Caliph in power there.'

'Let me interrupt you there. Do we have any intel on what happened to the Saudi Royals? Or how this Caliph came to power?'

'None, Sir. But I have a theory.'

'Go on.'

'Well, the extended and less productive members of the Royal family, many of them, and especially lots of the minor Princes, were… well just a bunch of hypocritical, whoring, liquor drinking parasites. So, in some ways it would be logical to expect that they were removed as unworthy of enlightenment. Or another option is that they were killed by the Caliph and his supporters very early on, before there was time for them to reconsolidate their power base.'

'A quick coup you mean?'

'Exactly, Sir.'

He nodded in general agreement, 'Sound reasoning. Go on, Major'

'OK… erm, so, for North Africa, I don't see them having great influence, although they'll probably expand north into Europe over time and life will then improve for their masses. But their populations don't allow them to do more than spread out thinly or become new pilgrims for Europe. Whether it's advantageous for viable states like say Morocco, to move a sizeable portion of its population to Spain is less certain. It will probably happen. There are benefits but they don't change the balance of power. In West Africa, Nigeria is an interesting case. They'll have lost maybe half their population so there's more to go around now and so the country might be content to reap the bounty, or it might be expansionist. Time will tell, but their oil is no longer such a prize. Either way, at ninety-seven million population, expansion is relatively easy to support.

'Then there's the influence of the extremist cults like Islamic State and others. Whilst true adherents to Islam know that these groups are deliberately distorting the Quran, they remain a threat. The only weird thing about them though is that there's no news I've found on what they're doing now. There doesn't seem to be much coming out of the region. Mind you, we're still practically deaf in our information access...' Cummins paused, clearly in thought.

'Go on, there must be other scenarios, Major?'

Cummins nodded, 'Absolutely. I looked at the new power brokers and tried to determine who is going to be the new U.S.A. in this world, the real superpower with capability to change things, if history and human nature leads to territorial expansions. The key countries remain those with large populations, intact infrastructure, democratic institutions, and military might. In order, I put the league table as Indonesia, so no change to my original thinking, possibly in alliance with Malaysia, followed by India, Pakistan, and then perhaps a true Caliphate in the Middle East if that survives and decides to spread out physically rather than through doctrine alone. However, I still concluded that the Indonesia and India Pakistan areas would simply thrive and be happy. They have land, resources, education, democracy, adequate food, sea access, in fact everything to thrive. They'd be crazy to put any of that at risk or in fact need to look too far outside of their current boundaries for further influence. They are the new superpowers.

'As for a new Caliphate-style group in the Middle East, they'll find it very difficult to expand their influence militarily or physically beyond that region. Their real influence is going to be in assuming the right to control the rest of us via their interpretation of the Quran in conjunction with the lessons from Revelation Day...'

'Whatever they might be,' Habbib interrupted.

'Exactly, Sir. History has too many examples of warfare between opposing ideas. The new question is what actions will be taken by those wishing to take control, or those thinking they have the only true interpretation of Allah's will, coupled with a desire to enforce it?'

'Hmm. So, no threat to us directly then?'

'Not militarily, no, but we face a much more immediate threat, Sir.'

'What?'

'Winter is coming, and I don't think we'll survive that enemy. I think we must migrate south, Mr President, and soon.'

RIAZ

Harry sat at his radio set, deep in thought, trying to come to terms with the latest information he'd received, as Riaz walked into the room, humming. *I grow to love this old man more each day. I'm so glad Charlie befriended him*, he thought. 'What's new, Harry?'

There was a pause before he answered, a little distractedly, 'I think something major is happening between the Caliphate and the Iranians.'

'Oh, like what?'

'Like a major war.'

'How do you know?'

'My contact in Saudi, the scared one, the one that is very cagey, he just told me a lot... before he was cut off. Seems like there's air attacks in progress, and maybe a ground battle too.'

'Oh no! What did he say, exactly?'

'That the Shiites have retaliated, and now there's a price to pay for the Caliph's proclamations against Iran. The key word for me was retaliation. That means that the Saudis started something, I'd guess, and now the Iranians have hit back and in a major way too.'

'Why'd you say that?'

'I could actually hear air raid sirens in the background. I asked if he was safe and he said it was okay, that he was many kilometres from the centre of Riyadh. But if I could hear the sirens then either he's lying to throw the scent off from anyone listening, or that was a pretty widespread bombing raid going on.'

'Could you hear explosions, Harry?'

'No, nothing like that. But he didn't seem worried by the air raid, just the possibility of being overheard, or at least that's how it felt to me.'

'Can you get him back on?'

'No point now. Whenever he's dropped off like that before, he waits at least a day before he signs on again. I'll try him tomorrow about this time.'

'Can I listen when you do?'

'Course you can, so long as you keep quiet. I don't want to spook my friend over there, he's pretty skittish already.'

The next day Riaz sat quietly whilst Harry tuned the radio and did his call sign procedure. There seemed to be a lot of static and it was almost seven minutes before there was any success.

'8ZT2, 8ZT2, 8ZT2, this is GSK7GB, Golf Sierra Kilo Seven Golf Bravo calling and standing by.'

Only seconds passed before a reply was heard, '8ZT2, 8ZT2, good morning, GSK7, over.'

That's a heavy Middle Eastern accent, Riaz thought. This is exciting.

'8ZT2, 8ZT2, this is GSK7, reading you strength 5. Good to hear your voice again. I was a little worried after the events of yesterday. What's the situation now, over?'

'Hard to say, but there seems to be nothing happening now. All activity and air raids have ceased and there's no commentary from the leadership either, over.'

'GSK7, so is there a war going on with Iran, over?'

Twenty seconds of silence, punctuated only by static, filled the room. Harry and Riaz held their breath, until finally there was a reply. '8ZT2, yes, I think so. It's hard to be sure, there's no TV news of it, but... the Caliph says that Iran attacked us first, but I don't know, over.'

'But you think that maybe it was Saudi Arabia that was the aggressor, is that right, over?' Harry suggested.

'Saudi Arabia no longer exists by that name. It is just The Caliphate, or sometimes The Caliphate of Mecca. I need to be careful these days. I think my radio conversations would be classed as illegal, maybe blasphemous even, over.'

'How could they be blasphemous, over?'

'Many things can be blasphemous, maybe more so now, since the Prophet's direction is being interpreted in different ways by different people, over.'

'What's your name, 8ZT2? I'm Harry, over.' Riaz looked at Harry in surprise, assuming the introductions would have been made months ago.

A pause. 'Just call me Zed Tee, like part of my call sign. I prefer that, please, over.'

'OK, Zed Tee. So, what's really going on out there, over?'

There was a noticeable sigh, as ZT started to talk, 'Things are not good. There is a lot of suspicion and recriminations and people spying on their neighbours, and family even. There are many people taken away and not always returning. After the death of the officials that tried to carry out the stoning of adulterers everything changed. At first it was for the better. But then it just became more hidden. No executions of people but there are stories still, of the bad treatment of those not fully supporting the Caliph's views. There's lots of talk against the Shiites still, and especially the regime in Tehran. That is being called the Devil's Spawn by the Caliph. I don't know for sure, but I think our army attacked the Iranians and was defeated, because there are too many rumours of missing soldiers and aircraft, and they can't all be made up, over.'

'That sounds bad, ZT, over.'

'It is. I need to go. I don't think long transmissions are good. Thank you for your friendship, Harry. Over.'

'8ZT2 this is GSK7. Thanks for the most pleasant contact, I hope to meet you one day. Seventy-three to you. 8ZT2 this is GSK7GB off and clear and listening for your final.' Harry sighed deeply and turned his set controls off.

'Doesn't sound good out there' Riaz said. What does seventy-three denote?'

'Oh, seventy-three is the code for best regards. Eighty-eight means hugs and kisses. No, not at all the time of peace and prosperity, Riaz. Allah can't be pleased by this,' Harry said quietly. 'I need a cuppa and a biscuit. Want to join me, Riaz.'

'Sure. Good idea.'

CHARLIE

Charlie sat with a scowl on his face in class. The so-called History teacher was clearly a fundamentalist, as his father would have described the type, and so he was being careful, as were the other kids too. No-one was game to make any open comments, and it was obvious that the teacher was becoming agitated by this.

'I will not accept this level of non-interaction from the class,' Mr Aziz said forcefully. 'We cannot learn in an environment of suspicion. We now live in a glorious world that basks in the favour of Allah, blessed be His name. There is no place for defiance. So, I will ask again, who can tell me the key lessons that should have been learnt by the infidels in the period leading up to Revelation Day?'

Silence ensued, and Charlie's desire to speak was getting stronger. As he considered sticking his neck out, as his father would have described it, the attention shifted to Mohammed Khatam, a tall boy known for his bullying behaviour.

'That the infidels should have converted to Islam, Sir?' Khatam said.

'That is not an answer. Obviously, that would have saved them, but I am looking for considered discussion, not platitudes that you feel I wish to hear.'

'Perhaps, Sir,' Charlie began, 'the Western world might have considered leaving themselves out of Middle Eastern politics and its countries. Although I suppose that might have meant that millions more of the faithful would have died at the hands of each other. Maybe we would even have seen a major conflict between Iran and Saudi Arabia, rather than via proxy wars fought between different terrorist groups. It could have meant that the conflict in Syria would have expanded elsewhere, maybe Iran would have developed its nuclear bomb and destroyed Mecca even. Left to itself, the Middle East has rarely been at peace.' Charlie's knees began to knock as he silently castigated himself for speaking out this way. Oh well, too late now.

Aziz had a look of horror on his face, fluctuating emotions seeming to twist his expression weirdly. The class looked at him and then at Charlie, waiting to see what would happen next. Almost twenty seconds passed, and then Aziz seemed to calm down.

'Thank you, Charlie, that is at least a considered response and quite an interesting one too. Have you heard these things discussed at home?'

Shit! Be careful now, Charlie. 'No, Sir, but I think I had heard them discussed on the radio a long time ago, before Revelation Day I mean. When there was talk about whether the West should get more involved in Syria, when all the refugee problems were happening.'

'Ah, yes, that was when the West pretended that it was not the cause of the Syrian crisis, and that its policy in Iraq had not been a factor. How stupid of them. But what do the rest of you think? Whilst these views might not be Charlie's own, what of the suggestion that Iran would have ended up at war with the rest of the Muslim world?'

Alia Kaduji spoke first, wanting to help Charlie out, 'I suppose there was years of bloodshed between the Shia and Sunni sects in Iraq, Sir, and Iran and Saudi Arabia didn't like each other, did they?'

Other comments followed quickly. 'That's right, the Iranians killed millions of Iraqis years before the Gulf Wars...'

'Iraq should have been split up between the Shia and Sunni populations...'

'Syria was all to do with its President being a tyrant...'

'Should have split Iraq up with a bit for the Kurds as well...'

'That Arab Spring stuff was a failure too, none of them countries was better off afterwards...'

'Always seems like the Arab world is the problem; you don't see fighting like that in Indonesia and places with democracy...'

'Enough!' Aziz called out, putting his hands up. 'Let us please have some order here. I am pleased that finally you have decided to take part in my class but let us take these issues one at a time.' The class became instantly quiet. 'Now, let us discuss the issue of Iraq's internal fighting between its Shia and Sunni populations. Was it not the fault of the Americans when they instilled a non-representative government there after deposing Saddam Hussein?'

The class remained silent, so Aziz continued, 'Well let me state that this was the case, although few of you would have been old enough to be aware of these things when they happened. It is true that Hussein was a tyrant leader and perhaps at first the people were glad that he had been removed, but then, as usual, the West meddled in affairs that they knew little about, and they imposed their views and ways on the country and alienated the people. This was the problem with the West. Their ways came with evil baggage. Even if their intentions were honourable to start with, and that is debatable, they always failed to understand the purity of Islam. After all, who cannot remember the claims they always made of Islam being allied to terrorism, rather than it being a religion espousing peace?'

Fuck it, Charlie said to himself, just go for it. 'Maybe the problem for the West was the way that those nutters following Islamic

State just loved murdering people and so it was hard to believe in the Quran being the book of peace that it is, when we, the faithful, failed to defeat that kind of terrorism, Sir.'

'You seem to have given these issues a lot of thought, Charlie. Your father must be well educated to debate these things with you.'

You're not getting me that easily, you prick. 'Not my dad, Sir, he never talks politics with us, just football, cricket and what's for dinner.' The class laughed at this, and for just a moment, Aziz seemed angered, but he controlled his facial expression quickly.

After class was dismissed and Charlie was kicking a ball around the playground with others at lunchtime, Alia dragged him away from the game.

'What the hell were ya doin', Charlie? Are you mad or summat? Don't bloody provoke Aziz, he's dangerous.'

'He was pissin' me off, Alia. I knew what he was gettin' at; it was obvious. But I'd just had enough, that's all. I needed to... I don't know... challenge him I s'pose. It felt good too,' he smiled.

'You're taking chances, Charlie. It's not worth it. Did you hear about that kid in class 7 that defied one of the biology teachers? The poor kid got caned! The teacher laid into him with a stick, bent him across the desk and beat his arse with it. The class said whilst he was screaming in pain the teacher's face looked like he was loving it. Fuckin' perverted bastard!'

'Shit, no I didn't know that. What happened afterwards?'

'Don't know, but the kid's been away ever since. But I don't think his mum and dad complained. Maybe too scared to do that. These new teachers, a lot of them anyway, they're crazy. You've got to be careful. Promise me?'

Charlie nodded, 'OK, I will. Thanks, Alia.'

'For what?'

'For looking after me. You're a mate, truly.'

'Is that all I am, Charlie?'

He looked confused, and then went red in the face. 'Well, I... I mean...'

'Have you got a girlfriend, Charlie?'

'No, course not.'

'Do you want one? Like me, perhaps?'

'Honest?'

'Girls don't offer if they don't mean it, you fool. I like you. Do you like me?'

'Of course; always have. We're friends, aren't we? We share secrets and everything.'

'We could share other stuff too if you want?'

'You mean... like...'

'No! Not that! God, Charlie. Kissing maybe, not sex.'

'I didn't mean that!'

'Then what did you mean, you liar?' Alia laughed.

'I don't know. But kissing would be nice.'

'OK then, but we'll need to be careful of course. I'll devise a plan and let you know.'

'Let me know what?'

'When we can have that first kiss. Now get lost back to your football.'

HABBIB

'Over to you, Major Cummins.'

'Thank you, Mr President. OK, well, as explained, we have little choice but to move south and consolidate our current New York and Washington populations where we can survive the winter and where there's infrastructure to support ourselves and thrive. Miami has been chosen. I looked at Atlanta and Charleston and New Orleans and Galveston, a few other cities, but Miami was the best choice.'

'What about hurricane risks?' George Saba asked.

'We'll have to live with it,' Cummins said.

Imran Malouf nodded in agreement, and added, 'We've looked at options for the exodus between aircraft and vehicles. Initially we'll send some aircraft down there with the advance party, but most of the population will travel by personal vehicles and buses and we'll utilise refrigerated container trucks for essential supplies, supplementing those as we get closer to the south, probably in Atlanta.'

'How long will the move take?' Habbib asked.

'Phase one for the aircraft group will leave in a week. We found enough trained pilots that were able to get to a level of competency on larger aircraft. So, there will be three Boeing 767's carrying 600 people, initially a day apart from each other, because of them being filled with technical people,' Cummins replied, 'but that will increase to 10 aircraft per day from day 3, growing to one per hour during daylight hours if the pilots can handle that. The road convoys leave in phases every two days. We have a lot of buses and can transport ten thousand people per convoy. The aim is to have two million people in Miami within 3 months.'

'Contingency plans?' Saba asked, looking at Cummins.

'For the road convoys, we're going to be using three different routes down there, one going from Washington towards Atlanta, one from New York towards Charleston and hugging the coast roads, and another roughly between those two routes for each departure city. Along the way, we'll pick up as much as we can from strategic locations of importance, like major distribution warehouses for food, medicines, and engineering equipment. We want to see what we can get from the CDC in Atlanta, although I have no idea what that might provide; maybe nothing.'

'You could be right about that, Major,' the President said. 'The Centre for Disease Control didn't carry too much in the way of stocks of medicines itself, rather than having the ability to coordinate them from other places and do the necessary work to define the risk and counter it. But it's certainly worth considering, so the idea makes sense.'

'Any push back from community leaders not wanting to make the move?' Sanchez asked.

'None, Amelia,' Cummins replied. 'Once we explained that there was a very high risk of starvation or freezing to death most people saw the benefits, as well as us ending the rivalry between the two cities vying for importance. If anything, there was some sadness at leaving the monuments that we have in both cities, iconic and historical. I think leaving Washington DC is a confirmation that the USA is not what it used to be.'

'Sadly true,' Habbib said quietly.

'When are you going down there, Major?' Saba asked.

'With the first aircraft team. I'd like to suggest that Ms Sanchez heads down with the third aircraft, Mr President. We'll need an admin coordinator ahead of the road convoys and my groups will be too busy with engineering related tasks to handle that.'

'Fine by me. You okay with that, Amelia?'

'Of course, Mr President; whatever's necessary.' Nobody gave away their knowledge or suspicion of the growing relationship between Cummins and Sanchez, but she felt herself blushing and hoped that she wasn't.

'So, now to Phase B, the occupation and consolidation of Miami,' Cummins continued. 'The engineering advance groups will assess the power stations, communications installations, marine bunkers for diesel fuel, condition of naval shipping and coast guard assets, general housing standards and facilities, applicability of State Government buildings for the Presidency and administrative offices, hospitals, schools and university campuses, and warehouses for food, fuel, medicines, emergency equipment, and other items. However, I think we also need to protect what we leave behind and try and... not sure what to call it... to make the White House and major historical buildings safe for a future when we can come back.'

'I understand what you mean, Major,' Habbib said, 'but that might not be possible in our lifetime, and I don't think we have the skills or material to achieve that aim.'

'You're probably right, Sir, but I want to at least attempt it.'

'Do whatever you can and if you need anything, let me know.'

'What does San Francisco think of this?' Saba asked.

Sanchez said, 'They concur, and more to the point they think there's a greater chance of re-establishing communication links by just concentrating on a single city connection.'

Habbib looked across at Imran Malouf. 'You look worried, Imran.'

'Yes, Sir, a little. I know you're skilled in the logistics issues involved in this, Major, but what happens to the road convoy vehicles if there's no power to assist refuelling them on route?'

'Good question. It's a real problem. We don't expect any power, clearly, so you're right to assume that the service stations won't have any ability to turn their pumps on. But we've played around with a fuel support vehicle with a diesel generator on it. We took it to service stations that have been long dead, without a power source. After a lot of thinking on the go, we've devised a way to repower the pumps. So, as far as getting the bowsers to work we've solved that problem. However, we might come across a few service stations that have insufficient fuel left in their tanks or have other technical issues that we haven't come across up here. The back-up we have is that we'll be travelling with full tanker trucks in the convoy, at least 45 of them, 15 per group. If we need to use the fuel in those we will, then refuel them as well, whenever possible. We don't want to get to Miami and be without fuel, because we'll be relying on diesel gensets for a while down there.'

'Any issues with having no air traffic control or navigation support for the flights?' President Habbib asked.

Cummins smiled, 'Air traffic control is not important, Mr President, 'as there's nothing else flying. As for nav, we managed to link into some satellites still operating and we can also fly by sight, if necessary, although the lower flying altitude for that would chew through the juice faster. But worst case, we hug the coastline all the way down there.'

'I guess Miami International will still have huge amounts of fuel stored too,' Malouf stated.

Cummins nodded, 'Sure, but I'm also hoping that the runways are clear, or at least one of them. Last thing we need is blocked runways when we get there.'

'That being a possibility is it more prudent to send an advance team by road to be safe?' Saba asked.

Cummins nodded, 'I did consider it, but we have more than one runway to use, so it would be unlikely to have all runways blocked. Plus, we have contingency and enough fuel for Fort Lauderdale, if necessary, even back up to Orlando at a pinch. Lastly, I had a look at Washington National and noticed that there were free runways there, so it's a calculated risk that I'm comfortable with.

'OK, thank you everybody; let's get back to work,' the President said, this time with a smile.

RIAZ

'Good morning, Freddy.'

'How are ya travellin' Riaz? Ready for another stimulatin' day on the engines?' he said with a smirk and a chuckle.

'How do you always manage to stay so cheerful, Freddy?'

'No point bein' a sour puss, eh. Make the most of it, I always say. Fight them battles you got a chance of winnin' and don't lose sleep over the things you can't change. That's one of the secrets of life, Riaz. I'll let you have that one for free.'

'You're very generous with your wisdom, thank you. So, what's our first task today?'

'The genset with the oil leak, I think. Probably just getting old. Might be a simple fix, hopefully. Plenty of spare capacity so no bother for the hospital to turn it off. If you want to grab the tools, I'll meet you down there with some more rags and a tarp.'

It took them an hour to fix the problem, after which they returned to the maintenance office and made tea and Freddy took out a packet of chocolate biscuits from a drawer next to their sink.

'I wonder how long the supply of chocky bickies will last, Riaz. I get a feeling that there aren't many people making new stuff. Do you agree? I mean, it seems like there's a general view that the supermarket stocks are unending, so we just go a little further afield each time we run out.'

'That's true. Apart from milk. At least there's dairy farming back up again, and animals for meat too, and eggs,' Riaz countered.

'Sure, but that's the easy stuff. What about engineering, or communications, transport. When are we going to find out what's really happening out there in other countries? I don't get why it's taking so long.'

'Hmm. Charlie says there's no information coming from his teachers either, so they don't know. I don't think we're being kept deliberately in the dark though.'

'Has Charlie said much about the teachers to you?'

'Like what?'

Freddy hesitated before answering. 'Well... look I don't know for sure, so if you were a lawyer you'd say this is hearsay, ya know. But I've heard that the teachers are very strict in the schools now, and a lot of the kids are frightened of them. Seems that we've gone back to the days of beating kids that step out of line.'

'Who has told you this?'

'No-one directly. But one of the nurses upstairs said that a lad had been brought to the hospital for an infection and when they examined him, he had deep welts across his arse, made from a cane. And eventually he admitted that he'd been beaten by a teacher for questioning the Quran. Apparently, it's common now, but the kids are afraid to tell the parents in case the same thing happens again. You might want to quiz young Charlie about it.'

Over dinner that night, Riaz decided to come straight to the point, but needed to bend the truth a little. 'There was a boy brought into the hospital this week with severe lacerations that were received by being caned at school. Is this sort of thing going on now at your school?' he asked, glancing at each of his children in turn.

Salina looked down at her lap and Michael averted his eyes from his father too. A moment later, Charlie said, 'It's happening. Some of the teachers are doing it a lot, others not at all.'

Mina drew in her breath sharply. 'What do you mean by a lot, Charlie?'

'Mr Aziz is the worst, a real bastard. Gets his rocks off with it I reckon. Probably beats a kid every third or fourth lesson. You can tell by his face when he's in a vicious mood. He enjoys it too, sick fuck!'

'Charlie!' Mina admonished.

Riaz ignored the expletive. 'Give me an example, Charlie, please?'

Charlie sighed heavily. 'OK then. There's a short kid, Paul Kotanda, African. I think his dad was from Kenya originally, so he's black. Nice kid really; very quiet. Aziz loves to throw Quran questions at him to get him into trouble, always looking for sneaky ways to phrase things so that Paul ends up being accused of blasphemy, or disrespect. It's total bollocks and everyone knows it. A few weeks back he ambushed Paul with some daft question and then went crazy with him and said Allah would make an example of him. He pulled him to the front of the class, bent him over a desk, grabbed his cane and started belting him with it, at least a dozen times. Paul was screaming in pain. Anyway, Mohammed Pavi stood up and told Aziz to leave him alone, calling him an evil shit. Aziz went over to Pavi and started whacking his arms and then laying into him. The class went crazy, all screaming and shouting. Then the Headmaster barged in and told Aziz to stop and for the rest of us to be quiet. Aziz went away with the Head, and we were left alone for the rest of that lesson period.'

'Surely there was follow up?' Riaz asked.

'Sort of. The Head came back at the start of the next period and said that he had faith in his teachers and that all of us should respect them and the role they play. We couldn't believe it, but no-one was game to say anything.'

'Riaz, this is awful,' Mina said.

Riaz nodded his head. 'What about you too; have you experienced violence from your teachers?'

Michael nodded, 'Not as bad as in Charlie's class though. A few kids have had their hands caned. One of the girls was whacked on her legs for not being covered enough.'

'But you all wear the same uniforms!' Mina said.

'She was told her dress was too short,' Salina said, 'so she got given three straps across each thigh. She had the welt marks for the rest of the day.'

'I'm not standing for this. I'm going to have it out with the headmaster,' Riaz said calmy, barely holding his anger in.

'No, dad!' Charlie said. 'That'll make it worse. They'll victimise us then'.

'If they do then I'll take you out of that school.'

'So what? There are only a few high schools near here anyway. And our teachers will probably pass on to other schools that we're troublemakers or something. It won't solve the problem, Dad,' Charlie said.

'He's right, Dad,' Salina agreed. 'It's better to just stay quiet and do what you're told.'

'I don't agree, Salsa. Bullies must be stopped and that's what this sounds like to me. Teachers being bullies, or power hungry. They are no different to wife beaters or criminals.'

'No, Dad, please?' Salina replied.

'Look at me, Salsa,' Riaz said kindly. 'What will be your opinion if next week you have your legs whipped by a teacher, just because he takes a dislike to you and wants to make an impression on the rest of the class, showing them that no-one is safe and that he has the power to inflict pain whenever he feels like it? Will you come home and tell us, or will you hide it and live in fear?'

She put her head down and started to cry.

'What would you say to the teachers, Dad?' Michael asked.

'Simple. I will tell them that if any of them lay a hand on any of you, I will personally go there and break their canes over their heads and beat them senseless for their child abuse. Then I will arrange for home schooling or open a school myself for like-minded parents. And your mum will run it,' Riaz said firmly.

There was a silence of disbelief around the table, and even Mina kept quiet, aware of her husband's tactics. Charlie spoke first, 'Would you really, Dad?'

'Absolutely. I went to school during an era when corporal punishment was normal. Sometimes I wonder whether some of the crime and delinquency we saw before Revelation Day could have been improved if the worst offenders were given a beating, I will admit that. But the problem with that approach is that it is too often abused by sadistic people that enjoy the power. The bad outweighs any slight good. Society in the west moved on from those days, and overall, it was better for it. I don't want to see us going back in time. That doesn't mean there isn't a place for punishment, but not this way. I won't have it.'

'Maybe now is the time to say something that's been bothering me, Dad,' Charlie said.

'Go ahead. Your mother and I will always listen to you; you know that.'

'OK. Before Revelation Day I always thought I'd finish school, get good GCSE results, hopefully, and go on to university, as you know,' Charlie began, pausing as his parents nodded their agreement. 'But it's not the same now. What the world needs is practical skills, not lawyers or stockbrokers or… I don't know, airline pilots even. I think I want to leave school.'

Riaz didn't answer for a while. 'That makes sense,' he began, but smiled as he saw the surprise on his younger children's faces. 'In part, but not really. Charlie, I agree that to go on to university, assuming there are enough lecturers to even run courses now, I don't know, might seem ridiculous. But some skills need proper training. Like medicine, for instance. Becoming a doctor still requires a lot of learning. Maybe being an engineer can be picked up from a mentor, like an apprenticeship. It depends what you want to do, or maybe on what the world needs the most now. Just because we have had our population decimated here, doesn't mean that populated countries are the same. I imagine that life in Pakistan, or Indonesia, is just like before, with education valued and the kinds of jobs remaining like beforehand.'

'What do you want to do, Charlie?' Salina asked her brother.

'I don't know anymore. I was thinking of medicine. But then I was also interested in being a journalist too.'

'Wow, pretty different, those two,' Michael said.

'I know, Bro,' Charlie laughed. 'Can't see much use for journalism now.'

'Can't you?' Riaz asked. 'Seems to me that reporting and telling the truth in this new world might be something very important. Maybe not as much as being a doctor, but more dangerous perhaps.

Don't make any decisions just yet. However, getting back to corporal punishment at school, and this bastard Aziz. I'm going in tomorrow to tackle this. If there's even a hint of this making your lives more difficult, you'll be leaving that school. Do you agree on this, all of you?'

'Of course, Riaz,' Mina replied.
'Okay, Dad,' Charlie agreed.
'Yep,' from Salina.
'Absolutely,' Michael added with a smile.

The next morning was bright and sunny. He looked out of the bedroom window and took a deep breath. *This is an omen. I must get this right for the kids.* He was quiet over breakfast, rehearsing his planned words. After Charlie, Michael and Salina left for school, he finished his breakfast and morning ablutions, kissed Mina tenderly and cycled to the school.

'Thank you for seeing me, Mr Kuris. I assume that being a Headmaster, you must be very busy.'

'That is not a problem, Mr Ahmed. What can I do for you?'

'I am concerned about the new tendency towards inappropriate corporal punishment being perpetrated by some of your more zealous staff members.'

Kuris blinked, his mouth open, not having expected such a forthright exchange.

'Please let me continue, Headmaster, whilst you gather your thoughts if I may. I am aware that some teachers, and Mr Aziz in particular, have been beating the students with canes, severely in too many cases. As I understand it, whilst Mr Aziz might, perhaps, have stricter expectations regarding adherence to Islam, this is still a place of learning that should be getting its students ready to take on the roles that the new world needs, and its emphasis needs to be on sound teaching and adherence to learning practical skills. Islamic inspired subjects are not going to prepare our children for the realities of this new world, where preparation for meaningful jobs is so important. If I wanted my children to learn the deeper tenets of the Quran, then I would send them to a Madrassa perhaps.

'Furthermore, from the information I have, it seems to me that Mr Aziz gains satisfaction from beating his students, and even orchestrates their transgressions so that he can pleasure himself via their punishment. If so, he must be removed from his role and severely reprimanded.'

Kuris started to pant, and his face had gone red as he clearly sought to control his emotions. 'Mr Ahmed, I can assure you that these allegations are completely without foundation. Mr Aziz might at times be disappointed by the attention of his students to the lessons. But he is a sound teacher, I assure you. Some of your... conclusions are unfounded.'

'Have you ever witnessed a beating by Mr Aziz?'

'No, of course not. I am not in the classrooms during lessons.'

'Then you have no idea at all about the effect his actions have, nor the pleasure he gets from his sadism?'

'You are making very dangerous accusations against one of my staff, Mr Ahmed.'

'Yes, I am. So, let me be even more plain. I believe that Aziz is a sadistic teacher, and that he gets sexual pleasure from beating his students. I also believe there are other staff members who have similar traits. You, as Headmaster, are ultimately responsible for the behaviour of your staff. I therefore hold you ultimately responsible for the actions of your teachers and the policy under which they work. Capital punishment was banned in British schools decades ago. This is still the United Kingdom, and the expectations of parents remain as they were before Revelation Day. If this resurrected and old-fashioned practice of corporal punishment is not stopped forthwith, then I will act against Aziz, and you. Do I make myself clear?'

'I run this school, Mr Ahmed, and the new world that we now live in, praise be to Allah, is different. We are quite rightly bringing back the discipline that Islamic teaching demands and the students must learn to adhere to in the new and glorious world. I am sure you cannot disagree with that, Sir?'

'Nonsense! I absolutely disagree with such rubbish. If we were not chosen by Allah Himself, praise be to Him, then we would not be here. Therefore, any changes to behaviour or belief should be unnecessary. Islam is a religion of peace and understanding. It is as modern as the world itself and does not need us dragged back to an earlier and more brutal time. So, again, Mr Kuris, I will be plain. Either Aziz stops what he is doing, as well as the other teachers that have shamed themselves with similar behaviour, or I will personally stop him, and you. This school will revert to normal modern teaching methods, or I will make it my goal to remove you from authority and I will bring charges against you and those responsible for the beatings, as sexual paedophiles. You need make no comment now. I will hear directly if any students are harmed further from now on. Good day, Headmaster,' Riaz said, as he stood and started to walk out of the office, leaving Kuris to poorly control his emotions.

KALIL

'What do you make of it, Sabal?' President Asif asked.

He contemplated the question, whilst assessing the look of slight dismay on his counterpart's face. 'Do we know that it is true?'

'All reports seem to confirm a major conflict evolving between Mecca and Iran,' Asif said. Mecca was now the standard vernacular for the old Saudi Arabia, although meaning more than a physical location and having expanded to be the spiritual centre of the Islamic world, as well as the aspirational and political centre. It was seeking to assume the political and religious position enjoyed by the Pope in Europe in the few hundred years leading up to the 16th century.

Kalil replied, 'Whilst there was always likely to be enmity between the Sunni's and the Shiites, I had hoped that a total Islamic world would perhaps see the end of that rivalry. After all, we need not fight over territory, surely.'

'Iran and Mecca, or rather the Saudi's, were always destined to vie for dominance, Sabal.'

'What have your sources found out?'

Asif shrugged, 'Not very different to the media reports. There was an air battle over Tehran and the Caliphate lost over 50 aircraft, whilst Iran had similar losses, but Iran had older aircraft and so they seemed to do better than expected. On the ground there has been a large tank battle to the west of Kuwait, without an obvious victor.'

'Once again the sands of Iraq have much blood to absorb.'

'At least this time it is not the Iraqis that are dying.'

'Not yet, but this could get out of hand, and the unstable Sunni-Shia peace we hoped for might be short lived,' Kalil said.

'Maybe I am naïve, Sabal, but I truly thought that when Allah spared the faithful it was proof that Sunni and Shia alike would bask in His glory, all of us having been chosen as worthy.'

'Not naïve, Ghulam, only human. What you wanted, and which should have happened, is completely logical, and just. But the avarice of man and the power lust of a few has clouded the glorious future we have been shown by the Prophet, praise be upon Him.'

'Maybe you will have that opportunity for a glorious future in the Americas, Sabal, whilst I stay here and protect our borders from escalation of the Caliphate-Iran conflict.'

'We should not worry about their war over the desert, Ghulam. The power of the new world is ours for the taking if we plan well for it. Let the Caliphate grind itself to stalemate across the sands. I will take the new pilgrims to America and secure it for us all. However, you must be vigilant against any sectional fighting spilling across the border. If we need to be ruthless with those that seek to extend their conflict into our territory, then so be it.'

'I have already strengthened the southwestern Pakistan border against potential Iranian refugees. At this stage there is nothing like that occurring. If anything, I would expect Iran to begin to make gains. They have greater manpower at their disposal,' Asif suggested.

'Perhaps, but their skill won't be to the standard of the British and American trained Saudi forces.'

'Skill alone won't be enough, especially when it is countered by an unwarranted self-belief and arrogance, often not backed up by ability. I have seen some of their officers when we occasionally trained together. They have no idea about hard work and leading from the front, Sabal.'

'Agreed. Much as we might prefer to ignore history, we both benefitted from the traits that the British instilled in us.'

'What outcome from their conflict is better for us?' Asif questioned.

Kalil looked a little surprised by his fellow President's change of tone to strategic considerations. 'You mean who do we prefer to win?'

'More than that, Sabal. A preferred winner, if such is possible, is only one consideration. Let us say that we are indifferent to a winner. Is it better for us if both sides are severely weakened, or is it better if one wins quickly and decisively?'

'Interesting question, Ghulam. We certainly do not want a winner to become more ambitious. So, in general I would prefer the Caliphate to lose, if not totally, then at least be severely weakened.

Their aspirations will then be significantly hampered. However, a strong Iran is a problem too, especially if it develops nuclear missile capability. A long and difficult war that exhausts them both might be best, as long as it does not spread.'

Asif stroked his chin, deep in thought. 'Yes, we agree on that. I wonder if Allah will allow this fight to continue.'

Kalil allowed himself a slight smile. So, you believe in divine intervention, Ghulam. I must never forget that.

AMELIA

'I don't know how I'll cope without you for two days, John,' she said breathlessly, in between kisses and the frantic shedding of clothing. They were in an unused office in an out of the way location in the White House that had become a regular place for hurried sex during the day. The secrecy of it continued to enhance their desire. It was quick and teenage-like and over in a few minutes. Their office sex was different to their intimate time together in either of their apartments.

'It's going to be a long two days, Amelia. I haven't abstained from sex for that long for a while now,' he laughed.

'Do you think the President knows about us?'

'Probably.'

'Really?'

'Haven't you seen the odd looks we get from time to time? Malouf and Saba must suspect, and the President's no fool. What does it matter? I think they'd approve.'

She looked wistful for a moment. 'I hope so.'

'When the migration is completed, life will be much better. We'll be in a working city again, with lots of people, and real things to do. It'll be busy but rewarding, and maybe we can get back to some sort of normality… maybe get married?'

'What?' Amelia's eyes widened and she looked intently at his face, trying to make sure that he was serious.

'I love you, Amelia. You must know that. I'm asking you to marry me. Will you?'

'Oh my God, of course I will! I do, I do, I do, Major John Cummins. I love you too,' she cried as she kissed him and held his face between her hands. They kissed and caressed each other for what seemed like a long time.

HEADING SOUTH

The President and White House staff flew to Miami in the first air contingent on the third aircraft, once the route was established and no issues experienced. The exodus to Florida proceeded well. By the time that the ninth air exodus of 600 people arrived, Miami was a functioning city again, if a little sterile and taking on the feel of a disaster recovery exercise. The initial road convoys had experienced little in the way of problems, beyond the few that had been foreseen. Food was easy to transport. It was then stored in large warehouses at naval and coast guard bases, with adequate freezer capacity run by diesel generators, now humming continuously. Two gas-fired power stations were back online, but diesel remained the main fuel supply. It was easier to find and control and took limited technical skill to keep the plants going.

At the end of two months, the exodus had exceeded expectations, partly due to growing confidence in night flying capability, which had doubled the movement capacity, so that 387,650 people had flown to Miami. This had to be cut back again as the limited number of pilots became fatigued. The road convoys were now constant, which produced a few headaches regarding refuelling stations causing traffic jams, but oddly, the people saw this as getting back to normality, rather than being an annoyance. New bus drivers were quickly trained in the basics and so the numbers arriving daily at the south of Florida by road, reached 15,000 at the peak. Drivers rotated, some sent back north with their empty buses, whilst others flew back and picked up a new bus and began the drive south again. There were no complaints of overwork, and the atmosphere was one of common purpose and high spirits. As service stations ran dry, others were found and put into operation. Fuel was plentiful.

By the end of November, most of the population had adopted a Florida lifestyle. Many of the apartments and some hotels at Miami Beach were fully occupied, as were similar enclaves in downtown Miami itself. Previous state government buildings were being utilised, electricity and gas supply was dependable again, a wider food supply was readily available, with only minor shortages, and morale was high.

Badiah Malaki was particularly happy. Not only was she one of the few trained journalists in the city, but she had almost open access to the White House staff, who still used that term, and she now ran a mini-media group that published a weekly newspaper, with her as Editor in Chief, a title she bestowed on herself. However, her sights remained on TV, and that aim drove her. A modern society needed TV access. The US needed to link into the wider world. The inability to achieve that still rankled, and she believed it was the 'Friscoes' that were thwarting her ambitions.

That largely tech-savvy Californian population that now surrounded Silicon Valley were equally disappointed that they'd failed to get the internet back up and running, along with social media and real news-gathering capacity. They also hated the term Frisco, just as the previous inhabitants of San Francisco disliked foreigners using that nickname before them. Badiah took a deep breath again, as she did each time the lack of connectivity angered her. It will happen, Badiah, she told herself for the hundredth time. Be patient. Eventually you will be famous and influential... and marry the President.

An hour later, she looked in the mirror. You look gorgeous, girl. Alluring enough to be noticed by the President but not too threateningly sexual or predatory. She left the apartment and made her way to the New White House, at 1700 Convention Center Drive, Miami Beach, previously the Mayor and City Commissioners' Office that had housed many of the previous municipal departments. Whilst not nearly as grand as the White House in Washington D.C., it was large and functional.

The world might have drastically changed, but the American psyche remained, and there were now armed guards at the building entrances. Four marines in dress uniforms were stationed at each entrance, although it was difficult to determine the threat that they guarded against. She wondered if they were even trained.

As a regular, her security check was cursory. However, this too provided a level of prior normalcy about it, and nobody minded, or questioned its rationale.

She was led into the Florida Office, sometimes called the Square Office, which was the new home of the President. Recreating a replica Oval Office was not on any priority list. The room was impressive, if lacking any historical value. The walls were adorned with the pictures that had hung in the Oval Office in Washington, and the furniture had also been transported there, as there was a desire for some historical continuity.

'Good morning, Mr President.'
'Good to see you, Badiah. Coffee?'

'Thank you, Sir; that would be lovely.' An aid filled two cups, already with cream, no sugar, as she liked it, and she sat when Paul Habbib indicated a chair to her. The aid left the room.

'I hear that your weekly newspaper is a success?'

'Seems that way, Mr President. Although it's hard to determine if a free publication can be adequately judged,' she suggested.

'Don't be so hard on yourself, Badiah, it's the quality of the articles and the feedback you get that determines the paper's worth, and that must please you?'

'Yes, Sir, it does, that's true,' she admitted, smiling, happy that he was aware of her achievement.

'So, what do you see as the mood of the people? What are the good signs and the bad?' he asked, now serious.

She didn't hesitate. This was a common update question. 'Well, Sir, the good is the continuing return to normalcy; shopping, swimming, driving even, buses running, heating, cooling, and lighting, even my weekly paper. All these things are morale boosters and each week they increase.'

'And the bad?'

'No internet, no continuous TV programming, no social media, no links to the outside world. In a nutshell, isolation. Biggest gripe is the lack of internet access though. Any progress on that, Sir?'

'None that you'd be happy with, although it's hopefully coming, as we've heard for a while now,' he laughed. 'You know, some people would see the end of social media as a good thing.'

She laughed too, 'I agree, and sometimes I'm happier with the return to real old-fashioned journalism...'

'But?' he prompted.

'But I miss TV too, and especially the lack of international news. I mean what is going on in the rest of the world, especially the high population countries. Are India and Pakistan and Indonesia ruling the world now? What's happening in the Middle East, Africa and Europe?'

'I wish I knew too.'

'Are there any plans to send a plane out there, Mr President, to see first-hand what's happening?'

'Not yet. Not until we have an idea first. Internet, or at least international access to information, somehow, is my priority as well. I have the same feelings of inadequacy as you about the lack of intelligence gathering. However, I'm happier day by day about the return to normalcy here. I didn't think I'd see that day. I didn't think I'd see people happy again. I mean genuinely happy.'

'Yes, that's true. They are,' Badiah agreed, then changed the subject, 'Mr President, what's the truth about the rumour that you're going to ban private gun ownership?'

He laughed. 'I didn't see that question coming. Your sources are correct. I am going to ban it. I do not want America going back to the bad old days. One day we will need domestic security again. When that day comes, I don't want any private citizen having the ability to kill innocent people or avoid capture by the police or military.'

'That's fair enough, I suppose, but some would argue -'

'Who?'

She faltered a little, 'Well, that doesn't matter, does it, Mr President? I mean...'

'Of course, it matters. I'd like to know what kind of people prefer to return to the old days of mass shootings every week, and a government being in bed with the NSA?'

'I don't think it's that, Sir. The comments I've heard, and believe me these are not widespread, are more to do with protection against an outside force. Sort of like the original reason for the Second Amendment, to protect the nation against a foreign aggressor, when there was no standing army.'

'That's naïve, Badiah. If there were a larger aggressor, we'd have no chance of defending ourselves. Don't report that! Any world power coming here could finish us off easily if that was their intention. We have an extremely limited, professional military and minimal skilled pilots or high-tech personnel to operate naval or air force assets. In any serious attack we would be defeated. The two arguments are incompatible. The next potential threat is more likely to be civil disobedience, as in a Shia versus Sunni conflict. Happily, that's not likely here; we're not the Middle East with those petty rivalries. However, I want to be a step ahead if such an awful day ever came. Do you understand me?'

She nodded, her face grave. 'Yes, Mr President, I do.'

'This should be a peaceful world now, but according to the odd amateur radio reports from the outside world, it seems that Shia versus Sunni conflict, or rivalry between powerbrokers in Mecca and Tehran might be happening. It's illogical. Allah, praise be His name, has spared us all. That alone means that He sees no distinction between Muslim sects; all are righteous, all are worthy, and all of us have been saved. That should mean world peace. If it does not, then it is men that are to blame.'

There was an uncomfortable silence for a few moments, before Badiah said, 'Mr President, I'd like to ask your opinion of something, if I may?'

'Of course. Go ahead,' he smiled, happy to see the topic changed.

'You know my background, Sir?'

'I do.'

'Well, I was wondering, now that we have a thriving population here, and things are becoming...'

'More normal?'

'Yes, exactly, Mr President. Well...' she hesitated.

'Spit it out, Badiah, please?'

'OK then. Well, I wondered if you could see me as... say, the national communications director, maybe for when we have TV up and running again, or even before then once we have any sort of modern news link restored. I just feel that my journalist background could help to provide that link once we have the means.'

Wow, talk about ambition! Damn, I must be showing my surprise. Calm yourself, Paul. Wouldn't you do the same in her place? Smile. 'You don't see a conflict between that... ambition, say, and the role that Amelia Sanchez has on my staff?'

'Oh no, Mr President, I don't see the two roles as the same at all. I'd never suggest replacing Ms Sanchez. She's well above my skillset. No, Sir, I meant a sort of being the official journalist, the spokesperson on TV. Let's face it, we won't have the luxury of multiple competing TV channels any time soon, and I think it's important when we can restore some level of broadcast service again, for the news to be delivered with an official sanction. The world has changed, and people will have a different expectation from the government. I think I can assist that process, eventually, when... well, when we have the technology back up again,' she concluded, looking a little flustered.

Not a bad answer, given being put on the spot, Kendall thought. 'Well, let me say that I will certainly take your suggestion on board. I too look forward to the day when we have the capacity for a daily dialogue with the American people again, and I see no reason why you couldn't assist with that.'

'Thank you, Mr President. I look forward to that day too,' she said with undisguised glee.

A few days later there was a more important visitor.

'He's here, Mr President,' George Saba announced, standing aside to usher in his guest.

A tall man, easily over six feet, entered the room, dressed in a blue pin-striped suit, a white shirt and red tie. He was beaming, but also clearly overawed, trying to glance around without it being obvious, and failing.

Please let your capability exceed your boyish looks. 'Mr Geiger, welcome,' the President said, offering his hand, which Tom Geiger shook with vigour.

'Thank you, Mr President, such an honour to be here, and to be flown here too. So long since I was on an aircraft. Makes me think back to old times. I can't really believe it.'

'Yes, well, apart from the airlifts we used to start bringing the population to Miami, you're the first person to be flown from Silicon Valley over here. I hope that these trips will become more common again. Anyway, please, sit down, Mr Geiger. Coffee?'

'Oh, yes please, Mr President, thank you.'

'Cream and sugar, Mr Geiger?' Amelia Sanchez asked.

'Yes, thank you. Oh, not quite, no sugar, please.'

Amelia had tried to calm Geiger down when he first arrived in the building. He was far too agitated by the occasion, and they needed his expertise and rational thinking, without him being too polite to speak plainly. She passed the coffees around as the small talk continued, aimed at making their guest feel more at ease.

'Amelia is our Population Liaison Officer, Mr Geiger. Although she's a lot more than that, and her background was in media, as I'm sure she's explained to you. So, she has better skills than most of us in communications and I thought she should be here too, to hear your views and explanations firsthand,' the President stated.

George Saba added, 'Mr Geiger, one of the major issues that people bring up, especially now that some normality has been restored, is about the lack of communications infrastructure. Phone lines, mobile networks, and the internet. If we could restore those, over time, then people would feel that life was returning, or that there was no loss of what a modern world expects. We want to understand how and when the Internet, especially, can be restored. Hence bringing you from Silicon Valley over to Miami.'

'Yes, well, thank you, Mr President, Mr Saba, Ms Sanchez,' he replied, nodding at each in turn. 'I really appreciate the trouble you've gone to, getting me here. I hope I can help. But this is not easy, and perhaps I need to try and explain the way that the internet worked, and why we no longer have it,' Geiger said, somewhat apologetically.

'Just tell it to us how it is, Mr Geiger. We need to be educated, before we can make any decisions,' the President said.

Geiger took a deep breath, then a slurp of coffee, draining his cup, wiped his mouth on the napkin by his side, and began to talk confidently. 'The internet is composed of four main things. Firstly, the websites, which are hosted all over the world, and which belong to each company or government, for example, and may be local or geo-located, with replicas all over the place, and you get pointed to them by where it thinks you are, within the website itself.

'The websites have end-users who connect to them. They are linked together by cables. Forget satellite, it's too slow and doesn't have large enough bandwidth. The cables generally are undersea between counties, and they are mainly fibre optic. There are lots of cables for redundancy around the Asia pacific region and multiple cables joining the regions to each other.

'There are DNS servers and routers which sort out what IP address relates to what website and how to get there. If there is a break in a network connection, BGP routing... sorry, that acronym stands for Border Gateway Protocol, tries to find another path, and tells everyone how to get around it.

'Theoretically, the internet can run without the USA and the EU, but lots of data would be missing, and you would only be able to get access to what is hosted in places with power and all infrastructure up. So, the lack of power supply was what killed things.

'Now most of the backbone was run by the big Telco's, which of course would have had back-up generators in place for short periods. But, for longer periods they would go dark and the BGP routing would try and sort it out based on least cost routes as far as it could.

'Those countries with power supply could get up anything hosted inside their country as most of it would end up at one or two main interconnect points, meaning control centres, before power is lost, but they would only have access to what was hosted in their country.

'So, effectively, when the US and Europe and major parts of Asia lost power, it was like... sort of blowing up the critical middle of the whole system. We need to reconnect the connections, but that needs immense amounts of power, to places where, I suppose, we no longer have population centres.'

George Saba was the first to speak when Geiger paused. 'Are you saying that we'll never get the internet back again?'

'Not quite. But assuming we have continuous electrical power to places where there's data located, or backed up, we would still only be able to get at our own data in those cities until they were connected externally.'

Silence met Geiger's last sentence, each of them trying to come to grips with what he was saying.

Amelia spoke first. 'So... for all intents and purposes... we're not getting access to the internet back anytime soon?'

Geiger gave a half smile, 'Yes, I'm afraid that's correct.'

KALIL

Admiral Muhammed Pereira enjoyed his position; that was plain. When he was on the bridge of his aircraft carrier, the Pakindesh Navy Ship, PNS Vikramaditya, surrounded by the might of the fleet, he was in control of all before him. The aircraft carrier was an old Russian ship, first launched in 1987, then updated in 1991 and renamed Admiral Gorshkov. It had been due for replacement by India for many years and had a troubled history of refurbishment issues and cost overruns. If the US had remained a military superpower, this Indian fleet would not have lasted more than a day in battle against it. The ship had limited on board armament and relied on its battle group for defence. Its Mikoyan MiG-29K Fulcrum-D aircraft would have been no match for the US Air Force. However, this was irrelevant now. In this new world, India's military was probably the best equipped, and Admiral Pereira was its commander.

However, his command of the Pakindesh invasion fleet was still subordinate to President Kalil. Kalil had shed his military rank now. He briefly elevated himself from Lieutenant General to General and considered making himself a Field Marshall. In the end, the position of President made more sense, and nobody questioned his distinguished military career and acumen. Sharing political power with his counterparts in Pakistan and Bangladesh was unimportant now. Ultimately, he aimed to become the President of the United States.

The month at sea was cathartic in many ways. He befriended Pereira, but maintained a healthy level of distrust as well, as was prudent. World trade, at least in the North Atlantic, was dead. The seas were therefore largely empty now, and the solitude had allowed conversation to flourish. He felt a little like Christopher Columbus about to discover the New World, although Columbus ended up in the West Indies, unlike Amerigo Vespucci, who at least provided his name to America. What would they find when they sailed into New York? American Muslims with open arms, happy to see other people? Would America have solved its problems well? Unlikely. A few million people of dubious skills would struggle to survive or resurrect their old lives. They'd be weak, like Americans had always been, without the benefits of their technology and their wealth. Whilst he hoped in part that Muslim America thrived, he doubted it. No. His fleet will be their saviours, bringing technology back to them, like the superior society they now were.

He stared at the sea, grey and choppy. Not long now, he thought. My destiny awaits, thanks be to Allah, praise be upon Him.

Admiral Pereira interrupted his thoughts, 'We will arrive in New York tomorrow morning. The advance team will fly in on the Sea Kings, reconnoitre Manhattan, and land on prominent buildings to set up observation posts. Special Ops teams will then determine the situation on the ground. Team 2, on the Kamov Ka-31's, will secure JFK. A company of marines in landing craft will traverse the East River to the Hudson and land at Battery Park on the southern tip of Manhattan. From there they will scout those locations we identified earlier and set up a staging post.'

Kalil nodded. 'I cannot imagine any resistance, Admiral.'

'I agree, but it is always wise to expect the unexpected, as you know all too well, Sir.'

'We only have 5 days to secure JFK before the aircraft arrive.'

'That won't be a problem.'

Less than 24 hours later, without a shot fired in anger, or by mistake, or in jubilation, Kalil felt cheated. New York was empty. Manhattan had been explored from north to south and east to west. Pakindesh marines, with supporting naval and air force personnel and assets, had landed in over three dozen locations and coordinated their investigation of the city. JFK airport was secure. The city was deserted.

At 3pm, there was a strategy meeting on the bridge of the PNS Mysore, a Delhi Class guided missile destroyer, with the number D60 on its hull. Along with its sister ships, the PNS Delhi (D61) and PNS Mumbai (D62), these ships were docked in the Hudson. Several frigates and merchant ships were progressively docking along the East River as well as the northern end of the Hudson. The island was no longer uninhabited.

On the bridge, President Kalil, Admiral Pereira, Colonel Kumar, and several other senior officers had listened firsthand to junior officer's reports of their findings around Manhattan. The senior officers were now alone, looking sombre.

Kalil spoke softly, 'You know, until this moment, I don't think I'd ever really understood what our new world was like. I thought I did. I experienced the sudden loss of population across India, the lower noise level of life, the changed demographics, and the loss of diversity. But that was tempered by the improvements; less traffic, greater wealth and opportunity, a new world order that would be better than the old world. But this,' he said, sweeping his hand over the horizon of New York City skyscrapers through the windows of the bridge, 'this is sterile desolation. The end of dreams and hopes. A wasteland, as if a neutron bomb had gone off, leaving only objects untouched, life extinguished. Do you feel the same, gentlemen?'

Kumar nodded, silently.

Pereira shrugged, 'In part, yes. I understand what you mean, Sir. However, I am also partly relieved that we have encountered no problems. I mean, we have the entire fleet here now, safely harboured, and all of our aircraft and personnel intact.'

'So where are the 4 million Muslims that used to live in the United States?' Kumar asked.

'If not here, where it makes the most sense for them to be, then either in Washington DC, or maybe California?' Commander Hukkeri suggested.

The bridge door opened, and a junior officer came in, saluted, and handed a written message to the Admiral, who acknowledged it. As he left and the door closed again, someone said 'That wind is the coldest I've experienced.'

Kumar looked up sharply, slapped his head, somewhat theatrically and laughed. 'It's cold!' he exclaimed loudly. 'Winter is going to be a lot worse. What would people trapped in Manhattan do in the winter now?'

Kalil smiled, suddenly understanding his old Adjutant's meaning. 'They would die here. Without any heat and power, they would suffer and die here. Ha! I agree, Kumar, they have fled south to survive the winter.'

'If that is the case, then Washington will be deserted too.' Pereira added.

'Every city in the north. But they could have gone to California perhaps,' Kumar suggested.

'Admiral, we need to reconnoitre Washington DC,' Kalil ordered, 'see if there is anyone left there at all. I doubt it, but there might be messages left behind, or at least some intelligence on where people have gone. California is possible, but where would you go if you needed to move a sizable population from the northeast of the country, in safety and the most easily?'

'The closest and warmest place with the capacity to feed them, and provide power, water, heat and services,' Kumar answered.

'Where is that?' Kalil asked those around him, already knowing the answer.

'Florida,' Pereira said.

'I think you're right, Admiral. It's closer than heading west and is probably easier to administer,' Kalil agreed.

Kumar looked less convinced. 'What about hurricanes down there?'

Kalil shrugged, 'True, that could be an issue, but even if they have gone south as an interim measure, it still makes the most logistical sense.'

'Does this mean that we rethink our phase 2 expansion to California?' Pereira asked.

'Yes, for now at least,' Kalil stated, rubbing his chin in thought. 'But send that recon group by air to DC and thoroughly check the main buildings we identified in the planning phase. Once they return, if the conclusions don't change, we head south to Miami. And for now, we delay the air migration too.'

CHARLIE

'You okay, Salsa?' Charlie asked.

'Sure... s'pose so.' Her face belied her words.

'You seem sad to me, little sis.'

She ignored the statement, giving away no facial clues either. 'Charlie, do you wish it never happened?'

'Every day I do. Every single day.'

'Really? I sort of thought that you were good with things now. You seem happy, especially when you're helping out at the hospital.'

'Salsa, I hate it. If I could click my fingers and return to the world before the deaths, I'd do it in a heartbeat. I miss it all; the people, friends and non-friends alike, football, tele, holidays, the news, cars, traffic, music, gossip, everything.'

'And Janice Donaldson, and Sarah?'

Charlie looked surprised.

'You loved her, didn't you? Janice, I mean. It wasn't just Billy you liked to visit. It was his sister that you mooned over.'

No point denying it now. He sighed. 'Yes, I think I did. But we never did anything. She didn't really look at me like that. Why would she? She was white and blonde and pretty and English, and I was the gawky Paki kid from next door. As for Sarah, well, we kissed but it was over.'

'I think Janice would have warmed to you. You're different now as well. Stronger, bigger, more... confident.

'Hmph! I might not be if things had stayed the same, Sis.'

'Yes, you would. Don't put yourself down, Charlie. How's it going with Alia Kaduji; still hot passion between you two?'

'Er... well... it's good, all good.'

'Alia really likes you. Maybe a bit more than you realise.'

'Does she? What makes you say that?'

'I can tell. The way she glances at you when you're kicking a football around. Her eyes follow you. She's hooked, Charlie. You should bring her home for dinner.'

'Isn't her family devout?'

'I don't think so. She doesn't give much away. None of us do now though. She was playing some Ed Sheeran music on a USB the other day and I asked her if she'd ever seen him live, and she had, at Wembley back in 2015 I think it was. I got the impression her family was like ours. You should meet her family. Be careful, of course, but I think they're OK.'

Charlie was smiling now. 'Hmm, OK I might just do that. I'll see what she thinks. What about you though. Any boys you like?'

'Maybe. Not sure. You know what's weird though? In the old days I'd have been scared to go out with a boy, coz, you know, they want sex, or at least they want to... explore, you know what I mean.' Charlie blushed, not used to his sister talking this openly. She was growing up fast. Salsa laughed at his expression. 'Charlie I'm almost 15; I know what boys want, and a lot of girls my age had already let them do stuff, before the deaths I mean.'

'Not Muslim girls?'

'No, of course not. Just the more rebellious Anglos. I thought they were crazy. I mean why let a boy stick his hand down your pants, or shag you, at fourteen or fifteen. I thought they sold themselves too cheaply. It wasn't like the boys respected them for it, just the opposite. Crazy to lose your virginity or your reputation like that. They thought we were frigid; such stupid girls,' she sighed. 'I still miss them though. They were funny at times. At least they got to experience sex before they died, I suppose.'

'Salsa, do you really think that Allah did this? I mean, why would we be the chosen religion? Islam isn't the oldest faith, and let's face it, Muslims were too fond of killing each other in the Middle East and blaming their problems on the west, or any other excuse for bloodshed. If I was a God up there somewhere, looking down on all the worst stuff in the world we had, I don't think I'd have done things this way.'

'OK then, what would you have done?'

'I haven't really thought about it like that. I suppose I'd get rid of bad people first, no matter what religion they were. That would set an example of how people should live, in peace, helping each other, not being violent or selfish, that kind of stuff.'

'Talkin' of bad people, have you noticed that those shit teachers that loved to cane kids have stopped? Dad's visit to the headmaster must have worked.'

'Yeah, I think you're right. Aziz has left. No idea where he went to, but that's been good. Seems like the subjects have got back to normal too.'

'So, what have you decided to do? Still thinking of being a doctor. Or tinkering around with boilers and pipes and generators and stuff?'

'I'm not sure.'

'You'd make a good doctor, I think. Do something that'll make you happy, Charlie. That's the main thing.'

'What about you? What's your passion going to be, Salsa?'

She shook her head, and looked a little sad, 'I don't know yet.'

AMELIA

'So how was your day, John?' Amelia called out from the kitchen as her lover walked into the apartment that they now shared openly. She liked to think of him as her lover, not boyfriend. They were too old for that. She liked the term lover; and he was such a good lover too. She started to feel the warm stirrings of passion. Be patient, girl. God, I'm becoming insatiable. She watched him walk over to the window and gaze out at the beach and the sea.

'Sorry, Amelia. Just wanted to get an eyeful of this view again. My day was good. I think the people I've recruited will do well as the new civil defence force. What about you? Still frustrated by the end of internet?'

'Yes. But more by the other communications issues. I thought we'd be able to get a limited mobile network up again, but Geiger was not exactly confident of that either.'

'What about a local TV service?'

'That might be easier, and Geiger is going to get some of the people in Silicon Valley to assist us,' she said as she wrapped her arms around him, and then they kissed. 'What's in the bag?'

'Contraband. Found it in a store whilst I was looking for other things.' He pulled out a bottle of white wine and a six pack of beer.

'John! We can't.'

'Why not? Because of the Quran? Amelia, I was never that devout, and neither were you from what you told me. So, we're not exactly about to be struck down by Allah, are we?'

'That's not the point. It's forbidden, and we're Muslim; you by choice, me by birth. Why would you risk it?'

'Risk what, exactly? The wrath of the Prophet, or the disdain of other people?'

She looked dismayed, and he regrated his comments, but before he could say any more, she composed herself and he waited for her to speak. 'OK, let me ask you this? Did you believe in the Quran and its teachings before you finally converted to Islam?'

'Yes, of course, otherwise I wouldn't have done it,' he replied.

'So, what makes you want to go against the Quran now, when you've adhered to it for years?'

He sat down heavily on the couch and put his head in his hands. When he'd regained his composure, he looked up and his eyes were moist. 'You're right, so right. I have no idea why I did this, brought the bottles home. What the hell was I thinking? I mean, I was never a heavy drinker anyway, even when I was younger. And I've seen what alcohol can do to people. Help me empty them down the sink,' he added, rising, and taking the bag through to the kitchen. He took the tops off the beer bottles and emptied them into the sink first, then repeated the process with the wine. 'I have absolutely no idea why I did this. Forgive me?'

'Of course. If you need... to unwind, or some stimulation after a hard day, I can help,' she said, and then her skirt slipped down her legs, and she unbuttoned her blouse and threw it aside, smiling.

'If this is the alternative to alcohol, there's no contest.'

'Glad to hear it, Major. I'll meet you in the bedroom; don't delay,' she added, laughing as she ran past him.

Thirty minutes later they were still locked in each other's arms, the sheets dishevelled. 'Why do we need a civil defence force, John?'

He was used to her abrupt changes of mood or subject, and it didn't bother him. 'Well, I suppose I'm just trying to get ahead of things. At present I don't think we do need one, not really. Crime is non-existent, people are generally content, and local disputes between neighbours are unlikely to escalate. However, eventually, as the population normalises, and we get back to some trading-type existence, there's bound to be minor issues that will occur, and for that I think it's prudent to be ready. For now, the CDF is more of a citizen's help force, rather than a law enforcement or crime detection body. I'd like to think we never need the old skills of a police force or military, but that would be naïve. Human nature, even now, after everything that has happened, will throw up some curve balls. Apart from that, I want to use my skills again, if possible. I don't exactly miss combat or military activity, but it did stimulate the mind and keep me fit.'

'You're still fit, I think, Major,' she replied with a smile. 'Why don't we test that a little more? Why don't you practice your push-ups again?' she laughed.

CHARLIE

The noise level from the game of football in the park was high, with squeals of delight from the players and the spectators. It was a mixed match, hastily set up by Charlie, Michael and Salsa and a dozen friends. There was seven-a-side, with floating goalies and the score was 3-3. The day was cold and grey, but dry, and the weather had no impact on the level of enjoyment. It had become a regular Saturday event. Sometimes there were enough participants for a full 11-a-side game, at other times hardly enough for two teams at all.

Initially a few of the kids didn't want the girls to play, but that was ironed out quickly, after the reasoning seemed to be related to their traditional parents' views of male and female segregation. Those kids were told they could leave if they wished, but as far as Charlie was concerned, and he was the game organiser, everyone was equal here, so accept it and play, or leave. Nobody left. The game was a link with the past and everyone felt similarly about that, but openly discussing missing the old days was an accepted taboo subject. Completely open conversation wasn't trusted yet; the rumours and experience of hard-line teachers and Imams was something many were wary of.

The pitch was in an area of Green Park that was far enough away from its perimeter streets to be safe from occasional adults that might take offence. But over the few months that the game had gained a level of regularity, it attracted a few dozen spectators, usually parents or siblings of the players. There was talk of an organised league being set up. Charlie started the idea off, arguing that every country in the world played soccer, and every Middle Eastern country attempted to get into the World Cup, with lots of Muslim countries being quite successful, like Saudi Arabia, Iran, Iraq,

Nigeria, Morocco, loads of them. So, this was nothing new, apart from him allowing girls to play of course.

As if to accentuate the value of girls, Salsa took a long cross from the wing, chested the ball down and started a run at the goal, deftly dribbled past a defender, feinting left then right, ran into space, saw that the goalkeeper was off his line and took a shot towards the left-hand post. The ball went a foot to the side of the keeper's outstretch hand as he dived, and it hit the back of the net to take the lead 4 to 3. The Razzle Dazzlers, as Salsa had convinced her brothers to call their team, went wild in celebration. After a counterattack failed to equal the score, it was half time and the teams split into their respective halves, and someone from the crowd brought out a bag of apples for them all.

Salsa still had a huge grin on her face as she took a large bite of her apple.

'Great goal, Salsa,' Michael said.

'Lovely dribble past the defender too,' Charlie added.

'I think we've got them on the run,' Salsa suggested, bits of apple falling out of her mouth as she spoke. Everyone laughed.

Their goalie, Muhammed, laughed the loudest. Most people thought he had a crush on Salsa. He looked around at his teammates and said, 'This is how it used to be for me, playing football on Saturdays in Birmingham, then going to watch Aston Villa when they were at home. God, I miss that.'

'Me too,' Jamil agreed, 'we lived in Leicester. When the Foxes won the Premiership in 2016, man that was cool. Right up 'til the end of the season we still thought summat bad would happen and we'd slip away at the end. But the team was fantastic that year. The atmosphere in the city for months, even a year afterwards, was brill. Even though we were pretty shit again the next season it didn't really matter. We had that trophy forever.'

Charlie nodded, deep in thought. 'If you all had the chance, and you could go back to before Revelation Day, just by clicking your fingers, would you?' he asked.

'Damn right, I would,' Muhammed said.

'Me too.'

'O' course.'

'Who wouldn't, mate?'

'Be careful, Charlie,' Salsa warned.

'Why, Salsa? Why should we be afraid to say these things? Everyone thinks them, or at least all the kids seem to. The adults are too scared to say what they think, but I bet most of them feel the same way.'

'Maybe so but it's dangerous. The teachers would say it's blasphemy, Charlie; we need to be careful.'

'Your sis is right, Bro. Too many crazy fuckers around that won't have a bar of any talk against the Prophet,' Jamil said.

'Why does hankering back to the old world mean we're saying anything against The Prophet?' Charlie challenged.

Muhammed shrugged, 'Dunno, Chaz, but that don't mean the Imams, or the heavies won't lay into you for sayin' it.'

'He's right,' Michael agreed, 'remember how some of those sick fuckers loved to cane kids just for not knowing enough of the Quran, or even arguing with them?'

'I know all that,' Charlie agreed, looking around to see who was able to hear them. 'I think this country needs to get its democracy working again. I don't want to live in a Middle Eastern dictatorship. We're English, all of us. We might have our differences, like Villa versus Leicester versus Manchester United,' he laughed, lightening the atmosphere, 'but we should protect the values that we grew up with. OK, enough of that for now, let's get back to the game and win this one.'

Everyone cheered, jumped up and started to make their way back onto the pitch, smiling. Salsa looked across at her big brother. He was hatching something, she could tell. But he also looked happy, deep in thought, but happy.

HABBIB

It was 10am and a bright and clear day, and the President was walking along the beach with his staff, barefoot and in shorts. This was now a regular Wednesday morning event, a midweek break from the office, and something that he had recently fostered to stimulate freethinking. He'd instigated a few rules. No saying 'Mr President', but he allowed them to call him 'Sir', as it was too hard to break the habit of hierarchy and deference to The Office. He had suggested that they call him POTUS if they preferred, but that was taboo, the acronym only used *about* the President, not to him.

As they walked along, the discussion was about local medical services and access to the higher technology hospital equipment that they needed to find more technicians to operate.

'I placed poster ads around the larger meeting places, Sir, and I think the word will spread that we -'

Amelia's words were cut short by the high-pitched scream of three military jets streaking towards them from the northern end of the beach.

'Take cover,' Cummins shouted, diving for the sand. The others were slower but followed suit as the aircraft flew over them. 'MiGs!'

'Whose are they?' Imran Malouf shouted.

'Russians?' George Saba suggested.

Cummins had jumped up immediately that the jets were past them and he scanned the sky as they turned and banked over the sea, coming back north, ready to make another pass. This time the White House staff stood their ground, looking up as the aircraft went north again and then banked once more to head inland, then heading back out to sea some minutes later.

'They look like Fulcrums, MiG 29's,' Cummins said, 'and unless I'm mistaken, they had Indian Navy markings on them.'

'Indian?' Habbib queried.

'I'm pretty sure, Mr President.'

'That's a long way from home,' Saba added.

'Quick, back to the office,' Habbib ordered, talking as they jogged, 'Major, you'd better gather whatever manpower you've recently trained.' There was no further conversation as the team ran, stopping briefly at the sidewalk to put the shoes on that they'd left there.

A few minutes later, in the New White House office block, there was frantic activity. People were arriving in groups and standing outside the building, some calling for answers.

Saba was almost literally pulling his hair out, clearly anxious, 'Fuck, we can't even communicate with whoever is out there.'

Cummins ran through the door, 'I have a crew ready to man one of those patrol boats at the quay. I'm planning to take it out and see if we can spot a carrier out there somewhere.'

'A carrier?' Saba queried.

'What? You think those jets flew all this way from India? They must be carrier-based. And if there's an Indian aircraft carrier out there then it will have a whole fleet around it.'

'Is this an invasion force?' Sanchez asked.

'Let's keep our heads, people,' the President said calmly. 'It was only a matter of time before the rest of the world came to visit us. We need to take it that way, at least to start with.'

Cummins nodded in agreement, 'That's right. We can't defend ourselves from any significant force, but let's keep our heads.'

'Well said, Major,' the President concurred. 'Let's at least keep our decorum. However, we should also use as much pomp and ceremony as possible too. Impressions matter. They don't need to know how weak we are. Who knows, maybe they've really come to assist us.'

'You're an optimist, Mr President,' Cummins replied.

'I'm a pragmatist. There's a difference. As for your patrol boat, I'm not sure that's going to make enough difference, but if you think it can be handled risk free, without you on it, then go ahead. But I want you here with me.'

'Let me just advise the skipper, Sir, and send it out a little way, just for show, perhaps as an escort boat,' he said, quickly leaving the room.

A few minutes later, Cummins returned and walked straight into the President's office, where the rest of the senior staff were speculating on the situation. He interrupted their conversation, 'The boat's headed out, Sir, and we have shortwave radio to contact them. It will probably not be secure though, as I've explained to the skipper.'

'OK, good. Sit down, Major. Coffee? Whilst we have a little time?'

'Absolutely. I could kill one, thank you, Sir.'

The President smiled a little, 'Amelia, you know how he likes it, and I'll have another too, please,' he added. Amelia went to pour them.

'OK, Major, what's your analysis tell you?'

'Sir, you don't send a carrier group half-way around the world for a diplomatic mission. Nor is it likely that it will be a rescue mission either. Rescue from what? There are only two reasons for a major force like the one I'm assuming is steaming here from just off the horizon, Mr President, and that's to colonise, or to stop someone else doing the same thing before them.'

'Who else?' Saba asked.

'One of the other new superpowers,' Malouf suggested, 'like Indonesia.'

Cummins nodded, 'I agree. They would be the only other likely country to seek to expand into the Americas.'

'That wouldn't make sense,' Amelia interrupted, causing a few raised eyebrows, 'I mean if Indonesia was to come here, they would head straight across the Pacific to California, surely?'

'That makes sense,' the President agreed.

'Maybe, Sir,' Cummins conceded, 'but we have no idea what's really going on in the rest of the world. Maybe Indonesia and India are already at war. Or maybe it's a race to get here between them and a Middle Eastern state, like Iran.'

'Irrespective of that, we need a strategy, and quickly,' the President said. 'Suggestions?'

'I have two helicopter pilots available, civilians but experienced. I have them on standby at the airport,' Cummins said.

'They'd be shot down if we approached the Indian carrier, surely?' Saba asked.

'As long as the approach was obviously from unarmed choppers and they were flown non-aggressively, and perhaps with white flags strewn below, I think we'd be welcomed,' Cummins said.

The President turned from looking out of the window towards the sea, a determined look on his face, 'OK, this is what we'll do. Major, I'd like you to take the two choppers out to the Indians. Advise them via open radio communication, perhaps on an international emergency channel, that you are an official US Government welcoming party and ask permission to approach and land. Before you leave, change your uniform, and take on the rank of Major General, if you can find the badges for it. Congratulations, you're officially promoted. Once you are on board their ship, invite their senior officers and diplomatic head, if they have one, here to the New White House; use that term.

'Amelia, quickly produce an official invitation on headed notepaper for me to sign and for General Cummins to take with him. Use whatever welcome message you think is best.

'George, get cracking on a welcome committee from our staff and maximise the ceremonial aspects, without going overboard. Send people out to arrange as big a civilian welcoming committee as possible to line the streets leading here. The bigger the numbers the better. We can't let them see how small our population is. We must show a level of population capacity for defence.

'Imran, as Secretary of State, normally I'd send you out to meet them, but I don't want us to put all of our key people out there together. Any problems, or comments, anybody?'

'I think we should have a few clearly armed guards nearby, Mr President, and some hidden armed personnel within your official party here too,' Cummins said.

'Agreed, General. George, please arrange that. Any last points before we get moving?'

'Sir, what if the Indians send their own choppers here first?' Malouf asked.

Cummins interjected, 'I'll deal with it. We'll recall and lead them here, but we'll take a long route around. Time will be short I think, maybe an hour at most before they take the next step.'

'Get going everyone, and good luck, General,' the President concluded before everyone ran off to their respective tasks.

KALIL

The two Mig 29 Fulcrums landed back on their carrier, 20 nautical miles off the coast of Florida and roughly due east from Fort Lauderdale. The pilots made their way to the bridge, saluted the Admiral and the President, and stood to attention.

'What's the situation?' Admiral Pereira asked.

Lieutenant Commander Thota answered, 'Very quiet, Sir. It didn't look overly populated at first, but as we made the second pass, people were coming out of apartments or onto their balconies, and onto the streets near the beach to look at us, some waving. There was no sign of land-based defence assets, although there were clearly naval assets in the docks, including three guided missile frigates, and a few Coast Guard patrol boats anchored nearer to the Port of Miami, and Miami Beach proper, but they all looked unmanned.'

'No reason for there to be any active defensive stance these days,' Colonel Kumar suggested.

'Any obvious signs that they were expecting visitors, Commander,' Kalil asked the senior pilot.

'None at all, Sir.'

'Did you expect something, Mr President?' Pereira queried.

'No, I didn't. But it further confirms that they have minimal, if any, communications capacity, as some of you suspected. Whilst I didn't think anyone down here would be aware of our New York and Washington visits, it tells me that they have possibly no intelligence gathering capacity either. And that leaves them, and subsequently us, with a slight dilemma.'

'What do you mean, Sir?' Pereira asked.

'I mean that they do not know of our intentions, and we cannot communicate with them.'

'So, we have the element of surprise, Sir, which is to our advantage,' Kumar said.

'That, Kumar, is a double-edged sword. If they have any defensive capability at all, then by flying in we invite a defensive strike, possibly,' Kalil replied.

Pereira raised his eyebrows, 'Our assessment assumed they had minimal defensive ability and that we would be met with open arms, or at least some level of relief, as possible saviours.'

'True, Admiral, but that was always the best-case scenario. The alternative was open hostility that we would need to overcome.'

'Easily achieved with the firepower we have available,' Kumar stated.

'Gentlemen,' Kalil replied, with a half-smile, 'our aim is to be welcomed as saviours, partnering with the Americans to bring them back into the modern world and making ourselves indispensable. Then we help them to populate and grow again, and ultimately, we take over, as a vine takes over its supporting tree.'

'And you think they will just accept that?' Pereira queried.

'Of course not, but we are two democracies assisting each other, and we have some common aims as well, which I will exploit,' Kalil said.

'Such as, Mr President?' Pereira persisted.

'Common enemies represented by those states that have little history of democracy or innovation. We represent the closest background to the Americans that they know of, and I say that with sincerity. We have nearly a hundred years of democracy and the rule of law, based on similar lines to their own, modern science and research ability, nuclear powered electricity capacity, western education and pluralist societies. We will be friends, and we will advise them about the threats faced by the Caliphate, and Iran, and Indonesia.'

'What threats, Sir?' Pereira asked.

'I'll have to think about those, Admiral, but there must be some,' Kalil chuckled, and then Kumar and the other officers in the room added their quiet laughter.

At Miami airport, the newly uniformed General Cummins, looked at his hastily attired helicopter pilots and his aid, all of them new to being in uniform. There had been an army surplus shop nearby that had a host of insignia and uniform options available to plunder. Once dressed, they had quickly learned how to look military and how to salute, but they were clearly nervous about it. 'You'll be fine, gentlemen. Are the white flags secured and you know how to release them?'

'Yes, Sir,' one of the pilots answered.

'Well done; that sounded just like the officer that your uniform suggests you are. OK, don't worry about anything other than looking friendly and non-hostile when we get close to the carrier that we're looking for. I hope that the radars on these choppers work, and we can track our way to wherever this fleet is. When we spot the carrier, we will make for it in a lazy approach, turning so that they can see we are unarmed. Leave all the radio traffic to me, but as I explained earlier, I might make some idle chatter that the Indians can intercept, to give them more comfort that we're friendly, which we are. Any questions before we get airborne?' Cummins asked, looking at each man's face in turn and keeping a smile on his own face. There were no questions and they each boarded their respective aircraft.

The helicopters were relatively new Bell 407GXP's with a range of 337 nautical miles and a maximum speed of 133 knots, so Cummins expected them to spot the Indian carrier group that he suspected was not far offshore, without any range issues. They had only been airborne for a few minutes when he began the rehearsed conversation that he'd printed and provided to the other crew in the second aircraft.

Cummins had decided to use the call signs 'Charlie Echo' and 'Charlie Delta' to match the last two letters of their registration numbers. 'Charlie Echo, this is Charlie Delta, I think we should find that the Indian Navy visiting us is northeast of here and hopefully less than fifty nautical miles distant. Keep scanning the horizon and let's see if we can find this friendly fleet quickly, over.'

'Roger, Charlie Delta, will advise if we see them first, out.'

Cummins smiled as he spoke just to his pilot, 'They should have picked up that transmission. We should soon find out.'

On the PNS Vikramaditya, the radio operator advised the bridge commander nearby of the American transmission and relayed it live so that the whole Bridge could hear it. When concluded, and Charlie Delta had signed off, Admiral Pereira spoke first, 'They are talking for our benefit,' he said confidently.

'I agree,' Kalil said. 'I would do the same in their place. They have limited communications ability so using an open channel like this advises us that they are friendly.'

'Shall we respond, Sir?' the communications officer asked the admiral.

'Yes. Guide them in,' Pereira ordered.

'Charlie Delta and Charlie Echo, this is the PNS Vikramaditya, call sign Pakindesh One, I say again, Pakindesh One, of the Indian Navy, do you read me, over?'

'This is Charlie Delta, Pakindesh One, we read you loud and clear and wish to land on your deck and to meet with your commander, over.'

On the bridge, Kalil nodded silently to the radio operator, who continued to transmit, 'Charlie Delta, Pakindesh One, we would be delighted to host you. Please approach on heading four seven six five degrees. You are eighteen nautical miles off our port bow. A clear landing area for 2 rotary aircraft will be marked out on the mid flight deck, over.'

'Pakindesh One, this is Charlie Delta. That is most appreciated. We will approach as requested, two minutes apart, out.'

'Charlie Echo, this is Charlie Delta, follow us in to Pakindesh One from the port side as instructed, over.'

'Charlie Echo, roger, out.'

Cummins looked at his pilot, 'Ever landed on a ship before?'

'No, Sir.'

'Nothing to it in this weather. And this is one big mother of a ship too. May as well be landing at Miami International. Deck hands will be guiding us in. Once you put down, take a few minutes to look like you're doing routine shutdown procedures just in case we need to pull up fast. But don't worry, I doubt that will happen. We'd have no chance getting away anyhow. I suggest we just look, listen and learn, and try and work out what they're really doing here, no matter what story they tell us, okay?'

'Yes, Sir, General.'

'Good man,' Cummins said, smiling, and then he started to hum to himself as he popped a piece of chewing gum in his mouth. It looked to his pilot like he was enjoying the ride without a care in the world.

The landing went like clockwork, with the two Bell 407's landing a few minutes apart in the centre of the flight deck. Once their engines were shut down, an escort officer, a young sub-lieutenant accompanied by a man-mountain of a chief petty officer approached Charlie Delta. When Cummins neared them, they both saluted, which he returned smartly.

'Good morning, Sir, welcome to the PNS Vikramaditya. Please let me escort you and your officers to the bridge. I am Lieutenant Chaddya, and this is Chief Vandarintam.'

'That would be a pleasure, thank you lieutenant. I am General Cummins, with lieutenants Patterson, Mohammed and Silwa,' he stated as the two pilots from Charlie Echo walked across to join him and his pilot.

The walk to the bridge took a few minutes, during which Cummins made mental notes. Tired looking superstructure, many signs of wear and tear, too many areas of neglected steelwork requiring simple rust maintenance, storage of materials not bad but could be better, crew well-tended, uniforms clean and pressed, no sign of fighter crews checking us out. Who will be in charge I wonder?

A soon as the Americans entered the bridge, an Admiral approached him, 'Welcome aboard General, I am Admiral Muhammed Pereira. May I present His Excellency, The President of India, Sabal Kalil?' he indicated with a flourish towards the immaculately dressed man besides him.

Cummins didn't miss a beat, 'Your Excellency, this is an unexpected pleasure; a great honour to welcome you to our shores.'

'It is kind of you to say so, General. May I also introduce my Adjutant, Colonel Ashraf Kumar? He has been with me since my own military days, and I must say that I still miss my own uniform at times like these.'

I wonder what uniform that was exactly, Cummins wondered. 'I know the feeling, Mr President,' Cummins responded. 'My staff here are lieutenants Joseph Patterson, Bihal Mohammed and Anton

Silwa. My name is John Cummins and I also act as the Chief Military Advisor to President Paul Habbib.' The appropriate handshakes, nods and platitudes were exchanged and then Kalil and Pereira invited the Americans into the wardroom.

As they walked, Kalil clicked his fingers in recognition and said, 'Of course, Paul Habbib. He was the previous administration's Chief of Staff, wasn't he? Now he is the President, which makes perfect sense.'

Cummins would much have preferred to stay on the bridge and quietly observe, but he also accepted that he'd be taken elsewhere, just as he'd have managed that himself in the Indians' position. Once off the bridge and settled in the richly decorated wardroom, which was clearly kept for entertaining rather than business, Kalil took control, with Pereira in the background.

'Naturally I imagine you are wondering what we are doing off the coast of Florida, General, and I will most certainly tell you all of this later. But first, please satisfy my own curiosity and tell me what happened in America after the deaths? We first made for New York and found it empty, as well as Washington.'

Cummins was hesitant, but there was little point in trying to obfuscate. 'Mr President, as you can imagine it was a time of great confusion and fear. Our population was decimated, communications was down, and we lost many of our technically skilled people across a broad spectrum of capacity. Once we had established the scale of loss the first task was to determine where the remaining population was located. This was concentrated in New York, Washington, L.A., San Francisco, Chicago, and Michigan State. The aim was to concentrate in population centres with effective logistics and access to future capacity. We decided on San Francisco and New York initially. Then the realisation of the problems of surviving winter if our power systems went down led to a change of direction, literally, and the east coast populations were consolidated, and we moved south.'

'That must have been a difficult decision from an emotional perspective, even though a very practical one, I imagine, General?' Kalil asked.

'It was, Sir, but once made, the logistics took all of our energy, and the move south went very well.'

'How did you do it, and what population is there living in Miami now? I assume you are all in Miami?'

Cummins hesitated a moment, 'Yes, almost all of us are here now, although a little more spread out than just Miami. We have arranged a few flights between San Francisco too, mainly for communications work and technical issues. However, the seat of Government is now in Miami. I am authorised to invite you to meet with the President, although I had assumed initially that was to be an invitation for the Admiral of course,' Cummins said and then changed the subject. 'Forgive me for asking this, Sir, but is it not dangerous for you to leave your country at a time like this, Mr President?'

Kalil smiled, 'A time like what, General?'

'Well, let's say a time of geopolitical uncertainty?'

'What do you know about what is happening around the world now, General? Do you have access to global communications at all?' Kalil challenged.

Be careful, John. This is a skilled adversary. 'Not to the level that we'd like, Sir, no. It would be most useful to hear of your own experiences since Revelation Day.'

'And I will be most pleased to explain all that I can to President Habbib at the earliest convenience. How shall we proceed, General? Do you wish to remain with us and steam closer to the Port of Miami, or would you prefer to fly back and arrange things ahead of us? We are at your disposal. This is a peaceful mission, General, not an invasion.'

Really? I'm not so sure about that. How to do this? 'Well, Mr President, as I'm not a Navy man, I must admit to being less than certain about the shoal conditions for a ship of this size. It might be prudent to stay offshore a little way, and perhaps come in via air. You'd be most welcome to fly back with me, Sir?'

'That is most kind, General, but perhaps a little cramped. However, I'd be pleased to fly alongside you in one of our helicopters. I'd also like to bring some technical people along too, to speak with your own technical experts, if that meets with your approval. This might be beneficial for you.'

'That would be good, Sir. Might I suggest that my lieutenants fly back ahead, to alert the President's staff so that they can make the appropriate arrangements for your arrival, and I will fly in with you?'

'Perfect, General, that would work well,' Kalil agreed. 'I will leave you to arrange for your own crew's departure and I will get my staff and briefing documents together. Please feel free to wander the ship. I am sure that Admiral Pereira can arrange for an escort to show you whatever you'd like to see?'

'Of course, Mr President,' Pereira concurred.

Cummins walked his crew back to their helicopters. He had ten unchaperoned minutes to give them instructions to relay to the White House staff once they returned. Clearly, he wasn't going to be allowed to hear any conversation between Kalil and Pereira, so he decided he might as well explore the ship and see what he could learn whilst aboard. Maybe his Indian shadow would be forthcoming if he could engage him in conversation.

His escort was Lieutenant Commander Thota, a man who was clearly not a conversationalist. 'Have you ever been to The United States, Commander?' Cummins asked.

'No, General.'

'I was in India only once, about ten years ago, and only in New Delhi, on a military exchange for a month. I was most impressed, especially with the Sikh officers I met. I suppose they have all died now?'

'Of course. Only the faithful remain in our Islamic world, General. Is it not the same in your country?'

'It would seem so. I meant to ask President Kalil about the term Pakindesh that he used. What does this mean?'

Thota hesitated, clearly unsure how much he should say. 'There has been an amalgamation of India, Pakistan and Bangladesh now, hence Pakindesh.'

How interesting. Yet Kalil is here. Supreme confidence of his position, or something else. 'So, President Kalil is the President of the 3 amalgamated countries?'

'It is a shared Presidency, with Ghulam Asif as joint President. He was the leader in Pakistan beforehand,' Thota answered nervously.

'I see. Well, that makes sense; I would have done the same. Presumably, Pakindesh is now the world's only superpower, and rightly so,' Cummins gambled.

'How do you mean, General?'

He took the bait! 'Well, let's see, India's Islamic population was around 200 million, 240 million in Pakistan, and 150 million in Bangladesh. Your countries were all working democracies, with solid military capacity, modern communications, nuclear power, an enormous navy and air force and army, and presumably with no remaining threats from China or Russia. Only Indonesia has similar capacity, but nothing like that of Pakindesh. You must be very proud of your new dominant world status, Commander?'

'We are, Sir, I mean...'

'You said nothing to worry about, Commander. I hope that we can work well together with Pakindesh. We have a lot to offer too, although not in terms of population of course. Your President is to be admired. I understand that he was a military commander before?'

'Yes, Sir, he was a General too, before Infidel's End.'

'Infidel's End? Is that what the rest of the world is calling it?'

'Of course, what else? We are free of the non-believers now, and all will be for the glory of Allah, praise be to Him.'

'Praise be to Him indeed,' Cummins repeated. And may He look after America especially, because there's no way that this armada is here just to provide aid.

HABBIB

Paul Habbib waited with his staff inside the New White House. He'd been briefed by General Cummins' helicopter pilots only an hour earlier. He was excited about hearing real news of the wider world after such a long time, although not sure he would be able to believe it all. At the same time, he was nervous of his first official welcome as one President to another. He had said a silent prayer to the memory of his friend, President Kendal, invoking his help, if such a thing was possible.

Two helicopters of the Indian Navy landed in an open area some 400 metres from the New White House. Habbib noticed that his staff looked as nervous as him.

'We need to hold it together, everyone. Look regal, look superior, look confident... no matter how you really feel,' Habbib said with a smile, eliciting similar responses from Saba, Sanchez and Malouf. Besides the entryway to the office complex were a dozen uniformed men. He hoped that General Cummins would handle any military protocol issues. Sanchez, aided by Badiah Malaki, had done a terrific job to get well over three thousand people to line the approach leading from the landing point. There were no handheld Indian flags available, but the atmosphere was genuine, with most of the civilian population taking this visit as a sign of normality returning, as incorrect as that was.

The Pakindesh group was led by a tall, distinguished man in an immaculately tailored dark suit. This was clearly the President. He was shaking many hands as he strode along, in his element, confident, smiling, in control. Next to him was another tall man, in a Colonel's uniform, equally smiling, but wary, looking through the crowd rather than at the faces. The senior naval officer, presumably Admiral Pereira, walked a few paces behind, and there were three other officers alongside. General Cummins walked to the right and slightly behind the Indian President, making the odd comment from time to time.

Habbib put his official smile in place as the party came within 50 metres of the steps. Cummins has done well. Now it's up to me to play my part. Guide me, Andrew. Let me channel your wisdom. A young girl, aged about 8, in a white party dress, walked out of the crowd by the steps and presented a bunch of flowers to President Kalil with a curtsy. Sanchez had created a masterstroke. Kalil was genuinely surprised and delighted. He took the flowers and then held the little girl's hand and kissed it. She bounded away back to her mother and the crowd cheered and clapped. The official party walked up the steps and the quickly rehearsed greeting performance began, as the crowd continued to cheer.

Habbib and Saba and Malouf had debated whether to speak to the crowd at this point but decided to delay that until after their initial talks. The crowd would have to wait, but they did not seem unhappy about that. Once the two official parties walked through to the President's official 'square office', some of them started to relax.

Habbib took the host's initiative, 'President Kalil, allow me to introduce you to my Chief of Staff, George Saba,' he began, as Kalil shook hands with each person in turn, 'Imran Malouf, my Secretary of State, and Amelia Sanchez, my Population Advisory Officer, an unfitting title that covers a multitude of skills.'

'Likewise, Mr President, may I introduce you to my Chief of Staff, Colonel Ashraf Kumar, Admiral Muhammed Pereira, commander of the Pakindesh fleet, and Lieutenant Commander Thota.'

After handshakes, pleasantries, and the serving of tea and coffee, the two groups sat opposite each other around a large coffee table.

Kalil put his cup of coffee down and said, 'Mr President, I would be dishonest if I did not say that I am sorry we could not have met at the White House in Washington, although the weather is certainly more conducive down here. It must have been a difficult decision to have to come south.'

'Before we go on, Mr President, why don't we cut the formality a little,' Habbib suggested. 'All of this Mr President for each of us will get tedious. Please call me Paul.'

'That is very gracious of you... Paul. Please call me Sabal, but forgive my officers for retaining the use of Sir, or they might have... is conniptions the correct word?' Kalil asked, chuckling.

Habbib laughed, 'Yes, conniptions puts it well, Sabal. I'm sure General Cummins would feel better that way too,' he said, glancing across at him and gaining a smile and a slight nod of approval in return.

'I am sure that you must have many questions, Paul. Please ask whatever you like, and I will try to answer you as fully as I can,' Kalil offered.

'Thank you, that's very gracious. I would be most interested to know how the world fares in your part of the globe, and elsewhere; what happened immediately following the deaths and how it came about that India, Pakistan and Bangladesh amalgamated?' Habbib asked.

'Well, we were probably little different to here in the US, when the day of Infidel's End occurred, as it has come to be called, although Revelation Day is gaining favour, apart from in the Middle East. There was confusion, dismay, disbelief, and then a realisation, although not immediate, that only the faithful had survived the apocalypse. I learned since that in countries like Pakistan, which suffered minimal losses, the deaths were not understood to be part of a global destruction of non-Muslims. But, in India, which lost most of its population, like here, the scale of the deceased was incalculable, even though it was the middle of the night and most were in their homes. However, unlike here, we still had a large workable population of 200 million people. I was the commander of the Indian Army's Western Command, headquartered in Chandimandir, in Haryana State to the northwest of Delhi. At the time I was on an inspection tour to my 11th Corps headquarters at Jalandhar, towards Amritsar, where I was visiting the 55th Mechanised Brigade staff. As you can imagine, I lost most of my men, but from the survivors I put together a spearhead and we went initially to Amritsar, further northwest. I wanted to see for myself if there were any Sikhs left alive. I was hoping so. There were not, so we made quickly for New

Delhi. There was some sporadic looting and rioting around the capital, mostly from confusion rather than criminal behaviour. We put down the unrest and restored order.

'Over the following few weeks there was a semblance of order across the country. I was in the fortunate, or possibly cursed, position, of being the most senior officer left alive. Clearly this was a time of plenty but also a time of suspicion and potential conflict. Whilst India was now extremely wealthy, with only 200 million people inheriting the wealth of over a billion, petty issues were still capable of erupting. Happily, we had good remaining communications links. There were border incursions from Pakistan, which I expected, given that they were largely untouched yet understandably mesmerised by the vacant wealth of housing and food and land for the taking across our border.

'I sent a message to the President of Pakistan for a meeting. Without boring you with details, over the coming months we agreed that an amalgamation made sense, with Bangladesh as well, and from that idea Pakindesh was born. My joint President, Ghulam Asif, is an astute man, who I am pleased to say is now a dear friend as well.

'Elsewhere, the world has not remained as peaceful. Unfortunately, the old rivalries between Sunni and Shia remain an issue, and there is conflict ongoing between Iran and the Caliphate of Mecca. Presently that seems to be at a stalemate, and largely an air war, with some minor land battles. However, it is difficult to get accurate information. I am unaware of similar conflicts elsewhere. There do not seem to be any problems in the east, and Indonesia and Malaysia are prospering well I believe. Like Pakistan, Indonesia will not have suffered much loss of people. As for Europe and Africa we have minimal information.

'The good news is, I think we've solved the issues of climate change,' Kalil said, laughing.

'Are there other territorial conflicts in the Middle East, Sir,' Saba asked.

'I don't believe so, but it is difficult to be completely sure. No, the main issue is the wish for power by the Caliphate. We think that the self-proclaimed Caliph murdered the Saudi royal family and then tried to consolidate his power base. Unfortunately for him the reduced communications networks make this ambition a little more difficult to achieve than he imagined, and the limited news from Iran suggests that there is little being achieved on the ground.'

'So, you don't think that the conflict will expand to other Middle East nations, Sir?' Cummins asked.

'No, General, I don't. There is limited wish for more wars and most people see the folly of such things in a world where Allah has spared us all. To fight amongst ourselves after His deliverance would seem to be somewhat blasphemous, don't you think?' Kalil suggested, glancing from face to face.

'I agree, Sabal,' Habbib nodded, 'but since when does sense win out against greed?'

Kalil shrugged, 'That is often true, Paul.'

Cummins decided to change topic, 'So what prompted this voyage to America, Sir?'

Hmm, you are a little impatient, General. I can use that weakness. 'Curiosity of course,' Kalil stated with a slight smile.

'With all due respect, Sir, I find that a little hard to swallow,' Cummins replied.

'I would have been disappointed if you did not, General.'

Habbib said, 'Well, if I was in your position, Sabal, I would be deeply curious about how America was faring with less than 5 million people, and I would want to expand my influence, before any rivals came here first. Am I right?'

'Of course, Paul. But we are not invaders; we are emissaries, with good intentions, although perhaps you have a healthy scepticism.'

'Humour me, Sabal. Just don't begin with "have I got a deal for you".'

'Well, let me first ask for some indulgence if you would humour me too, Paul? Tell me how you see your immediate future when other nations come calling?'

'You want us to tell you of our defence capability, is that it, Sir,' Cummins interrupted.

'No, General, I am fully aware of that; it is minimal,' Kalil replied. Before any anger followed, he added, 'Please hear me out. I do not wish to cause offence, nor am I casting any aspersions on the military traditions and past capabilities of the United States. However, under my command before Infidel's End, I had 6 infantry divisions, 1 armoured division, and 6 specialist brigades. This was in a country where we had a sizable Muslim population, albeit within a large majority Hindu country. After Infidel's End I was lucky to cobble together a fifth of a division from my 3 Corps. Your situation is comparably pitiful, with all due respect, Mr President. Anyone coming here will defeat you, and I mean anyone. The analogy would be like the Conquistadors against the Incas, but with the numerical superiority being with the Spaniards this time. I do not want to conquer the Americas. I want to assist you to recolonise them. I would prefer to do this as your ally. I want America again to be the superpower it was, and I am willing to share power to do it. This continent, of north and south, is big enough for both of us. Now, is there any more of this excellent coffee, Ms Sanchez?'

After the Pakindesh Presidential party had departed, to be accommodated in the penthouse suites of the Fontainebleau Hilton, pending further talks over a dinner limited to the two Presidents, Habbib, Cummins, Saba, Malouf, and Sanchez held a debrief.

'Your thoughts, George?'

'Smooth bastard, wasn't he?'

'Arrogant son of a bitch if you ask me,' Malouf added.

'Goes with the territory of holding all of the key cards,' Cummins said.

'Hmm, I don't suppose anyone thinks otherwise as to that?' Habbib asked.

'No question militarily, Mr President,' Malouf said, 'and no offence to you, General.'

'None taken, Sir; they could take us within an hour if they wanted to,' he agreed.

'So why don't they?' Habbib queried.

'No need to,' Saba replied. 'Better to have a compliant population under a puppet government than alienate them. And no need to kill innocents either.'

'We'd never be a puppet government!' Sanchez exclaimed.

'Relax, Amelia,' Habbib said, 'George means that we can't oppose them, that's all. We have no ability to thwart their plans, but they would much prefer us to be on side and assisting than hampering them.'

'What do you think Kalil meant by being a partner and having enough territory to go around?' Cummins asked.

Saba snorted in derision, 'He's bullshitting! Why would he share power with us, given his military and numerical superiority?'

'Military, maybe,' Habbib agreed, 'but numerical? How?'

'A civilian airlift?' Malouf suggested.

'Would take a long time to bring large numbers of people over here,' Cummins stated.

'Do you think he's being honest when he speaks of others coming too, like Indonesia?' Malouf continued.

'Why would they? Why would anyone?' Cummins asked.

Habbib stood up and started to pace the room, slowly, 'Curiosity is a powerful motive; it doesn't just afflict cats,' he joked, with a slight laugh. 'Wouldn't any other superpower want to see what threat we might still pose? Or perhaps just to make sure that we're as defeated, or depopulated, as they assume?'

Malouf shook his head, 'No, I don't buy that, Mr President, not at face value I mean. It cost a lot to put this armada together, and I mean political capital at risk. I think they probably were curious about maybe Indonesia coming across here. No matter what Kalil said about his co-President, surely you wouldn't leave home and assume you'll be welcomed back months later to share power again? I mean is it just me, or does that seem incredibly stupid?'

'What are you saying, Imran?' Saba asked.

'He's saying that the Indians are here to stay, I think, George,' Habbib concluded.

In Miami Beach, overlooking the sea from the top floor of the Fontainebleau Hilton, President Kalil was asking his team similar questions.

'They are weaker than I thought,' Pereira stated.

Kalil nodded. 'Although the numbers of likely survivors suggested so, I am still surprised, although I shouldn't be. I saw what the deaths did to my own command, and across India, so this should have been obvious. Yet a part of me somehow assumed the Americans would have had greater strength.'

'We could kill the officials and take over easily,' Kumar suggested.

'That would be folly, Ashraf,' Kalil replied. 'We don't need to remove their President and Office. We can use them, assist them, strengthen them... and absorb them at our leisure.'

'What about the pilgrims? Do we still land them in New York?' Pereira asked.

'That is a good question, Admiral. If it wasn't almost winter, I would say yes, but given the difficulty of taking over a city without power in a cold climate, for people that have never experienced such, well that might be worse folly. I will consider it over my dinner with their President this evening.

One of the reasons for using the Fontainebleau to house the Pakindesh entourage was because of its iconic status. The other was because it had been the first Hotel to attract a professional chef and reopen its kitchen, as well as now housing about three hundred residents, mostly singles, on the lower levels. The New White House had commandeered the upper floors early on, for the times when they would need to entertain dignitaries. Habbib had assumed that would be a long way off when it was first suggested. Now he was pleased that he had agreed. He wished that there was still a CIA organisation available to bug the rooms.

Sanchez had arranged for a private dining room and made sure that the chef was available and there was an adequate menu. Whilst the two presidents were dining together, the rest of the official parties were on hand to assist, although not eating together.

The menu had 3 choices of each course but both presidents chose French Onion soup, followed by a local fish, with potatoes, carrots, and green beans.

After the first course, Kalil laughed and said, 'You know, Paul, before Infidel's end I would have been drinking a French Bordeaux or an Australian Shiraz, even with fish. I loved red wine... and whisky, and beer. I do miss that.'

'I didn't really drink, not much, except to keep my wife company, God rest her soul. I don't miss alcohol.'

'I'm very sorry about your wife, Paul. I didn't know. My apologies for bringing up a sad memory,' Kalil said sympathetically. 'My wife was killed in a car crash a few years ago. I didn't get around to remarrying, but that isn't the same as your loss.'

'Tell me more about this power sharing concept you mentioned, Sabal.'

'No beating about the bush, as you American's say,' he laughed. 'Okay then. Let us lay our cards on the table, shall we? You have few people here, sadly. Maybe a million in California, and possibly twice that many here, and limited numbers isolated elsewhere. Effectively you are a two-city state, separated by thousands of kilometres of land mass, on different oceans, with minimal communications between you. That is the bad news. The good news is that you have infinite resources and access to high technology, as well as almost inexhaustible supplies of fuel and food.

'So, what can you do with this? The short answer is nothing. You do not have the skills to unlock this wealth, nor the need to either. Consequently, America will again become lazy and complacent. Until one day, the Indonesians will come knocking, or perhaps the Caliphate, although I seriously doubt that.

'I can provide an alternative. I can populate your country again. I can bring across millions of technicians, doctors, farmers, builders, scientists, academics, pilots, sailors, aircraft engineers; whatever you need. We can populate your nation again and get its power plants back up and running, its hospitals operating, its defence capacity rebuilt. Paul, I can bring over millions of people in less than six months and repopulate New York, Washington, Chicago, and other places for you, including major farming land. They would live under the US system of government if you wish. This will become India in the west. Ha! No, that wouldn't sound right, would it,' he laughed, 'we can't call them West Indians; we'll have to think of another term.'

'You're serious?' Habbib replied.

'Absolutely.' Kalil watched Habbib's face as the silence grew in length, the American clearly contemplating many questions.

'Tell me the truth about your relationship with… is it President Asif?' Habbib asked.

'Yes, Ghulam Asif. He's a good man. He was already the President of Pakistan when Infidel's End changed the world order. It would have been the easiest thing in the world for Pakistan to take over India. His military remained intact, his population jubilant, his ambitions starting to come to fruition. That was why I needed to go to him early, quickly, and change his mind, before he'd even made it up. I laid my plans out before him and he began to see the potential. I can see that I need to do more to explain it to you, Paul.'

'Yes, I think you do. Please, do explain it to me.'

'Let me take you on my intellectual journey, if you will humour me, Paul?' Kalil began, and then continued without pause, 'First let me say that the new world scared me. I don't mean from the perspective of a takeover by Pakistan, or anyone else, not in the sense that you'd expect. No, it scared me because in one day we lost all that was great about India, and oddly, I had never realised quite so starkly just how great India was. To foreigners, tourists, even official visitors, I am sure that India scared them. They could not come to terms with her immense population, her crowds, smells, tumult, and in your face abundance of humanity. They could not see beyond the poverty and the vast numbers of poor. But they could not appreciate the growth and the positive changes that had occurred in the past few decades, and the continued potential that was only made possible by India's diversity of people.

'All of that diversity was lost in one terrible night. Yes, of course there was now no ethnic tension to worry about, although that was never large in the scheme of things. So, over a few days of intense reflection, I realised that I did not want to live in a greater Pakistan. Pakistan had far more problems than India, and its greatest problem was its lack of diversity. Islam was holding it back, not allowing it to blossom. On top of that was its inability to purge itself of radical elements like the Taliban and fundamentalists in the north and rural areas. I could only see a tightening of freedom, and not because of Asif, but despite him.

'I do not want to live in a greater Pakistan, whether we call our amalgamated nation Pakindesh or something else; the sad reality that we face is stagnation and a lack of freedom. For now, no one has voiced this. Perhaps none of them sees it, not yet. Apart from the Caliphate versus Iran conflict, the rest of the world is probably still wallowing in its newfound abundance of materials, free homes and stored foods and fuel. In that respect, Pakindesh, as well as Indonesia, Malaysia and the more enlightened African states can do well, because they have not lost their widespread abilities, and especially agricultural capacity. For other countries, such as the United States, and probably many in Europe, they will one day realise that they have no ability to prosper, because they are too limited in their skills. When that occurs to them, there will be conflict, because people will need to congregate and when that happens, they will sadly fight each other, as their differences are accentuated.

'For that reason, Pakindesh and Indonesia and a few of the more enlightened Middle Eastern states will dominate the new world. In my humble opinion, Pakindesh is more likely to lose ground than gain it, and we might not keep pace with Indonesia's expansionism.

'Therefore, there is only one option to take control of the future. Diversity and freedom of thought. I need America's ideals and the diversity of Pakindesh's abilities and people. Only that combination will secure the world that I think we both hope to see again, Paul. Or am I wrong?' Kalil asked, spreading his hands in a question that seemed to seek hope.

RIAZ

'Are you sure of that, George; over?' Harry said into his handset.

'As sure as anyone can be these days, my English friend. There were a few weeks of fighting here, but mainly little fights, sort of like street gangs with big guns but little brains, if you understand me? Then, quite suddenly, it was over, and people have been saying that those armed men that supported Iran have disappeared now. I don't know if they are dead or left Beirut, or what; over.'

Harry thought what to say for a few seconds, 'Does that mean that Lebanon is peaceful now, that there's no other fighting happening; over?'

'Harry, this is Lebanon, not London. There has always been fighting. Maybe it was criminals much of the time, and sometimes it was factions fighting and killing for power. We've had Syrians, Iranians, Palestinians, all of them stealing and killing, some involved with drugs, others with arms smuggling. Today, for now at least, it has gone quiet. My nephew, he walks the streets a lot more than me, and he says that the worst men are dead, but he doesn't know who killed them... over.'

'Is there a functioning government in Beirut, George; over?'

'I suppose so. At least there is food everywhere, and people drinking coffee at street cafes, and the schools are open, and the hospitals too. For us this is maybe as good as it gets, maybe a little better than we've seen in the last ten years even; over.'

'Do you know what happened between the Caliphate and Iran, George; over?'

'Only rumours. I think Mecca lost, or at least they didn't win. A man I know said it was a bloody stalemate and that the two powers are tending their wounds. Who knows? Over.'

'Is any of this on your TV news? Do you see pictures of that conflict at all; over?'

'Harry, it is not like the old days, even here, where we lost less people. There are no regular TV programs. We get more news in print. That I like, it reminds me of when I was young, even if we are sceptical of what we read. The TV news is on every day at six, but we don't learn much of the outside world from that. Harry, I must go. I will broadcast again in 5 days. Take care, my friend; over.'

'Take care as well, George. I look forward to your next transmission, GSK7GB out,' Harry said as he shut down his radio and ran his hands through his thinning hair.

'What did you make of that?' Riaz asked from the doorway.

Harry physically jumped in fright, 'Jesus Christ! Riaz, you frightened me half to death. I didn't hear you there. Good God, lad, don't scare me like that.'

'Sorry, Harry, I thought you knew I was there. I just heard the last few minutes of your conversation. Is that the guy you thought converted from Christianity?'

'George? Yep, he's the one. He married a Muslim girl, years back he said, and had to convert first. His own family disowned him for it, so he moved out of the place he was born and into Beirut.'

'He seems less worried about people listening in than your Saudi mate?'

'Yes, I think he's quite well off too. He's talked a lot about places he's travelled to years ago, so I think he's more knowledgeable. Sounds to me like this is more evidence that the old terrorist groups have been removed.'

'Removed by Allah, you mean, Harry?'

'I do. It's like those that are spreading fear and death are... well, dropping dead, I think. I quite like the idea of that. Bodes well for the future really. Don't need those fanatic bastards here for a start.'

'Bloody hell, Harry, maybe that's what happened to Charlie's teacher, Aziz. He was brought into the hospital last week, dead on arrival from a heart attack. His wife was with him, and she had a horrible welt on her face, and other bruising, clearly from a beating. I happened to be in the ED, fixing a fuse, when she was told he'd died. She was hysterical, but I thought it was unusual somehow, not quite right. Now that I think back on it, her reaction seemed more relieved than grief stricken. I wonder if he was beating her and had his attack. Maybe Allah struck him down. Well, I'll be... Allah be praised indeed.'

AMELIA

Looking around the room, she made a point of holding each person's gaze for a few seconds before moving on. She knew that it unnerved some of them. Too bad. Is this going to be the usual boys' club discussion, without me getting a word in or being asked my opinion? Let's see. I can deal with it if I must.

'Do you believe him, Mr President?' Cummins asked.

'Oddly enough, I do. He was very open, surprisingly so, and his analysis did make sense,' Habbib replied, looking around the faces of his staff in the Square Office.

'What does he expect you to do or say, Mr President?' Sanchez asked.

'There was no ultimatum, Amelia. I don't think he's in any hurry either.'

'Do you think his whole team feels the same way, Sir,' Saba queried.

'That is a more interesting question, George. To be honest, I don't believe they know all his thoughts, no. The strategy might be known, and by that, I mean the immigration plan...'

'Don't you mean invasion plan, Mr President?' Malouf interrupted, clearly angered.

'I understand your meaning, Imran. No matter the definition, Kalil's thought process was sound, more so than I would have been able to determine myself. Either he's a master chess player and strategist, or... he's true to his word. If the latter, then he needs what we have more than those in his team realise. For them, and perhaps for the government he left behind, he's playing two games. They might have similar elements, but his long game is different. The question for us is how to profit from this?'

'What difference does it make, Sir,' Malouf said, 'we're about to be taken over, that's what matters, and -'

'Not necessarily, Mr Secretary,' Cummins interrupted, 'Kalil wants what we and India used to have, vibrant open democracies. He wants to resurrect that again, to escape the possible iron fist of fundamentalism choking off that future.'

'Very eloquent, General,' Malouf replied, 'but it's still a future that he wishes to rule, isn't it? I don't see you running his military for him, nor anyone in this room keeping their positions, with all due respect, Mr President.'

'You might be right, Imran, but unless you have a solution to what seems to be inevitable, I suggest you at least pretend to be on board,' Habbib stated.

Saba shook his head, 'No, Sir, Mr President, I don't think that's a good idea. It would seem somewhat unbelievable if we all went along with smiles on our faces. Better that Imran retains his healthy scepticism, don't you think, rather than make Kalil suspicious, as well as the rest of his group?'

'Hmm, yes, good point, George. Okay, Imran, play it straight. However, for all of us I suggest we consider what we say and how we say it, when with other members of their entourage.'

'He's a widower did you say, Mr President?' Cummins asked.

'Yes. Why?'

'Well... I wonder if we could set up a kind of dinner interview between President Kalil and Badiah Malaki. You never know, he might be interested, and in turn, she might be a useful ally in the long term.'

Saba laughed, 'A sleeper agent you mean, General?'

'You never know. Two attractive people, both ambitious, both single,' Cummins replied.

Sanchez coughed, knowingly, 'I think you might be on the wrong track there, General.' *Really, John, how could you suggest this,* she thought?

'You don't think Badiah would be attracted to Kalil?' Saba asked.

Shit! I can't stay out of this idiocy. 'Maybe she could be persuaded to play that game. But her intentions are... well let's say a little closer to home,' Sanchez stated, and then looked at each of her male colleagues, including the President. 'Oh, come on, gentlemen, don't be coy,' she laughed.

'Spit it out, Amelia,' Habbib said.

'Mr President, Badiah only has eyes for you, Sir.'

'What? I've never given any indication...'

'You don't need to, Sir, she is quite capable of planning her own path in life. Believe me, Mr President, she has her sights set firmly on you.'

Later, back in their apartment, Amelia lay with her head on John's thigh as he read a book held in his right hand and stroked her hair with his left.

'You knew about Badiah's designs on POTUS, didn't you, John?'

'No, I didn't actually. I tend to be a bit slow on the uptake with stuff like that. Plus, I haven't had much to do with her either.'

'Yes, you men are pretty dim I suppose,' she laughed.

'Has she ever talked about the Pres with you?'

'Of course not. She knows where my loyalty lies, John.'

'What has professional loyalty got to do with it?'

'I'm on the White House staff. She has predatory designs on the President. That means that if she succeeds, she becomes the First Lady, and above us all. She'd be extremely careful about her confidants. I doubt she's told anyone of her desires.'

'So how do you know then?'

'I'm a woman. I can read the signs that males don't seem to be able to. It's as clear as day to me. I can't believe that POTUS didn't see it.'

'His wife hasn't been gone long, Amelia.'

'I know. That's why Badiah hasn't made her move yet. She's waiting a year and a week I think.'

Cummins laughed, 'Really? You have her strategy down to that level of detail?'

'I do. After a year and a week, she will make her move. Two months after that, if POTUS is interested, she will let him into her pants. From there it's a done deal.'

'You know, I don't think I've ever been more impressed by your analytical ability, nor more scared,' he joked.

'Just you remember that, General,' she said as she turned over and leant up to kiss him. 'It's different for you though, John.'

'How so?'

'You can get into my pants any time,' she said, unbuttoning her blouse and starting to undress.

CHARLIE

'Charlie, I spoke with some of the doctors at the hospital,' Riaz said over dinner. 'None of them has any idea how a new medical student would be trained. There are no universities with that teaching capacity operating again. I asked if there was a way that they could train you themselves, but they didn't think they were capable. One of them said it was one thing to be a doctor but quite another to train one from scratch. I'm sorry.'

'Maybe you could train overseas, Charlie?' Salina suggested.

'That's not possible, Salsa,' Mina stated.

'Why not?' Michael asked.

'Where would he go, Michael?' Riaz said.

'Mecca?' Salsa suggested.

'Forget that!' Charlie snorted in derision, 'I'm not going there.'

'I think most of their doctors probably trained here or in America or Europe anyway,' Riaz commented.

'India perhaps?' Salsa persisted.

'I'm not going overseas into an unknown situation. Apart from that I don't know how I could anyway. You can't exactly hop on a plane these days, can you? Anyway, I don't want to leave you all. If I can't go to university here, then... well, I'll just have to do something else, that's all.'

'Don't get upset, Charlie,' Mina said. 'It's not fair, I know.'

He stood up, 'I'm sorry mum, I'm not hungry, I'm going out,' he said and left the table before anyone objected.

'Leave him be, Riaz,' Mina said. 'Everyone please finish your dinner, please. Let Charlie have some time alone.' A few moments later they heard the front door close.

'I'll talk to the lad tomorrow when he's calmed down a bit,' Harry said. They continued to eat in silence.

Charlie ran along the street. It was dark and cold. He didn't think where he was going but it became clear as he ended up a street away from Alia's house. He went around to the side and threw some small stones up at her window. She put her face against the pane and looked down, suddenly grinning as she saw him. He went around to the back door, and she slipped outside and into his arms.

'Come in,' she said.

'No, come out with me, please? I need a walk and I'd like you to come too.'

'Okay, wait a sec, let me grab a coat.'

A minute later she snuck out, buttoning her coat, and taking his hand. They walked away from the house, Alia looking once over her shoulder. 'It's okay, no one will know I'm gone.'

There was no conversation until they were in the next street. 'What's wrong, Charlie?'

He signed deeply. She stayed silent, waiting for him to compose himself, clearly upset. 'I don't think I can be a doctor. There are no university courses available and Dad said none of the doctors at the hospital seem able to train new ones.'

'Oh. Do you think that's true though? I mean there are other doctors, other hospitals. Surely there must be a way?'

'How?'

'I don't know. But we'll find a way. If that is your ambition, we'll find a solution. There must be one. You must have faith, Charlie.'

'Faith? In bloody Allah!'

'Shush, Charlie, keep your voice down,' she said, looking over her shoulder and around the street. 'You don't know who might be around.'

'I don't care. I'm sick of keeping my thoughts to myself, sick of the self-righteous Imams and the yes-men that surround them, sick of this new world.'

He looked across at her and saw that she was crying, the tears streaming down her face, 'I'm sorry, Alia, I didn't mean to frighten you, I promise.'

She sniffled, 'It's not that. I'm just sad for you. You deserve to train to be a doctor, you do. I feel the same as you do. I want you to be happy, that's all.'

They walked into a nearby park and went to sit on a bench in a gazebo. 'Are you cold, Alia?'

'A little. Let me sit on your knee so we can keep warmer, Charlie,' she said as she adjusted her position. He held her tight and nuzzled her neck.

'The only thing I want more than to be a doctor is you,' he said.

'I want you to be happy and fulfil your dreams, Charlie.'

'You make me happy,' he said kissing her cheek. She turned her face and let him put his mouth against hers, soon kissing intently.

RIAZ

Riaz approached Dr Jennings when she was on a coffee break. She was Iranian but her husband had been English, and he did not survive Revelation Day. She didn't seem bitter about it, but he had always felt that was unlikely, that she simply held a wall in front of her, to not show her anger about her loss, not only of her husband but her children too.

He explained the situation about Charlie and asked her advice.

'It's a dilemma, I agree. Some of the medical staff spoke of this recently too. It's not just the lack of new doctors being trained but those in research and support positions too. Our diagnostics ability is lacking, and screening tests are becoming a limitation in how we treat people as well,' she said.

'Is there any medical board in place now, anyone looking at training new students, Dr Jennings?'

'Not really, no. But I did suggest a conference be held, so that we can discuss the issues at stake. Unfortunately, Dr Gadkari believes that Allah will provide if we remain strong in our faith,' she said with some derision, looking over her shoulder and keeping her voice down.

'Perhaps I can help, Dr Jennings. I could raise the issue at the management meeting for the hospital next month. It's easier for me now because I have a reason. Maybe I can raise the urgency? Perhaps you could provide me with some details, properly... sanitised, so that the source is kept hidden?' Riaz suggested.

She thought about it for a few moments, looked again over her shoulder, nodded and said, 'Yes, I'll help you. We need to move ahead. Maybe coming from you it will seem less professionally threatening to Gadkari. But he has influence, you know that?'

'Yes, but I also see that the others don't seem to like him. I have no secret agenda, so I can speak more passionately, and I will. Gadkari doesn't frighten me.'

'No, I don't suppose he would. Is it true that you threatened the headmaster at your kids' school, and got some sadistic teacher removed?'

'I did, and I'd do it again. This is England not Afghanistan. We were all saved, not just the fanatics. In fact, I think most of the violent fanatics have since been... divinely removed, shall we say.'

'How do you know that?'

'We have a Ham Radio in my house, and we get news from the Middle East.'

'Really? Could I listen to it sometime?'

'Of course, if you want to. We live with an old man called Harry, he operates it, but he doesn't mind who listens with him. I'm sure he'd love to meet you. Come over any time you like. Come for dinner this week if you wish; my wife won't mind another guest, she'd love it. Please?'

She considered it, smiled, and said, 'Okay, I will, thank you, Riaz, thank you very much.'

'Make it Friday. You can walk home with me if you like, we're not far from the hospital. At seven?'

'Great, thanks, seven on Friday it is,' she said and then made off to the ward, smiling.

Riaz walked into the engineering area in the basement with a smile on his face. Freddy looked at him and returned the smile, 'What's up, Riaz, you look happy.'

'Do I? I suppose I am. Dr Jennings might be able to help me with Charlie's future. She's coming over for dinner on Friday.'

'Hmm. Hope Mina is okay with that,' he joked.

Riaz's face fell, 'You think she might not be?'

'Kiddin' mate, don't worry. Mina will love a guest, I'm sure. She liked feeding me at least.'

'Good point. Maybe you should come too, make it less threatening?'

'Threatening for who? You or Doc Jennings?'

Riaz laughed, 'Both I think.'

'I'll be there. Beats my cooking.'

When Friday came around, Riaz couldn't wait for the day to end. Mina had been more than happy to entertain Dr Jennings, as well as Freddy. She liked Freddy and found his irreverent sense of humour delightful. The three of them walked from the hospital, all wrapped up warm against the winter chill and wind. When they arrived, Mina opened the door before Riaz had his key out, and ushered them in out of the cold, took their coats and shook hands with Dr Jennings warmly. The kids and Harry came down the stairs soon after, as their parents and guests were talking. Introductions were made with Dr Jennings, who insisted they all call her by her first name, Amaya.

By the time of the main course, a spicy curry that Freddy liked, Riaz had deftly introduced the topic of Charlie's medical aspirations, and the difficulty he faced with there being no active university courses available to him.

'I'll just have to re-think my options,' Charlie said.

'You shouldn't have to, Charlie,' Amaya said. 'We need new doctors. More than that, we must train them or what will happen as we age and lose our capacity? I'm going to help you where I can, and your father has a plan too.'

Riaz interrupted her, 'Freddy, this is highly confidential, okay?'

'Lips are sealed, brother,' he confirmed, smiling.

'There's a hospital management meeting next week. I am going to raise the issue, and Amaya will add her views, which might contradict Dr Gadkari. He's a hard liner,' Riaz explained.

'That's an understatement,' Freddy said, 'the man's a fool. Always has one of those Allah will provide cop out answers.'

'Foolish perhaps,' Amaya agreed, 'but not a fool. There's a difference. However, he does rub people up the wrong way, and that might be our trump card, because the other members on the management team don't like him.'

'But do they fear him?' Charlie asked.

Amaya dipped her head in admiration, 'Now that, Charlie, is a very intelligent question. Yes, we do have to consider that. In the case of Gadkari though, I think the dislike outweighs the potential fear. For all of that though, he is a fine general surgeon. I might have to play to his ego. We will have to wait and see how he reacts.'

'Has he made a play for you, Amaya,' Freddy asked.

She blinked in surprise, clearly unsure how to answer, 'Er... I don't think he sees his colleagues that way, Freddy.'

'Gay, is he?' Freddy asked.

'Doesn't seem that way to me,' Riaz commented.

'You're an attractive woman, Amaya,' Freddy added, noticing her confusion. 'He's single. If he hasn't made a play for you there must be a reason. Unless he's intimidated by you.'

'Are you, Freddy? Intimidated by me?' she asked.

'Sadly, yes. You're too intelligent for me. Otherwise, I'd be buying you flowers and asking you out, probably,' he laughed, but nobody seemed fooled by the forced humour. Mina's eyes began to shine as she looked between him and Amaya, trying to hide a smile.

'I didn't take you for lacking confidence in your own charms, Freddy,' Amaya said.

For once he seemed lost for words, so Mina assisted, 'That's a challenge I think, Freddy.'

Whilst Freddy remained tongue-tied, Charlie jumped in, to his parent's surprise, 'Let me help. Amaya, I have this friend, he's very funny, a real gentleman, always willing to help others, a mentor to young people, skilled at his job, able to turn his hands to lots of problems, and liked by everyone. But he's sometimes quite shy and hides that behind a great sense of humour. I think he'd make a fine husband for the right lady. But she'd need to be different to him, I think, someone clearly intelligent, and kind, and someone that never worries about what other people think. Can I arrange an introduction for you?'

Riaz, Mina and the rest of the family stared open mouthed at Charlie's eloquence, then laughed. Amaya had a huge grin on her face. Freddy was embarrassed and avoided looking at Amaya. Harry was beaming, looking from Amaya to Freddy and back, waiting for the next round in the game that Charlie had launched.

Amaya cleared her throat to grab attention, looked directly at Charlie, and took on a serious expression, and a formal sounding accent. 'Well, Charles, thank you for the introduction to your colleague. I think he sounds intriguing. He could possibly be the man I have been looking for, perhaps a man that can take away some of my sadness even. I would be pleased to hear from this gentleman if you wish to pass on my regards to him. Tell him to contact me at the hospital if he wishes.'

'Okay Dr Jennings, I will do that, thank you,' Charlie replied, smiling.

'Tea or coffee, anyone?' Mina said, deliberately breaking the spell to return the conversation to normal, prompting their responses.

Harry was the next to receive Amaya's attention. 'Harry, what news is there on your radio from Iran?'

'Nothing direct, Amaya; I only have regular contacts in Saudi and Lebanon. There was an air war, or at least a limited engagement, over Tehran for the main part. But there might have been an air raid on Riyadh too. Seemed to be a stalemate overall. Then there was a land battle, but I don't know how big it was, and another stalemate I reckon. Since then, a month back now, it's been quiet.'

'Do you hear how life is in the Caliphate though? Is it... harsh?'

'Hard to say, except that my radio contact seems very nervous over there, much more so than the person I speak to in Beirut. He's relaxed most of the time. Do you have family in Iran?'

'No, Harry. My mother was from a wealthy family in Tehran, back in 79. She was a student here. When the revolution happened, her parents told her to stay here until things settled down. They were targeted by the revolutionary guard and her father was imprisoned. Her mother managed to escape, although she wanted to stay behind, but her husband insisted that she left. I think she was lucky; her husband, my grandfather, was killed. He'd arranged for money to be smuggled out though, so my grandmother was not too badly off. She fled here and was granted asylum. My mother finished her studies and became a doctor. She was my inspiration for medicine. My father was English, from Leeds.'

'So, was he Muslim?' Riaz asked.

'No, Catholic, but non-practising. It was odd really, my grandmother forsook her religion after the revolution; she hated the fundamentalists and it was her way of fighting back against them, in a small way. After she died, my mother began to take an interest in Islam, even though she had also married a Christian. I think my Maamaan-Bozorg, my grandmother, would have been proud that her daughter and granddaughter became professional women, but I'm not so sure she'd have accepted my mother's renewed adherence to Islam.'

'So how were you brought up a Muslim if your father was Christian?' Charlie asked.

'My father was an atheist. He didn't care what my mother believed if she was happy. When I started to follow my mum to the mosque, he didn't mind that either. We didn't go every week. My mum rather blew with the wind. She went from periods of devout behaviour, when she felt the pull of her childhood, to times of complete indifference. I started to take an interest a few years ago. I don't know why really. My husband was agnostic, but from a Jewish background. We agreed not to introduce any religion to our children, and I was happy with that. My interest started as an intellectual and historical perspective when I began to research my family tree. From there I visited a local Iranian Imam. We met regularly to discuss cultural issues. I was still not looking for God. About two years later, I realised that I'd begun to believe. I didn't even keep Ramadan; that would have been odd within my family. But, inside, I think I had found a spiritual acceptance. It brought me peace. How stupid that was! If I'd known that Revelation Day would kill my family and leave me behind, I would never have trodden this path. I do not feel saved, but cursed!' she exclaimed with a sob, covering her face with a napkin.

'I'm sorry,' Amaya continued, composed again. 'I didn't mean to bring the atmosphere so low.'

'You have nothing to be sorry for,' Mina said, 'in your position I would feel the same way. To be honest I do not understand what it is that left any of us alive either. We rarely visited a Mosque and were not in any way devout. I feel afraid all the time, that some fanatic will uncover us and want to make an example of us. It makes no sense to me.'

'Me either,' Harry added. 'I might believe in a God, but I was no Mosque attendee either. Why was I spared?'

'The house of the disbelievers,' Freddy stated. 'And yet, here we all are. There must be a reason.'

Michael, who hadn't said much at all during the evening, lightened the mood. 'I have a theory,' he said. 'I think Allah needs moderates. He needs people with good hearts, not prayer mats stapled to their knees. That's why he's removing the violent ones. He's against the lunatics as much as we are. We are the future, not the Mosque-addicted.'

Riaz was surprised by his quiet son's comments and pleased too. 'Mosque-addicted? Where did you hear that term, Michael?'

'It's mine, dad. I made it up. It means blind obedience without thought. It includes all of those people that hide behind the Quran rather than live its teachings.'

Amaya smiled. 'Bravo, Michael. You might have a poet or a philosopher in your family, Mina, as well as a future doctor. I am so very glad that you invited me into your home tonight.'

'You are welcome any time, Amaya,' Mina said.

'It's getting late. I might have to request another time to listen to your radio discussions, Harry, if you don't mind?'

'No problem, Amaya; any time,' Harry replied.

'Can I walk you home, Amaya,' Freddy asked.

'That's very kind of you, Freddy, thank you, that would be lovely.'

As their dinner guests left, Mina hugged her husband. 'That's a love match, Riaz.'

'Jumping ahead a bit there, aren't you? He's only walking her home,' Riaz scoffed.

Mina looked across at Salsa, who was nodding and smiling, 'Take note, Salsa, men are fools in the game of love. You'll see.'

KALIL

It was comfortably warm on the beach, and Kalil and Habbib walked without shoes, alone, their teams left back at the hotel, albeit keeping an eye on their prospective Presidents through binoculars. There was no need for bodyguards in this new world.

'Do you plan to return to India to manage this emigration that you hope for, Sabal?'

'It is already planned, Paul, as I'm sure you have surmised. However, you can have an impact on it. You can decide where the people go. Should they start in New York, or Washington, L.A., or Chicago? Or here? What do you need? What kind of people and skills would you like to arrive first? Doctors, scientists, engineers, power plant technicians, farmers?'

'Are you telling me that the... immigrants... are coming soon, no matter what we say?'

'Yes, Paul, I am. The first sea deployment has begun. There will be 200,000 civilians arriving in a month. We can also airlift another 60,000 people each month by air, with the vanguard beginning at your call. That is the contingent that I'd like you to determine. Tell me what America needs and I will supply it for you. Tell me where to send the aircraft and when and we can fill the skill gaps that you are missing. I don't want the seaborne population to arrive in cities without stable and reliable power supply or infrastructure. I want them to be welcomed by Americans in positions of authority, backed up by the resources I already have here,' Kalil explained. 'This is a partnership with your country, Mr President.'

'Really? A partnership that I have no say in approving. You've already expressed your desire for power sharing. In the corporate world that was called a reverse takeover. One day two companies are amalgamated, but by the end of a year there is always a clear winner, and the management team from the losing partner will disappear rather quickly,' Habbib stated. 'What is to stop that happening to us?'

'I will tell you simply, and honestly. I, Sabal Kalil, am why that will not happen. Because if Pakindesh takes over and simply floods America and removes your government, then I become just as vulnerable. As much as I have a good relationship with my co-President, Ghulam Asif, I have few illusions that he would not take over as sole President of Pakindesh with limited remorse.

'I am voluntarily walking away from Pakindesh to create something better, bigger, and much more interesting. You think that I want to take over America and usurp you; I can understand that. Do I want that? Not really. Will I do so? Perhaps. But only if the greater dream is thwarted. The Americas represent half of the world, Paul. If my dream for North America works, and you and I deliver it, then I wish to move on to Central and South America in the same way. I will rule South America, based on a similar democratic model.

'It always intrigued me why the USA did not forsake the Middle East and concentrate on the Americas when it had the chance. Your country did not need Middle Eastern oil, Paul. You propped up Saudi Arabia even though your non-domestic oil supply came mainly from Canada, Venezuela, and Mexico. Your greatest folly was to back your allies in the Middle East because of the immense arms sales you sold to them. You became a victim of believing your own propaganda. That led America into more and more stupid wars. You tried to bring democracy to places too foolish to understand the concept and with no history of it, ruled by narrow-minded zealots. If you'd have concentrated on the Americas alone and left the Arabs, North Africans, and Persians to kill themselves as they had been doing for centuries, you would have increased the wealth across all the Americas. That would also have reduced the desire for illegal migrants to seek their futures in your country.

'I am offering you an Americas-centric world. But, this time, we can build it better, without the failures of your past, without gun violence and racism, without the huge wealth gap between rich and poor. Perhaps even with a new constitution if you wanted to.

'The world is our oyster. We need to grab it with both hands, yours, and mine, and to keep it out of the clutches of fundamentalists. I tell you honestly, in all sincerity, that this is my dream. Will you join me on this journey?'

RIAZ

Freddy accosted Riaz as he arrived at the hospital on the following Monday morning.

'Great dinner on Friday, Riaz. Please thank Mina for me, it was a lovely evening.'

Riaz was surprised with this unnatural behaviour from Freddy, this formality. 'What's up, Freddy?'

'Nothing. What do you mean?'

'You seem... not on edge, but... I don't know. Are you sure everything is okay?'

'Never better. Truly.'

'Truly? There's a word I've never heard you use before. It's almost as if... oh, wait a minute, I get it. Mina was right. You're taken with Amaya, aren't you? Even your speech patterns have changed. You're smitten!'

'I don't know what you're talkin' about, Riaz. You're crazy, man...' Freddy began contradicting, but then stopped, grabbed Riaz by the hand and pulled him towards the stairs and down to the engineering rooms. As soon as they entered Freddy's warm sanctuary, he pushed Riaz into a chair and almost shouted, 'What am I going to do?'

'What are you talking about?' Riaz asked, dumbfounded by his friend's distress.

'You're right, Riaz. God help me, but Amaya's unbelievable! She's gorgeous, a genius, exotic, beautiful, sexy, yet down to earth, approachable... a Goddess. I can't stop thinking about her.'

'Wow. You've got it bad, Freddy. Really bad. Look, it's early days. She'll need time to be wooed. No woman can be expected to fall for you straight away, it's not realistic. She needs to be...' Riaz stopped abruptly as he saw the look of wonder and the huge grin on his friend's face.

'No, Riaz! You're so wrong, oh so blessedly wrong. The world is smiling on me again. Amaya feels the same... well, maybe not quite, but she will. It has started, Riaz. My path to happiness.'

'Calm down, Freddy and tell me what the hell you're on about.'

'I walked her home, as you know,' he began, noted Riaz nodding his head, and continued, 'we'd only got to the end of your street before we were holding hands. It's true, odd as it sounds. I don't know if I moved my hand towards hers or she did it first, but it was just so... natural... and warm and soft, and...'

'Get on with it, Freddy. What happened then?'

'Allah be praised for the cold night. I had to put my arm around her to keep her warm. That made the walk a little slower too, which was even better. When we arrived at her door, she invited me in for a night-cap, her words. I went in. We must have talked for two hours. I finally left there after midnight. I don't even remember how I found my way home. Riaz, she's one of the most amazing women I've ever met.'

'Freddy, I'm so happy for you. That's... what's wrong?' he asked as he saw the look on Freddy's face.

'I think maybe I scared her off. Or read the signs incorrectly. Maybe I moved too fast.'

'Why? What's happened since?'

'Nothing! I mean absolutely nothing. No message from her today, no notes at all.'

'So, you didn't see her on the weekend?'

'No. Stupid, I now realise. It was late and I didn't think of it being the weekend, for some crazy reason. So, on Saturday I came to work, just to see if she was here, but she wasn't. Nor yesterday either. And no word today. She must be avoiding me.'

'Not necessarily, Freddy.'

'She must be. Riaz, we had a spiritual connection on Friday, I know it. How could she not want to continue it?'

'How do you know that she didn't wait at home hoping that you'd have gone around on the weekend, but you didn't?'

Freddy's face fell. The look in his eyes being close to despair. 'Oh my God, you're right, Riaz. What a fool I was. Why didn't I go back to her apartment? She thinks I don't care and is avoiding me now!'

'Nonsense! You don't know that. Freddy, pull yourself together, you're acting crazy. Look, make yourself a coffee and let me go and investigate. Okay?' Freddy nodded and Riaz escaped to find some sanity away from him.

He went up to the third-floor ward where Amaya usually worked and asked the nurse on duty if she knew where Dr Jennings was. The answer made him smile and after extracting some more information, he headed back to what he was beginning to consider the nut ward of the engineering department. As soon as he entered, Freddy jumped up, spilt his coffee, and started to babble. He cut him short.

'Sit down, lunatic.' Freddy did so. 'Let me ask you a question. What did you discuss with Amaya on your walk home with her, or in her apartment? Did anything about work pressures come up?'

Freddy frowned, clearly thinking back. 'We spoke for hours, Riaz, on all sorts of subjects. She didn't want to talk of work, given the paper she was trying to finish. We spoke of other...' he paused.

'Penny dropped, has it?' Riaz asked. 'Brain cells re-engaged perhaps. Any chance she told you of how busy she'd be this week; where she would be today?'

'I'm an idiot! Her dissertation, of course. On post-Revelation Day stress and its health implications. She did tell me, yes... but, then she changed the subject and we got onto other things. But, yes, now that you bring it up, she did tell me she had to finish it for today.' He sat down heavily, slapped his own forehead, and sighed deeply. 'Sorry, Riaz. I guess I'm just love-struck.'

'Is that another word for dumb?'

'Touché, brother. I deserve that. Oh, Allah be praised though. She hasn't forgotten me.'

'Poor woman. I hope she knows what she might be getting herself into,' Riaz laughed. 'Perhaps we should do some work?'

'Of course. Oh yes, that's something else I forgot about. An old friend of yours is coming by today. A guy called Phillip Abuja from Crumpsall Hospital. He said you'd remember him.'

'Phillip? Yes, of course. I haven't seen him since Manchester. Where is he working now?'

'No idea, I just took the message. He'll be here at 10, he said.'

Phillip arrived a little earlier and when Riaz was called to reception he greeted his old friend warmly. They exchanged updates on their families and then Riaz introduced Phillip to Freddy, and they gave him a tour of their domain. It wasn't until they broke for lunch that Phillip explained the purpose of his visit.

'Do you remember the young Imam, Jeffery Buliya, Riaz?'

'Of course. If it hadn't been for him, I'd never had met you or be working here now.'

'What did you think of him?'

'I liked him. He was so different to any Imam I'd ever met, especially those stern ones from my youth,' Riaz laughed.

'What about his leadership skills?'

'Pretty good, I thought. I'd have followed him. He seemed able to bring everyone together. Mind you, his entry into the job was unorthodox, so that probably helped.'

'Yes, that's true. Do you think his adherence to the Quran would ever be questioned by older Mullahs?'

'I don't know. Why would it be? I mean, his dad was an Imam too, and he was clearly knowledgeable. Why are you asking all these questions? Is he okay?'

'Oh yes, he's great, honestly. I saw him last night. He lives in Chelsea now and has a good following of younger people...' Phillip paused. 'The thing is, there are some older Imams who are not happy with him, but younger people are asking him to become a civil leader.'

'Civil leader? What do you mean exactly?' Riaz asked, becoming apprehensive.

'Riaz, we have no civilian government. All the focus has been on moving everyone to London and getting society back up and running. As you know, there's still a long way to go on that. We've made progress though, and that's why there's starting to be a push to re-establish a government and administrative processes. Surely, you're aware of that?'

Riaz shrugged, a little embarrassed. 'To be honest I'm too busy getting things into working order and keeping them that way. We have a host of problems to contend with, without getting into politics, Phillip.'

'I don't agree, Riaz. Politics is how things get into order... or stay that way. You have kids in school, how is their education progressing?'

'Well, it's been sporadic. We had a problem with... well let's say some overzealous teachers being too strict in their teaching of Islam above the other subjects; and bringing back harsh punishments. I put a stop to that.'

'You did? How?'

'I went into the school and threatened the headmaster. I told him he had to rein in his abusive staff, or I would do it for him. I accused him of harbouring vindictive paedophiles. It worked. The worst offenders left, or they started to teach standard subjects again.'

'That's very interesting, Riaz. So, you saw first-hand how fundamentalist views were starting to be promulgated, and you stopped it. Congratulations.'

'Well, I think that's going a bit far. I just called into question a teacher's abusive behaviour. He was a sadistic man, and it had to be stopped.'

'Of course. But you did it. You stopped it before it became mainstream. Before this country started to drift towards an old style, Mullah-dominated society.'

'If I had been in the minority the outcome might have been different, Phillip.'

'Exactly! That is the danger, Riaz. That these fundamental elements will rise in power. We have no government in place. The only authority is the Imams and some institutions. But their emphasis is religious, not social. If we don't consolidate our moderate society then we might lose it. I don't want the UK to become like Iran after 1979 or Saudi Arabia in its treatment of women. Do you?'

'Of course not, but who says it is going down that road? Phillip, get to the point, because I realise you have one,' Riaz laughed.

Phillip smiled, 'I'm sorry, I was getting carried away. It means a lot to me. Okay, if you haven't been kept up to date, there is a push by some more radical Imams to form a government based on religious principles, with Sharia at the centre and civil liberties subordinate to that. Jeffery Buliya is working against them, but he doesn't have enough people willing to stand up and fight with him. The radical Imams naturally have those people that attend their Mosques. The less devout people, like you and me, don't congregate. So, we are deemed not to exist, or to be indifferent. Jeffery needs people to stand up and be counted. He needs you, me, and everyone like us to raise our voices. We don't have a lot of time. If we don't act, we will be overruled. I want you to come and meet with Jeffery tonight. Will you come?'

'Of course.'

'Good. Thank you, Riaz. Prepare yourself for a bitter fight though. This isn't going to be easy.'

KALIL

'You did what!' Ashraf Kumar exclaimed, before controlling himself. 'I'm sorry, Mr President, I didn't mean to criticise, I meant only that...'

'Relax, Ashraf,' Kalil said, smiling. 'You have been my adjutant for over ten years and remain my advisor now. More to the point, you are a friend too. I trust your judgement, most of the time,' he laughed.

'What does the Admiral think?'

'I haven't told him, and nor will I, at least not to the extent that I have explained it to you. Pereira is a good man, and competent. However, his political judgement is less so. I prefer to leave him to manage the fleet and logistics and not worry himself about longer term politics.'

He walked over to the window. 'A beautiful view from here, Ashraf,' he said, as he gazed over the azure sea beyond Miami Beach. 'Forget the shock of my... longer term vision, Ashraf. What is your assessment of its potential?'

Kumar rubbed his chin and began pacing the room, a habit that Kalil was familiar with, so he sat down again and waited for his friend to ponder uninterrupted. Almost two minutes passed when he stopped pacing, sat down again opposite Kalil, and nodded. 'I think it will be alright, Sir. I think President Habbib will take you at your word, eventually. He will see the benefit to America of our immigration. He will use them to make America a power again, or at least he will aspire to that goal. He needs all the things that you have offered him.'

'He won't see this as an invasion, a takeover?' Kalil queried.

'Not for long, Sir, no. He is a pragmatist. He comes from a political system where compromise is necessary and normal, rather than a strong man approach. Nothing was done here without a long process of negotiation with elected officials, and even between parties. We often saw the President as a spent force when he lost the majority in their Congress. Habbib will be happy that he is past those days. Yes, he misses them, of course. But he looks to the future. Your plan presents him with a lower threat scenario. He will grab onto it with both hands. He needs to believe in it. If he doesn't, then you just take over anyway. You have provided him with a... a... vision that he can believe in. He needs to believe you, so he will. That is my opinion, for what it is worth.'

Kalil looked into Kumar's eyes and kept his gaze there, unblinking for some time. 'Ashraf, just to be clear, my friend, what I told the President is what I really mean. My plan is real. Do you understand that?'

'I do, Mr President, I do. But this is not the same plan that I think President Asif has in his mind, is it?'

Kalil considered the question for a few moments. 'No, possibly not. But, then again, Asif's motive is different. He needs me gone so that he can rule Pakindesh. He never expected me to return, and possibly would be unhappy if I did. He will support this plan because it is better for everyone concerned; him especially. The plan is sound, Ashraf. History will see it as the master strategy of the age of Revelation. Do you doubt this at all?'

'No, I don't, Mr President. I don't doubt anything that you put your mind to.'

'Good. Now, as far as Pereira is concerned, I will provide him with a... somewhat tempered version of the plan. No need to worry the admiral with geopolitics and strategy.'

'What about their General, Cummins?'

'Good question, Ashraf. Yes, what of General Cummins? Will he believe in this plan, and will Habbib let him in on it, or will he keep it closer to his chest, I wonder. Time will tell, but the next level of talks could be interesting.'

RIAZ

The façade of the handsome Chelsea house, a Georgian-looking, 3-storey building with large windows and ornate stonework was impressive. Similar in many respects to his requisitioned ex-embassy residence, but older. He chuckled to himself. *Haven't we all come up in the world now, thanks be to Allah?* Then he checked himself, realising that he rarely thanked Allah unless consciously stating His name for the sake of appearances, and especially in meetings with more devout people. He hesitated before crossing the street, staring at the large red wooden door with its gold scroll-worked handle and knocker. *What is Jeffery going to want from me?* He felt apprehensive, and his 'little voice' as he termed this level of premonition, tempered his enthusiasm to see the young Imam again. He took a deep breath and walked across the road.

The door opened within a few seconds of him knocking.

'Riaz! So glad you could come,' Phillip Abuja greeted him.

'Phillip? I didn't know you were going to be here?'

'I wasn't at first, but Jeffery asked me to come too. He thought you'd feel better with me here. Was he right?' Phillip laughed.

Riaz smiled, 'Yes, I suppose he was.'

'He normally knows what's what. As I think you will soon hear. Come along, he's in the drawing room,' he said unselfconsciously, leading the way.

On entering he noticed there were several other people in the room, three women and four men. Jeffery immediately came over and greeted Riaz warmly, smiling broadly as he shook his hand. 'So good to see you again, Riaz. Thanks for coming. You're just in time. Mark!' he called out to a man in jeans and a sweater, of light

Indian complexion, in his mid-thirties and clean-shaven. He came over and stood in front of Riaz, smiling widely.

'Is this your engineer?' he asked as he looked intently into Riaz' face, not challenging, rather more in an enquiring manner. Jeffery nodded.

'Pleased to meet you, Riaz. I'm Mark Catchpole, and before you wonder about that, my dad was someone who felt that changing your name to something very English would be useful. He was probably right in that respect, coz none of us kids ever failed to get job interviews,' he laughed.

'You're a Londoner then?' Riaz commented.

'Yeah, accent gives me away, so I decided not to wear my West Ham shirt tonight though,' he laughed again. 'Where are you from?'

'Manchester.'

'Not originally though?' Mark prompted.

'No, Iran until just after the revolution, but my parents were from Pakistan,' Riaz added.

'Before my time, mate, but I've read about it of course. Sounds like a bad gig back then. That's what we don't want to happen here, Riaz. That's the reason for this gatherin' tonight.'

Just then, Jeffery Buliya clapped his hands to gain attention. 'If you'd all like to move into the dining room, we can sit around the table. Please feel free to take some food and drinks from the sideboard as you go through.' The room emptied quickly, the majority clearly comfortable enough to do as requested and put some food items on plates and pour teas or coffees or take a soft drink on the way through.

It took a few minutes for everyone to settle, with the Imam taking the position at the head of the enormous 14-seat table at the far end, with Phillip Abuja at the opposite end, next to Riaz. Riaz looked at the other people around him. Four seats remained empty.

The Imam wasted no more time, coughing quietly to gain attention and then talking whilst he cast his gaze on each person deliberately, inviting each of their smiles. 'Welcome once again, all of you. I sincerely thank you for coming and for your support and vision, which matches my own, and for which I hope we will find many supporters across the country. It has taken me a while to find some of you. Others have come to me directly, or via convoluted paths that suggest Allah's hand is involved somehow. I certainly hope so, for we will need His help if we are to achieve our common aims. But first, let me introduce the newest member of our growing club, Mr Riaz Ahmed,' he said, gesturing with his hand as he continued. 'Riaz came to me in Manchester and offered his help in an engineering capacity, and I am pleased to say that he worked very well with Phillip to improve the situation at the hospital there, and he still works in that role here too.

'Riaz, let me introduce you to the team. But first, do you recognise anyone here?' Jeffery asked.

Riaz was a little taken aback, wondering how he could know anyone, but he looked a little more closely at the other people sitting around the table, most of them eating and drinking without any discomfort at being referred to. Some seemed slightly familiar, but he wasn't sure. 'No, I don't think so. Should I?'

Jeffery laughed, as did some of the people concerned. 'Possibly not, but it says a lot about the unenduring legacy of politicians, I think. Everyone else here was an elected member of Parliament before Revelation Day.'

'Really?' Riaz exclaimed. 'Oh, I'm sorry, I didn't recognise anyone. But then it's been a while since then,' he said apologetically.

'Don't be sorry, Riaz,' one of the women said. 'I'd be surprised if anyone knew us unless they voted for us. I'm Tasmeena Hikaka. Let me introduce my ex-colleagues, from both sides of politics,' she smiled. 'From your left, we have Mark Catchpole, Peter Sati, Jonas Mehmood, Julian Karra, Yasmin Hussein, and Naz Javed.' Each person nodded in turn as their names were given, and Riaz nodded back.

'All of us have Pakistani backgrounds,' Tasmeena continued, 'and yet, we were elected across different demographics, to left and right leaning parties, and not necessarily in Muslim dominated electorates. The fact that this happened confirms that the British were not inherently racist and that our society was pluralist, open, and moderate. The fact that three of us are women confirms the egalitarian nature of British politics. The fact that we are all here tonight and have been talking with the Imam for some time, is because we are equally worried about the potential rise of Islamic fundamentalism potentially eroding the freedoms that we have taken for granted.' She paused, which gave an opening to Mark Catchpole.

'Riaz, don't let my name fool you, nor my accent. My background is Pakistani, like most of the population left alive in the

U.K., I'd reckon. But unlike the old days, we see this not as a right versus left political game, but a moderate versus Mullah power play, present company excepted, Jeffery, with respect,' he laughed.

'Go on, Mark,' the Imam encouraged.

'Yeah, okay, so the way this team sees the current situation is that the country is likely to be taken over by radicals, and we want to stop that, and we need people like you, those that don't really visit the mosques, to take a stand.'

In the pause that followed, and before Riaz could react, Naz Javed, possibly the most striking of the three women, added her voice. 'Let me just add something for the benefit of Riaz, before we overwhelm the poor man,' she began, gaining a laugh from Jonas and Yasmin. 'In my case I was elected as a Tory. People assumed I leant that way because we were naturally conservative in outlook, being religious. That was strange, because my parents rarely visited a mosque, and it wasn't until I began campaigning that I started to take more interest and go myself. I apologise to the Prophet, praise be His name, for my cynicism. I freely admit I was currying votes. However, before I digress...'

'Yes, would the Member for self-aggrandisement please get to the point,' Peter Sati interrupted.

'Keep your shirt on, Peter,' Naz responded without taking breath, 'my point is that there's a bloody big difference between religious conservatism and economic conservatism. I was an economist, but the current aspiring power brokers are religious zealots. Well, some of them are, anyway. I don't want to see the nation go down a fundamentalist road. But if we don't counter them, and quickly, we will lose.'

Jeffery stood up, to regain the room. The sudden silence was impressive and Riaz again realised that the Imam's presence was significant. He might look like everyone's next door neighbour, but he was clearly in control, as well as being genuinely admired for his easy-going manner. 'The thing is, Riaz, and I am addressing you only because you are the newest member of this group, if I can assume your ongoing support,' he began, not pausing for acknowledgement, 'we need the input and dare I say the non-political, er... common sense and measure of the people's mood, that I hope you can provide. Only three of us in this room have no formal political background. The rest are potentially tainted by their past experiences...'

'What do you mean by that?' Riaz asked.

'Ahah!' Jeffery said, smiling, 'Straight to the point. Well done. Only you and Phillip live in the real world. The rest of us, and I include myself, sadly, tend to believe our own publicity, if I can use that euphemism. We're too close to the power game, or rather, we're too far away from the masses. We don't really know what people like you, who we term the moderates, really think. We don't know what the average English person will do if confronted by an election dominated by candidates that are either Mullahs or religiously -'

'Fanatical,' Mark interrupted. 'That's right. Jeffery is being a bit modest. He's no fool, as you know, but he's right regarding how people will vote, assuming they're given that option anyway.'

'That might be optimistic,' Tasmeena suggested. 'This is a very different world now. We don't even know if our view is right, that the majority aren't visiting mosques. If they are, then they're probably hearing a lot of fundamental stuff from pulpits. There's no counterview, no moderate voice, nobody pushing the British agenda.'

'British agenda?' Riaz queried.

Phillip explained, 'It's what we termed the continuation of the British way of life; democratic, moderate, fair, socially responsible and open.'

Jeffery nodded, 'That's right. If we are taken over by those pushing for Sharia, then the life we knew is over. You saw first-hand what happened in Iran after the revolution. You know how bad things can go, and how quickly the majority can lose their freedom. We need your experience, and we need your help to recruit the wider public. Will you join us?'

HABBIB

'Thank you for coming, General.'

'Of course, Mr President.'

'Coffee?'

'Thank you, Sir,' Cummins said, slightly surprised at being waited upon.

'I wanted to have a chat with you, General, and to gauge your opinion on my discussions with Kalil yesterday.'

'Of course, Mr President. Are we waiting for the others?'

'No, this is a discussion just between you and I, and for the time being it must remain that way. What Kalil told me yesterday was... well, quite a story. Or it was visionary. But I'd like your opinion too. So, let me paraphrase Kalil's vision. They are going to import millions of people here to recreate a strong America, but under our system of government and with our constitution and ideals. Unless I want to update the constitution that is. But he's going to facilitate the means for the U.S. to get back to a vibrant working entity, and he wants us to tell him what skillsets we want delivered here first, but assumes engineers, scientists, power plant operators, IT experts, communications people and farmers.'

'What's in it for him?'

Habbib laughed. 'Yes, well that's the question isn't it. I do believe his vision and his rationale. He wants to populate the Americas, let us run the north and he will move on to colonise South America, and together the Americas will become the power base of the new world. He doesn't believe there's anything for him back in India, or Pakindesh I should now call it, and his co-President there wouldn't want him back as competition. That makes sense. He also genuinely feels that if he doesn't achieve this then Indonesia will be here next. He also doesn't trust the Middle East. I'm with him there.'

Cummins rubbed his chin and then went over to the side table and poured himself another coffee, the first having been quickly gulped down, and began slowly pacing so as not to spill it. 'So, you think he's trustworthy on this plan, Mr President?'

'I do. I can't tell you exactly why, but I sense his ambition. I think he's one of those visionary leaders that sees a larger goal for himself. He doesn't need us. Let's face it, his advance party could wipe us out in an afternoon. But he's offering us this continent to run, with his people doing the work.'

'But we'd still be a puppet government, surely. I mean, if he didn't like the direction we went in, he'd take us out, wouldn't he?'

'Maybe. But really there's no need for conflict, from his perspective. Our people need, or rather they want, to get back to the lives they had before, at least in materialistic ways. Everyone wants to feel safe and secure, with access to food and shelter. Once that's fulfilled then they consider the next hierarchy of need, and with the background we all have here that soon becomes a return to the best of what we had; education for our children, a good health system, and a first world lifestyle. They will follow anyone that provides that or is at least heading in the right direction. If that isn't me, then it will be this new Indian Messiah.'

'I have a feeling that your Cabinet isn't going to be as supportive as you, Mr President.'

RIAZ

'Riaz!' Phillip Abuja called out across the hospital main entrance. 'Quick, come with me,' he ordered, half jogging towards his colleague and heading back outside the doors.

'Where are we going?'

'I just got a message from Mark Catchpole. Something momentous has happened. We need to head for Westminster, come on, I've got some bikes over here,' he said, pointing to the wall to his left.

When Phillip was in this kind of mood it was best to go along with him and get the details as they unfolded, so Riaz smiled and took the bike offered to him. They had only ridden a few metres when the next part of the untold story was provided. 'You're not going to believe this but there's a French guy just arrived from Paris and the pollies have arranged a briefing session so that he can advise them of the situation across the channel. I got us an invite to listen to him too.'

'Really? That's great. Real contact from another country. Thanks, Phillip.'

'You are part of the moderate inner circle now, so I couldn't leave you out of it. Anyway, Mark insisted that you come too. Jeff's going to be there as well.' Half an hour later they rode over the bridge and into the Parliament building. It was strange just being able to wander in, and they were met by Yasmin Hussein and Naz Javed as soon as they'd propped their bikes against the wall.

'Glad you could get here, guys. Come this way,' Naz ordered and led the way to an anteroom on their left. She opened the door without knocking and as soon as they were inside, Riaz realised that all the moderate inner circle, as Phillip called them, were already assembled and seated. There was also a very tall man, well dressed in a suit and tie, with clear North African features, standing at the front of the group with his arms folded, looking a little apprehensive. Riaz and Phillip were introduced to Monsieur Yusuf Bertrand, as an emissary from Paris, and they quickly sat down to listen to what was going to be a formal presentation of sorts.

'Ladies and Gentlemen, thank you for making yourselves available to listen to me and accept my status as the French Ambassador, although perhaps somewhat unofficial. It is a pleasure to meet with you all,' he said in French-accented English, but clearly well-educated. 'I am here mainly to make contact and to see if we, France and the United Kingdom, can assist each other in this new world with so few people, and many challenges. Would you like me firstly to tell you what happened in France and what our situation is now?'

'That would be very useful, Mr Ambassador,' Naz Javed said. Riaz quickly glanced around the group, assuming Phillip or Mark might have been the main spokesperson, and a little surprised at Naz taking that role. However, none of the rest of the British politicians seemed surprised at this.

'Please call me Yusuf, as my Ambassadorship is not quite official, given the lack of formal Government remaining in place in France,' he said, smiling, then continued without pause, 'however, what we do have now is an informal government made up of 30 people with skills that we believe are most important in getting the country working again. But first, some background. As you might suspect, I was not born in France. I was brought up in Algiers and my father was a local politician. He took on a role in Paris in the 60's, after the civil war that created so many problems between France and its old empire. I went to university in Paris and so was not in any way like so many Muslim migrants that entered France over the following fifty years or so. We were wealthy, educated, spoke French well and lived in an upmarket area. We, me and my brother and sister, were encouraged to succeed and to learn other languages, apart from French and Arabic. I chose English, my sister Italian, and my brother German. But I digress, my apologies.

'The reason for telling you this background is because it has allowed me to be heavily involved in the administrative challenges in Paris and why I was chosen to come over here to talk with you. Our population is probably larger than yours now. We think there are about five million people in Paris today, with another million or so living in Marseille. Almost every person that had lived elsewhere in France moved to Paris or Marseille quite quickly. There are undoubtedly other pockets of people elsewhere, but we don't really know. It was obvious that most of the Muslim population was in Paris and therefore the city had the greatest opportunity to start to operate as a thriving city again. We also had the luxury of many nuclear power stations that continued to work unmanned for long enough to allow us to find engineers that could keep a few of them on-line. This also meant that we had working systems like sewage plants, water works and other infrastructure. This doesn't mean that we avoided other problems, naturally. We haven't been able to get the trains running and we have continuing issues with agriculture and fresh food cultivation, and no operational aircraft either, for lack of pilots. Whilst it is good to have most of the people living together in a major city for some things, others are made more complex. Excuse me, Naz, can I have some water please?'

'Of course, Yusuf,' she said, getting up to grab a glass from the sideboard, fill it from a jug and hand it to him. 'Take a break from talking for a minute and we will fill you in on our own experiences here.' She and her colleagues then took turns to provide a similar outline of the British situation. After that there was more interaction.

'How are your hospitals working?' Riaz asked.

'Reasonably well in some ways, but we have limited surgical capacity. Is it the same here?' Yusuf asked.

'No, I think we are perhaps better off, because there were so many Muslim medical practitioners, doctors, nurses, and scientific support staff, that we managed to have a working hospital set up quite quickly, once we sorted out the power failures,' Riaz answered.

Yusuf smiled, 'Yes, I think perhaps the French version of equality was somewhat less than the integration over here. We clearly had less migrants in higher positions, at least in some professions anyway.'

'But you seemed to have better engineering skills, or at least a wider workforce to tap into than us?' Phillip suggested.

'Perhaps, although maybe our people were lower-level managers, yet higher skilled practical personnel. I don't know, but whatever the reason we did get back to operating modern infrastructure faster than one would have thought possible.'

'What about communications, internet, mobile phones, television and radio broadcasts?' Naz asked.

Yusuf shook his head, almost embarrassed, 'Unfortunately not. We cannot get internet access or any useful links with the wider world. We also haven't managed to get the phone system back up and working, and we can't seem to get broadcast capability for TV or radio, which is extremely frustrating.'

'So how are you communicating with everybody in Paris,' Phillip asked.

'A weekly printed newspaper, delivered to street corners and cafes, and large billboard posters.'

Jeffery Buliya laughed, with genuine mirth. 'So, there is a renewed need for good journalists again.'

'Perhaps,' Yusuf agreed, 'but a much greater need for telecommunications experts.'

Yasmin Hussein gave a slight snort of derision, 'I have thought for many months now, that what we have inherited, in some ways, is the result of coming from a world where everything was at our smart phone fingertips, and so our level of education continued to be dumbed down, until there were so many people that knew more and more about less and less. Then one day we arrived at a place where too many of us knew everything about nothing!' she laughed. 'But that was okay because we congratulated ourselves that at least it was all politically correct. What a bunch of absolute fools we had become.'

'Perhaps, Yasmin, now is not the time to go down that road, much as I agree with you,' Jeffery said in a calm and comforting way.

She nodded in agreement, 'Yes, perhaps, Jeffery. Thank you.'

Yusuf had watched this brief exchange and smiled, in solidarity. 'I think you are right, Yasmin. As some people loved to say, especially after some tragedy or ridiculous situation, that "the world had gone to hell in a handbasket", or some such weird American saying. But we have a chance now, praise be to Allah, to put things right, and to get the world on track again, don't you think?'

Jeffery took the opportunity to have his voice heard first, seeing that almost everyone wanted to make a point. 'Mr Ambassador...' he began, pausing for effect after his formal opening, 'clearly, we agree with that, of course. However, that leads me to a question uppermost in my mind, if you can inform us, perhaps. What is the situation in France regarding the level of... let me call it devoutness? As a clearly educated man, I would imagine that you are more supportive of the benefits of open government and inclusiveness and equality, now that such benefits are available to all? Has France taken this path now, or is it leaning towards fundamentalism?'

'Hmm, I think this is what the British like to call getting to the point, or not beating about the bush? Let me be equally frank with you. The interim French Government is redrafting the constitution to form its 'Alpha' Republic. 'We have moved away from a numbering system for our Republics now. I am fearful of the direction of this first post-Revelation Republic. It is leaning towards a fundamentalist agenda, with Sharia in place and a hard-line attitude to dissention. It reminds me of post-revolutionary situations across the Middle East and North Africa after the Arab Spring; almost all of which were failures, or at best, had disappointing outcomes. There are many of us that are fighting against this, but we will lose I'm afraid. We don't have the numbers, and sadly, most of the original Parisian population now in control of the agenda was uneducated and drifting more and more into fundamentalist activity or terrorism, to counter the discrimination that they lived under before. They see this new world as proof that their direction has been endorsed by Allah himself. If I cannot change this view, and the newspapers are largely controlled by the clerics, real ones and newly self-appointed, so my influence is extremely limited, then France will become another Iran or Saudi Arabia.'

'Is that the real reason you have come across the Channel, Yusuf?' Naz asked.

'Yes, I suppose it is. If you have a more moderate view, then perhaps I can use that knowledge to counter the French situation, or at least report on the benefits here. If my French colleagues don't agree and I cannot influence them in a moderate alternative, then I can escape here instead. If though, the U.K. is also moving to a fundamentalist future, then I have no idea what I will do.'

Mark Catchpole took control during the lull of thinking around the group. 'Yusuf, you are lucky that you have managed to meet in this room, the entire moderate political team in the country. Moreover, this group includes seven of us that were elected Members of Parliament. We too want to continue with a pluralist, moderate, non-fundamental future. We are still to fight that battle, but if France is too far along that path, then we need to act fast here. I have no idea if we can help you, but perhaps you can help us.'

HABBIB

President Habbib had welcomed his Cabinet into the room and given them a slightly shortened version of the speech and vision that Kalil has presented to him on the beach, and then called for comments. The room remained stunned for almost 30 seconds.

'Surely you don't believe this plan, Mr President?' George Saba asked.

'Yes, George, I do. We are not needed. Let's be frank here. If Pakindesh wanted to take over, they can do that this afternoon. We present no credible force to stop them, and we don't provide very much that they need either. Have you looked out of your windows? That's a carrier group out there, with enough fire power to destroy us fifty times over. They don't need us, meaning those of us in this room, except for the sake of appearances and friendly relations. Look at it from Kalil's viewpoint. Back in India he has competition, from a Pakistani President with greater military power and population. He can't achieve much back there except wait for the inevitable battle for control with Indonesia one day. Or he can wait and see if the democratic world he knew will become subjugated by radical Middle Eastern thinking. Either way it's less than his massive vision, and yes, massive ego too. I believe him. I think we either work this to our advantage, as offered, or...' he threw his hands up and shrugged.

'You go along with this too, General?' Imran Malouf questioned.

'I do, Sir. I see the benefits, and I see the difficulties of any alternate idea. We are being offered a prize here. We just need to mould it properly.

'But what does he get to gain from keeping us as the government?' Amelia said.

Cummins stood up and faced the group. 'I've been considering that too. He does need us. We are the only ones that can keep the population on side, quiet, and obedient. Without our endorsement and support he's likely to get some resistance, civil and military. Now, yes, they can suppress that in an afternoon. But it will remain below the surface, a potential thorn in his side. He has known conflict, and war. And he knows what a dedicated revolutionary, or terrorist group can do. It's a situation he wants to avoid. He's a supremely confident man, and he's known military success and command at the highest level. He's also been able to keep his competitor President at bay. That takes skill, and charisma. I think you're correct, Mr President, his vision is real, and it does make strategic sense.'

'As your Chief of Staff, Mr President,' Saba began, pausing slightly, 'I think we're playing with fire. Even if Kalil's plan, or vision, call it what you want, is genuine, we're still being taken over. Do you want to be a puppet, Sir?'

'How would you play it, George?' Habbib countered.

The rest of the group looked at Saba and waited for him to react. 'Well, I... I'd need to think about it some more, Mr President, of course. I realise this is difficult. Perhaps when they return to India to escort the new arrivals here, we could overcome their smaller group by befriending them and then sabotaging their ships. I'm not a military expert, Sir, but we can't be helpless, surely?'

Cummins made a noise that left his disdain in no doubt, but immediately regretted such openness. 'They won't be leaving, none of them. The new arrivals are already on their way. They'll be here in about 4 weeks. Maybe in New York as well as Miami, and other locations in between. This carrier group isn't returning to India soon. If I was Kalil, I'd determine whether we believe his vision, and let's continue to call it that so that we don't fall into any bad habits when we speak with him. If he decides that we are a threat to his dream then we, this government, is as good as dead. We've all said as much; he doesn't need us. We are convenient and we would be helpful to him. I don't quite have the President's faith in this, but I do agree that we have little alternatives, for now anyway.'

'Thank you, General,' Habbib said. 'I'd like us to think differently now. I'd like you all to go away and put a wish list together, of what people you'd like to see come here. What skills do we need the most? What material items are we short of, if any? Where would we be best supported if we could control the immigration of say five million people in the next few months?'

'Five million!' Sanchez exclaimed.

'That's right, Amelia. Kalil is planning on building the population of the US and later South America to a viable level as fast as possible. Don't forget he has the whole of Pakindesh to recruit from, which is more than five hundred million potential skilled migrants, with a lot of military capacity to protect them, and aircraft to move them around. He'll be populating California too. This country, in whatever way we can keep its ideals and history intact, has been offered a lifeline and a map back to self-sufficiency. Yes, George is correct in that this does not come risk free. But let's use it to our advantage, or at least survival. And lastly, add to your shopping list this idea too; what political changes to the U.S. Constitution and style of government would you change to make our country work better than it did before?'

'None, surely, Mr President,' Saba stated.

'Really, George? You really think that our government and way of life was the best it could have been? Or that it wasn't hindered by an Constitution, politicised to a point where it discriminated against a better way of life for our citizens?'

'I take it you have some examples that are close to your heart, Mr President?' Sanchez asked.

'Many, Amelia. Here's a few. The Right to Bear Arms was deliberately misinterpreted from its historical intention, which was to allow the newly formed nation to raise a citizen militia to protect the country from foreign invasion. It had absolutely nothing to do with allowing citizens to hold arms for their own sake, and over time that position became ridiculous when so many Americans decided that having a home full of automatic weapons that could kill so many, so effectively, was a right. Our Founding Fathers would have been horrified at the result of that Amendment. Do you think it wouldn't have been changed if they'd have known that a future nation would witness mass murder on a weekly basis, resulting in over 30,000 deaths of innocents and children a year?'

'I agree with you on that, Sir,' Cummins said. 'We had one of the worst records in the world for violent crime, and a total inability to debate the issue logically, because of the political influence of the NRA.'

'We had a pretty poor report card on women's rights too,' Sanchez added, 'especially the right to abortion on demand, for women to have control of their own bodies, spared from the religious right to impose its will on us.'

'I'd be careful of that one now, Amelia,' Malouf suggested. 'This is a religious world now; Praise be to Allah,' he added as an automatic add-on, without sincerity. 'I think the days of abortion are over.'

The President put his hand up to end the discussion. 'Let's not get into detail on this now. But I do want you to consider changes to our way of government, which would improve the lives of all our citizens, and especially allow for new immigrants to feel attracted to our way of life. We are talking about people that are used to a British-based Parliamentary democracy. That system has many good things about it, as does our own. Now is the time to discuss these, between us, so that we can present a united front when the time comes, and one which benefits us, or at least protects us. That's all for now. Thank you all for your time. General Cummins, could you remain behind for a moment?'

Sanchez, Saba, and Malouf left the room. 'Got a little hotter than I expected,' Habbib said.

'Really, Sir?'

'Really. Do you think that George was serious about the idea of resistance against them?'

'Maybe, but he clearly has no idea about the threat level.'

'Honestly, John, am I being naïve here? Am I buying into Kalil's vision too easily?'

'It's not my place, Mr President.'

'I'm making it your place, John. This is a new world. Whilst I appreciate that we are all keeping up appearances, as they say, and that my position as the President is being accepted, in all honesty we are playing a new game now. This isn't the old United States. We are clinging to a dream, like nostalgia overtaking common sense perhaps. So, I'm asking you for an unfiltered opinion now, with no respect for rank, warts and all.'

Cummins took a deep breath and sighed, then resurrected his pacing habit. Habbib allowed him the time and waited, leaning back in his chair. 'OK, Sir. I like Kalil, and I believe that he believes his vision. It does make sense, and it gels with a military man used to power. It's also sensible in relation to distancing himself from the Pakindesh politics, as he explained them. What I don't quite get though is why he'd accept the U.S. political system rather than one he's more used to. Maybe it doesn't really matter, because he sees it as unimportant, at least for now, and by accepting our system, or at least pretending to, he knows we'd be put at ease. But leaving that aside, I'd have to say that I see mainly upside for us.'

Habbib nodded, 'Me too, John. In part, that's what worries me. It seems either too easy, or too... stupid. But I generally class myself as a decent judge of character, and I'm drawn to the man. Are you?'

'Yes, Sir, I am. But I thought that was perhaps just because he's a military man and exudes capability, which I tend to accept more than I would from a politician... present company excepted of course.'

Habbib laughed. 'Don't worry, John, in this new age I see politicians being somewhat less than useful, compared to someone that can get telecommunications back up and working.'

'That's a good point, Sir. Kalil is going to have to deliver on his promises quite quickly, not so much for us here, but all those immigrants are going to want a better life, and right now, it might be that their better life is back in India and Pakistan.'

'I don't think that will be a problem. It's not as if they will starve here. And the options for housing are pretty good, by comparison I'd guess. No, I'd imagine that these pioneers are looking forward to a brave new world, and they will support Kalil for as long as his vision is progressing.'

'You might have a problem internally, Mr President,' Cummins said quietly.

'You mean George?'

'Yes, Sir, I do.'

'Don't worry. His bark is worse than his bite, as they say. George speaks his mind, and I like that about him. But he's loyal, and genuinely worried about us being a puppet government. Which is a good thing to be worried about. But for some reason I seem to be more excited than worried by this coming storm of people.'

RIAZ

It had taken weeks of planning, including the technical back-up and the advertising and administration, but the 7 elected Members of Parliament, plus Jeffery Buliya, Riaz, and Phillip Abuja were about to address a crowd estimated at more than 30,000 people. They had chosen to host the event at the Chelsea football ground and a small dais had been set up on the pitch. Phillip Abuja had set up a sound system with a microphone attached to 4 large music speakers. There were ten chairs in a semicircle behind the dais, 5 on each side of it. All the crowd had been directed to the seats on the western side, with capacity for others to each side of that stand, on the goal sides, or they were encouraged to stand or sit on the football pitch in front of the stand. Riaz had arranged for 50 footballs and some volunteers to run a small kids' coaching football session at each end of the pitch. The aim was for a fun, light-hearted event for the kids whilst the serious issues were explained to their parents and other adults.

The posters that had been put up around the city and in the newssheet stated:

IT IS TIME TO GET BACK TO A WORKING DEMOCRACY AGAIN.
WE HAVE ALL BEEN CHOSEN AND ARE ALL WORTHY, AND SO WAS OUR WAY OF LIFE.
WE HAVE 7 ELECTED MEMBERS OF PARLIAMENT CAPABLE OF RESURRECTING THE GREAT BRITAIN WE WERE PROUD OF.
IT IS TIME TO GET BACK TO WORK AND TO DETERMINE OUR FUTURE ONCE MORE.
IT IS TIME FOR THE RESSURRECTION OF OUR DEMOCRATIC, OPEN, FAIR, MODERN SOCIETY WITH EQUALITY FOR ALL MEN AND WOMEN
IT IS TIME TO RE-ENERGISE OUR ESTABLISHED SYSTEMS OF EDUCATION, HEALTH, AND DEMOCRACY.
MEET YOUR ELECTED MPs AT CHELSEA FOOTBALL GROUND ON SATURDAY AT NOON.
SPEAKERS WILL INCLUDE OUR MPs: MARK CATCHPOLE, PETER SATI, JONAS MEHMOOD, JULIAN KARRA, TASMEENA HIKAKA, YASMIN HUSSEIN AND NAZ JAVED.
THERE WILL BE FOOTBALL COACHING SESSIONS AND GAMES FOR THE CHILDREN.

The group had decided that Jeffery Buliya should act as MC, introduce himself, and set the tone of the event, before then passing the microphone to Mark Catchpole and Tasmeena Hikaka, who would alternate their comments to show equality of the sexes and add tonal variety for the crowd.

At 11:55, Jeffery Buliya looked at the other nine people huddled together, trying to look nonchalant, and somewhat failing, and said to them, 'I think it's now or never everyone. It's kick-off time.'

'Break a leg, Jeff,' Mark Catchpole laughed.

Jeffery went to the dais and stood on the little stool-cum-step behind it, gaining some height. He switched on the microphone, which immediately squealed, and Phillip instantly turned a knob and moderated the volume. He visibly took a deep breath. The crowd went quiet, apart from the kids at either end of the pitch laughing and kicking balls around. 'Good afternoon to you all. My name is Jeffery Buliya. I'm from Manchester originally, and since Revelation Day I've been working as an Imam up there, and more recently here in London. My father was an Imam in Manchester too.

'Today is not about religion. But I wanted to at least set the stage for the more important people that will address you shortly. The most important thing that we can all be proud of since Revelation Day, is that every single one of us was found worthy by Allah, praise be to Him. If that was not the case, then we would not be here. Every one of us, no matter how outwardly devout we were, or were not, has been chosen. There is no need now to worry about our level of devoutness, or our level of adherence to the Quran, or whether we choose to attend a mosque daily, weekly, monthly, or never. Because we have been chosen. That does not mean that we cannot do better, be more charitable, help our parents, attend school, strive to learn all that we can about the world, be kind, be inclusive, and laugh often. We have been spared, and the full enjoyment of life is there for the taking. We are all different too. Different in our political views, different in our backgrounds, and from very different families perhaps, as well as being of different persuasions, including those in our community that are gay. But look around you. All of us have been chosen. Therefore, none of us or our chosen ways of life are wrong or to be denigrated. If they were, we would not all be here together.

'We now live in a world without the need for discrimination. I say the need, and that is what I mean. There is no need to discriminate because of differences between us. Think about that and be thankful that this way has been shown to us.

'I now wish to introduce you to Mark Catchpole, the elected MP for the seat of Gillingham. Thank you,' he concluded and there was a beginning of applause which grew louder and lasted half a minute.

Catchpole took the microphone and steadied himself on the dais step. 'I wish I'd been standing here before Revelation Day, because I was a Chelsea fan and that would have been fantastic. But I'd also like to say that whoever your team was, I do miss the Premier League, and there's no shame in that. We should not fall into the trap of believing that those things before Revelation Day were all bad if they no longer exist. We are now in a world with a small population, all of us chosen, as Imam Phillip just said, and it is purely due to the few of us remaining that many of our old institutions are no longer here. But to say that football was bad is as silly as saying that satellite communications was bad. That is ridiculous. And for that reason, we here addressing you, who are the remaining representatives of the British Government, meaning your elected representatives, whether we were based in your electorate or not, are a solid link to the past and we are also a link to the future.

'The democratic way of life we enjoyed has not gone. It's just been delayed until we, collectively, all of us, can see a way forward. Let us look at what we have achieved together since consolidating our population here in London. We have an operating hospital with trained and dedicated nurses, doctors, surgeons, and administrative staff. We have over a hundred working primary and secondary schools. We have food distribution systems back in place. We have resurrected farming enterprises. We have operating power, water, and sewage systems. We have social events and family gatherings. I believe we are ready to be a working country again. But before I bore you senseless, as we politicians can be guilty of doing,' he paused to allow the smattering of natural laughter to continue for a while, 'I'd like to hand over to Tasmeena, who was an elected MP in Bolton, Lancashire.'

There was a gratifying round of applause, and the group started to relax a little as Tasmeena took the dais. She smiled and then waved to the crowd, and many waved back. 'So lovely to see you all here today, truly. I don't want to bring the atmosphere down, but I do need to tell you some things that we have learned recently, from radio transmissions as well as a visit from an official in Paris.' She paused for effect as there was clear interest in this change of topic.

'The biggest loss that many of us seem to feel is communication. We've lost the internet and mobile phone coverage and television broadcasts. Hopefully we will get these back. But we do have what many of you might remember as Ham Radio enthusiasts, and from them we know some of what is going on out there in the wider world where their populations haven't been so severely impacted. So, I'd like to use my time up here as a sort of long overdue news service.

'There is a power struggle going on between Iran and Saudi Arabia, which now calls itself the Caliphate and is seeking to be the dominant force in the Middle East. There seems to have been conflict between those two countries and an air war. It looks like a stalemate now. The conflict is based on the old Shia versus Sunni antagonism. If that's the case then it unfortunately shows the ongoing stupidity of both of those regimes because all of us have been chosen by Allah, praise be to Him, and any conflict of this sort is an insult to Him. But it does show that human weaknesses have remained, and this world still needs to be protected from narrow thinking and prejudice.

'A government official from Paris visited us last week. He did not have a good story to tell. He advised that France is becoming fundamentalist and that this has impacted on progress there. He urged us not to follow that path. He told us that the problem in France, and especially Paris, was made worse by the lack of education of many of those now in power. But he believed that here in Britain we had a much better chance of a decent path to normality, because our backgrounds here were more diverse and mainly from countries in the sub-continent where democracy was vibrant and our level of education and positions in society were higher. And this made those of us sitting here today think hard about what future we want and what we already take for granted.

'What our visitor told us was true. We do have advantages over many other parts of the world where their populations have been decimated. We, all of us in this stadium today and across London, have had the benefit of a decent education, without limitations on our employment or aspirations. We were not discriminated against, apart from by those few racist idiots that were in the minority. Even some of that anti-Muslim feeling we experienced from time to time was often linked to home-grown terrorism, by those misguided fools that thought that blowing up innocent fellow citizens would somehow help distant causes in the Middle East. That was totally stupid, and it made our lives here worse.

'We do not need to go down those ignorant or narrow-minded fundamentalist roads. We are free to create our own future, and that can and will be bright and joyful. We are here today to talk to you and to urge you to embrace our democratic, open, educated, and free futures, for yourselves and your children. I want to ask you all, now, to stand up and applaud if you agree with us, that we should not be taken down a narrow religiously restricted path. We have all been chosen and therefore we are free to continue to take our better path to a happy life, with whatever amount of religious activity we choose, or reject. Are you with us?'

It wasn't immediate, and there was an obvious sense of nervousness within sections of the crowd, but within about twenty seconds it started. The crowd began to rise, and to applaud and to shout, joyfully. Some remained seated, until the overwhelming support took over and by that time there were no people still seated.

As the crowd noise continued, Jeffery Buliya took to the dais again. 'Thank you. Thank you all,' he shouted. Please take your seats again.' A few minutes passed before the crowd was seated again, and he waited patiently for the noise to settle, then smiled broadly, and he applauded the crowd, 'Thank you all. It is gratifying to know that we have your support. Our aim is to get Britain back to a thriving and vibrant world centre. As an Imam, I am happy to answer any questions of faith that you might have and wish to voice today. I am aware that there are some Imams, a few at least, and some of you perhaps, that have taken a more conservative view of this post-Revelation Day world we have been gifted by Allah. That is understandable. But it is misguided in my opinion and locked in the past. Before Revelation Day we struggled to voice our faith to others. We felt alienated in countries where we were the minority. Some adherents of Islam believed in violent Jihad and strict interpretation of the Quran. In part this was due to upbringing, or indoctrination by fanatics, who preyed upon mainly poor and uneducated people who had been left behind by their societies. Yet, those of us that were born in the West, or spent our formative years in the democratic world, would never have accepted the limited lives allowed to our subjugated brothers and sisters in places like Saudi Arabia, or Iran, or Afghanistan. Those regimes are not ours and their view of life is not ours either. Wherever our families originally came from is irrelevant today. We are British, we are free, we know what living in a democracy means and what having a voice means. These things must not be lost. Being the chosen people now, we have a duty to preserve the way of life we had, and to export its benefits to other places too. Now, does anyone have a question? We have some people amongst you with roving microphones. Tell us what you think, ask us whatever you want, and feel free to argue if you wish. That is what freedom means in a just society that we treasure. The ground is yours,' Buliya concluded, opening his arms in a wide gesture of encouragement.

It didn't take long before people started to stand up and wave, to gain the attention of the dozen young people that had been asked along as helpers, including Charlie, Michael and Salina Ahmed and their friends.

A man in his thirties was the first to have a microphone handed to him. 'Thank the Prophet that you came here today. This is a weight off my mind. I have been worried sick that we were going to end up like in Iran after the revolution, with the stoning of women in the streets and strict Sharia Law imposed. We must fight against that kind of world. I am with you,' he shouted, then handed back the microphone as the crowd cheered him.

Salina passed her microphone to an older man, perhaps sixty. 'I am not going to disagree with what you said about a free society, my young Imam. You spoke well, all of you. But I am less sure that we should downgrade our adherence to Islam just because we have been saved. Who is to say that this is not a test by the Prophet, praise be to Him, to see if we remain worthy of Allah's grace? Maybe we need to be more devout.'

The crowd's murmuring this time was less supportive and there were some boos, until Buliya started to respond, 'Sir, I thank you for those words, because I do think that you have voiced a worry that many people have. And it is a good question. Are we being tested in our faith? My opinion, in part, is that before Revelation Day we were indeed expected to be faithful and to encourage others to see what we saw in Islam. Converts were welcomed. But we also suffered from radicalisation of our youth and those misguided people that believed that killing infidels was holy. The problem with Islam was that it was controlled by the Arab world. They saw their interpretation of Islam as the only way, and for many of those countries in the Middle East they looked down on the rest of the Islamic world. Their arrogance and strictness did not suit people in democratic countries, or where women had more freedom, not just in Europe, but in Indonesia, India, Pakistan, Bangladesh, South Africa, for instance. We must resist a slide into strict adherence of our faith by conservatives. It is dangerous and led to more deaths of Muslims than others. We were our own worst enemies in that respect. I was once asked by a Christian friend, what would happen if a terrorist act was perpetrated on the United States, which killed say eighty thousand people at the Super Bowl, and the U.S. retaliated and dropped a nuclear bomb on Mecca? I explained to him that there were fundamentalist lunatics out there, like Islamic State, which wanted that outcome. They wanted a third world war of Islam against the Infidels, because they believed that Islam would triumph and that they had nothing to fear, and they heralded such a day. Can you imagine that level of utter stupidity? The outcome of such a conflict would have been the death of tens of millions of Muslims. Thankfully that perverted future never eventuated. We are better than that, and Allah, blessed be He, is allowing us to follow this future and this freedom of thought and life.' There was a long and rousing cheer and sustained applause for more than three minutes until Buliya managed to calm the crowd again and continue the question session.

A woman in her twenties asked, 'Do you think that women now should wear the hijab or burqa?'

Buliya said, 'No, unless they really want to. Historically the burqa or niqab was only worn by the Prophet Mohammed's wives. It is not a requirement of the faith. Its usage was encouraged by the Arab world more than elsewhere. I see no need for it.' More cheers followed.

Another elderly man stood and was passed a microphone. 'You worry me, young man. In the world that you see, or want, I think perhaps there would be nobody attending the mosques. Is that what you want? You'll be out of a job.'

'Sir, I want the continuation of a free society, without coercion to pray. If many people that never attended mosques, or rarely, have been chosen along with the most devout of us, then that tells me that the Prophet, praise be His name, is satisfied and we have been provided with a world that can be heaven on earth, if we don't stray into bad behaviour. If the mosques become empty historical buildings, then that might be part of the plan, who knows. But in my opinion, if we live good lives, with pure intentions, we will continue to be saved.'

There were many more questions along similar lines for more than half an hour, and then a teenage boy asked, 'What do we do if our own Imam tells us that you are a false prophet and should be silenced?'

Buliya stood quickly. 'That is the question that I feared and waited for, my young friend. There might well be some Imams that want a strict, Sharia-controlled interpretation of Islam imposed on all. They will see me, and your elected representatives here today as a threat, to their positions, and in their opinion, to the faith. Whether you were born here or migrated to Britain, we had the privilege to be free to live as we wished. Freedom of religion and belief and thought is sacrosanct, and none of us should be forced to live in a narrowly focussed way that is the opinion of a select few. That kind of world will make slaves of our women, uneducated servants of our children and violence perpetrated against anybody that is seen as being disobedient, just because of their curiosity and desire for intellectual debate. I am not a violent man, but I will fight against that kind of world, and so should you.' Buliya sat down but was clearly emotional, and the crowd erupted in support.

A few hours later, when the crowd had dispersed and the democracy team, as they were now calling themselves, was gathered back at Riaz's house, the mood drifted between sombre and ecstatic.

Mina had provided a lot of food, and everyone had been on a journey from famished to satiated, allowing for discussion to be calmer. There was agreement that the afternoon at Chelsea had been a success and that the crowd reaction broadly vindicated their own aims for Britain. But they also saw the threat posed by conservative clerics, which was obviously being presented by people that had heard some fundamentalist opinions of the meaning of Revelation Day by their Imams.

'I think we are fooling ourselves if we think that the older Imams will just accept this,' Catchpole suggested, again.

Peter Sati and Jonas Mehmood were the most emphatic about fighting physically, if necessary, against threats. But they were reminded that no police force existed, or military, and that it would come down to numbers and that the majority would want freedom from the thought police, as Julian Karra called the fundamentalist preachers.

'So, where to from here?' Tasmeena asked.

'I've been wondering about that,' Mark said. 'I think we need to call for elections of more MP's so that we have more representatives for the size of our population, and therefore more supporters that will defend democracy.'

'What if the fundamentalist put themselves up for election and try to grab their chance to gain the majority? Our democratic system could be used against us,' Yasmin suggested.

'Are we kidding ourselves? There were maybe thirty thousand people at Chelsea today, and the majority seemed to be on our side...'Jeffery began.

'Or are we in danger of believing our own PR?' Naz interrupted. 'Let's face it, whilst it was a real buzz to be there and feel the general support, thirty thousand is a handful compared to the London population now, which is... what Mark?'

'Not sure but close to five million.'

'Let's be analytical about this,' Jonas suggested. 'We put out the details of the gathering only two weeks ago. We have no idea how many people read the printed newssheets. We don't know if the average Imam told his congregation to boycott the gathering. We also don't know if they might have sent spies to listen and report back, and so maybe the crowd became one of those preaching to the converted events that distorts the true level of support out there. Are we becoming paranoid or deluded by what we hope people think?'

There was a lot of nodding of heads and frowns around the table. Jeffery broke the contemplative silence, 'That was a good analysis, Jonas, in a way...'

'In a way?' Jonas questioned.

'Hear me out,' Jeffery continued. 'I think we need to be wary of getting too caught up in analysing the event like this, because there's no solution that way, and too many options to consider,' Jeffery stated.

'So, give up and full steam ahead regardless?' Mark asked.

'Don't put words in my mouth, Mark,' Jeffery replied. 'What I mean is... how to put this? We believe that the majority think like we do and will grab freedom and democracy over fundamentalism. We know that they are used to voting processes and won't want to lose that link to the past. We also know, I think, that pre-Revelation Day, mosque attendance was wrongly interpreted as providing a possible pathway to radicalisation. Yet the real data showed that like other religions, attendance reinforced the sense of belonging to the wider community. Mosque attendees were just as likely as others to feel that they had something in common with other British people, were more likely to have friends outside their ethnic group, and more likely to engage in mainstream politics.'

'Very interesting, I'm sure, Jeffery, and forgive me for saying this, but so what?' Peter asked.

Jeffery smiled, 'Sorry, Peter, I guess I shouldn't harp on about past studies, but they used to really interest me. What I am saying is that we shouldn't necessarily fear other Imams or assume that they all wish to push us down a stricter or conservative pathway. Most attendees were, and probably remain, moderate. I am convinced that we are in the majority, that's all.'

'I agree,' Mark said.

'Me too,' Yasmin added.

'Are you agreeing because you want it to be true, or because you've challenged your own desires and can back up your feelings?' Julian challenged.

'I feel it in my gut,' Mark replied.

'Could just be hunger,' Riaz interrupted. 'In which case you're about to be reinvigorated because Mina just cooked some more samosas and chicken.'

'Smells divine,' Naz said. 'I'm voting for Mina,' she laughed.

The discussion continued for another hour, interspersed with more food, a few jokes, and a consensus that there was no option but to push ahead and call for candidates to fill vacant positions in Parliament, which they estimated should be 50, if the population was five million and they aimed for one MP per hundred thousand constituents. The difficulty was how to go about the process.

KALIL

'I really enjoy these beach walks, Paul,' Kalil reiterated. 'I was once posted to Goa, years ago, as a Major back then, in command of an infantry company, and I often used to go to the beach when I needed to think, and I'd take off my shoes and wander down the beach, still in uniform. People looked at me a little strangely, but I became a regular sight I suppose. I found it a marvellous way to clear the mind and think through a problem.'

'Do you have a problem now?'

'Ha, straight to the point as usual. Very American; I like that.'

'Is it? I guess we do tend to be 'get to the point' people I suppose. Or maybe impatient?'

'No, not impatient, Paul,' Kalil paused and Habbib remained silent. 'I wouldn't say I have a problem, no. I think maybe it is just that you and I have a similar... leadership challenge.'

'Oh, and which is that?'

'We must convince our people that neither of us would be better served by taking control rather than sharing the future. Or do you disagree, Paul?'

Habbib remained silent as he thought how to respond, and Kalil allowed him the time. 'Have we arrived at another point of needing to be frank with each other, and therefore very trusting, Sabal?'

'Perhaps.'

'It's easier for you, Sabal.'

'Why is that?'

'Because you have the power. You could take what you want today and there's very little that we could do to stop you, and you know it. So why don't you? That's the question that some of my team have.'

'A reasonable question, and one that many in my team pose also. Maybe we should both put these... belligerent types, in a room together to sort it out,' Kalil laughed, and Habbib did too.

'My team are worried, and I'm sure in our place you would be too. You hold all the cards... or rather all the firepower and ammunition. What do you need me for?' Habbib asked.

'That's the question my side want to know as well.'

'OK then, let's be more specific,' Habbib began, 'what is it about the U.S. system of government that makes you accept it? Your Parliamentary democracy works well. Why impose our system on your people. Where's the advantage in it?'

'A very good question, but one with a simple answer. The people that we are bringing over as immigrants are coming for one main reason, to become Americans, in their minds. It is the dream of America that attracts them, even though we know that none of that exists anymore. But they expect to see it, and at first glance it will be here, in its icons and cities; even empty ones. They will see your roads and freeways and infrastructure, and the relative calm and quiet. They equate those with greater freedom, even though that is a mirage and was never true.'

'Never true?'

'Of course not. Your society was probably the most unequal democracy in the world, apart from India perhaps. The gap between rich and poor was extreme. Blacks and Hispanics were treated badly, and even poor white people... what did you call them... white trash, I believe... were living in abject poverty. Your health system was prohibitively expensive, and law and order were a battlefield. Gun violence was out of control and your politicians were held hostage by big business and vested interest groups. By comparison, India was a paradise, for the middle classes upwards.'

Habbib started to respond, then thought better of it, sighed, and changed track, 'I'm not going to defend the United States, because it doesn't exist anymore, but I will never say that to my team, partly because it would seem like a betrayal of our history and all that we worked for, and partly because... well, what's the point now?'

Kalil nodded. 'I am sorry that I spoke so judgementally, Paul. It wasn't meant that way, truly. I simply wanted to show the disparity between a dream and reality. Dreams are important. They not only provide hope, but also hold things together, even when our conscious brains tell us otherwise. It is an important survival skill.'

'So, you are happy to have your people live here under the U.S. Constitution?'

'Paul, to blatantly misquote Scarlet O'Hara; frankly, Mr President, I don't give a damn,' Kalil said and then laughed uproariously, and he was still chuckling to himself a minute later, as Habbib shook his head and smiled.

'In fairness to your question, Paul, whilst I truly don't care that much regarding which political system is pursued, it would make more sense to adopt a Parliamentary Democracy, I suppose. But there are a great many elements of the U.S. system that are better, at least as far as your Bill of Rights is concerned. But the Electoral College system was anachronistic and should have been updated, as should some of the Constitutional Amendments. However, these things are very difficult, I realise. Perhaps now is the time though, to take the better parts of our system, and yours, and from others as well, and make up a new Constitution that better represents the new world?'

'Actually, I agree with you, Sabal.'

'Good. Now, is there anything we need to discuss more, ahead of this afternoon's joint planning session?'

'No, I don't think so. Have you decided whether to have Admiral Pereira there?'

'I must. He has great insight on the logistic side, for the ship movements especially. Kumar will be there too, but it will just be us three. I don't wish to dominate the numbers around the table. And your team?'

'All of us. General Cummins, for logistical knowledge of course. Malouf, my Secretary of State, Amelia Sanchez, who now is heavily involved in migrant population issues, and George Saba of course.'

'Of course. Mr Saba is the most critical, I think. I do not begrudge him that. I'd be more suspicious if he wasn't. I would be happy to have him on my staff. You have a loyal ally there, Paul.'

'I know. Thank you.'

'Paul, I might say things today that... how do you say it? Stir the pot?'

'That is how you say it, Sabal. In what way?'

'I don't know, but I feel that it is going to be necessary. If I do, please don't get angry. Some things might be aimed at my side rather than yours.'

'As strange as this sounds, Sabal, I think I'm looking forward to this little game you play.'

'Will you be playing it too?'

'Very possibly.'

An hour later, but still an hour ahead of the scheduled logistics meeting, Habbib addressed his team. They had all eaten lunch together and now had coffee, tea, water or a soda.

'I know you want to know what was discussed on our walk today. To be honest, not very much of substance. The only conversation we had which got a little testy was when he criticised America and suggested that our country was less than the beacon of light to the world that we thought it was...'

'The prick!' Saba shouted, 'As if fucking India was a land of opportunity...'

'Calm down, George. What he said was pretty much true, and he just highlighted all the inequities in our society that we were aware of and tried to solve, with great difficulty. He similarly acknowledged India's issues too. But the point I was coming to, was his explanation of why he was comfortable with the U.S. system rather than the British one. He said it was the dream of America that was attracting most of the migrants coming here, and that therefore accepting our system would be welcomed, warts and all. He also said he didn't really care which system we chose to adopt in the long term but that we had an opportunity now, an easy one, politically, to grab the best bits of any political systems we wanted, and to update the Constitution and the way our government works and make it fit this new world. In that regard, I think he's right, and it's something that we should think hard about. What do you think?'

Malouf was the first to speak, 'I agree. This is a unique time. Those of us in this room, plus whoever else we wish to invite, could rewrite the Constitution, and fix up a lot of stuff that we couldn't before. Why not? Makes sense to me.'

'No fucking way, Imran,' Saba responded. 'We had the best system in the world-'

'Bullshit, George!' Habbib said, stunning everyone. 'Let's not blind ourselves to reality and rewrite history for the sake of nostalgia. Our system had many faults, and there's no need to make a list. Only a fool would ignore the opportunity that lies before us. I'm not saying we dive into this now, but we should not ignore the benefits.'

'I agree with the President,' Sanchez said. 'We owe it to the people and ourselves to make anything better that we can. We have been chosen and it is expected of us to improve the world now.'

'I'm calling a halt to this now, but I suggest, George, that you think about it later, when you're calmer, please?'

'Of course, Mr President.' His face betrayed his continuing antipathy.

'OK then team, let's go over the points we want to make before the Pakindesh trio arrive.'

At 2pm, Amelia Sanchez invited Kalil, Pereira and Kumar into the 'Square Office' and invited them to drinks, and pastries. All of them did so before sitting across from the Americans around the main conference table.

Habbib had decided to take control and opened the discussions. 'President Kalil, you asked us to provide a list of desired skills for the migrants, which we have done, and I have those here for you,' he said, handing across copies to each of the three men sitting opposite the Americans. He continued as they perused the list, 'As you can see, the main skills are listed and then a statement on priority, any issues to note, and minimum numbers required. Miss Sanchez, perhaps you'd like to go through the list?'

Sanchez immediately took control, 'Thank you, Mr President. Gentlemen, the clear priority is in engineering skills and especially power plant operations, whether nuclear, gas or even coal, as well as gas-related infrastructure, from pipeline engineers to compression plant and refrigeration related knowledge. I've also added petroleum engineers, at several levels, from domestic gas station skills to refining plants. There's an annex at the back with locations of plants that we wish to start up again and the people numbers related to those facilities, with an extrapolation into support personnel needed if the plants are not currently close to populated areas. We've concentrated these on the east coast from New York to Miami, with cities further south being more important for now, unless of course you wish to populate New York before next Spring. But clearly winter up there is not going to be very hospitable, so we suggest leaving that until it warms up.

'After the engineering numbers and linked support staff are the following categories: medical, which I've split into MDs, or what you call general practitioners, and I've based that on a ratio of one doctor per 10,000 people. Is that achievable?'

Kumar answered, 'I think it might be a stretch to begin with. We assumed a one to 50,000 ratio, which is closer to a best case Pakindesh average for major cities, but we can look to improve that over time.'

'OK,' Sanchez accepted, 'what about my nurse and specialist numbers?'

'Nurses are no problem, but I think we need to take some risks for the specialists. Whilst we don't know for example, how many heart surgeons are needed, or oncology surgeons, we can look at the statistics for general surgeons and people like orthopaedic specialists. I will send the details home and we can assess what we need in the general population and take that as a starting point. However,' Kumar hesitated, looking at Kalil, 'Do you think, Mr President, that there will be some pushback in Pakindesh when we start to recruit so many highly qualified people out of our hospitals?'

Kalil contemplated the question and rubbed his chin before answering, 'Possibly. I think the argument I need to prosecute with President Asif needs to be based on us linking migrant numbers to their equivalent ratio in the population. So, whatever is normal in Pakindesh per 100,000 people is what he's likely to accept, because then there is no net decrease at home. But I think we can increase the engineering numbers if we allow for short term contracts for specialists.'

Habbib interrupted the conversation, 'Are you saying, President Kalil, that your counterpart is not completely on board with your plans?'

'Not at all, but he hasn't seen hard numbers, and it will require careful explanation. I am not worried, if we don't adversely impact the standard of living and availability of services at home. Otherwise, in his place, I would reject it too.'

'Back to you, Amelia,' Habbib said.

'Thank you, Mr President. I don't think it's necessary to go into detail around some of the other categories I have listed, and you will note I have included air traffic controllers and pilots, both fixed wind and rotary. However, I am struggling with farming resources. I really don't know how to determine what we need, what should be grown, or how many people are needed to do it all. Can anyone help with this?'

Pereira spoke for the first time, looking quizzical, 'Why don't you ask the farmers here?'

There were a few embarrassed glances between the Americans, until Malouf said, 'There were no American Muslim farmers, Admiral. Lots of different ethnic groups were involved in the farming sector here, from old established Texan ranching families to the Amish in Pennsylvania, Mormons in Utah, and hundreds of thousands of poorer Mexican and other Hispanic people spread across the country. But it was an area devoid of our faith.'

'Why?' Kumar asked.

'The short answer, Colonel,' Habbib offered, 'is because most of the American Muslim population was first or second generation, and we, or our parents, came from a more urban background, no matter what our original nationality was. So farming was not an area attracting migrants, and it is low paid as well, unless you own large tracts of land. Hence, no Muslim farmers.'

'I see. I suppose that makes sense, Mr President, thank you. Does that mean that followers of Islam here were wealthy?'

'Not necessarily. Or I suppose it depends on who the comparison is with. There were many Muslims that earned above $100,000, but also many earning less than $30,000, and the rate of unemployment across the board was higher in each career category than for the general population. But overall, I suppose one would have to conclude that Muslims in America did better than many other categories of workers,' Habbib answered.

'Like blacks and Hispanics, do you mean, Mr President?' Kumar asked.

Saba interrupted, 'Generalisations can be skewed, gentlemen. Can we proceed?'

Kalil nodded to Saba, 'Of course. Miss Sanchez, are there any other categories that you have listed here, which I must congratulate you, is a very comprehensive list, clearly with much thought and analysis behind it.'

'Thank you, Mr President. I suppose the only other area that I have to say is perhaps less than specific is in IT and communications. We have been provided, some months ago, with a complicated and discouraging explanation of why the internet is down and that it might not get back up again. This was from our people in Silicon Valley, who worked in IT. Can I ask whether this is the case in India, sorry, Pakindesh, too?'

Kalil frowned and said, 'Yes, sadly that is true. But I am not sure that our experts were quite that pessimistic. However, they might just wish to present a more upbeat picture to me. Regardless of that, would it make the most sense to send our communications and IT professionals to California?'

'Probably,' Saba said, 'but this takes us to the issue of who goes where, and when.'

'I have the proposed initial cities listed in Annex B on the last page,' Sanchez said, and everyone turned to that list. 'We concentrated on minimal geographic dispersion to start with and kept to cities with a milder Winter climate and within or close to Florida, which is why Tampa, Tallahassee and Jacksonville have the high numbers that you see. Further North, Charleston is significant due to its good port facilities as well as its proximity to farming land, and Atlanta was the city chosen for a major population centre due to its superior infrastructure. San Francisco and Los Angeles are assumed as stage 2 locations. In general, the assumption is that we'd repopulate coastal locations initially, apart from major farming areas, but keep the latter in the south of the country, and away from the tornado belt. The Gulf of Mexico cities are high on the list, and especially Galveston with its port and closeness to Houston. I was hesitant about Galveston. It was wiped out by a hurricane in 1900, killing 8,000 people, and took 12 years to rebuild. But then it survived another storm in 1915 and is no riskier a location than lots of other southern cities.'

'A very sensible list, Miss Sanchez,' Kalil stated, 'and not dissimilar to my own thoughts. Yes, we need to concentrate on port and coastal locations, with good infrastructure and access to food storage depots and power plants that can be reactivated quickly, preferably gas fired. When the aircraft arrive, we will send the high-tech people to California.'

'So, when does the armada arrive?' Habbib asked.

'Three weeks from today,' Kalil replied, ignoring the possible accusation within that description.

RIAZ

Jeffery Buliya, Mark Catchpole and Riaz met at the hospital a few days after the Chelsea football ground event. 'Still confident?' Buliya asked.

'No,' Catchpole said, frowning. 'It's too quiet. I thought there would have been some reaction from the more fire brand Imams out there.'

'How many are there?' Riaz asked.

'There's six prominent Imams pushing for Sharia,' Catchpole replied. 'Do you know any of them Jeffery?'

'Only by reputation. There is a Council of Imams, which I've attended twice, but those meetings were not focussed on religion at the time, rather than fixing up issues within their catchment areas and seeking volunteers to work, that kind of thing. Unlike pre-Revelation Day, when conversations often drifted into community issues and racism, or recent terrorist activity and trying to keep a handle on radicalisation.'

'Maybe we're being paranoid,' Riaz suggested.

'No, I don't believe so,' Catchpole said. 'This is going to be a major test of what direction the country takes, and those Imams with ideas of leadership beyond religious issues cannot allow us to move back to a secular, democratic society devoid of religious influence.'

'I tend to agree, Mark,' Buliya said, 'but maybe we are overly sensitive to all of this. This isn't 1979 Iran, or Saudi Arabia of old, or post-Arab Spring North Africa. However, better to plan for the worst rather than be taken by surprise.'

'Exactly,' Catchpole replied. 'So, we've created posters and news articles advertising for candidates to run in an election planned for 8 weeks from Saturday.'

Riaz asked, 'Is this going to be along the old party lines, like Labour and Conservatives?'

'No. We kicked that around the seven of us and realised that the old party politics is irrelevant, especially with the affluence we now enjoy regarding housing, schools, and resources. We have a good opportunity to rewrite the past and create a more equal society. It was an interesting debate, given that we were almost equally split between so-called right and left parties. We've decided to re-represent ourselves as Social Democrats, but we are stating that we are sitting members and therefore not up for re-election, because we will be needed to guide the newly elected MPs in how the process works. We're also abandoning the House of Lords.'

Riaz frowned, 'But that means no House of Review for law amendments.'

'That's true,' Catchpole acknowledged. 'But we felt that the old system was somewhat anachronistic and needed to be changed or abandoned. In a new country of five million people, with less contentious issues to debate, I think it's time to move forward. Does this worry either of you?'

'I understand the reasoning,' Riaz began, 'but there needs to be checks and balances, somehow. Otherwise, what happens if in the future, a dominant group takes the country in an extreme direction. How can that be curbed?'

'It can't be curbed by relying on an Upper House to protect us. That's not feasible,' Catchpole explained. 'If we head down an extreme path, then we've already failed. This is a new world now, and we need to move forward and have faith that many of the old problems, the majority in fact, no longer exist. Our first challenge is to pursue or maintain a path of a tolerant and moderate society, and then protect that position.'

'I agree,' Buliya concurred. 'However, we might need to consider a role for dealing with the faith, and before you ask me, I have absolutely no idea how that can be done, or whether the very idea brings its own dangers.'

'I don't like it,' Riaz stated. 'As used to be said before, in most modern democracies, there was a legal separation between so-called church and state.'

'True,' Buliya said, 'and maybe that's the best way to put it, as a separation between The Faith and The State.'

'So how do candidates put themselves up and how will the voting occur?' Riaz asked.

Catchpole opened a large notebook and placed it in view on the table. 'These are the key points, so far: 1. Candidates need to register their interest to run for election within the next 2 weeks; 2. They need to state their top five policy positions or areas of interest in order of preference; 3. They need to state their views on foreign policy -'

'Why?' Riaz interrupted.

'Because we want to know if they have leanings towards subjugating Britain's independence to autocratic elements in the Middle East, and this is a good way to try and tease that sentiment into the open,' Catchpole answered with a smile. Riaz nodded and smiled too as the MP continued, '4. They need to state if they have had any previous political experience and what that was; and 5. They are invited to comment on the draft Constitutional Direction Charter, which is this document here,' he concluded, laying down a piece of paper in front of each of them. It read:

British Constitutional Direction Charter (draft)

1. Great Britain is committed to a pluralist, democratic, equal opportunity future.
2. The country will have a single House of Commons, with no Upper House of Review, and with each Member of Parliament aimed at representing 75,000 to 100,000 inhabitants. (The first Parliament after Revelation Day might not be geographically aligned).
3. The Parliament will be made up of at least 45% male and 45% female Members, with the aim of eentually being 50% each.
4. There will be a separation of Faith and State in all decisions governing the nation.
5. Voting in elections will be compulsory for all adults over the age of 18.
6. Education of all citizens through to and including University (undergraduate and postgraduate) will be free.
7. Access to the Health system for all citizens will remain free.
8. Comment on weapons/arms needed. TBC
9. Comment on military service needed. TBC

'Your comments?' Catchpole asked. 'You look less than impressed, Riaz.'

'Oh! Do I? Sorry. No, it's just that... I suppose I was expecting something more... flamboyant... or closer to the U.S. Constitution document, I suppose.'

'I know what you mean,' Catchpole replied, 'but we don't need to go that far, and Britain never had a Bill of Rights charter either, so it's not likely to be expected by the population. But I know what you mean. I suppose it is a bit bland.'

'More that it's so, business-like perhaps?' Buliya commented.

'And if you aren't looking at an American-style thing, then why talk about weapons, or military service?' Riaz added.

'Yes, I tend to agree with you on those. Peter and Julian were quite keen. We did get into a debate you see, about protecting ourselves maybe from the French fundamentalists invading us if we stayed democratic.'

'That's crazy,' Riaz said. 'If the new world's already going to head down that kind of a path, then what was Revelation Day for?'

'Well said, Riaz,' Buliya agreed. 'I think those diversions, especially in a document of this kind, are an unwanted area for debate, Mark.'

'You're right. I'll push that with the others.'

'Never mind pushing it, I think this conversation needs to have us involved too,' Riaz argued. 'Let's not start with a politicians-only group. You need laymen in this process. The document needs to be citizen-initiated. So, it can be a good starting document for further debate, and that way it will deflect the possible drift into areas of faith and the interpretation of Revelation Day, which would otherwise play into the hands of the more radical Imams.'

Buliya clapped his hands and cheered, 'Well said, Riaz! Are you sure you don't want to stand for election? You're a natural. Honestly, you need to consider it.'

Riaz looked embarrassed, 'Not really my thing, guys.'

'I think Jeffery is right, this is your thing, truly. You should consider putting yourself up. We need your practicality and untainted background. Please consider it, Riaz.'

SALINA

She was reading an old and tatty childhood paperback book when Michael walked into her bedroom. 'What the hell's that thing?'

'An old Saddle Club story,' she said.

'Thought you'd got past those years ago?'

'I did, but it reminds me of my childhood. Happier days, you know?'

He nodded. 'Sure.'

'Haven't you got anything similar that you like to go back to?'

'Yeah. I flick through my Man United programs and pretend I'm at a match at half time and we're winning three nil.'

'I wonder if football like that will come back again?'

'I doubt it. At least not the way it was,' Michael suggested, then smiled, 'If it did though I'd stand a chance of selection for the Reds,' he laughed.

'Maybe not set your sights that high. How about Millwall?' Salsa laughed.

He threw a pillow at her and for a few minutes they continued a pillow fight and laughed like little kids. When they were panting and decided to stop and cool down, Salsa said, 'I want to be a journalist.'

'How?'

'What do you mean, how?'

'There are no real newspapers or TV anymore,' he said.

'Maybe not now but there will be, one day. Things will get back to... well, maybe not normal, but... modern again? Won't they, Michael?'

He thought about it. 'Yes, I suppose they must. But what would you report on?'

'Foreign affairs,' she said confidently.

'Really?'

'Yep. I want to travel and report on other places. Especially now. Don't you want to see what the rest of the world has become? Think about how the changes must have altered countries and outlooks.'

'Sure. Okay, but it might still be dangerous. Especially for a girl in some of those places if they've gone all fundamental. I mean you couldn't have done a job like that in lots of places in the Middle East before, and probably still won't be able to.'

'But we don't know that. And in many ways, it should become easier, less dangerous to travel, as a woman and as a Muslim. I want to see it all, and tell people about it, from my perspective.'

'Yeah, I can see you doing that, Salsa.'

'Want to come with me?'

'I think there might be a few dozen things standing in your way of this dream, Sis.'

'Like what?'

'Oh, like, lack of airlines, mum and dad, no papers or TV stations to work for, no experience, no money, you know, stuff like that,' he said as another pillow hit him square in the face.

Later, over dinner, Salsa raised her dream with the family, and Michael only added support, although the counter commentary was like his earlier views. Then Charlie changed the direction of the conversation. 'I think we shouldn't lower our expectations or desires. If we can't achieve what we want in this world then something has gone wrong. Revelation Day happened for a reason, surely. I'm going to be a doctor, and Salsa is going to be a journalist, and Dad will be an MP.'

'An MP!' Riaz exclaimed, drowning out any other responses.

'Definitely, Dad. They need you, as a practical and moderate man. And you're already on the inside with the others. Why not?' Charlie challenged.

'Yes, why not, Riaz?' Mina agreed.

'I have no experience of politics, that's why.'

'Nonsense,' Mina replied, 'you've been helping and improving things ever since RD. That's practical politics, isn't it?'

'Mum's right, Dad. You're doing what we always wanted politicians to do; make positive changes and help the public,' Charlie said.

'And all those MP friends you have now will back you, Dad, surely?' Salsa suggested.

'Maybe. But I like my job in the hospital.'

'Be honest, Riaz,' Mina replied, 'you're bored there already. Or if you're not, you soon will be. And anyway, there's a bigger reason too. You must get the education system back up and running so that Charlie can become a doctor. That's your job now. Make it happen, my husband.'

AMELIA

Amelia gave a gasp as she and John consummated their active morning in bed, after which they lay there looking at the view of the sea through the undraped window. It was a lazy Saturday, with no work scheduled before noon. 'I never get tired of that view,' she said.

'I never get tired of this view,' he said, looking at her breasts as he adjusted his position.

'You have a one-track mind, General.'

'Can you blame me?' he laughed.

She changed the subject, and the mood, 'I'm worried, John.'

He knew when she did this that there was no way back to intimate games or silly banter. 'What about?'

'Kalil. He worries me. Am I being stupid, or is he playing us all and we're going to wake up in a few weeks as quasi-servants in his new regime?'

'I can't explain why I have this feeling, and I know it's counter to everything that my military appreciation process of analysis tells me, and that I should remain deeply suspicious, but I do trust him.'

'Why?'

'What part of I can't explain this didn't you get,' Cummins laughed.

She looked at him and frowned, waiting for him to continue. 'Okay,' he said holding his hands up in mock surrender, 'let me try and put it into words, whilst I shower,' he said as he exited the bed and wandered into the bathroom.

She heard him pee loudly, flush the toilet, and put the shower on. She knew there was no point in rushing him. This was his way, and she loved all his ways. She decided to join him in the shower.

Afterwards, once he'd shaved and dressed and they were on the balcony, he answered her earlier question. 'I've met a few senior command officers in my time, and I mean those that have seen action and been in the front, at different ranks, and clearly know how to lead and more importantly, have other men follow them, no matter the danger.

'Kalil is one of those. He's a natural leader, secure in his position, and with an overriding ambition. I have no idea how that would have played out in India before, and whether he'd have gone even further, as a Muslim in a Hindu country, but he was made for command. But he's driven by a desire to make a difference. I can sense it. And his ambition is huge. But he doesn't trust those he's left behind, and especially because he needs them, or at least his co-President, Asif. Without the supply of people, more than anything else, his dreams will remain just that. So, he needs help, from over there and here. He needs other visionaries. Pereira isn't one. Kumar is loyal. I think they've been together a long time and Kumar would crawl over broken glass for Kalil.

'But Kalil needs other allies, and I think he's taken to Habbib, and the feeling is mutual. But specifically, he wants something that he doesn't have from his side. He wants a friend he can trust, and Habbib is his man.'

'I don't understand, John.'

'You've heard that old saying about the loneliness of command?'

'Sure. So?'

'It's true. When you get to the top you either fear people that want to take your place, or even kill you, or just tell you things they think you want to hear. Real advisers without another agenda are rare. And friends can be a danger to foster. I think Kalil and Habbib need each other. And Kalil can afford to befriend Habbib because he's really no threat. The reverse isn't necessarily true.'

'You mean The President might be betrayed?'

'Maybe not betrayed, but... perhaps disappointed one day.'

'And you, John, what do you think of Kalil?'

Cummins rubbed his chin and considered her question. She allowed him the time. She liked to watch him ponder. It was unselfconscious, and sexy as hell, she thought, supressing a smile as well as an urge. 'I think that Kalil might be the best thing to happen to America since Revelation Day. I think he could be the saviour of the Americas.'

'Wow!'

'I've surprised you.'

'Yes, but not by your statement, as much as your... foresight, maybe. You've been on this track for some time I think.'

'Yes, I have, Amelia. And I've questioned myself in depth. I'm not being disloyal to POTUS, and I'm damned well going to protect him from everyone, including himself. But there's a depth to Kalil that suggests true greatness. I've seen it rarely. I'd be lying if I didn't say I find it exciting. Well, maybe not that exactly, but... stimulating.'

'Imran and George don't like him. Do you sense that?'

'Ha! They hardly hide it. But it's not dislike. It's fear. They know they are outmatched, and they know, in their hearts, that there's not a thing they can do about it. That scares them. Partly I sympathise, because it's like being outgunned in battle and considering whether this is your own suicide mission, not a pleasant thought. But the bigger issue for them is loss of the political system that they know. They're only human.'

'Hell, when did you get to be so philosophical, General?' she laughed.

He smiled, 'When you brought me down to Earth, my darling.'

'Take me back to bed, John. Enough talking.'

Meanwhile, in the wardroom of the PNS Vikramaditya, Pereira, Kalil and Kumar were also discussing President Habbib. 'How does the man not burn with shame for letting us take over like this?' Pereira scorned.

'You sound as if you want them to fight, Pereira,' Kalil replied.

'I do, in a way. That would be honourable and allow us to take over as we wished, without the need for them and this... false negotiation. With respect, General; I mean Mr President; apologies.'

Kalil ignored the unimportant slip. 'We need them, Pereira. They can smooth the way forward for the integration and they have access to knowledge that is not so easy to research now. Anyway, I like Habbib.'

'Why?' Pereira asked with slight irritation.

'He's intelligent, and he's not foolish enough to dwell on what he cannot stop. He also knows that he needs our expertise. But I think he also sees our vision as more acceptable than anything else that might come his way. He prefers us to anyone from the Middle East, or Indonesia. He's visited India three times; did you know that?'

'State visits?' Kumar asked.

'No, family holidays. He loves India and Nepal and travelled with his family and spent time there before he went into politics. I think he's looking forward to a new vibrancy arriving,' Kalil laughed.

'But he must know that his days as the President are limited?' Pereira suggested.

Kumar laughed, 'Maybe he prefers to be Vice President of a vibrant nation of fifty to a hundred million people than a leader of five.'

'You are forgetting their background,' Kalil said, 'in the American system he would only have had 8 years maximum as a President, and he'd never have been in that position anyway, as a Muslim. He is only President now by default. Under our... partnership, he can lead for a much longer period and make a difference. We and our population and skills are the Americans' way back to civilisation and technology, which is something they not only understand but crave. What did you think was the most important aspect of our meetings yesterday?'

'How tightly they wished to keep the new population centres in the south,' Pereira suggested.

'Their priority for the skills was to get their communications and computer networks going again,' Kumar added.

'Neither.' Kalil replied. 'It was their total inability to know how to produce food again. They have been so far removed from the means of production that they are like children waiting to be taught. It might still be at a subconscious level, but they need us more than they realise themselves. But that will dawn on them very quickly. When it does, we will have another problem.'

'What is that?' Pereira asked.

'Making them feel needed. And the answer to that is to let them get involved in their growing democracy, constitution, and political processes. They need to be busy with government and logistics. With our help of course. Otherwise, the devil makes work for idle hands, as the old saying goes. Now, gentlemen, to work ourselves. When does the merchant fleet really begin to arrive with the first immigrants?'

'In four to six days, General,' Kumar said.

'Show me the initial plans,' Kalil ordered.

CHARLIE

'Any news, Harry?' Charlie asked as he walked into what he now called the radio room, which was really Harry's bedroom.

'A bit, Charlie. My Lebanese mate says that there's discussion in the streets there about the conflict between the Caliphate and Iran and that there seems to be factions forming.'

'What kind of factions?'

'He wasn't specific, but I guess along Shia versus Sunni lines.'

'I don't get it. If we've all been chosen, then why do those two countries still want to kill each other?'

'Everything is about power, Charlie. Those two are powerful as well as fearful of each other.'

'But why?'

'Good question. Probably because they've been fighting each other by proxy for years, and the Saudis saw themselves as the keepers of Mecca, of course, and they look down on Shia Islam. Especially the Wahhabi ultra-conservative Saudis, although they were losing ground after Mohammed bin Salman took over as Crown

Prince. But Iran feels intellectually superior and yet fears that the Sunni majority will want to eliminate them. Fear and power plays, Charlie; the essence of politics and war, unfortunately.'

'Do you think it will spread, Harry?'

'Perhaps, but I don't think it's a problem for us. Not for a long time anyway. So, what's up with you, young man?'

'Something amazing has happened.'

'Tell me quickly, coz you're busting to get it out, I can see,' Harry laughed.

'Remember doctor Jennings?'

'That Amaya that Freddy is sweet on?'

'Yes, and they're sort of together now, didn't you know?'

'I did, but I didn't mean to distract you. Go on.'

'Yes, well, she's going to help me train as a doctor. She's setting up a teaching program with other doctors and there's going to be a course starting in a few weeks. She said it will be a bit haphazard at first, whilst they sort out how to get the right mix between theory and practice, but that there's already fifteen medical staff committed to the idea, and I'm in.'

'Just like that? No, entrance exam?'

'No. She said that it will be a case of aptitude testing along the way, and a lot of book learning too. They don't know how long it will take to train a new doctor but that the students will need to be patient as well as adaptable.'

'Well, I'm right proud of you, Charlie. I think you'll make a good quack,' Harry laughed.

'We'll see, Harry. What do you think about dad going for election?'

'The best news I'd heard for a long time. Until yours today, of course,' he smiled.

'He'll make a good MP I think,' Charlie stated.

'I agree. The more moderates the better. We need practical men in the job, and women of course. Maybe your mum should run too?'

Charlie looked quizzically at his friend. 'That's not a bad idea, Harry.'

'Oh God, don't get me into trouble with Mina by telling her what I said.'

'I won't, but it's worth bringing up, maybe. I'll see you later, Harry.'

Charlie went to look for his siblings and found them kicking a ball around in the park nearby. He raised Harry's suggestion of their mother running for election.

'We couldn't have both parents as MPs,' Michael said.

'Why not?' Salina reacted. 'Mum would be just as good as dad at the job.'

'I know she would,' Michael replied, 'but if you had two members of a family going for election it would split the vote and then maybe neither would get up. Counterproductive.'

'Wow!' Charlie said. 'Since when did you two become so wise?'

'Stands to reason, Charlie,' Michael replied.

'I know, but I hadn't thought of it until you did, Michael.'

'Maybe we should discuss it with them anyway,' Salsa suggested.

'Yes, let's,' Charlie agreed. 'I'll bring it up tonight over dinner. But are you two saying that you think mum should be the candidate rather than dad?'

Salsa nodded, 'I think so. Michael?'

'Yep. Would be good for her. Dad has enough to do at the hospital, but even if he's getting a bit bored with it, I'm sure his skills will find other outlets. Plus, more women will set the tone for a balanced Parliament too, especially if there's a fundamentalist streak trying to impose its will.'

'Wow, you two really are maturing. It's going to be interesting to see what you end up doing in the future.'

'We've told you already, Charlie, we're going to be investigative journalists. Both of us.'

'Just checking that your wish hasn't changed. I can see that for you two. So, this is definitely a double act for you?'

'We think so, yes. We think we not only need to look after each other, but that we want to bounce ideas off each other too,' Salsa explained.

'Plus, a bit of protection never goes astray either,' Michael added.

'Why? You don't see this as dangerous, do you?'

'Who knows, Charlie. Let's face it, we don't know what the world out there is really like now, do we?' Michael said. 'We're stronger together.'

'Is this a twin thing, or do you really think that your two heads are better than one?'

'Isn't that always the case, Charlie?' Salsa asked.

'Hmm, yeah, usually, I suppose. Especially you two. I'd really miss you though.'

'Well, it's not going to happen soon, so I wouldn't worry too much for now, Chaz,' Michael replied.

That night over dinner, Charlie took the initiative. 'Mum, I think you'd be a better choice for an MP than dad, because we're going to need more moderate representation and more women will make it harder for the fundamentalists, if there are any, to infiltrate Parliament. Plus, I think dad's skills can be better used in the engineering sector. Don't get me wrong, Dad, you'd be a great MP too, but mum has advantages that you don't. You're better in admin and support, don't you think?'

Riaz looked initially crestfallen, then contemplative, and then he smiled. 'I agree. Mina, I endorse Charlie's recommendation, which I think is also Salsa and Michael's view, isn't it?' he said, looking at the twins.

'Yes,' they said in unison.

'Do you accept the family's support, my darling?' Riaz asked, a huge smile on his face.

'Yes, I do. Thank you all. The idea has been creeping into my mind lately, especially after spending more time with Tasmeena and Yasmin. I've been a bit down lately, due to boredom, I think. You kids are growing up fast, and you're busy at the hospital, Riaz. I have some good conversations with Harry during the day, but I need a purpose, and I think this is it.'

AMELIA

I'm beyond tired, she realised. She threw her large handbag to the floor as she entered the apartment in the Fontainebleau, and did as usual, walked to the window, opened the sliding door and went to gaze at the ocean and feel the breeze on her face. She lifted her arms wide and breathed deeply. 'Revive me mother earth. Give me the strength to get through these coming days and weeks. Protect John and POTUS from making any errors of judgement. Please let President Kalil be genuine. And give me a baby.'

She lowered her voice. 'Why do I do this, look to mother earth and not to Allah to help me? Am I unworthy? No, of course not, or I wouldn't be here. Why were we left alone here? What is the purpose of this... isolation, this homogenised... human disaster!'

The door opened and John walked in, smiling. 'I thought I heard you talking.'

'I was. To myself.'

'Oh. Did you win the argument?' he laughed.

She didn't smile, just sighed and her shoulders slumped. 'I'm just so tired, John.'

'Yes, I suppose we've all been flat out on the logistics for these migrants, and you more than most. I hope the cabinet appreciates your work, Amelia.'

'POTUS does, but probably not George and Imran; especially not George, chauvinistic fool!'

'Wow. Where's all this coming from, darling? Are you OK?'

She shook her head, and the tears started to roll down her cheeks. Within seconds she was sobbing heavily in his arms. He let her take the time she needed, without asking questions. After some minutes she took a deep breath, composed herself and raised her face from his now wet shoulder. 'I'm OK now, John, thank you.'

'Want to tell me?' he asked, clearly worried.

Do I? Should I? Will it help? She shook her head, 'I'm OK; it's nothing.'

'Well, it's not nothing, Amelia, clearly. You know you can tell me, don't you? I mean I'm hardly going to criticise anything you say. I appreciate you more than you will ever know. I will support you no matter what you tell me, truly.'

'Even if I say that I think Allah is a sadist for murdering the rest of the world, that I think this new world is a lot worse than the old one? Will you stand on that balcony with me and shout out that Allah is a false God, John? Will you?'

'I will if you ask me to, yes.'

'Do you agree with me though? Do you agree that he's a murderer that took our families away from us for no good reason other than Muslim pride and arrogance and... cowardice? That he knew his followers were inferior to the rest of the world and so he took away all those temptations that would have led to a better world, to science and learning and equality?'

'Amelia, Revelation Day took away my wife, and your family, and all our friends, and hundreds of millions of innocent children. Why is that not as bad as any crazed dictator or megalomaniac or mass murderer? The only reason I can think of is that there is a greater plan for us, and that we will be reunited with our loved ones somehow. If I didn't cling to that hope, then I'd be tempted to jump off that balcony. But there are upsides too, and I'd be less than honest if I didn't see those as well, even if the price has been so immensely high and meant the loss of my family, and yours.'

'What upsides!' she screamed. 'What possible upside can pay me back for my loss of family, John? Tell me that,' she sobbed. 'Yes, fucking tell me that...'

'You and me finding each other. The end of wars, I hope. The end of human pollution and land loss for animals, and hopefully solving climate change, and the end of poverty and racism, and crime. Those things will be better, surely?'

'You are just hopeful, John. And as for wars, well Iran and the Caliphate still are fighting each other. We don't know that those other things will last either do we?'

'No, we don't, that's true. Just as we don't know that we will have a baby, many babies perhaps, together. But I feel it. So, we will make a new family and we will guide our children into a new and better world, Amelia. We must. We just need faith, in each other first.'

She let more tears flow. 'I... no, I can't say it,' she cried.

'Let it out, Amelia. Let it all out now and then we can start to heal, perhaps. What do you want to say, or scream or shout?'

She shook her head, clearly fighting the urge to be open. He gave her the time to decide and just held her, nuzzling her neck, but not speaking. A few minutes later, she pushed him apart from her and nodded, 'Okay,' she said, then sighed deeply and continued in an unemotional voice. 'Here's the thing, John. I hate Allah. I despise Him, and I can never see myself attending a mosque again, nor praising His name, nor using those kinds of words. So, that makes me vulnerable, to His wrath, or punishment, if He exists. And that might mean that He punishes me through harming our future children, or you. I'm not sure I could bare that.'

The silence grew between them whilst John decided how to address the fears of the woman he loved. Finally, he said, 'Amelia, you were saved, presumably, assuming any of us were, and that this whole new world isn't just some bizarre... I don't know. Anyway, the thing is, that if there's a God, and if that superior being orchestrated all of this... resetting of the world, for whatever reason, then He decided that you were a worthy person to be in it, no matter what. If a God is all seeing, all powerful, all knowing, then you, and I, have been accepted, warts and all, haven't we? So, logically speaking, we are safe. Even if we curse God for taking away our loved ones, and all the things we held dear, He will know and accept that we will have these feelings of angst and loss. He would be merciful because He knows what he has had to do to take us along this road to whatever He has planned for us. If any God was to be so petty as to punish His creation for not understanding the new path He's created, then... well fuck Him and His plan.'

Despite her mood, she laughed out loud. 'Now I know why I love you so much, General Cummins. No-one else would put up with me like you do.'

'Ditto, my darling. So, are you okay now?'

'No, I'm not. I'm clearly wearing far too much clothing, and so are you, so give me a baby,' she said as she started to undress.

HABBIB

Attending the pre-migrant logistics planning session was President Kalil, Admiral Pereira and Ashraf Kumar, plus the entire U.S. cabinet team.

Amelia opened the briefing, as predetermined. 'So, I can confirm that the first city to be populated by the Pakindesh migrants is Charleston, South Carolina. We will be sending 1,053 advisers and migrant support personnel volunteers to the city tomorrow, by road, who will meet the advance technical party from Admiral Pereira's team. I know that you have all read my briefing paper, but just to highlight the reasons for Charleston again, this city used to have a population of about 130,000. It has good infrastructure, excellent deep-water port facilities, several power stations that we hope can be back up and running quickly, and a large amount of warehouse storage capacity close to docking locations. Housing is well contained within a manageable area to enhance the feeling of community and to support the first influx comfortably. In addition, the weather is mild in the winter and pleasant in the summer and has similar humidity that many of the new migrants are used to. Proximity to Florida is a bonus and access to good fertile farming areas are available too. Did anyone have any questions?'

Kalil spoke immediately, 'Miss Sanchez, can you just outline some of the power station statistics for me, and how it is expected that we will be able to get these running again? I know that some of that information is in your outline, but it might be useful to kick that one around.'

'Certainly, Sir. As I outlined in the paper, South Carolina had 4 nuclear power plants supplying 52% of the electricity, with up to 45% coming from coal plants and up to 17% from renewables, mainly hydro and some biomass. However, there was an increasing amount of gas-fired electricity production too, although the source of the gas was from the Gulf Coast pipeline through Georgia, and we don't know if this will be easily resurrected in the short term. Similarly, we don't know the state of the nuclear plants, but that was why we asked for nuclear power engineers from your people to help assess that on site. The nukes are reasonably old, I suppose. Catawba is 2,310 megawatts, operational from 1985; Robinson is 741 megawatts, older, built in 1971; Oconee is old too, built in 73, with 2,554 Megs. Those 3 were operated by Duke Energy. Then there's V.C. Summer, of Dominion Energy, with 966 Meg, built in 85. However, on arrival we hope to be able to utilise the hydro facilities first, especially the pumped hydro units to get the power system reenergised. But, again, we need your help on that.'

'That's in hand' Kumar stated. 'We have sufficient power station engineering teams in the first group of specialists to arrive. But an earlier assessment can be carried out by some of the power plant technicians within the Naval contingent.'

'What kind of people are in this migrant support team you speak of and what do they hope to do, and how?' Pereira asked.

Amelia didn't like Pereira's tone but ignored it. 'In that team will be doctors and nurses and general medical staff who are going to assess the situation at the Medical University of South Carolina hospital. It's the largest, or was, and is centrally located. There will also be people with engineering skills, as well as mechanics, dentists, teachers, chefs, all sorts. Do you have any concerns, Admiral?'

'No, that's fine, Miss Sanchez; I was just trying to get a feel for things, that's all.'

George Saba decided to shift the emphasis back onto the Pakindesh officials. 'So, for my benefit, gentlemen, can you provide a feel for what kind of initial support your migrant influx will need the most when they arrive, and perhaps what expectations they have?'

Kalil jumped in, with a slight laugh to lower the tension, 'George, I think it is most truthful to say that our migrants have no expectations at all, although they will have been given some history and geography lessons on America on their voyage. But many of them will either be expecting to arrive in Hollywood, with iconic American scenery before them, or some other unrealistic vision of the land of opportunity. I think they will be very happy with the accommodation they receive, and they will be ecstatic to be off the ships and on dry land. They will wander around in a daze for a few days, I think, and they will be very grateful to receive whatever American hospitality is afforded them. If they are met with kindness and open arms and comradery, I believe that they will feel that they are fortunate to be here. Apart from that, this will be a learning curve for us all.'

'Well said, Sabal,' Habbib acknowledged. 'We should remember that the migrants are taking a huge chance coming here, to the unknown as far as they're concerned. In many respects no different to our own family histories. America was founded on immigration, from across the world. The common thread has always been a desire to better their lives. This is no different.'

'What about language difficulties?' Saba asked.

'Minimal, George,' Kalil said, 'because all initial migrants had to have a good command of English to be accepted, apart from the farmers, who can communicate through the others.'

The remainder of the discussions was on fine detail and pairing of personnel between the Admiral's crew members and American specialist volunteers. After a light lunch, the two parties split up and Sabal and Paul went to the beach for their debrief and some privacy.

'It went well, Paul, I think.'

'Yes, I agree. There will be some technical challenges, especially in relation to getting power stations and gas pipelines re-energised. But if the migrants are patient and not too demanding, or too unrealistic, then I think it will be manageable. The list of families and their numbers was useful to pre-allocate accommodation, and the pre-advance party of medical and power station plant operators will work well in prioritising those facilities and services. If we have power, we have the start of normalised life again, as we found here when we moved south.'

'I admire what you achieved here, Paul, truly. Whilst we also struggled in India after Revelation Day, we had a sizeable population to assist with the shock, and we hadn't lost anywhere near as much modern-day support systems. In a way, we awoke with the lights on, whilst you awoke in the dark, my friend. That must have been terrible.'

Paul nodded, not speaking, and Sabal allowed him the time as they walked in the sand. 'What happened to your family, Sabal? You don't talk of one.'

He shook his head, looking away, across the sea. 'No, I don't. It is still painful. My wife was Hindu, and our children, 2 boys and 2 girls, were brought up as Hindus too. When we were married, my family accepted my choice. They loved Shanaz as I did. She had a heart and soul that endeared her to all. It was also a practical marriage, for my career I mean, although that was not a factor in my choice. I think I loved her from the moment we met, although the courtship took its time. Her family was probably less enamoured of her taking a Muslim husband, but my military position added respectability, and when I advised her father that I was open to our future children being Hindu... well that changed their views, although there was still suspicion, and rightly so. What father would not be nervous about a mixed marriage in India.' Sabal paused, sighed, and became misty eyed but averted his gaze away from Paul. 'Anyway, that choice has proved to be my undoing, and so I lost my family along with so many other billions of people on that terrible day.'

So, you and I are the same, Habbib considered? You must also hate the God that did this to us. Do you? Is that why you want to come to the Americas, to escape such strong Islamic... euphoria? Before he could formulate a question, Sabal pre-empted it.

'Did you hate Allah for taking your wife and family, Paul? I did.'

He stopped walking and faced Sabal, searching his face for the person behind those impassive eyes, now looking moist. 'I still hate Him. Do you?'

'How could I not? I forced all of that to the back of my mind in the aftermath of that day. I had to. I needed to survive, and I had a job to do. So, I worked, and I schemed, and I made myself push my despair to the back of my mind. But now, that... resentment... comes to the fore more often. And you?'

'The same I suppose. I can never forgive the God that did this and took my family from me too. But what choice do we have other than to seek a meaning in this new world, this... empty canvass. All I can do is hope that I will see my family again one day. Maybe, if this is a test, we will both see our families, if we do good work. Or maybe I'm stupid... delusional.'

Sabal laughed, without humour. 'We have no choice, Paul. We must go on and we must make things better. That is our salvation and our curse. But we must not forget our lost loved ones, nor in any way denigrate them or their own pasts. For a moment back on that day, I considered ending my life too. But if I had then there would have been no-one left to remember my beautiful family, and that I was not prepared to accept. So, I chose to live, and succeed, and remember. That is my revenge. The best revenge is to live well. I hope.'

RIAZ

Jeffery Buliya was uncharacteristically angry. 'We knew that there would be retaliation from the fundamentalists! We should not be surprised. No opposition might have been worse, and meant secret plotting against us,' he said, almost to himself, as he perused the faces of the group around Riaz's dining room table.

Riaz let him blow off steam, as he thought. *He needs this. It might be good for him to get this angry at last. His calmness was always unrealistic, or naïve, but endearing for all that. There was no way that the hard-line Imams would take our election lying down. No need to say that. Vent, Jeffery. You must.*

Mark Catchpole prepared to speak but Riaz placed a hand on his arm and patted it, hoping he'd get the message to remain quiet. There was a faint nod from the MP. Mina walked back into the room with lemonade, cake and tea and started to set it on the table, without interrupting Jeffery.

'We need to decide how to react. This is a test for us. Do you all agree?' Jeffery asked, his face stern, unsmiling.

'Of course,' Mark answered. 'What is your counsel, Jeffery?'

He took a deep breath, then scratched his head with both hands, like he was attempting to salve a deep itch. 'I think our response must be along democratic lines, not religious. We need to appeal to the public's sense of fairness, and control of their own affairs... but without attracting a religious or blasphemous counterattack.'

'The Imams might call for a boycott,' Peter Sati suggested.

'No, they won't do that,' Tasmeena Hikaka countered.

'Why not?' Jonas Mehmood asked. 'If they called for one and it worked and minimal numbers of voters turned out, then they would prove that democracy was not favoured by the population.'

'No. It would backfire, Jonas,' Tasmeena continued, 'no matter how poor the turnout, there will still be enough voters to make the process work, which just means that the power of the radical Imams will be weakened. No, that's the easier outcome to manage. The worst outcome is that they tell their followers to vote, and then put their own names forward as candidates, to take control that way.'

'Will they, Jeffery?' Riaz asked.

Buliya rubbed his beard and scratched his chin. He sighed, scratched his head, nodded, then said, 'Very possibly. And if so, then Tasmeena is correct, this would be a more difficult problem. But only if they fielded enough candidates of course.'

'We can defeat that tactic if we have public debates,' Mina stated from the other end of the room where she'd been leaning against the fireplace. The certainty in her voice surprised almost all of them.

'Go on, Mina,' Jeffery encouraged.

'I'll explain it like this,' she said confidently. 'Let's say that you are a regular mosque attendee where the Imam is either radical or has been coerced by more senior clerics to toe the line. So, he has put his name forward as a candidate, and he asks... no, let's say... he demands the support of all of those that he leads in prayer. His followers, apart from the extreme believers of course, will probably feel bullied. More to the point, they might feel that they are about to lose their free will and democratic rights. This isn't the Middle East. That attempt to coerce people to do as they are told will not be welcomed. But nobody will say anything. They will nod and make the right noises of course, but when the day of the election comes along, they will vote the way that they want.

'Now, if leading up to the election, there are a series of open debates between candidates, the radical Imams cannot avoid those, or they will be seen to fear the process, or be less sure of their arguments. That is where we will make major inroads, especially if people in the crowd ask questions about the future, like how they will get global trade going again, or the resurrection of air travel, or the Internet, or reopening universities to train doctors. Anything that widens the debate to real life and away from faith-based commentary. Once they have been shown up in public, well their campaign is doomed.' Mina sat down at the table as she concluded her argument, and Jeffery clapped his hands and comments flowed from everyone in the group.

Ten minutes later, when the group was under control again, Yasmin Hussein smiled broadly, laughed and pointed her finger at Riaz. 'I'm sorry, Riaz, but if there had still been debate about whether you or Mina should run for office, I think that question has now been answered.'

'I have never underestimated my wife,' he said with a grin, 'and woe betide anyone that does.'

Mark Catchpole tapped his fork against his glass to gain everyone's attention again. 'I think Mina has eloquently set out our strategy direction for us. We need public debates, and we need to drive the discussions to those things that people miss the most and where we can create positive nostalgia for the Parliamentary process.'

'Agreed,' Jeffery stated. 'And I wish to thank Mina again for brightening my mood and providing a clear direction.' Everybody cheered and clapped, and Mina found it very difficult to remove the smile from her face.

AMELIA

Watching the ships approach the coast of Charlotte, South Carolina was an intensely moving sight. It felt like the rebirth of the world; civilisation returning in many ways. Was this the right thing to do? Was this an opportunity or a threat? Not that POTUS could do much about it anyway. How could they have thwarted a force of this size? Was Sabal Kalil to be trusted? She liked him, and so did John, and his judgement was sound. She didn't like Pereira. Too arrogant, struts about more like a conqueror and has no claims on that score. In the old days he'd have been a minor player, no matter whether he commanded a carrier group or not. Those Indian ships would have been no match for the US Navy, or so John said, and he'd know. Pull your head in, Amelia, this is a civilian migration, not an invasion, remember. As the Statue of Liberty proclaimed: "Give me your tired, your poor, your huddled masses yearning to breathe free, the wretched refuse of your teeming shore. Send these, the homeless, tempest-tossed to me, I lift my lamp beside the golden door". Maybe not quite the same imperative now, in this brave new world. Good God, Amelia, stop with the literature quotes, get your head back in the game. You have work to do.

That was the last time she had off for free thinking for the next 4 days. At the end of that period, she was physically wrecked, but immensely satisfied. Her team, including the American volunteer welcoming party, plus the help of the Pakindesh advance group that flew in a day ahead of the migrants disembarking, had worked 20-hour days with limited rest breaks or food stops. But the morale was fantastic. The sense of comradery surprised her the most. This was how migrants were supposed to be treated and welcomed. It was the smiles that invigorated her the most. There was no pushing or impatience or anger. The sense of community was what surprised her the most. It was like there was an undercurrent of… joy. And hope too.

The people coming off the 47 ships, which now took up almost all the available berths closest to the passenger sections of the port, plus a fair number of commercial berths, had been efficiently organised. This was no haphazard arrangement, and it was a credit to the significant Pakindesh military planning. Kalil had done far more work on this than she'd realised. He and Kumar were clearly hands-on commanders, and their attention to detail was inspiring.

The next challenge was to move those migrants that were to be America's farmers out to the identified farms that had been designated as easiest to support and survive the winter more favourably, or so she hoped. The Carolinas could be very cold too, and the Pakindeshers, as she'd started to call them, would have minimal experience of an American winter.

She was broken out of her daydream by the advance of Kalil, flanked only by a single guard, unarmed. 'Ms Sanchez? How are you fairing today? You looked very tired yesterday, I thought.'

'Oh, did I? I'm well, thank you, Mr President. And pleased to see how well everything has gone. Your organisation is amazing.'

Kalil smiled. 'You know, I do think that we will need to get away from the formality of office titles. I realise it will take time and retraining ourselves. But I feel that this new world needs to be more… egalitarian. Do you agree?'

'Yes, Mr President... I mean...' she stuttered.

Kalil laughed. 'Don't worry... Amelia? I know this is hard, and I don't expect you to be comfortable calling me Sabal. Plus, it might not sit well with my own staff I suppose. But I will think on this and talk to your President too. There must be a way to be less formal, without losing dignity.'

'Formality does have its place, Sir, surely?'

'Of course. Perhaps I am being naïve. Anyway, down to issues if you will. I have seen the logistics plan for the movement of the rural families and their support elements, but I have a question. What is a normal winter in these areas? I can't Google that information anymore, so we need to revert to real knowledge, if you will,' he said with a smile.

'Well, around Greenville, where we've sort of centred the logistics base for rural production, the temperatures are mild. Winters tend to get down to just above zero Celsius, on average, a bit lower than that for the mean lows. Summers are the humid period with rains that can get high at times. We're not so prone to cyclones as other areas, like Florida and the Gulf States, but if they happen it'd be more likely around Springtime.'

'Thank you, Amelia. I need to see my staff now. I bid you a good day in your efforts,' he said, smiling, with a slight bow of his head.

'No problem, Sir,' she answered, as he walked off. Now there goes a true leader, and a very clever diplomat too. He knew I wouldn't be able to call him by his name, naturally. Yet he was able to use mine. Is that arrogance, or politeness, or manipulation, or what? Pull yourself together girl. Call it harmless flirting, whatever. Time to get back to work.

SALINA

Michael walked into his sister's bedroom unannounced, as usual. She spoke to him as soon as she heard his feet, without looking behind her to check it was him, 'What's up Michael?'

'It's Charlie,' he said, trying to disguise his voice, failing.

'Good try twin brother. You know I can feel you before you get here. Or maybe it's the smell,' she laughed.

He chuckled too at the regular joke, 'You need some new material, Sis. What're you doing?'

'Contemplating life, or more the future really,' she sighed.

'Spill it.'

'I want to see the world, Mikey; always did, as you know.'

'Sure. So?'

'Will I be able to now?'

'Why not?'

'Well, duh. Things like no flights, ships, trains. And can't hitchhike when there's no people on the roads either. I am really narked that we're going to live and die in this city, without going to all those cool places we used to dream about. Remember them?'

'Of course,' he said with some sadness.

'Prove it then. Name our top ten,' she challenged.

He laughed. 'Sis, the top ten changed all the time, every time we saw some new wonder of the world type program.'

'So what? Name any of our top ten contenders then.'

'OK. Umm... the Taj Mahal. Petra in Jordan, Iguassu Falls in Brazil, and Rio, and... the pyramids of Egypt, and Niagara Falls and Victoria Falls. We loved waterfalls, remember. Oh yeah, Angel Falls in Venezuela too. Japan, Australia, an African safari, Madagascar to see the lemurs...'

'Don't forget Paris and Rome and Venice and Prague and Moscow and Iceland and New York too,' she laughed, happy to resurrect their memories and plans from happier times.

'And sporting events too,' Michael added, 'an FA Cup Final at Wembley, a U.S. baseball game in New York, an Australian Rules match at the MCG, a cricket match in India, an Olympics anywhere, ice hockey in Montreal. Not sure where we thought all the money would come from to see all of that though.'

'Yes, you do. We were going to work our way around the world and report on it all, write our own travel blog and get paid for reviews.'

'That's right, we were. How could I have forgotten that part. You the writer, me the photographer,' he said, becoming quiet and frowning.

They stayed silent for a few minutes, each deep in their thoughts. 'Well, why can't we still do that, Salsa? I know there's problems with travel, but the whole world isn't dead and there's still some big countries with lots of people. Surely, they will get things going again. I mean I don't know about Internet, but the world can't fail to find an alternative, not now they've used it so much. I mean, people will be crying out for that again. It's only a matter of time. Same with planes and travel. I mean, it'd be like losing the wheel, but knowing how much it advanced the world, so people would remake it again.'

'I'm not sure you can compare the wheel with Internet and global air travel and tourism, Michael.'

'Why not?'

'Because the stupid religious nuts would find a way to call such frivolous activity blasphemy or such like. Then, anyone calling out for that stuff would be locked up, or worse,' Salsa said with some anger.

'Mum will help stop that.'

'Mum? What are you talking about?'

'You heard her the other day when they had that meeting. She's going to get elected, and the other moderates, and then things will get better; back to normal, in some ways at least. But she and Jeffery and the MPs, they'll get us back on track to a normal kind of world, you'll see.'

'You're an optimist, Michael; always have been. But I hope you're right. I can't go on living like this. I feel like I'm drowning at times.'

'Keep our dreams alive, Sis. We must.'

HARRY

He fiddled with knobs and dials and all he could hear was static. This isn't good. Something bad is happening between Iran and the Saudis; must be. No radio traffic out there for almost a week now. Why? Is this how it was in the pre-electronic age? Waiting for a physical messenger to ride in with news of far-off wars and strife? And how was that verified back then anyway, I wonder. Maybe there was less suspicion of subterfuge. He chuckled then. Idiot, Harry, there was more bloody political crap going on between royal houses and dynasties back then than in this century or the last. No, there's summat wrong out there, my lad. I'd bet my house on it. One or t'other of those power brokers has done something dramatic; maybe both. If there was a clear victor, then that'd be the one crowing about it. So, it must be a stalemate. Maybe like the Iraq-Iran wars and they've fought themselves to a standstill and no-one is game to declare victory yet.

Riaz walked into the room and Harry filled him in on his thoughts.

'So, what if Iran did make a nuclear bomb. Would they use it against the Caliphate? That would be almost suicidal, surely. The rest of the world would ostracise them if they destroyed Mecca.'

Harry shook his head, 'Wouldn't need to be Mecca, just Riyadh. That would make a serious statement and shake the old Saudis completely.'

'Maybe so, but the Saudis had a much better air force, more modern American planes and better training too. They'd surely inflict massive damage on Tehran in retaliation?'

'That's what I'm suggesting, Riaz, and that's maybe the reason for the radio silence; too much damage to both sides.'

'You could be right, Harry. What are you going to do?'

'I'm going to keep hunting for other radio operators and see if there's any real news out there. I'll let you know if I hear anything. Might try Pakistan, although not sure if they'd have had many Ham enthusiasts,' he chuckled. It took Riaz a while to understand the pork joke.

Three and a half hours later, after declining anything to eat, but accepting some toasted cheese sandwiches from Mina, Harry did find a new contact from Pakistan, although he called his country Pakindesh and had to explain what the amalgamation of the three countries was all about.

'So, what have you been able to confirm about the conflict, Imran?' Harry asked, using plain speech as his new source seemed to prefer talking that way, although from time to time the lack of saying 'over' did contribute to saying things again and trying not to speak simultaneously.

'It is hard to say, because most people here are on the side of the Caliphate, even though the old Saudi regime was less than friendly to guest workers from here. So, I don't believe that the reports of a big Caliphate victory over the Iranian Shiites is necessarily true. But neither is an Iranian destruction of Riyadh. I am an educated man, Harry, and before Infidel's End there was no way that Iran was powerful enough to take on the Saudi Air Force. If it was a ground conflict then, yes, the Iranians would be stronger in numbers, if not in weapons, and probably more fanatical. But then again, the old days of unflinching belief in their Ayatollah and walking into Iraqi machine gun fire with a plastic key around your neck to enter paradise would be completely stupid and a reason to overthrow the current regime. Iran is a young person's country, and its government was close to economic collapse before the world changed. They have a bigger population but minimal reasons to fight, unless seriously threatened.'

'But that's the point isn't it, Imran? I mean the Caliphate seemed to be trying to get a decisive victory against the Shiite minority in the world, or so I was led to believe. Wouldn't that be enough to cause Iran to fight for their survival?'

'Only if the Caliphate could achieve that, maybe. My impression, for what it is worth, is that the world is still coming to terms with all of us being saved by Allah, no matter our sect. So, if Allah has spared not just the Sunnis and Shiites, but also the Ahmadis, Alawites, Mutazilites, Ajlafs, and Arzals, Takfiris, Wahhabis, and Sunni Madhabs, and maybe even the Druze, then any threat to Shiites would be lower down the list of conflicts.'

Harry considered the argument, although deciding not to show his ignorance of nearly all the minor sects that Imran named. 'I understand your point, but perhaps the Caliphate wanted to strike first against its main rival for Middle East control?'

'Perhaps, Harry. Anyway, the point is that I think we can accept that some major air battle occurred between them, and the outcome remains uncertain.'

'Of course, Imran. So, is this sort of thing creating conflict in… Pakindesh, now?'

'No, it isn't. I don't know how to describe it to you, but the greater level of interest has been in the mass migration to America.'

'What? What are you talking about?'

There was a laugh over the airwave, then Imran coughed and seemed to catch his breath. 'I apologise, Harry. Of course, I forget that news is hard to come by in Europe now. That alone seems strange to me. I don't know how best to describe this, but I'll try, and as briefly as possible. After Revelation Day, and the amalgamation of our 3 countries on the Sub-continent, there was a plan put forward by the President of India, Sabal Kalil, endorsed by the President of Pakistan, Ghulam Asif, and a proxy President in Bangladesh, in the days when they decided to share power, for Pakindesh to send a major naval contingent to America to repopulate it, on the assumption that its surviving population would be less than 5 million people. Contact was made with the surviving Americans and its government, which had moved to Florida to survive the Winter. Since then, there has been an ongoing migration of skilled people from here to America, and the estimate is that there are now about 2 million of our people living there, with more arriving each month, mainly by air now.' He paused for this news to sink in. Harry wasted no time.

'So, are you saying that the U.S. is now part of Pakindesh?'

'Not quite, Harry, but I suppose in a way, it is. The American President, whose name I forget, is still the Head of State, but I suppose President Kalil wields the power. It is an amalgamation of interests. That is how Kalil described it, and he is over there and working with the Americans to get things working again. That is how the news has been relayed here, anyway.'

'Bloody hell! This is hard to get my head around, Imran. Look, I need to process all of this. Can I please keep in touch with you?'

'Of course. It would be my pleasure, Harry. Next time I will be asking more questions about Britain, but for now I will sign off. I am always listening about this time, but not on Wednesdays or Fridays. I bid you a good evening over there. Salaam.'

The radio went silent. Harry sat stunned, no longer too interested in the Middle East. America being repopulated by Pakistani, Indian and Bangladeshi skilled migrants in their millions! How bold a move was that? This Kalil bloke must be a visionary. Damn, what was the Paki President called? Bugger, I need to tape these conversations, or at least take notes. Daft idiot, Harry. Wake up. You're the eyes and ears of the UK now. Who'd have thought it?

ASIF

The last encrypted message from Kalil was satisfying, for several reasons. Firstly, he now doubted that his co-President would ever return to Pakindesh. That suited him very well, and had always been the plan, for both men. No need for internal political conflict now. He would rule Pakindesh and Kalil could take over the new virgin America, in a time and method of his choosing. Second, Pakindesh was now in a very strong position to take, grow and keep control of North America, which would lead them to global supremacy, rather than have Indonesia expand in that direction. And third, not that it was currently necessary, but the Greater Pakindesh influence would have access to all of America's military hardware. It would no doubt be decades before the true treasures of the American continent could be utilised, but that was fine, there was no hurry. This was a relatively peaceful world now, apart from whatever was happening between Iran and the Caliphate, and if Allah decided that mutual destruction of those two nations that were defying the new World Peace was justified, well that was for Him in his infinite wisdom to arrange: In Sha' Allah.

So, what to make of Pereira's coded message. Surely, Kalil would assume that Pereira was communicating with him; I would. I don't fully trust the Admiral, no matter what his background, Pakistani or otherwise. He's too clearly ambitious, and he likes to think of himself as the most accomplished Naval commander left alive now. Hah, maybe he is. But that doesn't make him astute; he's too arrogant for deep analysis. He's no match for Kalil, and he probably knows it, although fools himself that because he's Navy and Kalil was Army, that the need for Naval supremacy in the new world trumps all. He's a fool, but a useful one. No, what Pereira fails to understand is that whilst I like to get information from him, to expand on what Kalil tells me, he has missed the key point in our Co-Presidential arrangement. He thinks I am playing politics. He thinks that I might wish to one day remove Kalil. He's so wrong. Sabal Kalil is the closest I have now, or at any time, to a true friend whose judgement and ideas I respect and admire. He will do what I could not, and it will all be to the benefit of Pakindesh, here and in the Americas.

So, Pereira thinks that Kalil has befriended President Habbib and that this could cloud his judgement and allow the Americans to rise again and maintain control. A foolish conclusion. Does he think nothing of the population numbers? Whoever remains theoretically in power is unimportant, especially in these new expansionist times. Kalil's intellect and vision is so far beyond Pereira's as to be indecipherable to him. He chuckled and smiled. Ah, Sabal, my friend. You have given me a jewel beyond price, and yet, one day, yours will be so much the greater. History will speak of your vision. I might get a footnote. And a footnote granted to me by you. Still, you have a few challenges to overcome, and I look forward to reading the biased views provided to me about you. It is like a good novel, where one craves the twists and turns, yet remains allied to the hero of the story, wanting him to succeed. I never would have thought I'd be happy to be subordinate to another man's intellect, and not be intimidated by him.

Now, let me look at Kalil's new logistical demands. He wants thirty commercial pilots that are Boeing 737 qualified, to expand regular air routes to the West coast, another 50 general surgeons, 4 heart specialists, and another hundred nurses, 200 high school teachers, 100 high-level computer programmers to assist with Internet database recovery, 20 commercial helicopter pilots, enough crew to man 10 commercial deep sea fishing trawlers, and he wants these people sent out on the next available flights, or as soon as possible. Plus, some textbooks comparing Parliamentary democracy with the workings of the U.S. Constitution, and peer reviewed arguments comparing democracies and republics, and any analysis of the Swiss Canton referenda system. Hmm, that last one was going to be hard to find in the New Delhi general library. So, what are you looking to boost your knowledge on with these tomes, my friend? Attempting to make a hybrid of the U.S. system and ours? Maybe you need to get some Americans on side first. I wonder.

There was a short knock on the door and one of Asif's staff walked in with some pages in his hand. He was agitated.

'What is it, Sanghamita?'

'Sir, we now have some anecdotal evidence of the conflict in the Middle East, which has been cross-referenced with 3 sources.'

'Yes? What do they concur on?'

'It is possible that Riyadh has been destroyed by a small nuclear bomb. Retaliation against Tehran probably did occur, and the entire Caliphate Air Force was involved. Some sources are saying that it was like a suicide mission, with major damage inflicted and at least a hundred thousand casualties. Those facts seem credible and supported by radio traffic and mobile phone discussions as it was being played out. There is also some speculative commentary, but...'

'Just say it!'

'It is possible that Mecca was targeted too.'

'Good God! Call out all military units to maintain peace. And get me General Samara, immediately.'

'Yes, Mr President.'

HABBIB

'Miss Malaki, it's been a while since I saw you. What have you been up to?'

'Yes, Mr President; I've been to Charlotte, Sir. The new immigrant arrival program is going well.'

'So I hear. There looks to have been excellent logistics cooperation and good working relationships evolving.'

'Yes, Sir, and from what I saw, the immigrants were very happy. No complaints about waiting in lines to be allocated rations or accommodation or jobs or anything. I spoke to as many people as possible. I was surprised how good most people's English was, but maybe that was part of the initiation process for them?'

'Possibly, although I'd be surprised if the rural migrants spoke English.'

'Maybe not, Sir; I didn't get a chance to interact with them. But the more technical people were quite open, and thrilled to be off the ships, which is understandable, I suppose.'

'Did you experience anything, or hear anything, that should be worrying to me?'

'Uh, no, Sir, nothing that comes to mind, although I wasn't really thinking along those lines. Is there anything specific that you'd like me to... well, investigate?'

'No, no, nothing. But occasionally it's those snippets of conversation, overheard by chance, that provide different insights into what I'd call the 'official line'. It is always hard to get the truth, unadulterated, from advisors and aides. It's like they think that unfiltered analysis shouldn't be presented in case I would be annoyed by it. Yet, clearly, it's the exact opposite. I need the ugly truth, as they say, warts and all.'

Malaki giggled. 'Sorry, Sir, I was just remembering that comedy, The Ugly Truth, with Katherine Heigl and Gerard Butler. Did you ever see it?'

'I don't think so, no.'

'It was very funny. Oh!' she said suddenly, stifling a sob, a tear forming and then falling down her cheek.

'Are you OK, Badiah? What's upsetting you, so suddenly?'

She took a while to compose herself, then sighed heavily. 'I'm so sorry, Mr President. It was just... well... you know... one of those nostalgia thoughts. That there won't be any more of those films made, or that kind of funny irreverence, or...'

'I understand, Badiah, truly, and it's quite alright. I feel the same way, truly. I too miss the old days of movies and sport, and Internet, and normality.'

'But that's what keeps worrying me, Sir, the feeling that by missing those things, that we're being... blasphemous, perhaps?'

'I honestly do not believe that Allah would take such human feelings of loss, for family, friends and everyday pastimes that were innocent, as an afront to Him or this new world He has delivered to us.'

Once more, Badiah started to shake and put her face in her hands, seemingly inconsolable. Habbib put his arms around her shoulders to comfort her and held her until she recovered. Then there was an embarrassed moment between them.

'Thank you, Mr President. I'm sorry to have lost it then. I didn't mean to... well...'

'It's fine, Badiah. Maybe you should go on home and relax for the rest of the afternoon. We can continue the interview later.'

'Thank you, Sir. I will, if that's OK,' she agreed, and made her way out of the office and the building. Once on her way back to her apartment, and unobserved, she smiled. Now he's calling me Badiah. That's a step in the right direction. And his arms felt wonderful around me too. Good progress today, I think.

MICHAEL

What will I do if Salsa goes away to see the world? Is it safe? Will it be OK? Can I lose her? No, I can't. So, I need to be useful to her, as well as to protect her. We are one person. People that aren't twins don't understand our bond. She's so determined, but so stubborn too. If she goes off alone, she's going to get into trouble, I know it. She doesn't recognise danger; never has. Like that time that she was confronted by those two dickheads on the way back from school a few years ago. I mean, knowing some Krav Maga self-defence skills is one thing, but kicking them both in the balls and kneeing one in the face was a bit extreme. And what was her thinking? That there was "A Clear and Present Danger", as Tom Clancy wrote, whose books she loved, unlike most girls, and that one must strike first against an external threat before you lose the initiative. What a gutsy and scary woman my sister can be. That's another reason that I love her, and why I need to be with her, wherever she goes.

HARRY

Harry was deep in thought. This isn't good, the Iran Saudi shit fight. If Iran wins it might make retribution worse if there's a Sunni versus Shia global civil war. Surely Allah won't allow that to happen. We are all chosen, so rivalry like that is stupid, always has been. Would He allow his subjects to fight each other, after creating a single Islamic world? Surely not?

AMELIA

'John,' she called across the room.

'Yep?'

'Are you worried about the immigrants now?'

'Not the immigrants, no. Why?'

'Well, it all seems to be working so well. I mean, we might have regular air travel again soon, and possibly even the Internet, and a resurrection of other technology. But I still have this nagging doubt in my mind, that we're being played. And I don't know why because I do trust President Kalil. I mean, I know that he's effectively taking over, yet I don't see that as being all bad. Am I crazy, to think like that?'

Cummins smiled, rubbed his chin, and contemplated his answer, knowing the kind of things that worried her, yet needing to be completely honest too. 'Part of me sees this as a classic invasion by a force that wishes to be seen as benevolent. Another is that we're being played and maybe we'll be eliminated once Pakindesh takes full control. And yet, I don't really believe any of that. So, am I a fool, or have I read Kalil correctly, that his grand vision for the Americas is driving him and that we remaining Americans can be useful in his ambitions? I don't know.'

'But what does your gut say?'

'That we ride Kalil's coat tails and enjoy it, and especially the more rapid return to the 21st century technology we took for granted.'

'Me too. Are we being disrespectful, or traitors to just go along with Pakindesh taking over though?'

'Amelia let's be honest here. The United States ceased to exist when we were left with under 5 million people, no modern technology, no self-defence capacity, and limited useful remaining skills. Moving down to Florida and escaping a freezing winter was a major achievement, but what were we going to do next?'

'Sure, I agree with all of that. But, as a military man, surely you must feel... emasculated?'

He laughed, long and loudly. 'Sorry, I don't know why that made me laugh, but it felt good, nonetheless. Look, my darling, jumping from a Major to a General in a few months was the most rapid rise in achievement I've ever had, no matter that it was all bullshit and just one of those last man standing quirks of fate. Do I feel like my military position will be ignored? Sure, I guess so, in time. Do I care about that? No, I don't. In this new world I truly hope that the old military conflicts are just things to discuss in school history subjects. I don't expect to have to fight again or kill people for political reasons that I might not agree with. I am fully looking forward to building a new and better world, more equal, more supportive of the poor, and without so many of our old prejudices. In short, I welcome Kalil's vision and hope to be able to assist the new regime in whatever way I can.'

'You have no idea how happy that makes me feel. One more question?'

'What?'

'Are you looking forward to being a father this year?'

TEN YEARS LATER

SYDNEY, AUSTRALIA

Intan Probowo looked out across the sea from the balcony of their Potts Point apartment, and called to her husband to join her, 'Ahmad, come and look with me?'

He smiled but was also slightly irritated. 'It's the same view every day, Intan. Beautiful on a sunny day like this, yes, but the same.'

'How can you say that? It has a life of its own, this sea, powerful one day, calm the next. Blue, then green, and so deserted most of the time. Our sea back in Jakarta was not like this.'

'We were nowhere near the sea there. It took hours to get to a decent beach then, and we only saw it at street level.'

'Exactly, my love. That's what I really mean. Who would have thought, five years ago, that we would live here, up so high, so close to the water, so fortunate, wealthy even? Allah be praised.'

'Indeed; Allah be praised. God is great. He has delivered the world to the faithful.'

Intan suddenly shivered and rubbed her arms.

'Are you cold, darling?'

'No. Not that. Just that feeling again.'

Ahmad smiled, humourlessly. 'Your ghosts again?' he joked.

'Yes, sort of. I feel their presence sometimes, as you know; the people that used to live here before... before...'

'I know. But they didn't suffer. I know it. Allah was merciful. He removed the infidels without harm. The stories told by the surviving Muslim Australians are all good ones too, with almost a million of them surviving well, before we moved here too. If that wasn't the case, we would feel a malevolent spirit here. Isn't that what you've always said?

'Yes, I believe that. But it is still sad. So many people gone, without a chance to convert to Islam and live.'

'There were many chances, Intan; we've discussed this before.'

'I know we have, but I don't believe that. I wish that Allah had made his presence felt beforehand, to allow the infidels to know His power, and what was coming. Don't you, Ahmad?'

'I don't know. Here we are, with all of this. How could that have happened if Revelation Day had occurred differently?'

'I don't know. I just hope that we are not inflaming the dead of this place by being here, that's all.'

'We are not. Put that out of your mind, please. You must, Intan. This privilege was offered to us because of our work for the government. When the President decided to move the capital to Sydney, you said you wanted to be a part of that migration. Remember?'

'Of course, and I'm glad we did that and came here. It's been better for the children, everything… apart from the cold winters. So different in every way, but so special too. Those Australians were very lucky, but more so the survivors I suppose.'

'Some say those that were removed were selfish. So much land and resources for so few people. No wonder they were wealthy!' Ahmad scoffed.

'Not all of them. You've seen the old run-down houses too.'

'Ha! Intan, their poor were still millionaires compared to our poor. Is that not true?'

Changing the subject, she asked, 'Do you still think it was stupid of the President to move the capital from Jakarta to Sydney?'

'Maybe,' Ahmad considered. 'The plan was to move the capital anyway, to Borneo, but we needed to move people north and south, I suppose, to spread out and make use of the new bountiful resources of land, housing, farming and fishing, mining and space. And all these coastal cities and towns are now alive again, with wealth and an easier life for everyone. We have fifty million people living in Australia now, and more coming, all with a better lifestyle than they had in Java and Sumatra. It made sense to come here for the resources. But to move the capital here? That I am not so sure about. But I do like our own life here.'

'Me too. Is it wrong to pray for the souls of the infidels, Ahmad?'

'No, Intan. Of course not. It is compassionate, and you are a very compassionate woman, which is one of the things I love about you.

SALINA

Michael was sitting in a café on Avenue Atlantica, looking at Copacabana Beach across the road, wondering at how Rio de Janeiro would have looked before almost the entire population was from Pakindesh. The sunlight was invigorating, warming his soul, with the breeze cleansing his lungs, strengthening him. The sea was slightly choppy, whitecaps dancing, the odd seabird diving for something unseen. Every time he arrived in a new place, especially one as iconic as Brazil, he couldn't help but mourn for the loss of an entire race of people, who he so fervently wished he could have met, experienced, laughed with, danced with, cried with. He sighed deeply, once more silently castigating Allah.

His mind retracted to the business at hand. The coffee wasn't great. Not bad, but certainly not of European standard. He admitted that he was a bit of a coffee snob, a love that he first adopted in Istanbul years before, not for the strong Turkish coffees but the milder blends, and without sugar, plus a dash of milk. Later he learned that these were closer to resembling the long macchiato, of the Italians. He looked around for his sister. She was late. He read the eNews on his tablet as he waited, and listened in to the conversations nearby, almost all of them in English, with what was now recognised as a SAMPAK lilt, for South American Pakindesh; not to be confused with their North American cousins' NAMPAK accent and its slightly different cadence.

The table behind him was discussing something that was creating an argument.

'She's a bitch, no respect for the President and all he's done here,' a middle-aged female said.

'How can you say that when she's not even had an interview yet? How do you know that she'll be disrespectful? She's just as likely to be charmed by Kalil, as all others are,' a male suggested, with a slight chuckle.

'Did you see that interview she did with the French President a year ago?' a different female asked.

'Exactly, yes,' the first female said, 'she made out that he was a dictator, just because their government was delaying elections.'

'Well, she was right, wasn't she?' another male said. 'And her opinion caused the French to bring forward the election and the President was ousted. So, she brought down a potential dictator by force of argument and debating skill. Isn't that what we want from an investigative journalist?'

'I don't care about that. If she disrespects President Kalil, she'll have me to deal with,' boasted the first female.

'Ha! And just how are you going to do that, dear sister?' asked male two.

Michael smiled, wanting to join in, but enjoying the banter, and not at all surprised that it was the men that supported his sister and the women that didn't, until they met her, usually. Jealousy? Or deep-seated female subjugation to the role of a male leader? Would the slight dominance of men in political positions remain, apart from the half dozen women that had broken through that barrier? He looked at his tablet and saw that the time was getting on. Should he divert Salsa to another meeting place, away from the opinionated women behind him, or watch how things unfold when she gets here? She's a big girl, and supremely talented in debates. Let's see how this goes down, he decided, smiling.

A few minutes later he saw her getting out of a driverless electric taxi. She was as elegant as usual, dressed in an A-line grey skirt, sandals, and a pale aqua blouse with three quarter sleeves and a V-neck. Her favourite shoulder bag swung by her left side, and she adjusted her sunglasses, pushing them back onto her forehead, confirming his location as she crossed the almost empty road.

'Sorry I'm late, Michael.'

'No problem, Salsa,' he said, rising and kissing her cheek. 'What time are we doing Kalil?'

'Three, at the Palace.'

Michael tapped the table with his index finger twice and winked, then pointed his thumb in the direction of the table behind him, but out of their sight, and then put 2 fingers up followed by a thumbs up sign, then 2 fingers down, followed by a thumbs down sign. Salsa knew the signal – table behind had discussed her, 2 in favour, men, 2 detractors, women. Game on!

She wasted no time, interrupting the table behind her brother, smiling broadly. 'Excuse me,' she said to them, 'I'm sorry to interrupt you. I'm Salsa Ahmed and I'm lucky enough to have been granted an interview with your President this afternoon. I just wondered if you'd be kind enough to tell me what you think of him? I always like to gain some local views before I meet a Head of State, to see what local people think of him, so that I can ask him some questions that you might like presented. Would you be interested in talking to me?'

Michael smiled, having watched this tactic many times. His sister was a charmer, and psychologically brilliant, as well as having a superb memory for facts, figures, names, and quotes. He knew that she'd win the two females across within ten minutes and have them all eating out of her hand before he could consume another coffee.

An hour later they were walking on Ipanema Beach, carrying their shoes, enjoying the feel of the sand, watching people playing ball games, swimming, laughing, and joking. There were very few women wearing Hijabs or scarves. Bikinis and board shorts were common. Brother and sister linked arms as they walked.

'I wasn't really listening to your chat with the fixated four, Salsa. Assume you turned the sisterhood around, and had the men worshipping you, as usual?'

She slapped his chest with her free arm, in jest, 'You bugger, Mike. Making fun of my communication skills. You make it out to be a trick, rather than my use of logic to educate the masses as I travel around,' she laughed.

'So why did the chicks not like your style, or did they hide their previous comments?'

'No, they actually admitted that they didn't like how I'd spoken to President Yusuf Bertrand and believed that I had accused him of being a dictator. I explained that I liked the man but was worried that his slide into becoming a potential dictator by interfering with the electoral cycle would be worse for France, and that he should trust the people to make the right decisions in these things, or we would sink back into the terrible times before Revelation Day, and that we were all better than that now. I told them that he was grateful for the wakeup call and that we communicated regularly, and are friends, despite him losing the election.

'What a charmer you are, Sis,' he laughed.

'Enough of that. What's the plan for later?'

'Usual stuff. I'll film him manually, with another unit on a tripod from the other side and set up the third camera on you.'

'Inside or outside?'

'Depends. If we have a quiet outside option that adds to the visual impact, I'll take it.'

'Sounds good, as long as we don't have noisy birds like that time in Nigeria last year.'

'Oh hell, don't jinx me, that was bloody awful; almost ruined the whole interview. We were lucky that the Nigerian Opposition Leader had a sense of humour, and the time to redo it all,' Michael said with a smile.

'Well, it was in his interest of course,' Salsa reminded him.

'True, and it turned the tables on the incumbent too, so you made another lifelong friend.'

'I'm not manipulative, am I, Mikey. I mean, you'd tell me if you thought I was being… less than fair, wouldn't you?'

'You know I would. Even if it caused us to argue, again. I'm your sounding board, always, and I'll keep you in line if you drift off the goal of honest reporting. We agreed to that before we started doing all of this didn't, we?'

'Yes…' He waited for her pause to expire as she thought through things, familiar with her moods. 'Thank you. I couldn't do this without you.'

'Yes, you could. Cameramen are easy to get.'

'You're more than a guy behind a lens, Michael, you know that. If we didn't debate all the interviews ahead of time, and decide where we're going next, or how and when to upload them to IslamNet, we wouldn't be this successful. We're a team, always.'

He nodded, thinking. She picked up on his sudden mood change too, another twin thing. 'What is it, Bro?'

'Just thinking of the future…'

'Not the kids and romance thing again! Oh, Mike, we're only 25, there's loads of time for all of that, and…'

'I know. It's… nothing, don't worry.'

'Fed up with casual sex with myriad female admirers?' she laughed.

'No… never that,' he laughed. 'I'm just tired, Salina.'

She glanced at his face, always worried when he reverted to her full name. She knew this was coming, although she couldn't remember when she first realised his growing homesickness. 'There's only one more interview scheduled after here. Then we can go home. OK?'

'Sure. Thanks.' He glanced across at a couple, hand in hand, who, years ago, he'd have described as Indian, or Pakistani, but now were Pakindeshi, the world's most prolific ethnic group, its dominant socio-economic population, most scientifically and socially advanced, and most open and inclusive. So far removed from their heritage pre-

Revelation. Do they realise how much of their fortunate life is due to the foresight of Sabal Kalil? And Ghulam Asif too of course.

She interrupted his thinking. 'Do you miss England, Michael?'

Did he? And if so, what bits of it? 'I s'pose; some things. Mum and Dad of course, and Riaz. The changing seasons. London sights, even though we didn't really grow up there. But then in other ways I hate it.' He sighed deeply, not wanting to remember.

'Do you still hate God?'

They'd had this conversation many times, but it always returned. Salsa was less critical than him, less discriminatory, more forgiving. She had become more glass half full, whilst he'd seen his glass half empty at best, diminished by what had been lost to the world. 'It's not that I hate Him, Salsa. I mourn not only for what was lost, the good and the bad, but that so many people over time will never know how the world really was, and that the new history being taught is skewed, false. If we lose the honesty about the way the world was, then we... I can't explain it. You do understand, don't you?'

She leant up and kissed his cheek. 'I do, totally,' she said.

'Prove it. Put it into words, Miss Interviewer,' he challenged, half-heartedly but seriously wanting her perspective.

'Hmm, OK.' How to appease her brother, acknowledge his grief, yet raise his spirits. She did understand him, but she'd evolved a little more, maybe because she'd found a niche that fulfilled her, more than it did him. 'Michael, there are multiple facets to trying to explain the pre-Revelation world to those that were too young to have experienced the wonderful things we had. It's like trying to create the euphoria of 67,000 people at a mid-week Manchester United European Cup match at Old Trafford against Barcelona and winning it 3-Nil. Or experiencing an Ed Shearon concert, which was the highlight of my teenage life. The loss of the man and his talent, such a good man too, gone for eternity just because he didn't believe in the same God as our ethnic group, yet knowing that we were equally disbelievers as well, or at least non-practicing, and yet we were spared. It's all our non-Islamic friends, doomed despite their goodness; people who were just trying to get by, love their kids, have a laugh, kick a ball around, go to a movie, hope for a better world too. So yes, I do understand, because I agree and equally mourn with you for those things that have gone, Michael. I do, truly. But we are here, now, in Brazil, and -'

'South American Pakindesh,' he interrupted.

'Whatever... we are here, together, about to interview one of the world's most influential leaders, and we'll be watched by hundreds of millions of people. And then we'll fly to Washington, and then London, and go home in style. Would that have happened in the old world?'

'No, it wouldn't, probably, but...'

'No buts, Michael. Mourning the past is OK, and valid. But mourning the future is a cop out and disingenuous, and you know it. Honesty of reflection cuts both ways.'

He wanted to argue more, but he knew she was right. He needed to accept that his nostalgic grief was skewed, and that was as bad as the rewriting of history by so-called Islamic scholars, fixated with portraying the world in a way that was not truthful. All of that was what his sister was fighting, in a way, although never her intent. She focussed the spotlight on truth and was possibly one of the more valuable influencers of thought, and especially female emancipation, still lagging in the world. It was time to move on and help her. 'Salsa... you're right. I'm OK. Let's nail this interview.'

They booked a driverless cab and set the destination for the Presidential Palace. Like most visitors, they'd also been to Corcovado, and to Sugarloaf by cable car, but now it was time to work. The drive was short, and like most cities around the world, traffic was minimal, exceeded by self-navigating electric-assisted pushbikes and scooters. As they approached the Palace gates Michael enjoyed the lack of any heavy contingent of guards. There were two men on the gate, who watched them as they exited the car, retrieved two sports bags from the boot and then walked towards them. They were clearly expected and were not even asked to walk through a metal detector or be patted down; a simple ID check was enough. The building façade had a resemblance to the White House in Washington DC, apart from the lack of a lawn area, and had probably been a Consulate for a past wealthy nation. A golf buggy was waiting on the other side of the gate, and they were assisted with the small camera bags, then sat in the rear and enjoyed the light breeze on the way to the house.

'President Kalil is in the garden so we will take you directly there,' the senior guard said.

The side of the house was covered in ivy-like plants on one side and a magnificent yellow Banksia climbing rose opposite, before the foliage became more tropical and dominated by palm-like bushes and trees. When the buggy stopped, a young woman with a tray of cool drinks stepped towards them, smiling. 'Would you care for a cool drink?'

'Thank you, I would,' Salsa said.

'There is fresh lemon and lime, sparkling mineral water, or orange juice?'

'A lemon and lime would be lovely,' Salsa said, accepting a tall glass.

'Me too, thank you,' Michael agreed, shifting the weight of one of the sports bags on his shoulder, which prompted another staff member to help, who took the bags from him.

They were escorted further into the walled garden and towards a gazebo and asked to wait, as the President would only be a few minutes. Then they were left alone.

Sabal Kalil was one of the most recognisable men in the world, revered by many, adored by more, and known to be able to charm almost anyone, with his intellect, manners, cogent arguments, and obvious achievements, all done without any need for bloodshed or wars or heavy policing. As he approached his guests, they both stood, automatically. Salsa had told herself not to be intimidated or charmed into giving him an easy time. She had her reputation to consider. But he was attractive and charismatic, and she needed to get inside the man behind the charm offensive.

Pleasantries aside, they all sat, Kalil first, and Michael explained that he needed to set up two fixed cameras, but that when the interview began, he would move around to get close ups, and hoped that this would be OK. It was.

As he worked with tripod set-ups, Kalil took the initiative. 'How have you enjoyed Brazil, Salina?' She must have looked surprised, so he added, 'We do still use the historic names for each country area, which have been set up as administrative boundaries you know?'

'Yes, I did, actually,' she recovered. 'But somehow I expected you to welcome me to South American Pakindesh, rather than Brazil, Mr President.'

'One of my greatest mistakes I still think, was to call the continent North and South American Pakindesh,' he laughed. 'What the hell was I thinking? I think it might have been because of the debate with my staff about where we would set up the official capital in the south, and there were arguments about Argentina versus Brazil versus Chile etc. So, we nicknamed the continents NAP and SAP. If I'd been into alcohol, I could have claimed that I was drunk at the time. Unfortunately, those awful long-winded names stuck and now we have the interminable debate about what to change them to.'

'That's quite funny, Mr President. Perhaps we could replay that exchange? I didn't get it recorded,' Michael said.

'No!' both Kalil and Salina said, each laughing.

'OK then,' Michael acquiesced. 'We're rolling.'

'What, no make up for me?' Kalil joked. 'Must I look this old?'

'Hardly that, sir,' Salina replied. Kalil smiled.

'Firstly, thank you very much for the privilege of this interview, Mr President...'

Kalil interrupted, 'Why don't we shorten the formalities? Much easier if you call me Sabal, and I'll call you Salina, or do you prefer Salsa?'

'Oh! Either is OK with me, Mr... Sabal, I mean,' she stammered.

'Good. Go ahead, Salsa.'

She recovered her composure quickly and went back to her planned questions. 'Is it true that when you first came to Rio, you made it a priority to protect Corcovado's Christ the Redeemer Statue, and if so, why?' 'A good question, Salsa.' Kalil acknowledged. 'Because it has historical and aesthetic importance. It was an icon of Brazil's past, eventually classified as one of the modern wonders of the world. It deserved to be preserved. And it had interesting cooperative ingenuity too; a French sculptor, built by a Brazilian engineer, in collaboration with a French engineer, and the face sculpted by a Romanian, so, a very multicultural enterprise. But what I find most interesting is that that the engineer, Heitor Levy, was Jewish, but he almost fell to his death when working on it, and after the accident he converted to Catholicism, believing that Christ saved him. Levy even wrote the names of his family members on a scroll and kept it inside the interior part of the heart of the statue. Catholics said that the conversion of the engineer was a literal example of one of the promises of the Sacred Heart, that people who spread that devotion would have their name inscribed forever in Christ's heart. Now, clearly, I take this as an incorrect belief, but that does not diminish from its historical, and allegorical message, which is that there is a divine being watching over us. Who that divine being is, we have now settled, Allah be praised. But we should not denigrate truly devout behaviour and adherence to our creator.'

'Nothing like that statue or other feats of human endeavour, engineering and reverence should ever be destroyed. All of humanity is enhanced by such examples of human evolution.'

'But you were criticised in many Islamic clerical quarters for that. Why do you think those that opposed you are so afraid of the symbolism?'

'Because those clerics were, and some remain, uneducated religious Luddites. To be afraid of historical truths, and especially pre-Islamic history and archaeology, is like denying humanity's evolution from East African hunter-gatherer tribes to migrations north and east, and human progress from stone age to iron age and all other great leaps forward. To consider destroying Corcovado's statue would be no different to destruction of the pyramids of Egypt or the Greek Parthenon; totally irrational, and criminal. What would be next?'

'But there has been great destruction of cathedrals, synagogues, Hindu and Buddhist shrines and other non-Islamic history. So, are you fighting a losing battle in this area?'

'No, I don't believe so. There have been minimal destructive practices across the Americas, and across Pakindesh too, compared to the Middle East and in parts of Asia. Those initial losses of historic buildings were stopped quite quickly once post-Revelation Day calmness prevailed. Luckily, the world was assisted by a great number of rational and educated people, who saw the idiocy of actions to remove historical evidence of other religions. But it still saddens me that there are people with such little education or foresight who, nevertheless, hold some positions of power. Hopefully, they will be replaced soon.'

'Why did you choose Rio de Janeiro rather than say Buenos Aires, or Brasilia or Mexico City even, as the SAP capital?'

'Don't you find it beautiful here, Salsa?'

'Yes, I do. So, was that it, for beauty's sake?'

'In part it was, truly. But there were also practical considerations. As a physical location it was perfect for shipping and trade from Europe and Africa, both by sea and air. It also has an excellent climate, not as cold in the winter as BA, more rainfall than Lima and Santiago, coastal, so better than jungle cities like Brasilia or Bogota. Therefore, a healthy choice. I think President Habbib is envious of us too, freezing up there in Washington in the Winter, and boiling in the summer.'

'Is your friendship with President Habbib still close?'

'Extremely. Meeting Paul and becoming close friends and confidants early on was critical for what has become the most successful recolonization of anywhere.'

'Some people wonder about why you assisted the USA to recover, albeit with Pakindesh migrants, rather than just take it over. Some say that your romantic side took over and brought you down here earlier than might have been prudent?'

'I'm not clear about the actual question hidden in that, Salsa, but let me try to address it,' he said, putting up his hand as she tried to rephrase.

'I think on the journey to America I was formulating my longer-term plan before I even realised that this was happening in my subconscious. It is true that the initial plan was to populate the USA and get there before Indonesia or Malaysia, who I thought might have similar intentions back then. There was vast wealth in the Americas, and I do not mean the military hardware that so many people have used as a criticism for our migration, which they term an invasion. The USA was non-viable. Five million people with limited skills would have perished there quite quickly, or if not, then they would not have advanced or recovered sufficiently, and there are few of them who would argue with that. Paul and his team did a tremendous job of relocating to Florida, which perhaps saved them from freezing to death in their first winter. Pakindesh rescued the nation and brought them skillsets that they did not have, from farmers to nuclear power plant operators to health workers. I did not need, nor intend at the time, to take over as President of the U.S. That nation really ceased to exist except in history, but that fact needed to be discovered by themselves, before they could advance into what is now, I believe, a better nation, as North American Pakindesh, than was ever the case for the USA. It has a better Constitution, and lifestyle, as for all of the Commonwealth of Pakindesh Nations, with universal health care, no guns, no armed police, equality of the sexes, smaller government, free education to all levels of capability, and so many other benefits undreamt of in the old USA.'

'Perhaps, Sabal, but that too is a little disingenuous, don't you think? I mean, no matter who took over the USA, it was always going to be a better, richer, more pluralistic nation when sharing its vast wealth across its current 80 million people.'

'Partially true, Salsa. But in my place would you have rewritten the Constitution as Paul and I did, or accepted it as it was and tried to mimic what was a dead nation?'

Salsa looked at Sabal with surprise, realising that the question was genuine, and needed a response. He gave her time, and she used it. Almost 20 seconds later she said, 'No, I wouldn't have changed it, I would have rejected it, and installed a simplified Pakindesh Parliamentary Democracy, with all of its advantages, but denuded it of many of its bureaucratic and historically anachronistic hang-ups.'

Sabal laughed and clapped his hands. 'And perhaps that would have been better, perhaps. But Paul Habbib wouldn't have liked it done that way. My aim, and Paul's, once we'd become friends, was not to usurp the historical value and image of the pure American ideal, but to improve upon it and rid it of the baggage and inability to update its most outdated constitutional amendments that had dragged it down, along with its intransigent capitalist errors. And that, I believe we did, over the first 3 years. Do you agree?'

'Yes, actually I do agree. I think you pulled off one of history's finest political achievements post-Revelation Day, truly. Whether there was more good luck than good management isn't for me to say though.'

'Nor I, Salsa, nor I. We shall leave that to future historians I suppose. Shall we move this conversation on to other areas?'

'Good idea. Hmm. Were you surprised that Indonesia didn't come west and compete for the Americas?'

'Partly, but not completely. Remember, the world was left with one point seven billion people. There was more than enough of everything for all nations, without conflict...'

'I'll come back to conflict later,' Salsa interrupted.

He nodded, and continued, 'Indonesia's Government sat in the centre of a target-rich environment, as we used to say in the military. It had vast expanses of Asia to the north, the Philippines to the east, and Australia and New Zealand too. More than enough to tempt them. On the balance of probabilities, we were not going to be fought for the Americas.'

'Okay, but if that was your view, then why rush to populate South and Central America before the job was complete in the North?'

'You tell me; you're an intelligent analyst, why do you think I did that?'

Crafty bastard! But, oh so likeable. Be careful, Salina, don't lose your investigative traits to his charisma. 'There are two possibilities, overall, I think...'

'Which are?'

'One: you had become as curious and mesmerised as the old explorers, wanting to keep going into the new unknown, pushing the boundaries, before someone else beat you to it. Or, two: you had become comfortable that Paul Habbib would take the same path that you had intended for yourself, and so could leave the North in good hands, to follow your lead, safe in the knowledge that the risk of it coming undone was small, especially as the population would soon have a Pakindesh majority, and military control, if necessary. With that safely achieved and progressing, you were free to expand your plan, populate the Southern continent, and set yourself up in a virgin new world. You could become the new Conquistador explorer, but a peaceful one, without the need to subjugate any locals.'

Sabal clapped his hands, genuinely impressed. 'To an inquiring mind, the solution, or rationale, whatever you wish to call it, is obvious now. But perhaps I was not as understanding of my overall subconscious desires as simply as you just portrayed it. But yes, in effect that was the reasoning.'

'And has it been as satisfying as you'd expected?'

He nodded, 'Pretty much, yes,' he said with a genuine smile.

'So where to from here, Sabal? What is the next challenge for a man of your skills and vision?'

'Not where you might imagine, I think. I do not desire further... conquests of land or power. What I want, and you might laugh, or just not believe me, is to improve the lives for all of those living in the Americas, and to create as close a utopia as is humanly possible. We live in a world of suddenly immense wealth and resources. These can be exploited in the old-world ways, with old-world thinking and consequences, or in new-world altruistic, humanist ideals, without prejudice, war, poverty, and greed.'

'Isn't that a little simplistic and unrealistic?'

'Why?'

'I could simply say because of human failures and the unfortunate elements of selfish behaviour.'

'Or...'

'Or... because what you hope for is so far removed from human history as to be, maybe unobtainable, or... likely to lead to a benevolent dictatorship, followed by a non-benevolent dictatorship.'

Sabal frowned. 'Is your faith in humanity that low, Salsa?'

'I am only 25, Sabal. I have seen a lot of the world, in the past 5 years especially. I have seen the best and worst of post-Revelation Day changes. So, my expectations have been tempered by what I've seen, I suppose. For that I apologise, if my cynicism offends you, but I hope that your vision and actions continue to nurture the future and are then adopted by others. But maybe I can put this into a question rather than explain myself. What do you see as the major risks to your continued success?'

'You have a knack for deflecting the hard work to me. Your journalistic skills are impressive. You would have made a good field commander,' he laughed. 'So, let me see if I can live up to your probing mind. Some risks are easy to state, and fall into old-world practices, such as: one, a takeover by a rival who is less altruistic and just power hungry; two, profligacy taking over from hard work and sustainable ideals, so greed and laziness allowing us to fail to evolve, both socially and scientifically; three, a slide into fundamentalist or extremist thought, as happened in the Middle East initially; and four, the unknown.'

'What unknown?'

'If I knew then it wouldn't be unknown,' Sabal laughed again.

'No, seriously though, what unknown?'

'I am serious. It was long before your time, the best accidental explanation of unknowns, I think. Have you ever heard of Donald Rumsfeld, albeit before you were born?'

'Maybe. Remind me?'

'He was the Secretary of Defence in the US Government in the George W Bush Presidency in 2002. In answer to a question from a journalist about what the Government knew about Iraq and so-called weapons of mass destruction at the time of the second Gulf War, he paraphrased intelligence information into 3 categories, starting by saying that there were things that they knew they knew, and then there were things they knew they didn't know, but that there were also things that they didn't know they didn't know, and that human history could turn on the latter unknown unknowns. Some people thought he was crazy, but it was a very clever way to express the problems, and limitations, of military intelligence.

Whether he realised it was clever, or it was a fluke, I don't know, but it became an oft-quoted statement. So, in that vein, it is the something 'out of the blue' that I will probably never see coming that could destroy my dreams, Salsa.'

She blinked, not quite sure where to take this discussion next. He was mesmerising her and she wanted to break that spell and get into something harder hitting. 'Erm... not that it's likely, but if there was a military... clash, say with Indonesia perhaps, could you defend the Americas?'

The question clearly took him aback. He cupped his chin, rubbing it in thought, either mock or real, she wasn't sure which. 'It will never happen, so the question is rather foolish.'

Shit! 'Foolish because there is no need for conflict in our new world, or foolish because mankind has now evolved to a new enlightened position?'

He smiled. 'Both of those reasons, but especially the former. Why would any nation seek conquest of a far-flung region? What would be gained?'

Time to retreat. Bloody silly question: I should have known better. 'I agree, Sabal, but I needed to hear it said. I have been places where old fashioned war-like comments are still made, and whilst I see no evidence of that kind of paranoia here, I wondered whether your military background might have left you still planning for worst case scenarios, no matter how... absurd?'

'Yes, well, the Shia versus Sunni conflicts that saw decimation in Iran and The Caliphate do not trouble the world now, unless you think differently? You travelled to Iran last year, didn't you?'

'I did, yes. Although it was many years since the conflict between them, and each side still accuses the other of being the instigator, I was still shocked at the devastation. As you know, Tehran, Riyadh, and Mecca were effectively destroyed. I can understand the anger against Iran for destroying Mecca. But I could also understand why Iran felt the need to strike back after the air assault that laid waste to half of their capital, even though they destroyed Riyadh first. Who started it, or who should have known better... well, will we ever know? Let's face it, those two regimes had been prosecuting a proxy war against each other, through terrorist backing for decades. There was fault on both sides. The Caliphate was clearly seeking to dominate the new world, or unduly influence it perhaps. But maybe you have a different view? I was only a teenager when all of that happened.'

'No, your analysis is quite sound, Salsa. That event was a power play that had been brewing for decades, or centuries some would say. At least now there is no ongoing discrimination against the Shia, or other sects, by Sunnis. I have seen firsthand throughout Pakindesh how the sensible acceptance of each other has brought peace and prosperity. It was something I worried about for a time. Part of my delight in helping to create our new world throughout the Americas was to leave behind all of those petty discriminations.'

'That's interesting, Sabal. And it leads me to my last question. What do you see as the key challenges for the future, and how do you think the world will progress?'

Sabal laughed loudly. 'You don't like to give your interviewees an easy final question, do you?'

'Sorry, no, I don't,' she laughed.

'Hmm. OK, let me think about that.' He went silent and Salsa allowed the silence to extend.

'The key challenge, just one, is to improve the world significantly, and to accelerate our advancements globally, without leaving any person or group or country behind another. To achieve as close a Utopian future as we can, and not to squander the riches and opportunities that Allah has provided for everyone. We must not fall back into old ways, prejudices, inequalities, and human weaknesses. We have a unique opportunity to create a better future, one not dominated by greed, or power plays, and one where we can share knowledge and cooperate across all fields, especially science and technology. The Arab empire of the tenth century was a beacon to the world. But it became insular, and Islam consequently lost its position in the world when it withdrew by the end of the eleventh century, and retraction from Spain, influenced in part by North African fundamentalism. Science and technology and forward thinking do not threaten Islam. Nothing does now. As such, we can progress. In another century there is no reason why we cannot reach to other planets, at least in our own solar system, in the way that the Americans and Chinese sought to do, if that is the will of Allah of course,' he smiled, pausing.

'But to achieve this, we must progress wisely, systematically, with foresight and planning, and above all else, global cooperation. We are all Muslim, but we are not all on the same page. To emphasise what I mean by that, Salsa, can you tell me how you found the state of our religion when you went to Iran and Saudi?'

Salsa was caught out by the question, tried not to show it, and failed.

'I'm sorry to have dropped that on you without notice, Salsa.'

'No, no, that's fine, really. I just need to think back to my reflections when I was there.'

'Of course. Take your time, my dear,' Sabal smiled.

She took another half minute to consider the question, and to try and remember her feelings at the time. 'Hmm. I remember my overall feelings being of… horror… and waste… and stupidity. Yes, overall, it was the stupidity that got to me. So many people killed, and so much destruction, and all so unnecessary. For what? How could Sunni and Shia continue to hate each other when they had all been saved by Allah, and therefore proven to be worthy? But then, of course, that was the point really, wasn't it? They weren't worthy. They had been given a chance, for peace, for reconciliation, for brotherhood, and they squandered it. And yet, you know what I felt throughout, after looking through the ruined cities and crumbling monuments and mosques? Satisfaction. I know that seems weird, but I did. It was as if I was looking at Allah's justice. He gave and He took away again. And He was right to do so. And clearly, too, Mecca was not necessary, or He would have saved it of course. That too was a statement, that the whole world is paradise, and that placing undue emphasis on a single location, historical or not, is backward looking, and now we must look forward. As you have said too.'

'You are very perceptive, Salsa, well more than your short years would suggest. So, when you wandered the living parts of Iran and Saudi, what did you make of the opinions of the Mullahs?'

'The Mullahs?'

'Yes. Did they impress you, repulse you, or what?'

'Er… well… there were no Mullahs, Sabal.'

'None? What had happened to them?'

'Are you testing me? Is this a game? There were no Mullahs because they'd been removed too, those that might have survived the war, if any. You know this, surely. After the conflict, as far as the survivors would say, the Mullahs, Imams, all clergy, apart from a small handful, which were classed as radicals, meaning those that didn't follow the regime or the government, died. Any that tried to resurrect the conflict, apparently, died trying. Then the conflict itself died out.

Some people said that they saw clerics physically drop dead from heart attacks or in physical pain. Others said that they just disappeared. It was hard to really know where the truth lay. But, by the time I visited, which of course was many years after the conflict, there was no religious influence at any level of government, in either country. And there were no pilgrims visiting the ruins of Mecca either, or Medina, which was only partly damaged.'

'Thank you, Salsa, that confirms my own understanding too. So, tell me, in all the other places you have visited, which is more than most people these days, and is a credit to your tenacity and sense of journalistic vigour, how would you describe the state of religious fervour?'

'Why do I feel that you are now interviewing me, Sabal?' Salsa laughed, seeking to gain some thinking time.

'Because I am, of course. You are one of the most interesting people I've met since Revelation Day, and your perspective is unique, relatively.'

'How so?'

'Well... and I hope you'll forgive me for digging into your background for this,' he began, and she nodded in ascent, 'Your own family experience truly is unique. Or rather, your success, despite your background, is unique. Your background itself is a common one. What I mean by that is that you come from a family that is classed as British migrants, although you and your brothers are thoroughly British, born and bred. But you were classed as Paki's. Isn't that the term that was used in the U.K. for migrants from Pakistan?'

'Yes, but my father was originally born in Iran, but of Pakistani parentage. He left after the 1979 revolution.'

'Of course. Nevertheless, you were all considered Pakistani, even though only your mother was born there, true?'

'Yes.'

'How often did you visit the mosque when you were growing up?'

'What difference does that make?' Salsa said with rising irritation.

'Please, Salsa, I am not attacking you, just leading to a point, if you'll allow me?'

She took a deep breath, 'OK, please continue.'

'Thank you. As I understand it, you never, or hardly ever, visited a mosque as a child. Is that true?'

'Yes, that's true.'

'So, after Revelation Day, your family, like millions of others, was left bewildered, as survivors, in an Islamic world that felt alien to you. Correct?'

'Yes. So?'

'So, you no doubt felt like imposters. I imagine that your parents wanted to protect you from... what shall we call it... an inquisition? That questions might be raised about your level of devoutness perhaps? And therefore, your safety might have been at risk, or your freedom, maybe.'

'I don't know about that, but yes, my father was quite concerned that we... keep up appearances outdoors and not draw attention to ourselves. But over time we realised that there were thousands of people like us, almost a majority.'

'Yes, I have read your mother's biography.'

'What? Oh, of course you have. Silly of me. So, you know what we went through. We weren't that different to lots of other people all over the world, were we?'

'No, you weren't, I agree. But in a world of plenty, without war, apart from those early small conflicts, and such stellar achievements of so many people and nations to get ourselves back to where we were before, in the important ways, don't you find it extraordinary, that those that were most devout, even fundamental, have fared the worst? Or maybe have just stagnated, and lost their influence, whilst the non-devout have prospered so much. Have you considered this?'

'Yes, I have. I'd have been a fool not to have come to the same conclusion, wouldn't I? Given my own background especially.'

'And you are certainly no fool, Salsa. So, what is your conclusion?'

Her face was no longer smiling. Her suspicion, and her angst, was increasing and she'd lost control of the interview, not that it mattered; it was still a fascinating discussion. 'My conclusion, Sabal, is that Allah, praise be His name, wants us to succeed and push the boundaries, to boldly go where no one has been before, to discover new things and new worlds, and to seek knowledge.'

Sabal laughed and clapped his hands. 'Very good, the play on Star Trek I mean. But still accurate. Yes, that matches my own belief too. But to be specific, all of us have been saved, possibly as you said, to explore the universe, unencumbered by religion. We are all the chosen people now, and we have to be worthy, much as the Jewish people were definitely worthy, considering how much science, knowledge and progress they created in the world, yet were victims of so much unwarranted hatred,' he said, then paused as he saw her expression. 'What, this surprises you, my comment on the Jews?'

'Yes. I mean, I don't disagree, especially when one looks at their tremendous scientific and medical achievements and the number of Nobel Laureates they produced, from such a small population. But I've never heard any Muslim admit that, especially since Revelation Day.'

'That's a digression, to make a point. The point being that we, mankind, need to push the boundaries. The Islamic world didn't do that very much. We were too caught up in victimhood, infighting, and suspicion. Yet after Revelation Day there was a radical shift. Not immediately but quite quickly. How long was it before your mother entered politics?'

'Oh, erm... maybe a year or so?'

'Yes. So, on Revelation Day, your family was frightened of the future and whether you would be victimised, maybe even killed. You were a young teenager so I'm sure your parents kept their worst fears from you, but do you remember those days?'

'Of course, and yes, there were lots of discussions and rules about how to behave outside and to be careful of what we said, especially when we went to school in London.'

'That's right. Your parents were wise to be careful. And yet, after a year or so, your mother entered politics, your father had an influential job, your elder brother was studying to be a doctor, and you were formulating your future to become an investigative journalist, with your talented brother here as a film editor. Could that ever have happened if religious adherence had remained important, or influential?'

Salsa sat back in her chair and pondered. 'No, it couldn't, naturally. But that's not a new thought. What's your point, Sabal?'

'My point, Salsa, is that religion, as a concept, is practically dead. Allah has made Himself redundant. He has shown us the way and departed. The world is ours now, free of doctrine, if we choose to live that way.'

MICHAEL

How do I approach this? She's going to get defensive, but it needs to be said. Twins should be above the kind of sniping that will happen. I hate it; always have, but... shit! Grow some balls, Michael. This is a team issue; she's not the managing partner.

'What's up?' Salsa asked as she walked into the room, a towel around her wet head, wearing tracksuit pants and a cotton T-shirt with drip marks from her hair drying on the shoulders.

Just dive in and go for it, Michael. 'That interview was crap, Salsa.'

'What? Are you kidding, that last part was an enormous scoop, Michael. Don't pretend you weren't equally shocked by his Allah comment?'

'Forget that part for a minute. The rest was trite, a boring conversation, with you being mesmerised by his sex appeal. Salsa, he ran rings around you, dominated the debate and never allowed you to get into anything controversial. And if you don't believe me, then tell me which part of the interview, apart from his final statement, could be used to stimulate viewers into watching it all?'

'Just because it was like a fireside chat, I still got into the man's character, opened him up for people to see the real man, and what he'd achieved and how he'd thought his way through the process, as well as his insights on threats from other countries.'

'What threats? He practically told the world that he was ahead of other leaders, a visionary, deal maker and all-round good guy, whilst closing any door you tried to pry open into deeper discussions... not that you tried all that much.'

'Fuck you, Michael! If you think you could do better, then you take the lead and I'll hold the camera next time.'

'Don't get defensive, Salina,' he countered, and put his hand up in front of her face as she started to respond again. 'Answer these questions before you come back at me, OK?'

She pursed her lips, crossed her arms, and sat still, clearly seething but allowing him to make his argument.

'Answer yes or no to these points. Did we learn anything inciteful about Paul Habbib?'

She thought about that one, then reluctantly shook her head after 15 seconds.

'Did we learn anything at all about the economy of South America, or comparisons between different parts of the continent?'

'No.'

'Did we learn anything about the way that his government actually works and controls the disparate parts of the continent?'

'No,' she sighed.

'Did we learn anything at all about the real relationship between Kalil and Ghulam Asif, or how the two of them came up with the amazing coup of taking over the Americas?'

She put her hands over her eyes and gave a muffled groan of self-rebuke. 'Fuck!' she shouted.

He let her rant for a while, pacing the hotel room as she did so. Some minutes later, she sat down heavily, put her head in her hands again and said, 'God, I'm so sorry, Michael. It really was shit, wasn't it? How the hell did I come away from there thinking I'd got a good interview?'

He stayed quiet. She looked up at him. 'Did he play me? Did I fall for his charm offensive? Am I that pathetic?'

'No, you're not. And I know you well enough to know that you weren't allowing yourself to be deliberately seduced.'

'Meaning what?'

He laughed. 'Meaning that he's not your type. He might be attractive, intelligent and charming, and one of the world's most influential men, but that's never got any other similar candidate into your knickers, so I can safely assume that he won't get there either.'

'You bastard!' she said, laughing as she threw a cushion at his head, missing, then pushing him on to the bed and jumping on top of him, play punching his chest. A minute later they both lay there, laughing and breathing hard.

'Is the interview retrievable?' she asked, sitting up again.

'It's usable because of the last part, which is a game changer. Trouble is, I'm not sure we can, or should, play it.'

'Are you kidding? That's the only good thing we got; you basically just told me that, remember?'

He nodded slowly but retained a worried look. 'What's wrong, Michael?'

'Where have we been lately that there's still religious influence at government levels?'

'Lots of places.'

'Name them, Salsa.'

'OK. Nigeria. Pakindesh itself...'

'Really? I don't mean active mosques, but political participation and influence in decisions and policy. Yes, there were many people involved in religious practices, and more so in the old Pakistan and Bangladesh parts rather than in Delhi or Mumbai, for instance. But commerce and day to day politics was not influenced by religion, was it?' he suggested.

'No, I suppose not. But, Michael, when we are all Muslim, there's no need for political interference, surely?'

'That's naïve, Salsa. Did Iran and Saudi Arabia, and Egypt, Indonesia, or Malaysia keep their politics and religion separate before Revelation Day?'

'Indonesia and Malaysia did, maybe not Middle Eastern countries.'

'No, they didn't. Not really. They had to play the part of supporting religious sensitivities, just as much as the old America courted its religious right, because those people had money, power, and influence. The same was true in Israel. If either the right or left parties had been able to take power without doing deals with the religious zealots, they'd have found a possible way to peace, but those Israeli lunatics living on the West Bank made the peace process impossible, whilst at the same time being disliked by the average Israeli, because they didn't do military service and had dozens of kids living off welfare. Politics is a dirty business, or rather it used to be. I agree it's less so now. But that's because we live in a plentiful world now, with no true poverty. So, religion is no longer the last refuge of the disenfranchised because there really aren't any now.

'So, what Sabal said is pretty accurate,' he continued. 'In a world where we are all one religion, all accepted by Allah, really accepted, since Revelation Day, there is little need to practice adherence. Obey the law and be good people, sure. But, seeing as how we experienced the demise of those that were viciously cruel, or serious criminals, we've become that rarest of all things, an evolutionary first, an altruistic society free from conflict. But, dear sister, if we go and broadcast Sabal's last statement, there is a pretty good chance that all hell will break loose and every religious lunatic still breathing will want to kill him for blasphemy. Is that what we want?'

MOHAMMED ASIF

Mohammed Asif considered the meeting with Masud Sabri of Uighurstan as the most surprising he had experienced in all his political life. The other delegation leaders, from Kazakhstan, Kirghizstan, and Uzbekistan were much as he had expected, mainly due to their political backgrounds and positions of power. But Masud Sabri was different. In some ways he was like Kalil. He was a visionary. But he had risen from nothing, unlike his own dear departed father, Ghulam, or Kalil even. Perhaps because the Uighurs had been so cruelly treated by China and had never been close to running their own lives before, there needed to be a natural leader to take control after Revelation Day. But to have moved all his countrymen, the fifteen million Uighurs and the disparate thirty-five million other Chinese Muslims, across China to a handful of pre-chosen cities and then to have created a democratic nation so quickly, was breathtaking. Populating only the coastal areas from Shanghai to the Vietnam border had made immense sense. But how many other leaders accepted that excess land was not necessarily of benefit, and could be ignored or left alone?

But that was history. What Sabri has just offered him, once they were alone, was unprecedented, and intelligent. He was gifting the region of Tibet to Pakindesh, in return for a defence and cooperation treaty. When he had heard the offer, he was sure he'd been mistaken. He initially questioned whether this man was truly giving him control of Tibet and practically the rest of the Himalayas, whilst effectively tying Uighurstan politically and militarily to Pakindesh? It was staggering, but also well thought through.

Uighurstan was incapable of defending its vast and underpopulated territory. But it controlled enormous Chinese naval and military assets. These were useless without the skills, and manpower to use them. Sabri realised that one day, perhaps not for decades, Indonesia would move further north and potentially try to take control. Its history pre-RD, in Irian Jaya and East Timor, and its expansion to Australia and New Zealand post-RD, made this clear. Sabri wanted Pakindesh to train his future army and navy but provide the human assets in sufficient strength to utilise enough Chinese naval ships and land-based assets to protect Uighurstan from invasion. He also wanted there to be what he termed shadow students at each military rank and across all strategic assets, so that there would be capable Uighurstan officers within the next ten years to take control of their national self-defence.

Asif had tried to be as blasé as possible in accepting the offer, but Sabri laughed and had said "I know this is unprecedented, and very much will be seen as a one-way gift or enormous value to you. But, President Asif, you must also see that by tying my country to yours in this way, I will secure our future, at minimal cost, for all time. This is a symbiotic relationship and will never become one of parasite and host. I offer you eternal friendship, but the offer is not without cost for you."

They had consummated the deal over the next few hours, and then Asif had called Kalil to give him the news and to gain his insight. Kalil was equally delighted, but faster on the uptake than Asif had been in seeing the quid pro quo required to make this all work.

The three leaders had then worked out many of the details between them in the next few hours.

Asif now made the follow up call to Kalil that he'd promised earlier.

Kalil answered the video-call, smiling. 'Am I looking at the man that has now taken much of China into his territory and wonders how much more good fortune awaits the people of Pakindesh?'

'Holy hell, Sabal! Could you ever imagine this?'

Kalil laughed. 'Allah be praised, my friend. We are leading the world. And all without conflict. Who will come to us next to add to the bounty of Pakindesh?'

'I don't know, Sabal, but I am always worried when life gets to be too good. Pride comes before a fall, and all those other proverbs of warning seem to be in my head. But truly, this has been another momentous day. I just needed to see you again. I will leave you to the joys of Rio and meet with Masud for dinner. Take care, my friend,' he concluded, ending the link.

MINA

Shuffling through some of the papers on her desk, Mina was startled by the desk phone ringing and picked it up with some irritation, but immediately calmed herself when she recognized her husband's voice.

'I just had a message from Michael. He said that he and Salina are expecting to be back in three weeks' time. There's an interview pending with the US President next week, and then they need to determine when and what they put to air, but that they want to talk to you before they do that, to get some political advice.'

'Oh Riaz, that's wonderful news. Three weeks isn't long to wait. But what does Michael mean by my advice?' Mina asked.

'I have no idea, but he wanted me to give them some options for when you'd be free to talk to them.'

'Oh, OK, I'll have to check my diary of course. I'm meeting with the European Union President tomorrow, but apart from that I should be able to schedule a call. I'll send a message to Michael. How did they sound?'

'Tired, excited, looking forward to coming home though, and especially to see us and Charlie again.'

'I can't wait to see them, Riaz. It's been far too long.'

She ended the call, sat back, and thought of her youngest children. Not children anymore, of course. Accomplished documentary writers, with a huge following now. Michael had told her that their podcast interviews on IslamNet were regularly listened to by over fifty million people, and they sold their video interviews to multiple channels and made a lot of money from them, but they were far more concerned about access and influence than payment, especially Salsa. She still worried about Salsa, even though the world was safer and calmer now. But the twins' time in the Middle East had worried her the most, although less so now. She'd had a lot of anxiety about their trip to Mecca, especially after they broadcast the destruction wrought on the city by the Iranians.

That broadcast was five years ago and there was a lot of anger afterwards, against both Iran and the Caliphate, or what remained of them. The world felt that those two regimes had destroyed its most sacred place due to pride, power struggles, and out dated enmity between Sunni and Shia adherents. When Iranians started arriving in Europe, to escape the aftermath, there was a lot of unrest, and some violence against them. But unlike the pre-Revelation Day era of Syrian refugees fleeing into Europe, the Iranians just found largely uninhabited cities to take over. So now, Warsaw, Belgrade, Sofia, and Bratislava were essentially Iranian cities. Tehran was abandoned. Medina was now the most important pilgrimage city, then Jerusalem.

Southern Europe was transformed too. Over a hundred million people from North and West Africa now lived in Spain, Portugal, Italy, Malta, Greece, France, and Croatia. When she met with European Heads of State these days it was hard to accept that they were rarely European at all. But oddly, each re-populated nation had willingly accepted its historic persona, rather than that of its new migrants, at least in some political ways. The European democratic values had been resurrected, and still dominated. So, in Malta, which was almost totally Libyan-populated now, the language was mainly English, not Arabic. The country's new inhabitants respected the Island's historic links to the UK, and the value of English as a working language for Europe. French was as equally used as English, Spanish much less, German hardly at all, having been replaced by Turkish, being the majority ethnic background of most of the surviving migrants. The other European languages were essentially dead. Mina believed that English dominated due to the influence of Pakindesh and its migration of the U.S., and as the rest of the world was not interested in learning Indonesian-Malaysian Bahasa, numbers ruled the day. But she was still surprised at times that Arabic usage had been ignored except in the mosques. Initially that had not been the case, until after the Iran-Caliphate War, and the follow-on impact of the deaths of so many radical clerics. There had been few clergy willing to fight or argue too vociferously for Arabic to be the official language of the world – the numbers did not make sense.

A knock on the door interrupted Mina's thoughts, followed by the entrance of a woman carrying a tray with a tea pot, cups and a snack on it. 'Good morning, Prime Minister.'

'Good morning, Yasmin, how are you today?' Mina asked.

'Very well, thank you Ma'am. Am I too early for your tea?'

'Never. I hope you'll join me today?'

'Thank you, Ma'am, I do have time today if you like?'

'Definitely. I need your input. I'll let you pour whilst I finish this and then I'll join you,' she replied, finishing an email she was typing. Then she came to sit by the small coffee table where her secretary had poured tea for two and placed some biscuits on side plates for them.

'What can I help you with, Prime Minister?'

'It's teatime, Yasmin, remember?' Mina admonished her secretary, meaning they needed to talk as equals at this time of the day.

'Sorry, Mina, you know I find it hard at times to talk as equals,' Yasmin replied with a common excuse.

'No matter. Now, I need your opinion on something. If you had to state your three biggest fears or worries for the future, here or across the world, what would they be?'

'Good heavens, Mina, no pressure,' she laughed. 'How long have I got to think this through?'

'I don't want you to dwell on it, just talk off the top of your head. Don't worry about priorities, just say whatever comes into your mind, and we can delve deeper later. No analysis, just say whatever comes up.'

'Ok then... overpopulation by migrants that won't become or feel British... the religious fanatics getting more power or starting an uprising of some sort against women and people that they call Godless... loss of medical and scientific advancement... war of any kind... losing our heritage...'

'What do you mean by that last one?' Mina interrupted.

'Well, things like losing historic building and castles and things, because they're British and not admired or understood by foreigners for their historical value.'

'OK, go on.'

'Er... well, I suppose one of my biggest... not fears exactly, but it's the loss of things that were important to so many of us before Revelation Day, even if we didn't value them enough, but now that they're gone... well, I really miss them,' Yasmin said with a shrug, then picked up her cup and sipped her tea, watching Mina's face for a reaction.

'I think I know what you mean. My kids used to talk about this a lot; still do. I remember Salina crying about the deaths of Justin Bieber and Beyonce and Ed Sheeran and their music. Charlie never got over the end of football, and even though it's back again, he says it's not the same. I can't tell you how often he says he misses Football Focus and Match of the Day. Michael, oddly, misses foreign languages, which amazes me, as he wasn't exactly any good at speaking any. And they all moaned often at the loss of the Internet, although we all did. But the kids criticised IslamNet when it started, constantly calling it rubbish and a poor imitation of the real Internet, as they called it.'

'Well, they're right there, Mina! Lots of us think that IslamNet is missing most of what we had access to before. There are conspiracy theories everywhere that say that the clerics and Imams had a hand in deleting most of the data and files that didn't fit their view of the world.'

'Yes, I've heard that. It might be the case, or it just might be that the Pakindesh IT experts that created IslamNet from what they could resurrect out of American databases, just couldn't get everything back,' Mina stated.

'Really?' Yasmin queried, sceptically.

'I know you're suspicious, and you might be right. It is what it is I suppose.'

'But that's exactly my point,' Yasmin began to argue, then laughed, 'well, it was one of those things I meant to say anyway. We just don't know what was lost and what was destroyed. That's the real fear, I think. Everyone loves your Prime Ministership, truly. But lots of people still worry that you're too soft on fanatics and aren't progressive enough at getting back some of the things we all loved.'

'OK, point taken on that, but this is my question really. What do you want back, enough to put resources into it, whether time or money or political capital?' Mina challenged her secretary.

'Can I think about that and get back to you?'

'Of course, but I'm serious. I too hear chatter around the place and on the street. Your fear or anxiety about immigration impacting British institutions is a common one, but silly, given that none of us would have been here in the first place without immigration. So is the fear of re-radicalisation, although I'm less concerned with that one.'

'Why? Surely that's a big threat, isn't it?'

'I don't think so. Don't you remember all the news about the deaths of fanatical clerics after the Iran-Caliphate War? There were so many reports of the deaths of clergy across the world. Some people thought it was a new Revelation Day and that Allah was unhappy with the whole human race. But then it settled down and we realised that the moderates remained in place. Have you forgotten how calming that period was? It was only 10 years ago, Yasmin.'

'Yes, I do remember, you're right. How weird, to forget those days. I suppose it shows that we do forget too easily, and then worry too much, maybe?'

'A very human issue, Yasmin. We have short memories at times. That's something I need to think about. OK, back to work. Thanks for the tea and chat, Yasmin.'

'You're welcome, Prime Minister. I'll take the tray out. Call me if you need anything.'

CHARLIE

'I've never lost a patient before, Freddy. I'm just shattered,' Charlie said. He was sitting in the maintenance area of Freddy's domain, which was a common hideout to debrief and chat, and had remained a useful sanctuary throughout his medical training period and now through his residency position at St. Thomas' Hospital.

'Charlie, you knew that this day would have to come. No-one's a miracle worker, right? And the lady was seventy-eight didn't you say and was in poor health for years. You can't save everyone.'

'I promised her she'd be okay, Freddy. I shouldn't have, I know, that was stupid.'

'Not necessarily, if it brought some comfort. I mean, you didn't promise that to her relatives, did you?'

'No, of course not, I know better than that,' Charlie confirmed, rubbing his temples with his eyes closed.

'Headache?'

'A bit of one, nothing worth taking a pill for.'

'Coffee then?'

'Thanks, Freddy, that'd be good.'

'So, when's the dynamic duo due back in town?'

'In a few weeks. They're doing an interview with Paul Habbib on the way home.'

'Mixing with the rich and famous, eh? Not a bad life I reckon.'

'I spoke to Michael last week. He sounded tired. Said they needed a break and that they weren't sure about how to air the last interview or something. I got the impression they might disagree about it, but he wouldn't elaborate.'

'Does that happen much, fighting together I mean?'

'Not often, but when it does it can be a real shit fight, let me tell you. People say that twins are more closely bonded than other siblings, which is sort of obvious I suppose. But when they fall out or have disagreements you don't want to be caught in the crossfire, and especially not be asked to take sides. If you did that, you'd be the loser after they made up again. I learnt that hard lesson early on,' Charlie laughed.

'Really? I always thought Salina was so calm, and Michael rarely even raises his voice.'

'Hah, why do you think Salina got nicknamed Salsa, Freddy? Because she can hit you like a red hot chili when you least expect it. A girl not to be trifled with, believe me.'

'Is that right? How old is she now?' Charlie looked at Freddy and saw an odd expression on his face. 'Going on 26. Both.'

Freddy shook his head and handed a coffee hug to Charlie. 'Bloody hell, 26 already. Is she… I mean they, looking to settle down? Done enough travelling for a while, I mean?'

'I don't know about that. They've got a huge following and love what they do. Come over when they're home and ask them yourself if you want,' Charlie suggested.

'I'd love to, Charlie, thanks.'

Charlie looked at his watch, gulped down his coffee and excused himself, dashing off back to the ward, leaving his friend deep in thought.

SALINA

'Okay, Michael, let's look at this dispassionately,' Salina suggested.

'Go ahead.' This will be interesting, he thought. A back-down? Or a serious debate on the issues he raised in Rio? She'd been a bit distant for a while in Brazil, and only brightened up a little when they flew to Miami for this break and some beach time ahead of going to D.C. to meet Paul Habbib.

'Do you agree that Sabal Kalil is an intelligent man?'

'Of course.'

'And strategically astute?'

'Undoubtedly.'

'Not prone to dumb mistakes or underestimating opponents?'

'Clearly.'

'So, therefore, he would not have made his comments at the end of the interview without prior consideration, and in full awareness of how those words might be taken if it goes public, which he also knows will be the case. Agreed?'

'Agreed, but…' Michael raised his hand to stop her interrupting him, 'number one, that doesn't mean he's infallible. Two, his acumen might be slipping, after over 10 years in charge. And three, he might be hoping for a dramatic reaction, for which he has a plan, maybe, but fails to consider the fallout. And...' he raised his hand again as Salina began to open her mouth, 'we too have a responsibility, or duty of care, in what we report, so...'

'Bullshit, Michael! We are journalists and we report without fear or favour, and always have. What duty of care?' she challenged.

'A duty of care not to create strife for ratings, and inadvertently get people killed.'

'That's rubbish, mister high and mighty. First off, you might be overestimating our influence...'

'Ha! Coming from you, Salina, that's rich. You're always crowing about our influence, and it being a good thing,' Michael countered.

'That kind of influence was meant to be regarding our global pull of viewers, not our political capacity to create change, directly. We've never been into that, nor should be. We're independent, aren't we?'

'Yes, of course, but we're not infallible, Salsa. At the very least don't you think that we should ask Kalil if he realises that his words could create problems out there in the more fundamentally zealous nations?'

She frowned; her lips pursed tightly together. Think before you speak, she told herself. 'I wonder,' she said softly. Michael remained silent, knowing that she was at some sort of decision crossroad. A minute later she added, 'Should we send him a copy of the edited interview, and ask if he's okay with it going to air?'

'Wow! Now you've got me reconsidering. We've never given that right of veto to anyone else,' Michael said, now pacing the hotel room.

'Michael, we've never been in quite this situation before. I mean knowing that our work could create problems, in contrast to getting the truth out there. It's not the same as when we reported on the Iran-Caliphate war and decided to add our thoughts to it. That was a reporting style change we thought through ahead of time, and it was right to show the world the aftermath of sectarian stupidity then. But is this different?'

Michael stopped pacing and went to the laptop on the desk. 'Let's look at the last statement Kalil made again,' he said, rapidly scanning the interview to the end, then hitting play. Kalil's words moved them in the same way as when first uttered:

"My point, Salsa, is that religion, as a concept, is practically dead. Allah has made Himself redundant. He has shown us the way and departed. The world is ours now, free of doctrine, if we choose to live that way."

They each sat, silently for over a minute, considering the potential impact of that conclusion to the interview. 'Thumbs,' Michael said, instigating an old family game. 'One, two, three,' he said, at the end of which they each showed a thumbs up or thumbs down, much like the paper, rock, scissors game. They both had their thumbs up.

Salsa nodded her head. Michael did the same, then said, 'Okay, it's a go. We air it without recourse to Kalil.'

HABBIB

'That interview with Kalil caused some anger, Badiah,' Habbib stated. 'Should give me an idea of how Salina Ahmed might question me later in the week, on whether I agree with his view or not.'

Badiah looked up from her laptop, and considered her husband's comment, before speaking. 'Are you worried about her?'

'No, not at all. Do you think I should be? You were the journalist. Is she a threat I should be wary of?'

'Possibly. But probably not. You're right, tonight's interview will give you an idea I suppose. What would you consider the worst question she could ask?'

'Hmm, let's see. Whether I think that Kalil is mentally stable? Or whether I agree that it's time to move on from religiously based societies?'

'Okay,' she said, 'let's go with that. I'll play Ms Ahmed. So, answer that second question.'

'Well, it would be disingenuous to deny that there are many people around the world that are not devout, nor attend a mosque, or practice the teachings of the Quran diligently. And clearly there has been no divine retribution for these transgressions, or habits...'

'Not sure about calling devout behaviour habits, Paul,' Badiah coached.

'Point taken. Let me consider this more carefully later, and we can play out a mock discussion then.'

'Of course, darling. I forgot about your meeting with the PM.'

It had taken Habbib a while to accept his less powerful position of being President within a Parliamentary Democracy, and therefore being less involved in policy and decision making than the Prime Minister, who wielded more power, but after his three years as Head of State, before the new Constitution was enacted, he had been glad to leave the role and associated stress behind. It still amazed him that the last two U.S. Prime Ministers, from different sides of the political spectrum had each left him as President. His attendance at this morning's meeting was nevertheless unusual, but he'd accepted the Prime Minister's invitation without seeking a reason for it.

After being driven from the White House, Habbib walked into the Cabinet Room of the Capitol Building and nodded to those in attendance as he made his way to the centre position on one of the long sides of the oval table. Pleasantries were made and he looked around the room. It always pleased him that his old colleagues, George Saba, Amelia Sanchez and Imran Malouf, had earned and maintained their higher roles in the Government, respectively now as Trade Minister, Social Services Minister, and Foreign Minister. They were joined around the table by the Prime Minister, Malik Shah, the Treasurer, Pervez Ali, and two female Ministers, Fehmida Jamali for Environment and Progress, and Dr Rubina Dawar for Health.

'Good morning, everyone,' the Prime Minister greeted them, 'and thank you, Mr President, for attending our meeting today.

Habbib nodded and replied, 'My pleasure, Prime Minister,' as he settled into his seat.

Malik Shah seemed to command respect easily, and Habbib liked him personally. He looked at Habbib and said, 'May I once again suggest first name lack of formalities, for the sake of expedition, ladies and gentlemen?'

'Agreed, Malik,' Habbib replied. Everyone else concurred.

Malik Shah wasted no time on pleasantries, looking around the table, smiling, and then began, 'Welcome all. Fehmida, you have an update on the plastic pollution initiative, I believe? He looked across the table to a late thirties, pretty, slim woman, with long black hair tied in a ponytail, intense green eyes, and a serious expression. She finished arranging her paperwork and then sat back, looking confident and smiled.

'Thank you, Malik. Yes, and happily all good news. The initiative to utilise ships from the dormant multinational fishing fleets to harvest the millions of tonnes of floating plastic garbage in the oceans has gone better than expected. Over three hundred ships are now employed, from twenty-four nations, and there has also been progress on commercialising fifty-two new incineration power plants at coastal cities to use the majority of the waste. Despite the recent language against President Kalil from some of those nations, the initiative remains well supported and growing.

Imram Malouf coughed to gain attention, scratched his head and said, 'Yes, well that takes us to the key issue on the agenda, today, Malik. Not good news from Indonesia. They have taken a stern position and are using strong language against the Americas, after Kalil's interview bombshell about religion being dead and Allah making himself redundant. Forgive my language, but what the fuck was Kalil thinking! Even if he believes it, why go public? The Indonesian commentary is not good, and the Middle East is going nuts, rioting in the streets, and burning effigies, talking of a war against Pakindesh...'

'We know this, Imran,' Saba said, 'but I thought things had quietened down over the past week. From what I saw on blogs, there seems to be some more intelligent debate now on what Kalil meant. I even heard a comment about the possibility of a goal set by Allah for humanity to take control in His name, to prove our worthiness, free of religious doctrine.'

'Come on, George,' Malouf scoffed. 'It's irrelevant what more educated or Liberal people say, when put up against the masses in countries with insufficient history of freedom of speech, and where the Mullahs ruled by fear, or ran the only educational options in poor rural regions. Pakindesh itself is keeping quiet too, despite young Asif making calming comments, but he doesn't have the backing that his father commanded. Kalil wouldn't want to travel back there any time soon.'

Habbib coughed, to gain attention. 'You all know that Sabal and I have a true friendship. Over the months that we worked most closely together, I came to know him quite well, and respect him. He's not a man that rushes to judgement or to say anything that he hasn't thought through. I can't believe that his comment wasn't planned. He would have known exactly what he was doing in that interview. If you've watched it closely, which I'm sure you all have now, then you might have noticed that he came to dominate the discussion. For me, I think he was always leading to that position, or belief. It was no slip of the tongue, no unplanned slip. He knew the reaction it would cause. Have you spoken to him, Malik?'

'No, Paul. I take it you haven't either?'

'No, but I should, and probably before my own interview with Ms Ahmed.'

'I think that would be wise. Do that, Paul. We'll wait for you to report back. Okay, let us move on to IT. George?'

'OK. IslamNet is at 80% recovery of the pre-RD Internet database. However, this is always going to be difficult to confirm, and there is ample evidence of database destruction attempts by some regimes, notably Indonesia, Malaysia, and Nigeria. That might be futile, given database backups and redundancy, although we don't really know where all that backup was. Debate still rages in many places about the value of the original database, and those seeking complete transparency of historical knowledge and information are actively calling the database the History of Pre-RD Mankind, or HPRM. Objectors, particularly those preferring to rewrite history, are using malware to destroy historic electronic documents. We've seen a lot of destruction of libraries and museums across Europe. On top of that is the attempt to rewrite history and distort twentieth century information, specifically in relation to the Holocaust, and the creation of Israel and the treatment of Palestinians. Similarly, the role of the United States in the Gulf Wars and the downplaying of 9/11, and to the dismay of many, the emergence of a sector of people that still look upon the old Taliban in Afghanistan as saviours and heroes rather than terrorist supporters and subjugators of women.'

Habbib interjected, 'Some of this has been going on well before RD itself. Iran and other extremist governments always pretended that the Holocaust didn't occur. The disturbing issue for me though, is the old lesson that to deny or not learn from history is to be doomed to repeat it. Just because we are now in a peaceful and largely egalitarian world does not mean that we should forget the factors that led to Revelation Day itself.'

'I agree entirely, Paul,' Malik Shah stated. 'As for the Taliban, well, given that they ceased to exist not long after RD, I cannot understand who would want to resurrect their memory.'

'What I still wonder about,' Habbib said, 'is why Pakindesh doesn't absorb Afghanistan into its greater nation?'

Malik Shah smiled, 'They don't want that kind of headache, Paul. If the Afghans do not seek to integrate, then why create problems for oneself. There is nothing to be gained from assimilation of a largely tribal population into Pakindesh, even if it is now female dominated. President Muhammed Asif assists them but keeps them at arm's length, which is probably wise. I think his father would have been proud of young Mohammed. He certainly surprised many world leaders when he he was elected after his father died. Ghulam left behind high expectations, and Pakindesh continues to prosper. Anyway, please continue, George.'

'Thank you, Malik. OK, food production. Rather than go into details let me say simply that production is higher than ever, distribution and export has exceeded targets, and no adverse issues are anticipated. Exports are split evenly between SAP, Europe, and Africa, with domestic consumption at 17 percent. As an aside, for those that like to hear this stuff, since hardly anyone lives near the prairie lands now, the Bison numbers are growing markedly, over a million now, and elk and wolf numbers are healthy too, as well as bears and mountain lions.'

'Is this a problem for visitors though?' Fehmida asked.

'Not really. Unlike Americans, Pakindesh migrants are not into hunting and visiting the mountains much,' Paul answered.

Malik looked across at his Treasurer and smiled, 'Your turn, Pervez.'

'What can I really say? GDP is increasing, trade is expanding, as George outlined. The social pact of equal pay for all work performed has not created a problem between professional people and menial workers, which was the key criticism of the idea five years ago, and for which I was asked last meeting to take a closer look at the program. I did that and we interviewed the extremes, being surgical specialists and university lecturers versus garbage truck drivers and rural field hands. Many of us assumed that a brain surgeon would object to his pay being the same as for a vegetable picker. Whilst we were surprised that it was not, we looked more deeply at the rationale and why, now, this system can work and yet not be tainted by historical attempts to do things like this under communist ideology. We all know why communism failed, so I'll not go into that.

'The number one reason why this experiment works, is because we all live in an abundant world now. With free housing, cars, many consumer goods, clothing etcetera, all thanks to full and plentiful warehouses to supply the previous 350 million Americans, now going begging, this world has no link to the one we left behind.

So, whilst there is still a strong driver for education, the old drive that linked education to earnings has been decoupled. People either wish to be educated for its own sake, or for a more meaningful or challenging life and career, or they accept a simpler life free of stress, knowing that they will not starve or be unable to afford medical care and access to education for their children. I looked at the current levels of college and university degrees held by people working in non-professional roles. It is fifteen percent. Think about that. Pre-RD it would have been close to zero. But we now have significant numbers of people with higher education course qualifications that choose a simple life on the land or in menial, lower stress jobs. Why? Because they can. Because we have de-linked survival from job status. I urge you to start having coffee shop conversations with the people working there when you get the chance. I've been doing it and believe me it is a wonderful eye opener. Last week I was educated about Friedrich Nietzsche by a barista. She eventually took a break from her work to explain the concept of synchronicity to me.'

'I love the perspectives you bring to this table, Pervez. Whilst that is a happy note to conclude upon,' Malik said, 'I do wonder for how long such a utopian situation can last. I'd like to suggest that we consider options for consideration if, or when, our country is challenged. Please be ready to talk to this topic at our next meeting.'

After the meeting concluded, Paul Habbib left the room deep in thought.

MOHAMMED ASIF

'What are you thinking about, Mohammed?' his wife, Julia asked.

'Whether I should go to the conference with the President of Uighurstan, or not.'

'Why wouldn't you?'

'I'm not sure there's a benefit, and there's also some unrest because of Kalil's comments in his interview. I think my father might have been able to talk Kalil out of saying what he did?'

'I think he was speaking from the heart. It is what he now believes, and he's always been a man to be open.'

'Don't be a fool, Julia,' Mohammed said with more irritation than he'd meant. 'I'm sorry, I didn't mean to bite your head off, but I am annoyed at Kalil. Why stir up the faithful? To what purpose?'

'Clearly he had not thought through the impact of his words?'

'That's where you're wrong, my darling. Kalil always thinks and plans before he speaks. It might seem open and spontaneous, and charming. But he is the cleverest man in politics in the world. He knew what he was doing and saying. But why say it at all?'

'Why don't you ask him?'

'I want to. But I can't.'

'Why not?'

'Because if I do, then I will be drawn into whatever game he is playing, and whilst I admire him, and count him as a mentor, because of his close friendship with my father, I fear this... development.'

'Why? Why are you frightened, Mohammed?'

'Because this world is still fragile. Yes, we have everything we need. The people are happy, satisfied, for the most part. But we are still full of anger in places. I've seen it. The madrassahs are full, preaching, looking for greater meaning. Seeking more influence. The old enmities between Sunni and Shia are not completely gone. Any excuse to reignite the flames could occur out of nowhere. What do you think these currently quiet scholars, fanatics in waiting I call them, could do if someone called for a holy war against Kalil's blasphemy?'

'Blasphemy? Really?'

'I've heard them, and had it reported to me as well. Kalil is living in a false paradise compared to cities like Peshawar, or Quetta. The poor and uneducated might now be wealthier, well fed, able to find jobs and homes, and wives... but the old pull of the mullahs remains. Oddly, some now seek greater meaning than before Revelation Day.'

'I can understand that. We have experienced the biggest miracle... or sign, in the history of the world. Rather than answer the faithful's questions, the event has created more confusion for some. They might have expected that only the devout should have been saved. But Allah, in His wisdom, saved all Muslims. I have heard the street talk too. I know that this annoys some people. Those that have been devout all their lives feel cheated, of their rightful place as spiritual leaders.'

'My apologies, Julia. I should have known that you were aware of these... disenchantments.'

'I still think you need to speak with Kalil.'

'Maybe you're right. If he has properly thought this through, then I might as well understand his thinking. And if he hasn't... well, better to discuss the possible problems, I suppose.'

Julia walked over and kissed her husband on the cheek and hugged him. 'Good decision,' she said, smiling, then left him alone.

Muhammed Asif looked at his watch, quickly determined the time in Brazil and decided there was no time like the present. He went to his desk and set up a video call to Kalil's private email address. Surprisingly, he answered immediately.

'Asif junior? This is a pleasant surprise. I am happy to hear from you, my friend.'

'Sabal, it has been a little too long, although I did watch your interview with Salina Ahmed.'

'Ahh, I wondered how long it would be before you accused me of stupidity,' he laughed. 'Your father would have been onto me immediately. I do so miss his counsel, and friendship. Anyway, that is the reason for your call I take it?'

'Yes, it is. What were you thinking? And don't tell me it was an unrehearsed remark, Uncle Kalil. I know you better than that.'

'Yes, you do, that is true. And I won't play games with you either. I respect you too much for that,' he paused, but continued when there was no interruption. 'I suppose the truthful answer is that I genuinely believe what I said. I think that Allah, praise be to Him, has moved humanity to a new phase, one of... well, let me call it, self-enlightenment. Or self-control perhaps. I think we are being allowed to... manage our own affairs, without divine interference. The time of the Mullahs and the interpreters of the Quran and all faith-linked discussions is over. It is time to evolve, together, peacefully. Do you disagree?'

'Do you seriously expect me to answer that question, Sabal?'

Kalil laughed, 'No, I suppose not. But what is in your heart, now that you've had time to think about this, and don't pretend that the idea has not been playing on your mind for the past weeks. Be bold, my friend. It is just you and I talking now, and this is not like the chats we had when you were still in university, when you never wanted to follow in your father's footsteps. I am glad you changed your mind on that at least. Your Presidency is thriving.'

'Sabal, if we were in the same room together, and I was certain of there being no eavesdroppers, or listening devices or spies threatening us, even then I would be nervous of answering that question. And you should have been much more discreet in your interview. What made you say what you did?'

'I have told you. I believe it to be the case.'

'So! Do you think that will appease the masses? You've put a price on your head now. Every crackpot fanatic will be after you. You'll be lucky to see the year out. This could cause another holy war.'

'Possibly.'

'Possibly? Are you in any doubt? You are no fool...' Mohammed paused. Kalil remained silent. A minute passed. 'OK, I am calm again. Alright, tell me the plan, Uncle. How is this going to develop, at least in your mind? Tell me.'

'Thank you, my young protege. Let me do this my way; I always do,' he chuckled. 'Yes, you are correct that there will be unrest in the madrassah strongholds in places like Quetta, Peshawar, the remains of the Iranian and Middle Eastern states, some Gulf regimes, places in Indonesia, Malaysia perhaps, Afghanistan's anti-female old hands most definitely, Nigeria maybe. Unlike the old days though, there are far less of the uneducated poor able to be easily exploited. Still some, unfortunately. But the days of such easily manipulated young men with little to aspire to are gone.'

'Stop there, Sabal. Let me remind you that the image of terrorism being perpetrated by that class was always simplistic. We have all studied those days without rose coloured glasses on. The London bombings in 2005 were perpetrated by middle class men with good jobs and families, educated in Britain. Even the surgeon in Glasgow that tried to ram the airport with a car bomb. Those actions broke the simplistic myth that only poor, uneducated, easily manipulated peasants become suicide bombers,' Muhammed Asif countered.

'That is true, and you are correct in that we should not oversimplify the catalysts that create perpetrators of these events. But my overall theme is still valid here. We are in a different world, and it is one without the spectre of the all-powerful infidel that must be attacked. We have now escaped that victimhood stage of Muslim development. We are one people now and...'

'Wrong, wrong, wrong! Have you forgotten Iran and Saudi already? Where was the one people then, when they continued the Shia versus Sunni civil wars that they'd propagated for generations? You can't ignore the issues that don't suit your arguments, Sabal.'

'I can see that I need to get to the point and then debate your objections after that. So, first off, I accept your very valid comments. Yes, we have not eliminated radical thought and what I will term old fashioned ideologies. Irrespective of the shared wealth of the world and the paradise-like conditions that we share now, there will still be areas of unrest I suppose although most of those are political and linked to human greed or corruption, which sadly remain a part of the human condition. Unfortunately, too much of the Islamic world had limited experience, or true understanding, of the power and value of real democracy. So, please let me digress for a moment and approach this discussion from a different angle.

'I will make some observations, which will not be new to you, but perhaps have not been listed as a group before. Since Revelation Day we have witnessed the removal of most, perhaps all, radical clerics. The Taliban no longer exist. The most strident advocates for a strict interpretation of the Quran all died out within a year, seemingly from natural causes. People that attempted to, shall we say, thwart the introduction of democratic principles, or inclusiveness, also seemed to disappear or fail to find followers. Extreme misogynists also lost influence or died. The old royal families are no more, except for a few ceremonial types, but none have any power. Some were killed, I know, but most saw the need for change and adapted to it.'

'What's your point,' Asif interrupted again.

'My point is that there is unlikely to be any popular uprising of Islamic anger, or charges of blasphemy against me, and I would hope we will see an intelligent debate occurring.'

'You're mad, Sabal! Just because the fanatics seem to have disappeared doesn't mean that this campaign that you're on won't create a new cause for them. You might well have put back the secular roadmap by decades. This crusade of yours could create a new polarisation for enough people to start a war. And some of that might be orchestrated by regimes that want to decrease the power and influence of Pakindesh, here and in the Americas. You have given ammunition to those States, like Indonesia, and even the North Africans, to declare war on all of Pakindesh.'

'I am aware of that, naturally.'

'What! You want a war with them?'

'No, but we should not fear it, Ghulam.'

'Why not?'

'Because if I am right, any war perpetrated against us will fail, by the same kind of divine intervention we've already experienced.'

'Are you fucking crazy? On the one hand you say that Allah is letting us do what we want, to see what happens or something. Yet you then say that He will intervene to assist this process by destroying those that want to keep him in place as their Supreme Being. Do you not see the irony in that argument?'

'Of course. But think back to what we've recently discussed, with your father and afterwards, many times. All Muslims were saved, and vast numbers were not devout or even minimally practicing the religion. So, since Revelation Day there has been no identified divine support for the teachings of The Prophet, and no consequences for not adhering to the Quran. Do you disagree with that?'

Muhammed Asif sighed heavily, 'No, I don't.'

'So, why would Allah, praise be His name, change the direction of the path that He has put us on now?'

'Maybe because you've annoyed Him. Maybe He doesn't want your... analysis, to be aired like this?'

'Perhaps, but if so, then He would have made an example of me already, surely?'

'You have a bloody answer to everything, don't you?'

'I've been contemplating this for quite some time, Muhammed. I don't think we need fear this fanatical uprising you worry about.'

'And if you are wrong, my friend?'

'Then I humbly apologise and will prepare my forces accordingly.'

HABBIB

He was unaware of the coincidence, but Habbib's call to Kalil was only an hour or so after that of Muhammed Asif. Kalil had not only been expecting it but was anxious to have a conversation with his closest confidant. Habbib felt nervous, assuming a potential rift occurring if he was too forceful. A part of him was worried that Kalil might have lost his acumen. Above all else he did not want to lose the joy that he felt each time they had a robust conversation, and he remembered fondly his last visit to Rio for the Pakindesh American Leaders Forum.

His videocall connected immediately on a secure line and the screen in front of Habbib showed a smiling Kalil wearing an open necked lime green shirt.

'Paul, how wonderful to hear from you.'

'I suppose I should apologise for not calling you earlier. It has been too long, Sabal.'

'That is of no importance. I knew that you would need time to consider your position and thoughts before calling to scold me for my stupidity,' he laughed.

Habbib laughed too, smiling broadly as he immediately bonded with his friend, knowing already that Kalil had not lost his senses. 'I am glad to see you looking confident and like your old self.'

'What, you expected a dementia-ridden stroke victim, Paul,' he laughed again.

'I hoped not, and did not expect that, no.'

'Well, contrary to some quarters, I have not gone mad, nor am I seeking a religious war, so let me calm that fear, if you ever wondered, which I doubt.'

'Sabal, I never doubted your sanity, and it was clear in the interview that you remained on top of your game as an interviewee. Your rationale however... well, that is what I wish to learn more about, as I'm sure you realise.'

'I do. And I just had young Asif on the line too, equally worried. Well, maybe not equally, probably more than you. But then he does sit closer to the potential powder kegs of fanaticism than you do, and while he calls me Uncle, his relationship with me is not like his father's was.'

'True enough', Habbib conceded, 'and he's a little closer to old enemies or rival states than you are too. Unlike here in the Americas, he does have border issues to manage, and a larger population to control, as well as fewer linkages than Ghulam had.'

'That he does, Paul. So, are you going to grill me on my motives or how would you like to discuss things?'

'To be honest, Sabal, I think I understand your position, or at least your intellectual analysis of Allah's meaning for us all. The argument, or your conclusion of purpose, is simple enough to follow. However, it does leave you open to accusations of blasphemy, by specifically putting yourself above Allah by seeking to interpret Him. Would you agree with that criticism at least?'

'Of course, Paul. That is valid, but as the teachings advise us, "If the Quran was open to interpretation by all, each verse could potentially mean an unlimited number of things. This would as a result imply that God was the author of confusion, exalted is He from such absurdity!" Have you heard this ultimate criticism for what I will be accused of doing?'

'Of course. Most stridently from clerics in Asia and the Middle East, naturally. But you would have known that risk in advance of course?'

'Of course. But it's worth it. Ask me your most pressing questions, Paul.'

'Okay. What's the end game?'

'No messing around,' Kalil laughed again, 'I like that, and expected nothing less. Let me offer an apology in advance for throwing this back at you. Do you think that the world has advanced at equal pace in all places over the past decade?'

'No, of course not. But why would it when that has not ever been the history of the world?'

'Paul let us not confuse things with pre-RD times. RD changed everything. Therefore, it only matters what has occurred since then. Can you accept this premise?'

'Okay, keep going then,' Habbib allowed, his slight annoyance obvious in his tone.

'Thank you. So, what have been the most glaring setbacks to enlightenment, and what are the most positive changes?'

'You really make me do all the work, don't you, Sabal? But I'll play along with you. Let me think,' he paused. A minute later he said, 'Main setback was the Iran-Caliphate war and the subsequent destruction of Mecca, and Tehran. Then there was the various... let us call them... fundamental versus democratic disagreements, which seemed to result in a lot of deaths, by supposed natural causes, of hard-line clerics as well as Taliban and ISIS supporters and other terrorist groups, mainly Sunni supported. But after that there was positive progress across the world. There were, and still are, some fundamentalist actions by those that wish to rewrite history and destroy previous knowledge databases, but they are vastly outnumbered by people hankering for elements of past lives and information, and music, movies, sport, all sorts of nostalgia,' he paused, still thinking of further examples.

'Well done, Paul. A good precis, and I think you have covered the main points that I too have contemplated. So, let me use your list and extrapolate my own analysis if you will indulge me. First, the Iran-Caliphate war and the destruction of Mecca. Ignoring taking sides with either of those regimes, why would Allah, praise be He, allow for the destruction of Mecca from that conflict, Paul?'

'Hmm. Well, presumably because... it was no longer needed? Or it was time to move beyond a single dominant holy place?'

'Exactly! If Mecca remained preeminent, then its location, and whoever controlled it, would have inordinate power. Without Mecca, the entire world would or could be accepted as Holy Ground, equal in the eyes of God. Agreed?'

'That's one interpretation, I'll give you that, Sabal.'

'Do you have another interpretation?'

'Not right now, no. Not a satisfactory one.'

'An unsatisfactory one then?'

'A preference for Medina or Jerusalem to be the new holiest site or sites of course.'

Kalil considered that for some moments, and Habbib remained quiet. 'Yes, that is another possibility I suppose. But Medina didn't increase in importance, although Jerusalem did.'

'Of course, but that's because Saudi Arabia was decimated, and Medina was damaged too, whereas Jerusalem was less contentious, not being exclusively claimed by Sunni or Shia.'

'Or maybe because the once stateless Palestinians were suddenly presented with their own prize?'

'Why would that be important, Sabal?'

'Because it raised their somewhat tarnished status to the new controllers of the Dome on the Rock.'

'Are you forgetting the fierce fighting between the Jordanians and the Palestinians before the Jordanians relinquished their claim?'

'No, I'm not, but the Jordanians had no support, so they could never win, and they realised that within a week or so. It was never going to be like the Iran-Saudi conflict. And once settled it descended into peace quickly, didn't it?'

'And your point is?'

'That Allah allowed us to work it out for ourselves, and the loss of Mecca was not dwelt upon for long. Would that have been the case if its loss had occurred before RD?

'Those two options cannot be compared, Sabal. You're heading into poor arguments if you go down that track.'

'Agreed. So, let me move on. Your second issue was the various loss of radical clerics and fanatics and the move to democratic, pluralist governments. I therefore ask you, how likely was that outcome when there was such a lack of democratic institutions across the Islamic world, if not the whole world, pre-RD?'

'I disagree, Sabal. Yes, the Middle Eastern nations, and North African ones, were largely autocratic, but across India, Pakistan, Bangladesh, Indonesia, and Malaysia, these were successful democracies with vast numbers of people. I'd argue that most Muslims therefore lived in democratic countries, and especially when those in Europe and other parts of Africa are included.'

'Do you contend then that the expansion of democracy across the post-RD world was in safe hands and a likely outcome, Paul?'

'More so than not, yes.'

'Then why was it necessary for so many clerics and fanatics to be removed?'

'Assuming they were removed, rather than simply dying of natural causes during times of high stress,' Habbib began, '...then, perhaps any threat against advancement of a more pluralist society was against the post-Revelation Day plan?' he suggested.

'A plan, Paul?'

Habbib laughed, 'Have I been ambushed?'

'No, but you are astute enough to see where I'm taking this, aren't you?'

'To the plan being for freedom of thought, or freedom of how and when we worship? Something like that?'

'Yes. Do you disagree with my logic?'

'It's not the kind of debate that can claim logic, Sabal. This is an interpretation that stretches flimsy evidence into a premise that cannot be proven. Do you think this will convince the lunatic fringe that is calling for your head?'

'Perhaps not, Paul. But our brief history since RD shows that fundamentalists fare particularly badly in this new world. Whilst I have always believed that anyone claiming that God is on his side in any battle or war is a complete fool, it might just be true in my case. I am suggesting that Allah is pointing us down the road to freedom from religion to a future which should be determined by mankind alone. Allah is freeing us now from any strict doctrine, without adherence to the Quran, or the Hadith. Free to interpret His teachings as we see fit, individually, if our intent is love, and peace, and non-violence, and without harsh judgement for any transgressions upon Earth, with the knowledge that we will be fairly dealt with as long as our hearts are pure.'

"But what if you are wrong, Sabal?'

SALINA

'It's pouring,' Salina noted, morosely, looking out of the hotel window at the teeming rain, people dashing about with umbrellas, the Washington sky dark and foreboding.

'Just like yesterday,' Michael agreed, yawning, then stretching, reluctant to get out of bed. 'You're dressed. How long have you been up?'

'An hour or so. I slept well and woke up alive and full of energy. Do you want to go out for breakfast?'

'What, in this? Why not eat downstairs?'

'We can, Michael. Whatever you want. I'm just sick of hotel food, that's all. Aren't you?'

'Breakfast is the same no matter where we get it, but I'm okay if you need a change of venue. We've got rain jackets somewhere, haven't we?'

'Of course. We British never go anywhere without planning for rain,' she laughed, her mood suddenly lifted.

'Alright. Let me quickly shower and shave,' Michael said, throwing back the covers and making for the bathroom, dressed in boxer shorts. As siblings sharing a twin hotel room, there was a basic level of dress propriety that each maintained. A second room was only booked when one or the other had a sexual need to fulfil, and the signs were recognised without the need to spell out that it was time to accept a higher hotel cost. Twenty minutes later Michael appeared in jeans, a sweater over a T-Shirt, his favourite Hi-Tech boots in one hand and a Kathmandu rain jacket in the other. 'Where to, Salsa?'

'How about that funky coffee place next to the park?'

'Oh yeah, that's not too far. Got your jacket?'

'And an umbrella too,' she said, mock stabbing him with it as if fencing.

'Wow, you are in an upbeat mood. President Habbib might not know what he's in for today.'

'We need to go over the plan at breakfast; wargame it,' she stated.

'Naturally. I know the drill, Sis. Just let me get at least one coffee into me first,' he countered as they left the room.

Ten minutes later, a little worse for wear and shaking off the raindrops, they put the umbrella in a stand inside the door of the café, shook off their rain jackets and found a table by the window. By the time the waitress arrived they had perused the menu and were ready to order.

Salina ordered eggs Benedict and a latte, Michael opting for Belgian waffles with bananas, berries and syrup, no cream, and a long black coffee. There were only 6 other diners, and nobody close enough to hear their conversation. Salina went straight to the point, 'I think I need to push to get Habbib's views on Kalil's statement, don't you?'

'Of course, but why would he stick his neck out like that?'

'Because he's a close friend, and he'll want to protect Kalil from the fallout from his bombshell comments in Rio.'

'Maybe he won't. He might want to distance himself from Kalil.' Michael suggested.

Salina looked at her brother with disdain, 'Seriously?'

'Isn't self-preservation a basic instinct?'

'Are you saying that his assessment of risk, from global fanaticism, will override ten years of close friendship? No way, Michael. Apart from their personal bond, the Pakindesh Americas are dependent on each other. They sink or swim together, also backed by the Pakindesh subcontinent's might. The Pak-Empire must stick together, just as it has always done, which is why it remains the only true superpower.'

'You're making a huge assumption. You're equating SAP solely with Kalil. He might have created this American continental empire, but he's still just one man. If Asif junior and Habbib see him as a threat to their empire then he'll be sacrificed, just as many politicians past their use-by date are.'

She nodded her head, acknowledging her brother's point, then leant her chin on her clasped hands, staring into space. He let her think. A minute later she said, 'No. Not this time they won't.'

'Why not?'

'Because Kalil *is* Pakindesh; all of it. From Bangladesh to Pakistan and Alaska to Cape Horn. If he is shown to be fallible, or crazy, then the whole empire is at risk. He must be supported. If he falls then Habbib and Asif will too, and they could be potentially attacked on multiple fronts. Asif junior especially needs Kalil, he's astute but not his late father. Habbib is less vulnerable. No, this isn't one of those old political infighting issues that sees a leadership change as a regular occurrence. Kalil planned this, and even if he only explained his actions to Habbib and Asif later, he must have thought this through like a chess master, or the general he once was. He didn't get to be a Muslim Major General in the Hindu dominated Indian Army without supreme strategic and tactical skill and knowing how to play the long game, Michael. I think tonight's interview with Habbib is going to be extremely interesting.'

MINA

There was a knock on the door and the Prime Minister's secretary walked in, 'The Minister of Defence has arrived, Prime Minister. Shall I show him in?'

'Yes please, Yasmin, and we'll have tea too. Is there any of that fruit cake that he likes? If so, bring some of it as well. Otherwise, anything you think appropriate.'

'Yes, Ma'am,' she replied, then walked away to fetch the Minister.

A few moments later, a tall grey-haired man with a handlebar moustache was shown in, who nodded his head in deference, 'Good morning, Prime Minister.'

'Good morning, Peter, so good to see you. Please take a seat,' she said pointing to the chair opposite her with a coffee table between them with a few files on the edge of it. As he sat down and unbuttoned his jacket, she added, 'Tea is on its way. I'm hoping there's some of that cake you liked last time, but no promises.'

He chuckled, 'Your memory for detail puts me to shame, Prime Minister.'

'I doubt that, Peter.' Just then Yasmin returned with a tray containing a teapot, milk jug, two cups and two plates with some fruit cake, forks, and napkins. Yasmin left the tray, knowing that her boss liked to 'play mother' to put her visitors at ease, no matter what relationship she had with them, or how she planned to manage the pending discussions. Tea was a strategic ally she once told her secretary. During the pouring ceremony, she could assess the stage of nervousness or excitement of her visitors and plan her discussion. But today she was at ease, as was Peter Aziz.

He sipped his tea with satisfaction, then took a bite from his fruit cake, smiling as he savoured it.

'As good as last time?' she asked.

'Definitely. Thank you for indulging me, Prime Minister.'

'Well, I like it too, and it's nice to have someone to share it with, without feeling guilty of the calories,' she chuckled. 'Now. To business. How do you see tonight playing out, and what are the extreme outcomes we need to prepare for?'

'Well, PM,' he began, using the acceptable abbreviation of her title, and that she preferred, 'assuming President Habbib doesn't just deflect questions about Kalil's comments, there are only two options for him, support or condemnation...'

'Or downplaying them,' Mina countered.

'I class that as condemnation, on the grounds that it would be less than supporting, which as you well know, is like a knife in the back.'

'Hmm, maybe, although I take the point, no pun intended. Go on, Peter.'

'If Habbib supports Kalil, which we'd prefer, then it somewhat isolates the extremists, albeit giving them further targets perhaps. If he doesn't then it creates a rift across the whole Pakindesh empire, which would send a signal to anyone thinking of challenging their position, that the Empire has fatal flaws. That would, or could, lead to skirmishes along vulnerable borders, especially from Indonesia, less so from the Middle East.

'Indonesia-Malaysia, even supported by The Philippines, is no match for Pakindesh in a conflict,' she stated.

'No, that's true, PM. Even if supported from the north and east by the Stans and all Middle Eastern nations up to Turkey, Pakindesh would easily win a shooting war, and especially being nuclear capable.'

'Surely your analysis isn't suggesting things could deteriorate that far, Peter?'

'No, PM, not at all. We just looked at the balance of power. It would need Turkey to be a major combatant too, and that is not likely. Turkey's focus has been its broadening European empire for a decade now. It knows it would lose in a conflict with Pakindesh, and there's nothing to gain for them.'

'What about closer to home, for unrest I mean?'

'We don't see it, PM. If anything, we're far more aligned to Pakindesh, culturally and philosophically. 'Now, from a threat perspective, the UK has been left alone from African migrant moves, either because of the benefit of being an island or the strong cultural link to Pakindesh, which, thanks to your leadership, extended a treaty to us.'

'Yes, well, don't overstate that issue, Peter, it wasn't exactly any brilliance on my part, but rather the good luck of Britain having significant family ties to Pakistan and India and Bangladesh,' she said offhandedly.

'Maybe so, Prime Minister, but you clinched our defence when you invited President Asif to have a naval base here. The presence of their three destroyers and a carrier here is our protection.'

'Hmph, maybe. I hear my detractors are saying that I have handed effective control over to Pakindesh, and that I'm a puppet.'

'Some do, yes, which is a nonsense. Your master stroke was offering for the families of the Pakindesh military to settle here. Your supporters know that this meant we gained a free defence force, from their naval contingent, plus an army brigade and an air force squadron. That was clever, PM.'

'Well, it worked at least. We've never had internal street battles like France experienced ten years ago.'

'Exactly, and it's the French that would be more upset about this Kalil debate, being dominated by North and West African migrants that tend to be more devout.'

'Yes, I agree.'

'We no longer live in a world of major military conflict, and the old powers of the U.S., Russia, and China are gone. With very few exceptions, the old Middle East nations are peaceful and democratic. The Indo-Malay sphere is prospering and more concentrated on its colonisation of Australia, New Zealand, and the Pacific Islands, having expanded unopposed to the old northern limit of the Myanmar to Vietnam line. Nobody can seriously challenge the military might of Pakindesh.'

'That's true, and it still remains the only nuclear power I suppose?'

'Probably. There are nuclear missiles around Europe, but I doubt there are many people that could utilise them, or wish to, or at least I'd hope so. We don't believe that anyone outside of Pakindesh has the skilled manpower to operate nuclear submarines either.'

'I know I should really remember everything you've advised me on in the past, but would you mind updating me on the current state of African nations, Peter?'

'From a threat perspective do you mean?'

'Yes, just the overview, please. Pretend I'm a young university history student. It challenges my sometimes slightly off assumptions that way,' she suggested ingenuously.

'Well, the initial migration into Europe, from the northern and western African nations, and Turkey, happened by osmosis, without a plan, just people moving to a better place, to grab good housing and better agricultural land. Phase two was the in-fighting period, with the eventual winners being Turkey, now extending from Germany and along the Baltic Sea coast to Estonia, then south along the old Russian border to the Black Sea, including Greece, Albania, Croatia and all of Austria, Hungary, Czechia and Slovakia to Germany; like the re-emergence of the old Ottoman Empire but on steroids, PM.

'In the west, Spain and Portugal were an easy expansion of influence by the Moroccans. Algeria dominated the push to France and remains the ethnic majority of influence in Paris. Tunisia seemed happy with just Sardinia and Corsica. The surprise, for me, was the various Libyan groups in Malta and Italy being ousted by Nigeria. Although their weight of population and an odd amalgam of sub-groups became an easy grab. And yet that strong Nigerian population in Italy hasn't formalised its hold or taken on any Italian historical persona or government, and the Vatican City State remains a museum piece, untouched, happily, and surprisingly.

'However, once Turkey reached the capacity of its population to control its lengthening borders, there were places where the Nigerian diaspora proved more than capable of exerting its own control where it wished, whilst avoiding direct confrontation with Turkey. The Libyans, in contrast, don't control any regional or local government area anywhere in Europe, even where they have a strong ethnic presence in some cities, like Nice and Montpellier.' He paused for a moment, and the Prime Minister waited for him to continue.

'What we are less confident about is the internal power plays across the remaining states of North and West Africa. Some expanded by sea and sent their navies to South Africa, but there were no naval conflicts between West African states. Landlocked countries like Mali, Burkina, Niger, Chad, and the Central African Republic ceased to exist after their populations sought greener pastures, literally. There might have been some conflicts as migrations occurred, we don't know, as information flow in the initial years post-RD was very limited.

'Looking eastwards, Somalia split along clan lines, with many moving into the better agricultural and climatic regions of Ethiopia, as well as consolidating control of Kenya. Frankly, PM, there is limited ongoing intelligence about sub-Saharan Africa. Its population density is miniscule. Cape Town is a functioning city, but I don't know what its dominant ethnicity is. Windhoek and Luanda in the old Namibia and Angola were populated by West African migrants, but as for who wields the power now, we're not certain.'

'Thank you, Peter, a good summary. So, in brief, as far as being targeted as a Pakindesh supporter, we have nothing to fear externally, and less internally, unless we see some extremist behaviour like has occurred in France from time to time?'

'Yes, PM. But overall, Pakindesh must remain united, and Kalil continue to be supported by Asif and Habbib.'

The Prime Minister cradled her hands together, rhythmically tapping her fingertips as she thought. Peter Aziz remained silent, watching her. She looked across at her Defence Minister, alert again. 'How much of our population is a security risk?'

'We have sixty-three people that we keep a regular eye on. Of those, eight are higher risk, but not critical, PM.'

'Good. Increase whatever surveillance you have on them and keep me posted. Watch those eight, ahead and beyond of the airing of the interview that my daughter has with President Habbib.'

ADDIS ABABA

The President of Greater Somalia, Abdellahi Artan Dhulbahante, descended from the Darod bloodline, looked across the gardens from the balcony of his room in Addis Ababa. The view lifted his spirits, as usual. He took a deep breath and walked back into his room, which was cavernous, adjoining the bedroom and bathroom, with a desk against one wall and a coffee table and a settee against another. This used to be called the Royal Suite for the major hotel that it once was a part of.

He went to the bathroom and washed, then put on a long white robe, taking up his prayer position and fixing his gaze to the floor. He recited the opening chapter of the Quran, made up of just seven verses, then prostrated himself, palms open towards Mecca. He said *Praise be to Allah*, stood once more, recited another verse of the Quran, and repeated the procedure. At the end, whilst sitting, he looked sideways, first right and then left, cupped his hands together and said *Allah make me wise, forgive my sins, bless my parents and give them health, and please Allah, put my parents in Paradise. Please Allah, keep me on the safe path.*

He then took his prayer beads, a multiple of thirty-three, and said *Praise be to Allah,* thirty-three times; *God forgive me,* thirty-three times; and then *Gratitude to Allah,* thirty-three times.

A little later there was a knock on his door and immediately a tall man entered the room, carrying a tray with tea and some dates. His black Somalian complexion was glistening slightly with sweat. Abdellahi knew that this acolyte would never be comfortable in his presence. His name was Yusuf Isaq, his clan surname denoting his herder background and hence he would always be destined for subservient roles in Somalian life. After the tea had been placed on a table, he stood waiting for instructions.

'Is Artan Marehan waiting?'

'Yes, Sire,' Yusuf acknowledged, using a title that had come into practice only five years previously, after the clan disputes had lessened into an uneasy peace and most of the more distinguished clan families had migrated to Addis Ababa and away from Mogadishu and the coastal areas of Somalia. From that point on, many of the older and historic ways of addressing each other changed. The older generations did not like the changes, especially when ancient clan loyalties, and enmities, began to alter, allowing some lesser clans to achieve a better destiny than some thought proper.

'Bring him in, Yusuf,' Abdellahi ordered. Artan Marehan was his Chief Minister. His bloodline was also of the Darod, making him a natural ally of all the Dhulbahante and therefore unlikely to seek to overthrow his President.

Artan Marehan arrived, went through the formalities of greeting and was then asked to sit, take tea, and eventually the real discussions began. Some fifteen minutes into their conversation,

Artan Marehan reluctantly advised his President that there had indeed been discussions between clan leaders about the rumours of the blasphemy of the Pakindesh Presidents. All of them were deemed the same and there was no distinction between Kalil, Asif and Habbib, the latter most despised because of his American heritage, irrespective of his faith.

'Who were present at these gatherings, Artan?'

'Everyone, although in different locations of course. Hierarchy differences remained as always. The Isaq, Wersengeli, and Hawiye were the most vocal, but also the most stupid, having no clue as to the difficulty of attacking Pakindesh, which was their aim, calling for a Jihad, naturally. The debates amongst the Magan, Kenaidiid, Marehan, Dhulbahante and Isse were more pragmatic. They were equally angry, but aware of the impossibility of waging war against Pakindesh, or even against President Kalil alone.'

'Was there any discussion about the Government?' Abdellahi asked.

'You are safe, Sire. Nobody insulted your position, values, or right to rule. There was no call for Greater Somalia to seek a conflict, only to pray for the death of all Pakindesh unbelievers.

Once Marehan had left, Abdellahi paced the room, slowly, hands behind his back, thinking. His faith made him want to kill Kalil, because of his blasphemous remarks and therefore their deemed attack on Allah and the Prophet. The dominance of Pakindesh, on four continents, if its control of Britain was included, outraged him. Less so than the disastrous war between the Caliphate and Iran, although he was happy with the deaths of so many Shias, but the loss of Mecca and the demise of Arabia overall was a tragedy that consumed him. He had hoped one day to move north and take the Caliphate, sure that Somalia had the warrior capabilities, and numbers to achieve that. The Saudis were lazy and arrogant. He had dreamt of taking Mecca himself, and becoming a figure as famous as Saladin, during the crusades against the infidel Christian knights. When the holy city was lost, he was distraught, and it took him a year to get over the event and set new goals. Taking the major clans into Ethiopia and moving the centre of Greater Somalia to Addis Ababa had been worthwhile. Usurping Sudan over the next five years had also been satisfying, as was the subjugation of Yemen. But it still left him empty of his true goal, and there was no way that he had the strength or means to liberate Jerusalem. In his heart he knew that an attack on

Pakindesh was impossible, at least by military conflict alone. No, if there was to be any fight with Pakindesh, or Kalil, it had to be very well planned and supremely executed. It was time to plan, with Allah by his side.

HABBIB

'So, we are all comfortable with this approach?' Habbib asked.

'Clearly I am, Paul,' Kalil stated.

Asif sighed heavily, and his silence was not interrupted. Finally, he nodded, 'Yes, I agree. It is time, but I remain fearful.'

'And your thoughts, Mina?' Habbib pursued, conscious that the British Prime Minister had added little to the brief debate. She looked calm on the split computer screen in front of him.

She nodded her head. 'As I said earlier, I agree with the sentiment, and the conclusions, most of them, and will... toe the line, shall we say. But I do fear for reprisals more than you gentlemen. I am grateful for the offer of more military assistance though, so thank you again for that, Muhammed. I agree, of course. Good luck for this evening, Paul.'

'I am sure that your daughter will be kind to me, Mina,' he joked.

'I hope so, but I still urge caution. She can be a fire brand when she wants to be. But I am looking forward to seeing her home again next week.'

'Okay then. Thank you all,' Habbib said, 'and we will confer again next Wednesday at the same time.' He logged off the video call session and took a sip of his coffee. It was cold and he went off to seek a fresh pot, stretching his back as he rose from the chair. He was nervous of his pending interview. He knew not to treat Salina Ahmed lightly. She excelled in her profession and had earned a worldwide reputation on solid research, a killer smile, and a way of getting her subjects to let their guard down and talk more openly than might have been wise at the time. Kalil had given him some pointers and an interesting piece of intelligence, before the others had joined the call.

He was interrupted in the kitchenette by a secretary, 'Excuse me, Sir, but The Prime Minister is here.'

'Thank you, Shanaz. I'll be there in a moment,' he answered, taking a last gulp of coffee, wiping his mouth, and putting the mug in the dishwasher. There was little standing on ceremony in the modern White House.

As he entered the Oval Office, he saw Malik Shah perusing one of the paintings on the wall. 'Do you ever feel like an interloper, Paul?' the Prime Minister asked.

'Every day, Malik,' he laughed. 'What about you?'

'The same. I could never have envisaged this path for my life under any circumstances. Anyway, down to the issues at hand. I take it your expectations of the other Pakindesh leaders was as expected?'

'It was, and along the lines that you and I also assumed a few days ago,' Habbib confirmed.

'Do you have any exit strategies if it becomes necessary?'

'Not really. Once we head down this road, we have little option but to be bold, don't we?'

Shah frowned, 'Yes, I suppose so. Imran is the most concerned. I am a little worried about him. Has he spoken to you recently?'

'Yesterday. I agree, he is agitated. He concurs with the analysis, but thinks we're being… imprudent I believe was his word of the day,' Habbib said without humour.

'Yes, he said the same to me. You are greatly confident of Kalil, aren't you?'

'I am, Malik. He's possibly the most intelligent man I've ever met, and his ideas always make you sit up and think, even to question your own long held thoughts.'

'Well, let's hope his luck remains, as well as his acumen. I just wanted to wish you well. You have my support no matter what.' He stood up, nodded, and walked out of the room, leaving Habbib to his own insecurities.

MICHAEL

'I don't know why, Salsa, but looking out over the city depresses me. So many well-known monuments, although mainly from newsreels for us, I suppose. It's not like we remember Washington. They're false memories for us, really. London should seem like a greater sense of loss for us, shouldn't it, yet it doesn't'.

'Maybe because we live there now and all our London links are since RD, so there's an emotional attachment that is relatable, Michael.'

'Do you remember our reminiscence game, with Charlie?'

'Of course. I created it, after a lot of urging from him,' she laughed. 'I think Charlie realised that I was starting to brood and withdraw into myself. When he asked me what I would like most of all if I could control the world, I said the death of Allah, and then added and all the religious fanatics that hated non-Muslims. Charlie asked why, and I said that it was maybe those fanatics that had somehow created the genocide and that now we would start to see the subjugation of women and girls and life would become a living hell for females, like it was in places like Afghanistan.'

Michael nodded, 'Yeah, Charlie was very worried about your mental health, so he devised that game, for each of us to name something we missed. Didn't we start at 'A' and then go in alphabetical order?'

'Yep, and if we delayed by 5 seconds or more, we lost a point, and if the delay reached 10 seconds we were out of the game,' she remembered.

'That's right, Salsa, and Charlie started with Arsenal?'

'Yes, and I said Ariana Grande, and you said alcohol, which was cheating coz we didn't drink,' she laughed.

Michael laughed too. Wow, I do remember that, and the 'B's' had Boddington's beer, bunnies, and Birmingham Football Club, then Charlie said Chelsea, and you objected and said that we couldn't just use football team names as that was too easy,, and we limited ourselves to 5 football teams, and only countries that we had visited otherwise 'Z' would always produce Zimbabwe or Zambia.'

'Charlie was very good at keeping our spirits up, wasn't he?' Salina said.

'Hmm, he was. That game kept our past front of mind, and we never forgot the people and places and events that had been our reality growing up. I think in some ways it made the present then, and this last ten years, like an interloper in our lives, or perhaps an unwelcome rich relative that demands respect, without having earnt it.

By 9am the following morning, Salina had eight pages of notes and tips for the way that she wanted the interview with Habbib to progress. She had a premonition that this was not going to be dull, but provide another major upset, like Kalil had created in Rio only a few weeks ago. But in the back of her mind, she was also worried.

Kalil's bombshell had caused significant issues in many countries around the world, with fiery demonstrations in a few and calls for his blasphemous remarks to bring him to trial. Admittedly, most of these were orchestrated by anti-Pakindesh politicians, and religious leaders that saw the possibility of it assisting with a greater adherence to the Quran and boosting their declining mosque attendances, which had been falling steadily for years. A few street riots broke out, the worst in Lagos, Cairo, Casablanca, Jakarta, Mogadishu, and Tripoli. Europe was less strident, but a few minor demonstrations occurred in Istanbul, Berlin, Madrid, and Paris.

She struck out a few sentences of her notes, added others, chewed her pencil, tapped her teeth with it, stood up and paced the room, then made herself another lemon and ginger tea. At that point, Michael came into the room, perused the 'damage' to its cleanliness, realised the stage she was going through and asked if she wanted to wargame the interview.

'No, not this time, Michael. Part of me needs to have some strategies pre-set, and another to let it roll.'

'Any part of the script you want to bounce off me, Sis?'

She thought about it for a while, then said, 'Do you think I should push him to endorse or disavow Kalil, if he seems to be hedging or avoiding that issue?'

'No, I don't think you should push it too hard if it means creating a problem that might split the Pakindesh solidarity,' he suggested.

'Meaning?'

'I don't think it would be good to create, or maybe widen, any disagreement of positions between Kalil, Habbib and Asif.'

'Why?'

'Because Pakindesh is increasingly liberal, and we like its influence in the world, compared to other places we've seen, don't we? And then there's mum's position too of course.'

'Why would mum be impacted?'

'Seriously, Salsa? If there was any adverse impact on Pakindesh as a whole, then the UK is implicated. Our military security is invested in the power base of Pakindesh. It supplies our army, navy and air force.'

'But no-one is threatening the UK, Michael.'

'Not yet, but if the call to abandon adherence to the Quran grows, and if Pakindesh is at odds with the rest of the world on this, then the UK is just as much a target as the Sub-continent and the Americas.'

'From Indonesia or Africa? Surely not, Michael.'

'Salsa, if this thing grew to a major us or them, meaning Kalil's hypothesis of Allah fading into the sunset to allow humans to get on with things as they see fit, versus the fundamentalist version of the meaning of life, then this could become a major shit fight, and a shooting war, and it could become the Turkish Empire and North African dominated European states versus the UK as a Pakindesh outpost.'

Salina's face fell, as the realisation of the worst possible outcome of the immediate future struck her. Michael watched her assimilate many scenarios in her mind, her expressions like a silent movie. Eventually she said, 'This could be the biggest interview I ever conduct, Michael. Oh fuck!'

'Well, that's one way of putting it,' he laughed, attempting to lighten her mood.

'Michael, I can't stuff this one up. I'm not sure I can do this, honestly.'

'Yes, you can, you've done cutting edge stuff before. Don't freak out. Remember that Palestinian President that you took apart in Jerusalem, the one that denied the holocaust. You made him look like the right prat he was, and you weren't worried about offending the nation or us getting out of there alive then, were you?'

'No, but maybe I should have been. I've been reckless before, but my luck has held. Maybe I'll stuff this one up and people will get killed, or...' she shrugged.

'Steady on, let's not get this out of proportion, Salsa. I mean, yes, it will be an important interview. But you don't control the content; Kalil and Habbib do, and maybe Asif junior, and mum too. Let it flow. Whatever happens tonight will not be a definitive issue. Maybe there will be political fallout, or even a few shots exchanged in places. But, if Allah is watching then the future will be how He wants it, and Kalil and Habbib will have thought this through to the Nth degree, I promise you. Your job is to broadcast the messages and give those watching an opportunity to understand the issues and the arguments, and hopefully to be educated too. We've stuck the knife into fundamentalist regimes for many years now, Salsa. This is just another interview. We are the conduit, not the perpetrators of policy. Isn't that what you've always said?'

'Yes, I have. You're right, Michael. Thanks. Okay, I might have a nap before we need to go. Wake me in an hour, will you?'

'I will. Take it easy, Salsa. It will be fine, as usual,' he said as she walked off to the bedroom. He was confident that she'd be sharp again by the time he started to film. She always was, no matter how nervous she occasionally became.

A few hours later they were on their way. Habbib had sent a car for them. It seemed odd but not as intimidating as Salina had assumed to drive up the path to the White House, limited security formalities at the gate, thanks to the official familiar vehicle and its escort officer sitting next to the driver. Maybe because she'd been too young before RD to have much impression of America and the role and power that the US Presidents of the past held. It was a nice house, very aesthetically pleasing. But not in the same class as Buckingham Palace, which was not far from where they lived after first moving to London, and before she and Michael moved into 2 apartments next to each other on Canary Wharf.

Once at the door and being assisted with the equipment, they were led to the Oval Office to set up, in advance of meeting with the President, but watched by a guard as they prepared everything. There wasn't much to set up and the job was completed in twenty minutes. They then ran through a sound and vision check, adjusted the microphones and camera angles slightly and advised their watcher that they were ready. He radioed to someone and a few minutes later, Paul Habbib walked into the room, alone.

'Welcome to the White House,' he said, and approached Salina to shake hands, then did the same with Michael. 'Everything up to your standards, I hope?'

'Yes, Mr President, perfect, thank you,' Salina replied.

'And no technical issues, Michael?' Habbib asked, smiling.

'Perfect, thank you, Mr President,' Michael concurred.

Habbib sat in the chair opposite the twins and smiled broadly. At that point, a secretary entered the room, a young man in his thirties, impeccably dressed. Habbib acknowledged him with a nod. 'What say we get the nerves out of the way, have a coffee or other drink together first, then get into the official stuff?'

'I'd like that, Mr President,' Salina said.

'OK, what's your poison?'

'Is your coffee good, Mr President?' Michael asked.

'I think so, but you might not agree,' Habbib laughed.

'Sounds good then, coffee, please,' Michael decided.

Salina considered her needs, 'Erm, just a tonic water with lemon for me, please.'

'I'll join you in that, Salina. Thank you, Osman,' he said to the secretary, who then walked out of the room. The drinks arrived a few minutes later, as Habbib was showing them some of the paintings on the walls and explaining their historical significance.

'Have you enjoyed Washington?' Habbib asked.

'Yes, I have. I always do,' Salina said, 'especially the museums. I could spend days in the Smithsonian. You're lucky, as we are too in Britain, that your museums have been untouched by any overzealous behaviour after RD. Sadly, too many other museums and buildings have been destroyed around the world.'

Habbib frowned, 'Yes, I agree. The Americas are largely untouched, as you say, but some of Europe seem to have lost a lot, as have parts of Asia, India, China, and Russia. Who would have thought that so much could be lost so quickly?'

Salina was fidgeting and Habbib smiled, 'Don't tell me you're nervous, Salina?'

'No, Mr President, I am always like this ahead of an interview, because I don't want to pre-empt the discussion before the cameras are rolling,' she laughed.

'Not wanting to give the game away, you mean?' Habbib suggested.

'Not really, it's more that I don't want to start a discussion, get into a great debate and then have to try and replicate it again on film. It's never the same and I always miss the true spontaneity of a good interview.'

'Sounds like you want to get started, I think,' Habbib stated.

'Thank you. Are you set to go Michael?' she asked.

'All good for me. Mr President, I have set two fixed cameras so that I can switch between the two of you. This being a live feed, it's a bit more problematic, but I control the two screens from my console here,' he said, pointing out the various pieces of equipment. 'We still have seven minutes before we go live, but we will get the nod from the BBC who are sponsoring the interview, and I have a countdown on my screen here. We will go to their studio host two minutes before airtime.'

Salina and the President sat opposite each other, Michael a few metres from them and central to their chairs. He played with the camera angles a little more, adjusted some lighting and gave a thumbs up. His sister and Habbib adjusted postures and looked a little stiff in their chairs now, but he was used to that, irrespective of whether the interview was live or not. Salina was used to it all, but never took it for granted that there would be no stuff ups, so she remained alert, which some people took, incorrectly, for nerves. Habbib looked completely at ease.

Exactly on time the London live feed at the BBC went into its introductions and a few seconds after the agreed time Salina was live and made her introductory remarks, thanking the President for his time and the use of the Oval Office.

Without any preamble, Salina asked the most obvious question, and the one that the audience had waited for, in some form or other; 'Mr President, were you surprised at President Kalil's comments at the end of my interview with him in Rio recently?'

'I didn't expect that question so soon,' he laughed, smiling. 'I've known Sabal Kalil for over ten years now, and he often surprises me. I suppose he did so again in that discussion you had together.'

'Do you agree with his analysis?'

'Now that is getting right to the heart of it, Salina. But I think your use of the word analysis is on the money, as we Americans used to say. Kalil is a thinking man. He has depth and never takes things for granted. He would have thought very deeply about the issue before deciding to air his opinions as he did with you. He is also quite devout, despite what his new critics might believe. Kalil undoubtedly believes in our present situation being Allah's gift to humanity. Where he clearly disagrees with fundamentalists is in his analysis of this gift, what it means, and what future we should aspire to. But you spent time with him, so really, your opinion is also valid. What was your conclusion, after you had time to think about Kalil's comments?'

Salina was not ready to lose control of the interview so easily, but she saw no malice in Habbib's adroit deflection, so batted the ball back over the net, as she liked to think of it. 'I felt that President Kalil was deeply invested in his views of the world after Revelation Day. I detected no inkling of him being flippant, and certainly not blasphemous, as many are now accusing him. But do you also think that Allah is setting us free from the doctrine of the Quran?'

Habbib only paused for a few seconds before saying, 'Kalil's view, if I'm allowed to second guess him, is that there are significant clues, examples, and incidents around the world since RD, which have led him to conclude that Allah does not favour a strict adherence to the Quran and the Hadith. He believes that as we are now the only religion left alive, the need to adhere to such a restrictive set of rules is counter to human advancement. Kalil believes that the removal of so many mullahs, madrassah scholars, and especially the over-zealous subjugators of women, was a clear message from Allah. I must admit that the evidence around such changes does add weight to his proposition. Do you not think so, Salina?'

She knew she was going to be brought into the territory of making her own opinion known, and she had rehearsed her options, but now wondered how to balance the interview this early on. She couldn't allow Habbib to ambush her. He had to make his thoughts plain. 'Mr President, I'm just an interviewer, not a politician, or a scholar, or an expert on Islam. What do you think? Please tell us.'

'Fair enough. You are correct, that I have thought deeply about Kalil's conclusions, and after listening to his arguments, as well as the follow up of the past weeks, his arguments are sound. All of this has been debated so many times that it barely needs repeating. You know it all, all of us being saved irrespective of mosque attendance or Quranic adherence. 'Allowing the Iranians and the Saudis to almost eliminate each other, and their war destroying Mecca.

'Men in positions of power carrying out harsh penalties against women accused of adultery, or being rape victims, suddenly dying during their cruelties.

'I don't need to add to these examples, but they tend to support Kalil's view that the extremely conservative, Arabian-centric view of the Quran is no longer supported by Allah Himself. Perhaps I am wrong, but the evidence points this way, and Kalil's conclusions seem to be sound. After all, if Kalil was being blasphemous then surely Allah would strike him down, wouldn't He? But that did not occur. Allah is all knowing, all seeing, all powerful. If He is allowing Kalil to discuss these things, then can't that be assumed as tacit agreement?'

Salina further extrapolated the elements around the evidence that Habbib had used to add further weight to Kalil's hypothesis, without seeming to be biased or leading the debate. Then she asked, 'So if we assume that Kalil is correct and that he has accurately understood Allah's destiny for us, what might happen to thwart His desire for mankind to take this road, and to stand on our own two feet, free from a perhaps more stifling doctrine?'

'I can only assume that Allah will assist those of us that have seen His clear direction, so that we make the most of the gifts He has bestowed upon us; our intelligence, humanity, desire to live good lives, equality, education, technological advancement, and peace. If some seek to thwart these goals, or take us back to seventh century thinking, thereby diminishing us all, I think they might be harshly dealt with, as has occurred to others since RD that stayed living in the past, with narrow doctrinal perspectives.'

'But it is unlikely that the more fundamentalist or extreme adherents to the Quran will see it this way, Mr President. Won't that lead to conflict, as has sadly been the human condition throughout our history?'

Habbib smiled, 'Salina, if Allah wishes us to travel on the road that perhaps Kalil has accurately identified, then He, in His infinite wisdom, will assist us, and His preferred destiny for us all will prevail. If He doesn't, then we will be shown a different path, and there is no need for anyone to encourage violence in the place of intelligent debate.'

'Do you ever consider what the ultimate plan for humanity is, Mr President?'

'Of course,' he replied. She waited for him to add to that, the silence growing, as she nodded for him to continue. 'Well, I imagine almost everyone has considered that, many times. Who wouldn't? I suppose, for me, I like to believe that all of those that we lost on Revelation Day are still around us, maybe in a parallel world, just them, apart from us, perhaps equally confused about everything. Perhaps Allah deliberately split humanity apart to see which group would make the best world, going forward. Maybe that is the true test, a comparison of a pure Islamic world for us, and all other belief systems in their world or worlds, without us.'

'That's an interesting hypothesis, Mr president. I like that idea. Who knows?'

The interview continued for another fifteen minutes, with the observation made by Habbib that there was wide consensus across the Pakindesh world in support of Kalil. Salina then realised that the four leaders, her mother being one of them, had clearly decided on their solidarity already.

MICHAEL

Back in their hotel, after re-watching the interview twice more, Salina smiled. 'It went better than I expected, Michael.'

'Yes, I thought you were a bit stressed out about this one. I'm glad to see you smiling again, Salsa.'

'I feel better for mum now too.'

'What do you mean?'

'I thought she might either be caught in the middle of all this, or that the UK would be left without a political direction. If that had been the case, then there were more options for violence on the streets between fundamentalists and secularists.'

'But the UK hasn't had that kind of division, not really, Salsa.'

'You have a short memory, brother. Have you forgotten those teachers at school that would beat kids for perceived slights against Allah, or non-adherence to the Quran or insufficient knowledge of it?'

'Hmm, yes, I had I suppose. Long time ago, but now you mention it, we did play our part in the fightback didn't we, especially when dad got so angry and went and threatened the headmaster. I was never so proud of him as then.'

'That was nothing compared to mum's political campaign, and later fighting to be the PM.' Salina became contemplative for a minute and noticed that Michael was observing her. 'What?'

'Something's on your mind,' he stated.

'Yes. I was just wondering about all this positive change that our family has received. That could never have happened without RD, could it?'

'No, never. But what are you saying? Would you not turn back the clock if you had the chance?'

'Possibly, I don't know now. If you'd asked me a few years ago I'd probably have said yes, without thinking. But am I just missing all those things that we reminisce about, without weighing them up against life today?'

'You mean our little game of what we miss, versus the life we now have, which could not have happened otherwise?'

'Exactly, Michael. I mean there are not only our family's benefits, all of us together. But the planet is also better off, isn't it? Only two billion people alive now means that the environment has been provided with a massive safety buffer and time to breath, literally. Climate change is no longer an issue. Neither is deforestation, loss of habitat and biodiversity, fossil fuel pollution, over population in general, the destruction of the Amazon and Borneo rainforests. Even conflict has dropped off to insignificant levels.'

'You're not getting religious are you, Salsa?'

'Hardly! But I have found myself thanking Allah for our family's good fortune from time to time. Maybe I'm just a hypocrite,' she laughed.

'No, you're not. I know what you mean. Anyway, should we check the feedback from the interview?'

'Not tonight. I want to sleep feeling good about it. I don't want to read adverse tirades from pulpit-pushers calling for a Jihad. Tomorrow is early enough to read that kind of crap. I need sleep. I'm off to bed. Thanks, Michael, your camera and sound work was exemplary, as always,' she said, bending to kiss his forehead before walking to the bathroom. 'Goodnight,' she called again.

'Night, Salsa, sleep well,' he replied.

Left to his own thoughts, he wondered if he felt the same way regarding turning back the clock or accepting this life that they all had as being better. It was hard not to agree with his sister that they would never have achieved so much if Revelation Day had not occurred. But so much death. Was it not evil to accept such a loss of life as the price paid for their current success and happiness? Who is to say that he and Salsa might not have gone down a journalistic road anyway, and perhaps been equally as happy? They wouldn't have known any different. His mother could hardly have lamented not being Prime Minister; the thought would have been ludicrous. Charlie might well have still become a doctor. And Manchester United would have won more Premiership titles, surely. But there would have been a lot more human suffering, especially in the developing world. And in the Muslim world too, and especially for women, never mind the deteriorating environment.

Revelation Day was only the beginning of the changes needed. If most of the world could not now see that they were all on a continuing path to enlightenment, free of the coercion and dictatorial nature of those that could not see the need to bring the Quran into the twenty-first century, as a minimum, then will be further tests to pass.

He watched the interview again and was happy with it. So, why was he nervous about how it was going to be received around the world? His gut told him that there would be difficulties ahead. They needed to get back to their brother and parents and take a break for a while.

MUHHAMED ASIF

'Your daughter did well in her interview with Habbib yesterday, Mina,' Asif commented via the computer screen in front of her.

'Thank you, Muhammed. It seemed to go well, and thankfully, up to now there has not been too many demonstrations calling for Kalil's head, nor Habbib's. So presumably you and I are also safe, for now at least.'

'Yes, but I am not going to let my guard down, nor should any of us. I have decided to send an additional carrier group to the UK for your defence. I don't trust some of the Europeans, and especially Turkey.'

'Thank you, Muhammed, that would be most welcome. Which group is it, and where will it need to deploy?'

'It used to be called the USS Nimitz, part of the American 5th Fleet once, now renamed the PNS Humayun. I wouldn't say that it's in the same shape these days, and its air assets are less well honed, but there's still no major force outside of Pakindesh to seriously threaten it.'

'Do you see Turkey as a potential threat to us?'

'Not really, but it depends on whether the population rises in indignation, and even then, if the Government wants that kind of problem. Before RD I'm sure that Erdogan would have fanned those flames, when Turkey had deteriorated into his dictatorial plaything. He'd have been the last one to foresee being assassinated by a fundamentalist. He certainly was burnt by the fire he played with,' Asif laughed.

Mina frowned, not wanting to dwell into pre-RD politics that she was less than familiar with, although young Asif must have been channelling his father, as he was too young to remember the old Turkish leader. 'So where do you think any threat might come from if there is a large anti-Pakindesh coalition?'

'For you, France is the most likely source, but they are disorganised, and it wouldn't be government inspired. More likely an internal power play for relevance between the Algerians and other North African groups. I can't see the Moroccans caring too much.

They seem quite content in Spain and Portugal and are reasonably westernised anyway. No-one in the Middle East has the capacity to cause serious damage to us, but there's always the danger of lone-wolf attacks sponsored by fundamentalist regimes, like Nigeria or Somalia or Afghanistan. But none have the capacity to cause real mischief.

'We will continue to monitor the Indonesia-Malaysia Pact. But they generally have their extremists under control, and their massive programs on moving people into areas where their living standards increased exponentially, has completely changed the socioeconomics that allowed fundamentalists to thrive.'

Mina nodded in agreement. 'Have you spoken to Kalil since our call last week?'

'Very briefly. He was also happy with Salina's interview. I imagine you are anxious for your children to return home now?'

'Oh yes, it's been far too long since we were all together as a family.'

'Well, I sincerely hope that your family reunion is exceptional, Mina. I will speak with you on our next scheduled call,' he concluded, then ended the transmission.

She felt better now. Her anxiety level had been growing, even though Habbib had done well with Salina. Maybe it was because all of them had grown up in a world full of terrorism and war and strife, too much of it Muslim inspired, despite those that still liked to rewrite history and see the Islamic world as the victims. She didn't hold with that. But that was why she feared a repeat of extremism. Some people never changed their views, despite evidence, or the benefits of peaceful dialogue. She was having dinner with Charlie tonight. Riaz was going out with his hospital crowd. Charlie would get into a deep debate with her if she wished, he enjoyed politics and history, they both did. She looked forward to seeing her eldest son in a few hours.

ADDIS ABABA

President Dhulbahante was seething. The blasphemy of all those Pakindesh leaders. To seek to interpret Allah's will was a crime that had to be answered. His anger could not be quenched. His violent sexual assault on one of his female staff members had not helped. She had been bedded before and was not averse to rough sex, but he perhaps went too far last night. He couldn't get Habbib out of his mind and he raped and then beat her as a proxy for this new enemy. He had been in a blind rage, literally, and when he saw the welt marks on her back from his belt, he was ashamed of himself, partly because it also aroused him. He apologised to her and then sent her away, to be tended by the most discreet of his female assistants.

What to do about Pakindesh? It was his impotence against them that made him most irate. He was no fool and did not pretend that Greater Somalia had much capacity to influence the geopolitics of the world. He'd rejoiced after Allah's Revelation and Deliverance occurred. More so again after the short-lived Saudi Caliphate and the Iranian Shiites fought each other to mutual destruction. But the loss of Mecca troubled him deeply. For Kalil, and Habbib the American, to use that as a sign from Allah that His guidance was no longer necessary and that the teaching of the Quran and the Hadith could be abandoned, should have brought Allah's vengeance down on their heads. Why did it not? Why? There was only one reason. Allah wanted the faithful and most devout followers of His path to show these blasphemers the way. This was a sign, surely. Pakindesh was not all powerful, only Allah, and the Prophet Himself could decide the true path. Yes, this was a sign. Somalia's faithful were to be the catalyst that brought the world back to righteousness. Arabia had lost its historical position. African Muslims would now show the world the right path.

CHARLIE

'You look knackered, Dr Charlie,' Freddy said as he bumped into him in the corridor between two hospital wards, where he was slowly working on the rewiring. Freddy had penned the new form of address for Riaz's son even before he'd qualified as a doctor.

'I am, Freddy. But my shift has finished and I'm off to take a shower and then head to mums, for dinner.'

Freddy laughed, 'I love that. Off to mums! I don't know anyone else that could turn dinner at Number Ten with the Prime Minister into something ordinary.'

'It is ordinary, for us. But you know that.'

'I do. Just kiddin'. How is your mum, and I mean Mina, the down to earth lady I first met, not the PM?'

'Pretty good. I think she was a bit stressed leading up to Salsa's interview with Habbib, but it all went well so that calmed her down. What did you think of it, the interview?'

Freddy scratched his chin and scrunched up his nose, like he did whenever he was looking for the right words. 'She's the full package, your sister. I can't believe how the twins have developed into these global interview giants. It's weird. I still see them as teenagers, worried about the new world, and school and stuff. Now, they have more clout than even they could have imagined. Or did they? Maybe I just underestimated them as kids?'

'No, you're right, Fred. None of us could foresee this life for ourselves. We were all worried about it,' Charlie said, then looked past Fred and went quiet.

'You're doing that thing again, Charlie, going moody and broody on me. Live in the present, son, not the past. That has gone for good. This is the new, and better world. You have to believe that, surely?'

Charlie frowned. 'I do. I know. You're right. But I'm still allowed to grieve over people and things lost. Don't you, sometimes?'

'I try not to. My life is better, and the world is better too. And the people. I wouldn't go back, Charlie.'

'Me neither, Fred. So, what about President Kalil, and Habbib? Do you think they are right, that Allah is letting us get on with life without any need for prayer and adherence to the Quran?'

'When was the last time you picked up a Quran, or went into a Mosque, Charlie?'

'Hmm, it's been a while, I suppose.'

'What's a while, Charlie, five years? Or longer?' Freddy laughed but left the question open.

'I don't know. Maybe longer. I do fast over Ramadan though.'

'Good for you, but is that a way to realign your dietary habits or for religious reasons, Doc?'

'Bit of both, maybe. It's more of a family get together thing really.'

'Any guilt about that, Charlie?'

'No. What about you?'

'I've never given a toss about mosque attendance, ever. And I wasn't starting after RD either. If Allah left me alive then I said he must have approved of my life choices and inner goodness. Job done, thank you very much.'

'I agree. OK, gotta go, Freddy. See ya,' Charlie called as he wandered down the corridor to the stairs.

'Give my best to the PM, Charlie,' Freddy called out, and Charlie raised his arm in acknowledgement.

He trotted down the stairs, found his bike in the rack outside the hospital entrance, put some clips on his trouser legs, his pack on his back and cycled home, which was only twenty minutes away. Once there he had a shower and dressed casually for dinner at Number Ten. As he was about to leave, his mobile rang, and he eagerly picked up the call when he saw it was from Samantha, his current girlfriend.

'Sorry to delay you, Charlie,' she said, 'I know you're off to your mum's, but I needed to tell you that I've changed my shift for tomorrow, so I will be able to join you for that ride up the Thames if you like?'

'Oh great, Sam, thanks. Okay, I'll come past your place around eight if you like. Maybe we'll grab breakfast somewhere along the way?'

'Sounds good. Have fun tonight and I'll see you in the morning, Babe. Love you.'

'Love you too, gorgeous. G'night,' Charlie said as he disconnected the call and hurried out of the house, instantly thinking of Sam's beautiful face, and then reminiscing about Alia, his first sexual and true romantic relationship since RD. That had been a lovely time between them. Although consummated, many times over their intense six months together, he didn't regret their breakup. She was happily married now, with a child, and they occasionally saw each other and talked. But Samantha was the real deal. Maybe he'd pop the question this weekend. What was he waiting for? She was everything he wanted in a wife, and he was sure she felt as strongly as he did. They'd been together three years now, and although they each stayed over at each other's flats, neither felt right about moving in together permanently until they made it legal. It was an unspoken acceptance on both parts, but it was time now, he thought, and smiled broadly.

He walked a few hundred metres from home, took a tram for the ten-minute ride to a convenient spot and walked the last few minutes to Downing Street. There was one guard outside the door, who nodded at Charlie as he approached. They exchanged a few pleasantries and then the door opened, and he walked into the Prime Minister's official residence.

His mum was in the corridor and hugged him warmly and they both smiled. He kissed her cheek, 'How are you, Mum?'

'Great, Charlie. You?'

'A bit tired but all good. Looking forward to a few days off. Going on a ride up the river with Sam tomorrow.'

'Oh good. When am I going to be able to call Samantha my daughter-in-law?' she laughed.

That quip decided him, and he smiled, his heart suddenly lifted. 'How about tomorrow night, Mum?'

She looked shocked, pleasantly so, as her hands flew up to her face and she clasped them in front of her mouth and stifled a little yelp, 'Truly, Charlie?'

'Yes. I've been thinking about it for a while. It is time to make an honest woman of my little nurse.'

'Oh, your father will be so pleased. He loves her too. Have you said anything to Salsa and Michael?'

'Not yet. I only decided on my way here. I don't know what I was waiting for really. She's perfect, and I miss her any time we're apart, Mum. She makes my life complete. Was it that way for you and Dad?'

Mina smiled. 'Yes, I think so, but it took a little longer to realise that he was my soul mate, as they say. I've been very lucky with your father.'

'He has been with you, too, Mum. Who'd have thought he'd pull a Prime Minister,' Charlie laughed, teasing her deliberately.

'Well, it's not like – '

'Stop right there, Mum. I don't want to hear you say again that you're an accidental PM, only here due to the lack of quality options and all that rubbish. You're doing a great job, and the people love you, so enough self-doubt, OK?'

'Is that your diagnosis, Doctor?' she said, smiling.

'It is, Prime Minister. So, what's for dinner?'

'I made that Balti you like.'

'Excellent. Nothing like a home cooked meal. How did your kitchen staff take you invading their domain?'

'They know me well enough and that I like to cook personally for my son on those rare occasions you are free to join me. Now, let's go and eat, and then we can plan the wedding, Charlie.'

Over dinner, after they had exhausted marriage and wedding talk, but had decided that he must come back for another dinner the following night, with his fiancé, and when Riaz was available, the topic shifted to the Habbib interview.

'What will this all mean, Mum? Is there going to be a fight over this? Will the extremists start to agitate again? It's been years since they had any strong attempts to instil Sharia here, and all the Pakindesh nations are prosperous and calm. Will Indonesia-Malaysia or the Middle East players go to war over this?'

'No, that won't happen. They don't have a consolidated voice, are a long way from Pakindesh and the Americas, and frankly don't have the capacity to attack them,' she stated.

'What about Turkey attacking Britain as a Pakindesh ally?' Charlie asked.

'President Asif is already sending another Carrier Group here, to bolster our defences. Nobody can seriously harm Pakindesh or its allies, Charlie.'

'Maybe not in a conventional war or minor conflict, but what about terrorist activity, Mum?'

'Yes, we discussed that, all of us; Kalil, Asif, Habbib and I. We are not complacent. Kalil tends to believe that terrorist activity would be avoided by most nation states, and if it did become a serious threat then it might be thwarted by Allah Himself, even though even saying that seems to counter his belief in Allah losing interest in controlling us all,' she laughed, then added, 'Kalil is the most certain of this view, of course. I'd have to say that the rest of us are, shall we say, more dubious. Asif accused him of taking a massive gamble. Habbib believes that there is minimal likelihood of anyone in the Americas harming their own lifestyles. Asif is building his border security up, which is sensible. He was most worried about the more radical two smaller Stans, of course, but they just don't have the ability to harm Pakindesh,' she paused.

'What worries you the most, strategically I mean?'

'Well, as silly as it sounds, I did raise the historical context of a new Saladin, raising an army in the Middle East and Africa and sweeping across Europe like a twelfth century nemesis,' she laughed, without humour.

'Just for the sake of argument, if that happened, Mum, and I realise it would probably take years to happen, what would Pakindesh do?'

'Destroy them,' Mina said dispassionately.

Charlie sat back in part disbelief that this was his mother talking about a major war. She waited for him to say something. He considered his view on this revelation. 'How?'

'By every means at our disposal, Charlie. Kalil thinks that if it came to that, albeit unlikely, then if his hypothesis is right, Allah would assist us to destroy the threat well before it materialised.'

Charlie was shocked, and as his mouth fell wide open and he stared at his mother, she allowed him to get his thoughts in order. He gulped, took a breath, and said, 'So, we are talking here about a fight based on two views of Allah's will?'

'Yes. I suppose we are, Charlie.'

LAGOS, NIGERIA - ONE MONTH LATER

The planning had been detailed. The meeting in Lagos had been kept as secret as possible, but when the Presidents of Nigeria, Somalia, Egypt, Mali, Kenya, and Indonesia realised that they must meet face to face, to determine the true will of their people and many neighbouring States that they were also representing, an official subterfuge was needed. Lagos was a preferred venue to Abuja, the capital. Since RD, with a much smaller population, the city was far more attractive as a venue, enhanced by its coastal access. The meeting's rationale was an Africa-Asia Symposium on Disease Eradication. Five Health Ministers were present and had separate talks together on this topic, without realising this was a ploy, and that little would eventuate from their initiatives. Pakindesh officials, having heard of the symposium, wondered why they had not been invited, although several Indonesia-led think-tanks had occurred in Africa and the trade relationships between the continent and Indonesia-Malaysia were growing. However, that omission led to some discussion within the Pakindesh intelligence community.

After the covert discussions between the five nations had concluded, Presidents Dhulbahante of Greater Somalia, and Sintu of Nigeria, had a separate talk, away from prying eyes and ears, on a tiny boat off the coast, dressed as fishermen.

'So, were you satisfied by the conclusions?' Dhulbahante asked.

'In so far as they went, yes. But I don't give the plan more than a thirty percent chance of success,' Sintu stated.

'Why?'

Sintu shook his head, paused, then smiled. 'Indonesia sees this as a pure power play and cares nothing for the religious context that you espoused, hence them declining to take any active part. Kenya fears your growing strength and clearly classes you as a threat. Therefore, they are the least trustworthy and most likely to betray the plan, no matter how they supported you face to face. Mali was overawed by the occasion and surprised at their inclusion into the group. I'm sure you could sense their arse-licking attempt at supporting you, yet without any possibility of assisting the plan. And Egypt still sees itself as the head of the defunct Arab League and is living a half century in the past. In conclusion, except for Indonesia's military capability and desire for greater power, the concept would be dead before the end of next week. But you are no fool, so what did this meeting achieve for you?'

Dhulbahante clapped his hands and laughed loudly. 'Excellent! I could not have summarised this farce better myself. I knew that you and I would see eye to eye on this.'

Sintu looked incredulous, opened his mouth to speak, but was silenced by a hand in front of his face.

'I apologise, my friend, sincerely. I had expected almost the exact outcome that you so brilliantly described. So, let me explain how this will work, and after that, please give me your honest appraisal once more. May I?'

'I am intrigued. Enlighten me.'

Dhulbahante nodded in appreciation. 'Thankyou. First, your assessment is accurate, on all counts. But, if my plan works, then I need scapegoats. Mali and Egypt will fill those roles, one out of ignorance and the other out of undue pride. Kenya will assist because they fear me, as you noticed. And, yes, I too am wary of their potential betrayal, but I have placed some assets close to their President so I am reasonably confident that I will learn of any issues before they occur. That leaves Indonesia. I agree that they would potentially only be assisting as part of a bigger picture power play, of course. However, if the plan fails to assassinate even one of the Pakindesh leaders, then the retaliation against Jakarta, and probably

Kuala Lumpur, will be swift and decisive. Only Indonesia can provide the assets that this initiative could eventually lead to. Somalia cannot do this, nor Nigeria, and more to the point we should not be caught in the act, apart from having lower-level operatives involved. But I have complete faith in my asset, "Saladin".'

'Is he as good as you stated in the meeting?'

'Better. I have known him for many years. I am aware of more than thirty kills he has made, some in extreme circumstances.'

'What is his background?'

'French Foreign Legion, mainly as a sniper, then used to infiltrate extremist cells.'

'You mean he has betrayed Muslims for the infidel French?'

'Only when necessary to retain his cover. If it happened, they were martyrs. Collateral damage is necessary in a long war, or do you not agree?'

Sintu shrugged his shoulders, then sighed. 'Yes, of course. Allah will pardon him. Some of us are called upon to do difficult deeds.'

'Exactly. Anyway, the plan is now in play.' Dhulbahante looked out to sea; it was getting rougher and the boat was pitching, waves were splashing over the sides. Sintu sensed the Somalian's unease. He signalled the boatman in the rear to return them to shore. The motor was gunned, and the boat pointed back towards the beach. The speed increased to keep the bow higher out of the water and the spray diminished. The houses on the shoreline were getting larger and Dhulbahante's mood improved as the beach became closer. He concentrated on the blue of the water and tried to relax. A few minutes later the boat was safely tied up and the two presidents jumped from the boat and made their way to the end of the jetty. Here they walked in separate directions and were each met by their aides and quickly shown the way to their vehicles. The cars sped off, one to the west, the other eastwards. A few people on the beach noticed this but did not identify the passengers, only wondering why scruffy-looking fishermen would be travelling in expensive chauffeur driven cars.

Later the following afternoon, Dhulbahante was back in Addis Ababa. He asked for his military attaché to join him. When the two men had been served coffee and dates, the President said simply, 'It went well, Colonel, just as we had hoped. It is now up to the Indonesians, and Saladin of course.'

'I am pleased, Mr President. With Allah's help, in one month from today, Pakindesh will be severely wounded, and Indonesia blamed. After that, the faithful will once again rise and restore the world according to Allah's will, praise be to Him.'

CUMMINS

'Come in, John. Good to see you,' Habbib said, as they shook hands warmly. Once they were settled, opposite each other, with a low table between them, Habbib was all business. 'So, what was so urgent, and confidential, that it needed a one-on-one meeting today?'

'In my capacity as Secretary of Defence, I work closely with the other Pakindesh nations on all things military, including Intelligence gathering,' Cummins said, not waiting for any acknowledgement, 'so, lately we have become suspicious of several meetings that have occurred in Africa, which look... wrong.'

'Wrong?'

'I think that's the best way to describe it. The Pakindesh Security Service was the first to wonder about it. There was an unusual meeting on global health initiatives, sponsored by Greater Somalia, with co-chairing by Indonesia, recently held in Lagos, Nigeria. The other key countries present were Egypt, Mali, and Kenya. The agenda included malaria eradication, improved vaccine protocols for Ebola and Mpox, and other Africa-centric topics.'

'Doesn't sound out of place, surely?'

'Not at first glance, no. But present at the meetings were not just the health officials from those countries but their Heads of State too. But there were no additional staff, bureaucrats, secretaries, media, or any of the usual hangers-on. The health personnel met for two days but they didn't put out any press releases or invite outsiders. The various Heads met privately for half a day and then left before the end of the conference sessions. We have it on good authority that the Nigerian and Somalian Presidents met by themselves, on a fishing boat for three hours, clearly incognito.' Cummins paused as Habbib leant back and thought about the implications.

'It could be innocent, John,' he began. 'Two men with a previous friendship, perhaps, doing a bit of fishing, to unwind, before the Somalian returns home?'

Cummins shrugged his shoulders. 'Possibly. Except that, to our knowledge, they have never met before. They didn't fish, yet were dressed as commercial local fishermen, even though they later left in limousines. Plus, the countries present all have been critical of Pakindesh, and especially of Kalil since his interview.'

'So, what is your view, John? How sure are you of the intelligence provided?'

'Ninety percent. The PSS has good operatives in Nigeria, and Indonesia, but none in Somalia. They suspect that Somalia is the key player here, being the official instigator of the Health Symposium rather than Indonesia. That is a little odd. Somalia tends to be more fundamental in its approaches to health care. It still has a poor record in maternal health, has minimal risk to Ebola and Mpox, and less malaria impact than the other participants. Yet it put this agenda together.'

'If this was an attempt to discuss some sort of attack on Pakindesh, why would the fishing ruse have excluded Indonesia? Surely they are the largest player in the group?'

'True. Except that Nigeria and Somalia are closer in doctrine and rhetoric. Indonesia concentrates on trade and its link to expansion of power and influence, mainly in the western Pacific rim. There's no record of any recent links between Somalia and Indonesia. Somalia's direct control is from Yemen in the north to Tanzania in the south and includes Ethiopia and Sudan.'

'So where to from here, John?'

'We've increased surveillance where we can and are watching for any alteration in military behaviour for all of the countries discussed. As you know, Pakindesh moved another aircraft carrier group to the UK after Kalil's speech.'

'But you're still worried, aren't you?'

'Yes, Sir. I have my gut sense telling me there is more to this than it seems, and I can't shake that feeling.'

'Does Kalil know any of this?'

'He will later today. I sent someone down to Rio to meet with him and provide all that we have. It might be worth you talking to him tomorrow, Mr President?' Cummins suggested firmly.

'I can do that, but Kalil has a different perspective on threats, as you know. '

'Thank you, Mr President. If we learn anything more, I will let you know.'

When Habbib was alone again he felt agitated. It could all be nothing. Pakindesh was a formidable group of nations, with immense physical power, intelligence skills and resources across the globe, and many more supporters than detractors. But ever since Kalil's sentiment about Allah no longer being needed in people's everyday lives, the mood had shifted. I hope Cummins is wrong.

YEMEN

President Abdellahi Artan Dhulbahante was well protected by his security detail, even though there was no credible threat to him. One never could be too certain though, he thought. His history in this country was legendary, in those circles that remained fearful of his power. When a prior warlord of the Houthis, soon after Revelation Day, defied his attempts to subdue Yemen under Somalian control, Dhulbahante made an example of him. The man had four wives, three sons and nine daughters. Somalian assassins did as they were ordered, took the warlord hostage with his entire family, and then systematically raped all the females in front of their father and brothers. The father was then told to choose the order in which the women and girls were to be executed, so as to mercifully hasten their deaths. If he did not choose, then they would continue to be raped until they died, no matter how long that took, whilst his sons would be castrated and forced to rape their sisters or be killed slowly. After being given an hour to decide and knowing that there was no other way to end their suffering, he reluctantly provided the order of their deaths, from the youngest, a five-year-old, to the eldest, then his wives, and then his sons. When he was the last left alive, he had deep cuts inflicted and was left to bleed to death, looking over the carnage of his dead family. Dhulbahante had the photos and video footage of the event, which was released selectively to his enemies.

He now looked out over Sana'a, at peace with himself, mesmerised by the sight of the Al-Saleh Mosque in the early evening light. Its immense inner and outer areas could receive 44,000 worshippers, but these days the numbers had dropped significantly, apart from during Ramadan, which disappointed him. He waited for the man known as Saladin, and sometimes also as Al-antaqam, meaning Vengeance.

A non-descript man in his early forties, approached the square where Dhulbahante was sitting, drinking coffee, alone. His bodyguards were all around but well disguised, apart from the three nearest to him, who were deliberately vigilant and suitably alert.

The man walked purposefully towards him, then seemed to drop something from his hand and stooped to pick it up. Whilst bent over he tied his shoelace. He was professional and well-practiced, but Dhulbahante knew him from a previous encounter, years before the end of the infidels, during the proxy war in Yemen, between the Saudi's and the Iranians. As the man came closer to the table, he stopped, looked around, as if to identify somewhere he was looking for, then somewhat hesitantly came closer to Dhulbahante and asked in Arabic, 'Excuse me, but could you tell me where the nearest shoe repairer might be found? I am not familiar with this city.'

'Really? Where are you from, my friend?'

'I am not sure that I can answer that now. In these enlightened times, I feel like a citizen of the world. Is that not also true for you?'

'Perhaps, but I very much like living in the highlands these days. I have left deserts behind.'

'Perhaps I could join you for a coffee?'

'You are most welcome.' Dhulbahante raise his hand and clicked his fingers, clearly a predetermined signal to the café owner.

The visitor sat down, then said 'Now that the preliminaries are over, you can dispense with your... friends. I would appreciate that. You will be safe.'

'I am sure of it,' Dhulbahante replied, nodding to his guards, who retreated a further twenty metres away, still vigilant. 'The shoelace signal was well done.'

'One can never be too sure.'

'Wise.'

'Let us not delay. I received your request via my emissary. The target is achievable, especially now.'

'Now?'

'In these peaceful times,' he replied, smiling. He half raised his hand from the table as coffee was brought out. After they were alone again, he continued, 'The act is not the difficult part. The location and the target are insufficiently protected.' He paused as he sipped the coffee.

Dhulbahante said, 'Do I detect a problem, or some hesitancy?'

'Perhaps. I need to know what you expect to occur afterwards?'

'That is not your concern.'

'Forgive me but I must disagree. These times are not like those before Allah's deliverance, praise be to Him. There is minimal violence now, compared to any era ever known. If I do this, what will be the implications? I do not wish to be the catalyst for chaos. I must know why you wish this deed to occur.'

'Hmph. You have killed over a hundred men. Have you suddenly developed a conscience?'

'I am content with my conscience. My past deeds were linked to warfare and advancing the cause of Islam.'

'All of Islam? Or did you exclude the Shia when it suited you?'

'I have dispatched Shia and Sunni and other believers too, when it was necessary, as have you. Allah chooses to smile on us, clearly. Therefore, my past deeds, like yours, must have been forgiven. But this action might not be seen in the same light.'

'It sounds as if you are straying to the side of the growing masses of non-devout Muslims, who are no longer following the true path,' Dhulbahante said with rising anger.

'Do not misunderstand me. Some of your people, who I have worked with before, named me Ilham, because to them I was their inspiration, in times when that quality was needed more than guns. I did not take that name lightly. Even if I am known now more as Al-antaqam, rather than taking Saladin's name in vain, I do not kill indiscriminately. I am not an assassin for hire. My vengeance must be measured; it must be just. I take the path that I agree with, and I do not take life without regret. But, if this task is to be taken, then I need to know what will follow. To the best of your knowledge, or expectation, that is. You owe me this courtesy, if I am to be your deliverer of justice, as you see it. So, speak freely, and honestly.'

Dhulbahante was seething inside but keeping his emotions in check, he hoped. He was not used to being questioned, or disobeyed, ever. This man was one of the few that could achieve the mission he had planned. If he could not convince him then he himself was in danger of becoming the target. If that was the possible outcome then he needed to eliminate him now, here. But to give that signal to his guards was very dangerous, and perhaps premature. Think. His guest was calm, and took another drink, with his left hand. His right hand was in his lap. An overwhelming feeling came over him that it was close to a weapon that would kill him before he could raise a finger. A trickle of sweat began to run down his face, annoying him.

'Perhaps I understand you,' Dhulbahante began, slowly, playing for time. 'None of us are ungrateful for Allah's blessing of this peaceful new world we have been given the sole right to. To place that in jeopardy would truly be a crime, I agree. But there are forces at work that are diverting too many from the true path. Of this I am certain, in the same way that my heart sings when I am at prayer, or upon the sight of a magnificent mosque, or breaking the fast over Ramadan. I am sure you have these feelings too. The target is dangerous. He has misinterpreted Allah's benevolence. Since when have any of us sought to interpret Allah's will? Who would have the audacity to contemplate such blasphemy? I am certain that the removal of this man is the will of Allah, truly. Do you not also feel this? Are you happy if our devotion is weakened, year on year, until there is no adherence to the Quran anymore? Do you wish to see us degenerate into blasphemers, whores, alcoholics, like the now dead Saudi royal house? I cannot believe this. Tell me it is not true.'

'This coffee is bitter! Or it has become so, as I wondered about the true path whilst you spoke. I cannot be certain of what you think, or feel, or wish for. But I admit that there is a greater part of me that would welcome a more devout adherence to the Quran. If we are wrong, then this world is not meant for us. If we are right, then we will be saved and be welcomed into paradise. So, I will do this, on the terms agreed. In forty days, I will deliver the sign that you have requested. And you will then deliver to me whatever I desire in return,' he said, abruptly rising from the table, turning and walking away.

Dhulbahante breathed a sigh of relief, not sure if he could deliver to Al-antaqam what he wanted once he had eliminated the target. But he never intended to deliver the requested prize anyway, so that didn't matter. When the time came it would be Al-antaqam that was the victim of vengeance. His.

RIO DE JANEIRO

As the aircraft approached Rio, Malik Shah gazed in admiration of the symbol of the city, the Christ the Redeemer statue that dominated everything below it. He was not at all intimidated by the monuments of past religions or civilisations. He was grateful that in the Americas there had been sufficient time before Pakindesh expanded its influence and people, for the world to take a pragmatic view of history. If that had not been the case then there might have been appalling and uneducated destruction of icons like Macchu Picchu, Tikal, Teotihuacan, Chichen Itza, the Easter Island Moai statues, Mount Rushmore, the array of Washington DC monuments, and the tens of thousands of temples, cathedrals, churches, synagogues, and other examples of human development and history. What he'd seen of some of the initial uneducated behaviour of those that sought to erase non-Islamic history, especially across Europe and Asia, saddened him. He was looking forward to taking in the sights of Rio again.

Shah and Habbib were taken by limousine to Kalil's official residence, along with their secret service detachment of four men and two women. Some habits die hard, he thought. Habbib was far more at ease with their security detail than he was.

Sitting in the garden, sipping their respective iced teas, lemonade and coffee, Malik Shah began his official updates. 'Sabal, we have become concerned about a possible threat to you.'

'Really? Different to the usual ones?' he chuckled.

Habbib interrupted, 'Sabal, I think these are not to be taken lightly. Listen to Malik.'

'Go ahead, Prime Minister,' Kalil said more seriously.

'Our security services became aware of an operative called Al-antaqam. Have you heard of him?'

'Al-antaqam? Vengeance? No, I don't think so. Who is he?' Kalil asked.

'We think he was once a sniper in Iraq, on the side of a few different groups, largely targeting Shiite militia leaders, but was possibly trained by the French Foreign Legion before that, in West Africa, where he became radicalised. It's not easy to be sure. Anyway, he was seen a few weeks ago in Yemen, and had an interesting meeting, or so we think.'

'Think?' Kalil queried.

Habbib took over. 'Yes, it was a fluke really. Some of Asif's PSS operatives have been interested in President Dhulbahante. You know him?'

'Of course, he's that upstart trying to expand the influence of Greater Somalia.'

'Yes. He has become a man of greater interest to Asif recently, after he attended a Health Conference in Nigeria. None of it really made sense, so -'

Kalil interrupted, 'Yes, I am aware of that, from Asif. Sorry, I had forgotten all about it. It was just a few lines on a longer security briefing. Asif thought it was a front for Indonesia wooing a number of non-aligned states if I remember rightly?'

'Correct, Sabal,' Habbib said. 'Since then, the PSS has been trying to follow Dhulbahante's movements, and they placed people in Sana'a in Yemen when they heard he was going there for high level talks. But those talks didn't seem to occur, or not as we'd have expected them to, from a protocol perspective anyway. So, he was followed and was observed meeting up with a man later identified as Al-antaqam, or we are at least ninety percent sure of it being him. They had coffee together. The meeting was brief but intense, as far as the operative reported it.'

Kalil smiled, 'I am getting the feeling that you are reaching, perhaps. Is this not one of those two plus two equals five, assumptions?'

'Maybe, Sabal,' Habbib said. 'But after your interview comments, and the increase in anti-Pakindesh sentiment by fundamentalists... well, we can't be too careful, that's all.'

'Why do I get the impression that you two are here for more than walking on Ipanema Beach?'

Habbib laughed. 'Well, I do miss our beach walks, Sabal. Those Florida days of ours remain a very pleasant memory. But, yes, your radar is on track. There are other rumblings, which we preferred to talk with you face to face rather than electronically. Indonesia-Malaysia has put an aircraft carrier fleet to sea, heading east. These ships are from the newer ex-Chinese PRA Navy assets that were resurrected from their abandoned South China Sea fortified islands.'

'Well, we will get a lot of notice of them long before they cross the Dateline, gentlemen. And we both have a carrier group in the Pacific, so this doesn't really worry me. I think we are being a little old fashioned in our threat assessments, aren't we? Whilst I often revert to my younger, military days, let's not forget that this is a different world. There hasn't been a conflict outside of the Saudi-Iran war since RD. Idiotic minor skirmishes across some old borders, perhaps, or uncivilised power plays in parts of Africa, but there is no sense in this.'

'True, but Asif already sent one of his carrier groups to the UK to send a message to Turkey and France to calm their extremist groups. It would take too long to catch up with the Indonesians if he wanted to deploy a second group, which he doesn't. He's a little paranoid about these developments, and is tightening the home front,' Habbib stated.

'Yes, I got that impression too. He was a little subdued yesterday on our call. What else?'

'Three moderate West African military leaders died in accidents over the past week,' Malik Shah said.

'What!' Kalil exclaimed. 'I was not told of this,' he said with obvious irritation.

'We only found out the details just before we left DC,' Habbib said. 'Two were car accidents, and the third drowned on his daily swim, in choppy waters apparently.'

'Who? Where?'

'A Moroccan major general was the swimmer. The car crashes involved Tanzania's Opposition Leader, largely touted to be the front runner in their forthcoming elections, and the Norwegian Defence Minister, who has been closely allied to the UK for years, and recently entered into a Trade and Defence Agreement with the UK.'

Kalil stood and began pacing. He stopped, looked his friends in the face and said, 'I do not believe in coincidences like this.'

'Nor do we, Sabal,' Habbib said. 'And one more thing...' he paused. 'Al-antaqam has dropped off the radar. We can't locate him.'

'Where was he last seen?' Kalil asked.

Malik looked worried when he answered, 'Morocco.'

LONDON

'General Cummins, Ma'am,' announced the PM's secretary.

Mina Ahmed rose and left her desk to greet her guest as he was shown into the room, extending her hand, which he shook tentatively. 'A great pleasure to meet you, Prime Minister,' he said.

'I have heard much about you, General, both from Paul Habbib as well as Malik Shah. You come highly recommended.'

'They are very kind, Ma'am, I do my best.'

'I think you're being too modest, General, but let's cut the formality, shall we? It tends to slow things down, as well as irritating me. So, if you have no objections, please call me Mina and I will call you John, if that is okay with you?'

'Er... sure, Prime... I mean, Mina. Thank you.'

She laughed. 'You'll get used to it, John, believe me. Please, sit down, won't you? There is coffee for you, and tea for me, on the way, with hopefully some indulgent calories, which, sad to say, I feel a great need for these days. I dare say you might find Number Ten a little underwhelming, compared to the White House?'

'I like it. More businesslike, without the pretentions that can overwhelm visitors in the U.S.'

'Good observation. But I have to say this place certainly overwhelmed me when I first took office. But then we were all treading new ground, or I certainly was,' she laughed. 'It is amazing what we become used to.'

'So true. I was just a major in the Marines one day, then a general the next, kind of.' He stopped talking as refreshments were brought in and placed on the coffee table between them. The pots were left for them to pour themselves, and there were some biscuits, a few donuts, and a small cheese platter.

'Stuff your face, John, I intend to. Then we'll get down to business. My Chief of Defence and Intelligence, Martin Bashir, will join us shortly, he's been detained for a few minutes.' In between mouthfuls and sips, they spoke of family and recent experiences and general observations of life.

Martin Bashir arrived ten minutes later, took coffee, declined anything to eat and sat adjacent to General Cummins, whom he had met six months earlier, briefly, in Washington.

After five more minutes, Mina had skilfully assessed her guest, decided that she liked him and began to talk business.

'Right, let's get down to the core issues, please, John. Tell us what we need to know from your President and Prime Minister.'

'Yes, Ma'am, thank you for that,' he began, then smiled. 'Mina, our security forces, and I mean by that the entire Pakindesh Security Services, in the Americas, the Sub-continent and here in the U.K., have determined that there is a direct threat to Sabal Kalil, due to his interview with your daughter some months ago, and the rising level of anger with some fundamentalist factions, especially in the Middle East and North Africa. We believe that President Dhulbahante of Greater Somalia is the key orchestrator of this threat, but there are also indications that Indonesia-Malaysia might become involved, and an unknown number of North and West African countries. We have also detected some support from France, and Turkey. There is credible evidence to believe that an assassin, called Al-antaqan, meaning vengeance, has been hired by Dhulbahante to kill President Kalil. We also believe that this man was responsible for the three so-called accidental deaths recently, in Morocco, Norway and Tanzania.' Cummins halted as he took another drink of coffee, and to let the PM digest his initial comments.

'Why would an assassin with such an important high-level target waste his time eliminating three other people and potentially getting caught?' Bashir asked.

'Good question, and one that a few of us also asked. First off, he is supremely arrogant, and very confident of his abilities. Secondly, there is no urgency, so any deadline is one that he's likely to impose only on himself. And lastly, we believe that he wants to kill Kalil as publicly as possible, meaning – '

'During the upcoming Pakindesh Americas Symposium,' the PM interrupted.

'Exactly. If this assassination is the idea of Dhulbahante, then he will want a public execution that he can then say is the will of Allah, and use it to rally his supporters,' Cummins agreed.

'But rally his supporters to do what? And who exactly are his supporters?' asked the PM.

'Well, a Somalian operative was captured in Morocco, a few days after Major General Baksi's drowning incident. He told the Moroccans that he had been paid to observe the General's movements and report the times that he took his daily swims and who accompanied him. But on the day of the General's drowning, this man was most definitely not in the area. He also referred to the Followers of Allah's Vengeance. We are terming this vague group the FAV now.'

Mina frowned. 'I dread to think how the Moroccan's extracted this information. But back to my question, John. Who are these followers?'

'To be frank, we don't know yet. We suspect it includes radical elements in Nigeria, Indonesia-Malaysia, Egypt, Somalia, and Mali, as a minimum, but not necessarily their governments. However, it wouldn't take much to create havoc across Africa and for anti-Pakindesh feelings to be exacerbated. But the evidence is slim, apart from Somalia.'

'Then why has Indonesia sent an aircraft carrier group into the Pacific recently, and where is it heading?'

'As you know, we asked them, diplomatically, and they advised it was a routine naval exercise. It is currently a hundred nautical miles north of Polynesia.'

'I can't imagine that Kalil considers it a threat,' Bashir stated.

'No, he doesn't. And it isn't. Pakindesh America Pacific Fleet Command is more than a match for it. We have two carrier groups in the Pacific, one off North America and another off South America. And another two in the Atlantic, one north, one south. It would be madness to attack any element of Pakindesh, anywhere.'

'Yet Asif felt sufficiently worried that he sent me one of his precious carrier groups to bolster my defence,' Mina stated. 'He isn't usually worried by events in Europe, and the French are pretty disorganised as far as their factions are concerned. Turkey is more belligerent, from time to time, but, again, they are primarily diplomatically rather than militarily expansionist. For them it's more of a slow takeover and creeping influence game.'

Cummins nodded, encouraged by her level of knowledge. 'We agree. Thankfully our overwhelming advantage in satellite intelligence keeps us ahead, but these kind of lone wolf operations can evade all the intel in the world.'

'So, what's the plan? Why this face-to-face update, John?'

'Hmm. Yes, well, that brings me to my second item. I believe you had dinner with Admiral Pereira last week?'

'I did,' the PM confirmed. 'I usually invite him over on the rare occasions that he's here, and now that he's brought me the protection of his ships, it was the least I could do. Why?'

Cummins hesitated, started to massage his chin with his left hand and then abruptly stopped, clearly coming to a decision. 'May I ask how he seemed to you?'

'Okay, I suppose. He's fairly dry, as you know, not exactly the dinner table joke master,' she laughed.

'Was he alone with you?'

'No, he had another officer with him, a Lieutenant Commander Hussein. Pleasant chap. He engaged with my husband in a variety of discussions, from soccer to naval stuff. His wife has a baby on the way, and Riaz told him his life was about to change for good but for the better. What are you delaying for, John? What's on your mind?'

'There's no other way to say this, but the PSS in Delhi have some concerns about Hussein. He has been under surveillance for some time, but Pereira doesn't know that.'

'Why doesn't he?' Bashir queried.

'Because he's not a man that can hide his feelings very well. Asif and Kalil know, and President Habbib too. But not many others. The PSS think that he's been radicalised. Indonesia is finding out information that is highly sensitive, especially about naval movements, and detailed data that should be secure. Hussein might not be involved but the PSS don't want to alert him, so there are very few around him that are aware of this.'

'Let's say for now that Hussein is a threat. What could he possibly do, alone?' the PM asked.

'He might not be acting alone. But he is in a privileged position, so he has access to the fleet. If anything happened to Pereira and his senior officers, Hussein could theoretically seize control and create some damage. It is a long shot, I agree, and possibly would be a suicide mission, but nevertheless it is possible,' Cummins suggested.

The PM frowned, suddenly worried by Cummin's own demeanour. 'What's the worst he could achieve? Tell me, John.'

'An aircraft carrier ten kilometres off the coast of London, if there was a mutiny, and Hussein had control of its armament, even for a short period, he could decimate London.'

Mina Ahmed went white, and her mouth fell open in shock.

Bashir said, 'Then what the hell are we doing with this intel? Surely removing Hussein now would be prudent?'

'If we do then we might force their hand and then lose any chance of catching Al-antaqam in the act,' Cummins said. 'We have a plan, Prime Minister, but it needs your involvement, and there is some danger.'

'Tell me what I need to do.'

CHARLIE

It was rare for Charlie to cook, and more unusual for his siblings to be available to eat with him. Samantha, his fiancé, was leaving him to cook, as he liked. He'd invited Michael and Salina for dinner, as well as Freddy, and Tasmeena Hikaka. As one of his mother's youngest MP's, she was someone that Riaz felt might be a match for Michael, although she was eight years older than him. But Michael seemed to favour older women and craved intelligent conversation in his relationships. Charlie was always careful not to be too overt in his infrequent matchmaking attempts for his siblings, and clearly, he was no match for his mother's skills in that area, but he believed Tasmeena and Michael would be good together.

He also knew that Freddy, devastated by the sudden death from cancer of his girlfriend, Amaya, had intense feelings for Salina but would never make a move on her, as he was clearly intimidated and believed that she saw him more like an uncle figure rather than a potential husband. He'd relegated her to the role of friend, reluctantly, worried about harming his relationship with Charlie and Riaz.

Charlie realised that Tasmeena's political views matched those of Michael in many ways, and despite some key differences in outlook, they always enjoyed catching up. Maybe he was jumping to silly conclusions. Whatever eventuated, the dinner conversation would be lively. The twins could always draw a crowd, and it had been easy to get enthusiasm from Freddy and Tasmeena to join them.

They all mingled easily. Charlie watched the interplays. Freddy couldn't take his eyes off Salina but tried to mask it. She was aware of it but didn't make things uncomfortable for him, but did not move away from Michael to allow Freddy one on one time. Why was she doing that? Michael had gravitated to Tasmeena immediately and they took no time to get into intense discussion, and Charlie didn't bother to eavesdrop. He glanced through from his kitchen duties every few minutes to see what was happening as he stirred the three pots he had on the stove, relishing the aromas, tasting each in turn. The rice was almost done. The poppadums were perfect, the naan ready. 'Okay everyone, come and help carry these dishes in for me, please,' he ordered, and then handed dishes and plates to each of them, and took the last two for himself, as they automatically placed everything on the table and gravitated to a spot to sit. There was limited conversation for a few minutes, apart from praise for the spread, as they each dished what they wanted onto their plates.

'Wow, this is great, Charlie, as usual,' Michael congratulated his brother. 'I don't know about being a doctor, maybe a chef was your calling,' he joked.

'That was the reason why I agreed to marry him,' Samantha laughed, 'because it meant I would come home to a good meal, rather than having to cook it myself.'

'I hope I can find a man that cooks too,' Salina agreed.

An hour into the meal, all his guests having gorged themselves and again praised Charlie for his culinary efforts, the conversation came around to the Kalil interview, and then to the opinions within the group as to whether his bombshell comment had merit.

'I don't know about you, Tasmeena, but the rest of us here were in no way devout Muslims before RD,' Charlie said.

'Or after RD either,' Freddy concurred, the twins laughing in agreement.

'Well, as for me,' Tasmeena began, 'my dad was a fairly regular mosque attendee, my mum less so, and us kids, my two brothers and I, went maybe half a dozen times a year, mostly around Ramadan of course, and Eid.'

Michael smiled, happy to hear that Tasmeena's upbringing was also what he termed Muslim lite. 'The rest of us here have discussed this a lot,' Michael said, looking at Tasmeena, 'but was your family surprised that you'd all survived? I mean, did you feel threatened by the situation, worried that the more devout followers would out you?'

'Out us? Yes, that's probably the way we talked about it too, I suppose, thinking back. We were, worried I remember. But then the sanity of us being chosen to survive became more common as we realised that most of our community was, let's say, minimalist observers of the faith.'

Salsa nodded, and said, 'I can't remember when my fear of being outed went away. Probably after we moved to London and made friends in school and found out that nearly all the kids' backgrounds and family lives were similar. Then those harsh, fundamentalist-type teachers began to turn up and there was a sort of unstated war between the kids and them. It was brutal for a while. I was very scared in those days. It was so good when dad went and threatened those sadistic bastards.'

'Yes, I heard about that, from your mum,' Tasmeena said. 'It took guts for Riaz to do that.'

Charlie nodded, 'If dad hadn't seen what could happen, from his days in Iran before his family escaped from there, then it might have been different, but he knew more than us what the risks were.'

'Still took real guts though,' Freddy stated.

'I was never so proud of him than that day at school,' Charlie agreed.

'So, do you think Kalil is correct, Tasmeena?' Salina asked.

'About Allah letting us get on with life without bothering Him, you mean?' she laughed.

'Yes. Good way of putting it,' Salina laughed too.

'Hmm, well...' Tasmeena began, considering, 'the argument is valid, and the evidence is consistent. In particular, the demise of those in the early days that sort to instil the most conservative teachings of the Quran, Hadith and Sunna. That alone, such as the deaths of people that were preparing to stone women for supposed adultery, including rape victims. If that wasn't a sign I don't know what was.'

'What about the destruction of Mecca?' Michael added. 'For me, that was a key sign. With Mecca's status, there's no way that Allah would have allowed it to be destroyed. Nor would He have let the Caliphate and Iran destroy each other. It was as if that too was a sign that Sunni versus Shia differences should be forgotten'.

'Crazy to think that so many hundreds of thousands of Muslims have killed each other over the centuries for their different views on the succession after the Prophet Muhammad's death, praise be to Him,' Tasmeena said.

'You still say praise be to Him a lot, Tasmeena. Is it just habit, or is it a conscious thing?' Salina challenged.

Tasmeena was immediately defensive in her expression, glancing quickly at Charlie and Michael to see if they backed Salina. 'Well, I've never really thought about it. I suppose it is habit. Didn't we all become careful after RD to follow that tradition?'

'I didn't,' Salina replied.

Charlie wasn't going to let that pass, 'Bullshit, Salsa. You did follow the trend. We all did. Dad was adamant that we needed to espouse devotion and not bring suspicion on ourselves. I can remember the discussions we had. True, you didn't like it, but we did as dad said and made it a part of our speech back then. Don't deny it, Sis.'

'I agree with Charlie, Salsa. We did do that,' Michael concurred.

Salina looked annoyed not to be backed up by her brothers but let it pass. She wasn't sure why she'd baited Tasmeena but decided against pushing it. 'Sorry, Tasmeena, I didn't mean to sound critical.'

'Anyway, the Sunni-Shia fighting wasn't all that different to Catholics and Protestants killing each other over the centuries really,' Charlie suggested.

'Possibly not, Charlie,' Freddy agreed, 'But that was all over Henry the Eighth's sexual urges. So that was worse really. But another example of something that was a spat just between rulers, the Pope, and the King of England, yet it went on to create hatred between people and lots of wars. Madness.'xxxx

Tasmeena was nodding in partial agreement but clearly wanted to debate further. 'Sort of, Freddy, and there are similarities between the Catholics having the Pope as their intermediary to God, which gave so much power to the high priests, the way that the Shiites have Ayatollahs. I wonder though if Shia Muslims choosing to prefer the authority of hereditary rather than elected leaders, would have been different if their choice of leader had occurred and Muhammad's cousin and son-in-law, Ali bin Abu Talib, had taken over,' she suggested.

Salina was impressed. So, not an historical ignoramus at all, she realised.

Freddy looked a little lost and was watching the exchange between the girls like a tennis match. 'It's all beyond my knowledge I'm afraid ladies, much as I hate to admit it,' he laughed.

'Sorry, Freddy,' Tasmeena said, coming to his rescue amiably, 'It was such a common debate in our house between my dad and my uncle that it was kind of ingrained in us, even though it bored us senseless at the time. The history is that after the Prophet Muhammad's death, his close friend and adviser, Abu Bakr, became the first Caliph as His successor to lead the Islamic nation. What became the Shia, wanted a different result, and that started the rift, and it never healed.'

'Thanks for that, Tasmeena,' Freddy said, smiling. 'We never had discussions like that at home. Plenty of debate about Arsenal versus West ham versus Chelsea though,' he laughed.

'Now that's politics,' Michael said, chuckling.

'But irrelevant compared to Man United, Man City and Liverpool,' Charlie added.

'Don't, Charlie. You'll make me sad,' Freddy responded.

'Enough football nostalgia, boys, please,' Samantha said.

'Back to Kalil, Tasmeena,' Salina pursued, 'as a politician, what is your view of the possible outcomes?'

'Here, you mean. Or globally?' she queried.

'Both,' Salina pushed.

'I can't see there being much of a row here,' Tasmeena answered. 'Let's face it we don't really have much of a fundamentalist bent in Britain now. Different in France. They seem to often have mini skirmishes over there, but they seem to be factional issues between North African sectors of the immigrant communities in Paris, each vying for supremacy. I'd be surprised if there was much of a drama across Europe. Africa is probably more volatile. The old terrorist factions that were effectively just criminal extortionists in northern Nigeria, Niger, Mali, and Burkina-Faso became quasi-rulers, didn't they? So, they might use an anti-Kalil protest to win territory over less strict states, maybe.'

Salina nodded, 'Yes, the area is possibly the least advanced, culturally, compared to the rest of the world.'

'Who was that guy in Africa that went off his rocker about Kalil just after your interview,' Tasmeena asked.

'Dhulbahante in Somalia,' Michael answered.

'That's right,' Tasmeena remembered. 'He seemed a scary individual. Really a throwback to the pre-RD days, I thought.'

Salina agreed, 'Good description. If there has been an area that has not advanced anywhere near as much as it should have after RD, it is Africa. And it's the fundamentalists and the power-seekers that are holding the continent back. Political corruption did not end with RD, sadly.'

'The more liberal and educated in the population left the continent and headed for Europe though,' Freddy stated.

'True,' Salina agreed. 'Morocco is a standout liberal democracy, and Egypt seems prosperous and quite modernist too. I'd give Tunisia and Algeria eight out of ten. But the West African states are still quite volatile.'

'I thought Nigeria had become the leading democracy there?' Freddy asked.

'The government is pretty good,' Salina agreed, 'and the country is wealthy and modern in outlook, but there's constant pressure from its neighbours. From what Michael and I have seen over the years, and I admit it isn't comprehensive, Africa has benefited the least from wealth redistribution.'

'I thought Indonesia was struggling in that area as well?' Tasmeena asked.

'Not since they expanded north and south and the population density thinned out,' Salina said. 'I don't know whether they are managing their new empire all that well, administratively I mean. Let's face it, when your territory stretches from the Bangladesh border to Vietnam, north to China, plus Australia, New Zealand, and the Pacific Islands, that's a very diverse geography. Over a hundred million people have migrated from Java and Sumatra since RD. It's thriving. We loved it there, didn't we, Michael?'

'We did. Although there were places that we wished we could have seen before RD, like Bali. From what I had read, the island changed completely from its majority Buddhist past. Understandable I suppose. Overall, there was a kind of undercurrent of distrust by the Malaysian-dominated northern parts of the empire towards the more dominant Indonesian south. Common language, and religion of course, but Malaysia lost its British based government system and was clearly uneasy about the continuing nepotism of the Indonesian power brokers. That's how it seemed to us anyway.'

'Did you get down to Australia?' Samantha asked.

'Next on the list!' the twins said in unison, everyone laughing.

'Yes,' Salina added, 'we are due to go there next month. Should be very interesting to see what it feels like as an Asian nation now.'

'As soon as we arrive, I am going to shout out Aussie, Aussie, Aussie, and Salsa will call out Oy, Oy, Oy,' he laughed.

'That's sad, I think,' Charlie suggested. 'I always wanted to visit Australia.'

'Me too,' Samantha concurred.

'Yeah, would have been so laid back, I think,' Tasmeena agreed.

Salina nodded, 'Well, time will tell whether its past culture has influenced the Indonesians or not, I suppose.'

'How many Muslims did Australia have at RD?' Freddy asked.

'820,000,' Salina answered automatically, resorting instantly to her head for facts and figures, 'with 40 percent of them born there. The biggest populations were in Sydney and Melbourne. I'm hoping that the laid-back Australian identity still exists. We'll see.'

PEREIRA

'You called for me, Sir?' Lieutenant Commander Hussein asked, as he walked into the wardroom.

'Yes, Hussein, thank you. I read your outline plan for the mini training exercise. It was an interesting scenario, albeit perhaps a little unlikely. But then again, we should exercise our intellect in these ways. It will be good for the junior officers to stretch their thinking. Why don't you explain the scenario further, and your rationale?' Pereira suggested, motioning for his aide to sit down.

'Of course, Sir,' Hussein answered, sitting in the chair opposite the Admiral. 'I suppose I was just thinking about the fact that we are largely invulnerable here, and everywhere else for that matter. But walking around the ship and others in the fleet, it sems to me that the men are bored and becoming a little lazy.'

'You think my crews are lazy?' Pereira challenged.

'Not due to any character flaws, Sir. What I mean is that when there is no real threat of conflict, time is taken up doing routine maintenance tasks. All very important, of course. Then there are the occasional live fire exercises at sea, aircraft sorties, and safety related training, and firefighting drills etcetera. But we are not threatened with actual battle scenarios, and for very good reason of course. The wonderful thing about our world now is its freedom from major conflict. But that creates a problem regarding countering real threats. So, I thought about trying to devise a threat scenario that would challenge the men and stretch their thinking at the same time. If it was a sea battle war game, then I think they would treat it as a foregone conclusion and perhaps not be challenged to think outside the square. With my scenario unfolding in the way that I described, it would challenge the men to react in ways that they might not instantly consider and that way we could run a concurrent promotion assessment and see how the junior leaders emerge as the day progresses.'

'Very interesting, Hussein. And imaginative too. I like the scenario. I think it is worth doing. How long would it take you to put the whole program together?'

Hussein smiled, 'Well, Sir, I have been working on it for a few weeks now, and it is probably ready to go, with a few minor updates perhaps. But I think I could be ready to run it within a week, if that was to your liking?'

'It is. I will be very interested to see how it eventuates. What about the manipulation of the ammunition and missiles for your early mid-air self-destruction as part of the live fire exercise?'

'I have been working with the Chief Petty Officer, as he was an armourer previously, and he can adjust sufficient ammunition and colour code it for safety within the next few days, Sir.'

'Excellent. Then you have my authority to proceed. You can brief the senior officers the day after tomorrow if you wish. We will provide a warning order to the crews twelve hours ahead of the game.'

'Thank you, Sir. I will get working on the fine tuning today and give the Chief the go ahead.'

'Good. One other thing. I had a request from President Habbib. He has a nephew doing his military training at Annapolis, currently a cadet officer over there, and he asked whether I would take him under my wing for a month, to show him what life is really like at sea. He didn't want him to be posted to one of the American fleets because he thinks he'll be treated differently over there, and get too easy a time, whereas with me he will have to work. I agreed and he joins us tomorrow. This will be a good exercise for him to be involved with, so maybe he can be your shadow and learn from you?'

Hussein was a little annoyed to be asked to play babysitter but covered it well. 'Of course, Sir, it would be my pleasure.'

'Excellent. I'll introduce him to you tomorrow when he gets here, and you can show him the ropes. His name is Aaron Fadel.'

HABBIB

'Did Pereira buy it?' Malik Shah asked.

'Completely,' Habbib replied. 'My so-called nephew will be on board tomorrow.'

'I hope the young man is up to it. But I also hope that this whole threat is a red herring, as we used to say, Paul.'

'Me too, Malik. The thought of an old-style lone wolf attack scares me. I thought those events were destined for history.'

'Who is our plant really?'

'He is a twenty-five-year-old agent with excellent credentials as a close protection bodyguard. His age is misleading. His CV reads like an old Tom Clancy novel. He's a 3rd Dan in Aikido, and similarly skilled in Krav Maga self-defence, which he teaches at the FBI

Academy. Speaks French and Spanish fluently and has passable Arabic and is a marksman with a handgun,' Habbib stated.

'Will he have a handgun though?'

'It's been arranged, Malik.'

'Could be dangerous.'

'Not really. There's no reason to suspect him. I think Hussein might be quite disdainful of having him on board and might try to get rid of him during their naval exercise.'

'What's his name?'

'No idea what his real name is but he's taking the name Aaron Fadel, which is the name of my real nephew.'

'What if Hussein does some checking?'

'The FBI has uploaded false enlistment and report cards for him at Annapolis and used his real photos. He does look similar, which was a bonus. The real Aaron Fadel has been detoured away on a trip into the mountains and will be unobtainable for a week. It was a bonus to talk my brother-in-law into going trekking with Aaron, on some pretext that my sister made up,' Habbib laughed.

'Your sister isn't aware of the reason for this?'

'Of course not. It's her husband's 50th birthday coming up and I said we needed to detour him away so that we could plan a major event for him, and we told the same thing to Aaron, asking him to act as decoy.'

'You're a devious bastard, Paul. But of course, this means that you will actually have to plan this party now.'

'No problem, it's in hand.'

'Okay. So now we just sit and wait?'

'That's the hard part, Malik. Always is.'

CHARLIE

'Freddy, you have to make your move on Salsa,' Charlie urged his friend.

'Charlie, it will never happen. Salsa will never go for a maintenance engineer like me. I'm too old and too uneducated for her. What would we talk about, man?'

'Freddy, I'm going to tell you some classified information, which will both shock and excite you. But if you ever repeat this, to anyone, ever, even if in the future you are married to Salsa and there's a chance to repeat it, for whatever reason, it will mean the end of our friendship. Are you okay with that?'

'Sure, I'm cool with that. What is it, Charlie, tell me?'

Charlie looked at his friend's face, reminding him of an expectant puppy waiting for a food treat, and smiled. 'Freddy, I mean it. Michael would beat the shit out of me if he ever knew what I was about to tell you.'

'Are you saying that Michael is in on this too, whatever it is?' Freddy asked.

'Not in the way I think you mean. He told me something in confidence, but if I don't tell you, well it's a waste of info and a tragedy in the making.'

'Charlie, just spill it. Please.'

Charlie sighed deeply, thrust his hands in his white lab coat and started to pace up and down the electrical generator maintenance room. Then he stopped, looked his friend in the eyes and nodded, his decision made.

'Okay. Listen. Salsa and Michael talk politics and world affairs like we talk about the past glories of football teams. But they sometimes get into… well, let's say the juicy stuff. You know, relationships, sex, all of it.'

'You mean brothers and sisters talk about this stuff together?'

'It's a bit weird, I know. But they are twins, and they have a different kind of relationship to normal brother-sister stuff. They spend an awful lot of time together, and they, well… talk about their sexual… urges, I suppose is the right expression. I'm not saying that they pimp for each other when they are travelling, but they vet prospective partners for each other, sometimes. It was the day after the dinner, and Michael and I were having a rare heart to heart, because he wanted to know if he was reading the signs right about Tasmeena, and he didn't want to talk to Salsa about it because he was worried that Salsa would mention it to her, and he's not ready for that yet.

'Anyway, he started to laugh, like you do about an in joke and I asked what he was thinking about, and he said he'd tell me, but I had to keep it to myself, or Salsa would go crazy if she knew we'd discussed it,' Charlie paused.

'Go on,' Freddy urged.

Charlie sighed again. 'Okay... Salsa told him that every time she spends time around you...'

'Yes? What? Tell me, Charlie.'

He took a deep breath, hesitated, then said, 'She goes to bed so horny that she has to masturbate.'

Freddy looked shocked, and Charlie wasn't sure if it was in a good way or a bad way, so he stayed quiet and crossed his fingers behind his back and started to sweat.

Freddy's facial expression changed from its shocked phase to an enormous smile. 'She does fancy me then!' he exclaimed, clearly delighted with the news.

Charlie kept his expression as neutral as possible, although he wanted to shout his encouragement. Finally, he couldn't help it and said, 'She's mad about you, Freddy, you daft bugger. So, it's definitely time to make your move.'

Freddy clapped his hands, did a little jig and shouted something unintelligible. Then he stopped dead and his expression worsened again. 'But if I make a move now, she might realise that I know how she feels, and wonder how I found out, won't she?'

'Of course not. And for God's sake, don't ever tell her. You promised. I mean it, Freddy. Don't put me, or Michael in the shit. Understood?'

'Of course not, Charlie. I mean, how could I do that. How would she ever know?'

'She'd know if you ever brought up the subject of masturbation for a start, so strike that from your conversation list,' Charlie said.

Freddy looked suddenly worldly. 'Charlie, can you ever remember a situation in any of your... probably numerous sexual liaisons these days, where you brought that subject up with a girl?'

Charlie shrugged his shoulders. 'Okay, Freddy, point taken. No, you're right about that.' He looked at his watch, 'Damn, I'm late for my rounds! Got to dash,' he called over his shoulder as he ran to the stairs, bounding up them two steps at a time, and away from a very happy engineer.

MICHAEL

'So, do you think I should ask Tasmeena out, Charlie?'

'Clearly. Why wait?'

'I'm just not sure that long distance relationships work.'

'What long distance? You live three streets away from her, Michael.'

'When I'm here, sure. But how often is that the case, Charlie?'

Charlie considered that. 'Well, you are generally home every two to three months and you stay for two to four weeks, I think, so that's maybe four months a year that you are here. And I thought you two were thinking of cutting back and doing more domestic or just European work anyway, weren't you?'

'I'd like to. Not so sure about Salsa though. She gets itchy feet if we're home for longer than three weeks. She gets off on it more than me, I think. She tends to get deeper into the relationships with her subjects than I do. She'd miss that I think.'

Charlie wondered how to pose his next comment. 'That could change though. I mean if she met a guy that was here that could make her happy. Then she might want to stay at home more.'

'Maybe. But who?'

'Well, from what you said the other day, maybe Freddy?' Charlie laughed to hide his intent. 'Can't see Freddy making a move on Salsa though.'

'Can't you? Not even after what I told you the other day?'

Don't blow this, Charlie. How to play it? 'Well, I mean... if Freddy doesn't know about that then he might never ask Salsa out. You know how shy he is. I think he's intimidated by her. He didn't speak to her much at dinner the other night, did he?'

'No, he didn't. But you could tell him what I told you, Charlie.'

Charlie looked shocked but was worried that he might have overplayed the emotion. 'Really? Would you be okay with me telling him private stuff like that?'

Michael scratched his head, tutted, and then nodded his head firmly. 'Yes. I think you should. But only if he can keep it a secret, otherwise we'll both be in the doghouse and Salsa will be a nightmare to deal with. You know what she's like if she feels anyone has plotted against her or lied or kept secrets from her. Do you think Freddy could handle it skilfully?'

Charlie whistled, in relief and to gain time. 'I don't know. Freddy can be a bit of a loose cannon. I'd have to get his agreement to absolute secrecy before telling him anything first.'

'Maybe we need to tell him together and perhaps coach him in how to approach Salsa?'

'No way! He'd end up like a bad actor stuffing his lines. If this is to work then he'll have to decide how to approach her himself, in his own bungling way. Let me tell him if I can manage it. Leave it with me, Michael.'

'How do you think a relationship with Freddy would work out for her though, Charlie? I mean, what if it fails miserably. That would be worse maybe than...'

'What? Going on travelling aimlessly around the world until she marries some political leader that gets the hots for her? Would that work out? I doubt it. She needs a down to earth bloke, someone to cut through her bullshit yet adore her unreservedly.'

Michael nodded. 'You're right, she does. Okay, tell Freddy. But I hope we're not creating a monster here.'

'Me too, Michael, but if it brings Salsa happiness then it's worth it. Fingers crossed.'

AARON FADEL

I am Aaron Fadel. Fadel, Aaron. He looked in the mirror in his hotel room in London and tried to perfect his neutral facial expression. 'Good morning, Sir, I am Staff Cadet Aaron Fadel, reporting for duty,' he announced to the mirror. 'Thank you for the privilege of joining your crew for a few weeks, Sir.' Yes, it would do. Keep it simple. Your greatest risk is showing insufficient knowledge of your trade. But then it helps that at your supposed level of training you haven't been to sea yet for more than the odd day of familiarisation. Keep conversations to a minimum. Show awe, and fear, of the officers. Be deferential, but be inquisitive too, where it makes sense.

He'd been well briefed by a real naval cadet officer at Annapolis, and he'd familiarised himself around the base for 2 weeks in case he needed to answer any questions about his life there, and to make sure that his knowledge of how to wear his various uniforms was sound. He'd also spent two days at sea posing as a journalist on board a frigate to get some feeling for moving about a ship in choppy weather and understanding the routines. Not enough time but it would have to do. If Hussein is planning anything he'll probably try to get rid of me as an irritating shadow, by giving me some tasks away from him. That will be the hardest job, sticking by his side without it seeming out of place. If I'm sent off to do menial tasks it will be difficult to counter. I'll just have to trust in Habbib talking Pereira into keeping me on the bridge to observe the war games properly, and within his sight or attached to Hussein.

He practiced quickly bringing his right leg up and drawing his .25 calibre Beretta Model 950 automatic out of his ankle holster and aiming it and dry firing. The pistol had been delivered to his hotel via an embassy courier. Using the gun was his last resort if things went awry. The stopping power of the pistol's round was limited, but in close quarters it would be enough, hopefully, if it became necessary. But Hussein remained an unconfirmed threat, even if highly suspect. Trust in his arrogance, and disdain for lowly cadets, no matter my supposed relationship to Habbib. Be useful, if possible but not annoying.

MUHAMMED ASIF

The view over Ipanema Beach was spectacular from the penthouse suite of the hotel. Asif often wondered when he visited Brazil whether Kalil had won the prize for the most relaxed and rewarding location to be a President. His own options for his winter and summer palaces were Delhi and Islamabad, although he had a multitude of other escapes, in Srinagar, Kashmir, for total relaxation, Whistler near Vancouver for skiing, occasionally, which he preferred over European ski resorts. How lucky I and my family have been, and to have had a father with such insight, and trust in Kalil too. Will my children be as fortunate? They only know of conflict through history books and information on IslamNet. Praise be to Allah that we resurrected 80 percent of the Internet database, even if it did take ten years to achieve that. Stupid of the fundamentalists to want to destroy all that knowledge and history.

A knock on the door interrupted his thoughts and he turned away from the view of the sea and walked back from the veranda to the main room of the suite, as his secretary cum bodyguard walked in with a sheaf of papers under his arm.

'These just arrived from President Kalil, Sir, along with a message that he will be over in an hour.'

'Thank you, Safir,' he acknowledged, taking the material from him, and setting it on the coffee table.

'Can I get you anything, Sir?'

'No, thank you. I don't wish to be disturbed until the President arrives, except by him.'

'Understood, Sir.'

Asif scanned the paperwork, putting most of it aside, then noticed a sealed letter, which he cut open with a nearby paperknife. A single A5 printed page had the words 'March 9' and 'two' on it. Asif went to his laptop and opened a program called 'Redford'. He smiled, as usual whenever he was directed to these coded messages from Kalil, or other members of the inner circle. When his father, Kalil, Mina Amin, Paul Habbib and Malik Shah first set up their extremely discreet network it was Habbib that came up with the name for the program. Kalil asked why Redford, and Habbib said he thought it apt to remember Robert Redford in the film 'All the President's Men', about the Watergate scandal. The name had stuck. Each of them used a numeric keypad code, linked to their own predetermined code words. Two of his were March 9 and July 27, the birthdays of his parents. The second word 'two' added to that meant that he needed to add 2 to each of the four numbers of his father's year of birth, being 1927. So that became 3-11-4-9, and because it was an even number it was then reversed, to be 9-4-11-3. An odd number would have retained the order.

He logged in to his program and entered a separate password to proceed. He was then prompted to enter the new code, so he typed 94113. The program accepted the code, specific to him this one time, which had no allowance for errors and only lasted 20 seconds from correctly entering the first password. A message in clear text from Kalil filled the screen.

My Dear Muhammed, welcome to Ipanema. I look forward to meeting with you shortly. I received confirmation that Paul's nephew arrived safely and is on his way to meet the Admiral. Hopefully he will be taken in hand appropriately during their forthcoming activities. Our nemesis and his proxy have not been located, but arrangements are in place as discussed. If the next few days meet with foul weather, let us not drone on about it. The sun will shine again the next day I am sure, brightening up all those places that need uplifting. Hasta pronto, Sabal.

To anyone intercepting the message, it would be difficult to decipher its hidden meanings. So, Habbib's FBI agent is safe and about to board Pereira's ship. Dhulbahante and Al-antaqam have not been located, either in Brazil or elsewhere. And lastly, if all does not go well and any of the Pakindesh Presidents and Prime Ministers are harmed or killed, then there will be a drone strike against several key targets in Addis Ababa, Mogadishu, Cairo, Jakarta, Kuala Lumpur, Abuja, Lagos, Niamey, and Bamako. They had discussed whether to include targeting the capitals of Mali, Niger, and Egypt, three of the group which seemed potentially to be scapegoats rather than active conspirators, but in the end the consensus was to take no chances. Kalil's sign off, the Spanish for see you soon, was a pre-set code confirming that some European targets in France and Spain might also be included if any evidence of their involvement was proven.

No matter the power of Pakindesh in the world, they had not been involved in any conflict since RD, and there was a high level of discomfort about being seen to militarily strike against other nations. Their military presence, especially through its vast naval resources, primarily being the resurrected United States' Naval assets, could not be matched even by the combined resources of the rest of the world, and naval capacity was limited by most other nations. Similarly, the U.S. armoury's weapon stocks, from ammunition to missiles to aircraft and armoured vehicles was beyond comprehension in a peaceful, unpopulated world. But in over ten years it had remained impossible to eliminate what the Pakindesh leaders termed backward thinking. Or as Kalil termed it, Arabian-centred ninth century idiocy. So, here they were. The leaders of the most enlightened empire possibly ever seen in human history, being threatened by pre-RD mindsets and backward-looking agendas that still hated being unable to recreate the harsh living conditions that the Prophet Mohammad ruled over when he died in 632AD.

Asif took a shower, dressed, drank a lemonade, and relaxed on the veranda, waiting for Kalil to arrive. Twenty minutes late there was a knock on the door and Safir stood aside to let Sabal Kalil into the room.

'My old friend,' Kalil beamed, 'I am sorry to have kept you waiting. Paul and Malik are picking up Mina and will be here in a few minutes.'

'They are travelling together?'

'It is safe, don't worry. Their car is within a phalanx of security, and they are in a decoy vehicle too. If there is any fresh coffee, I would like some, please.'

'Of course,' Asif said as he ordered fresh coffee. When it arrived a few minutes later, he poured two cups, waving Safir out of the room.

Once seated, and alone, Kalil said 'You are up to date with my messages?'

'Yes. A little worrying to be unable to detect the two people of concern.'

'Agreed. I doubt that the instigator is in Brazil. But his agent is a worry. But we have two days before the ceremony. Let us not become paranoid.'

Asif grimaced, 'Easier said than done, Sabal.'

'Of course.'

'Let's wait for the others before talking of this more. Come, bring your coffee to the balcony. I want to get the most of Ipanema's views,' Asif said, leading the way. Once seated, he added, 'I was pondering earlier that you won the prize, coming here, leaving my father in Delhi and Islamabad.'

'Hmm. I don't disagree. It is enchanting here. But those early years were very hard, waiting for the population of Pakindesh migrants to arrive and grow enough to make the cities come alive again.'

Asif nodded, 'Well, you have done a wonderful job, Sabal. When you planned to migrate 150 million people across each of South and North-Central America, my father couldn't see it happening in his lifetime. I am glad he did live long enough to see your dream eventuate. An amazing achievement occurring quickly, safely, productively, and prosperously. And twenty million to the UK as well. The largest organised mass migration in world history, probably.'

'Plus, maybe another hundred million Pakindesh citizens that have expanded into our trading partner countries too. Spreading our views and influencing continued peace and moderation,' Kalil added.

'Hmph, Sabal, you've worsened my mood again, debating why we can't get our backward despotic African and Arabian cousins to understand Allah's gift to us all.'

'Not now, please. Enjoy the view and the coffee and let us wait for the others before we head down that road.'

'Agreed. My apologies, Sabal.'

'It's understandable. This issue caught us all by surprise.'

They watched the sea play against the sand, surfers and swimmers enjoying the beach and waves. Twenty minutes later, Safir came back with Paul Habbib, Mina Amin, and Malik Shah. Greetings were exchanged, hands shaken, hugs given, and small talk made as food and drink were brought in by hotel staff, administered by Safir. Once arranged, the world's most powerful leaders sat around the large dining room table, and ate and drank ahead of any serious discussions, by common, unspoken, agreement. There then followed a break for personal time to deal with ablutions, phone calls and emails before getting down to business. At that point Safir was asked to hold off on any interruptions except in an emergency, and they sat around the cleared dining room table to discuss their issues.

Kalil opened discussions. 'Welcome again everyone. It is truly a pleasure to see you all here. So, first off, the symposium does have several late apologies, and these might point to… let us say suspicions of unease on their parts. Whether it is fair to say that they wish to be nowhere near a potential area of unrest or conflict, we cannot say. However, these are the apologies that I have received, with the usual diplomatic niceties wrapped around their rationale for being unable to join us. It includes some of our prime suspects, such as the Presidents, Prime Ministers or Premiers of Egypt, Greater Somalia, and Nigeria, plus Kazakhstan, and France. The Sahel is to be represented by the current Chair of its Regional Governments, being Algeria and supported by Morocco's Vice President. Oman's President called me to say that he was concerned about recent border movements in Ethiopia and that he did not trust our new nemesis, Dhulbahante, and therefore wished to increase their diligence. Indonesia will be present, but that doesn't mean much. If they are a co-conspirator, they would be too obvious by their absence.

'So, down to details. The key address on the environment and technology sharing will be made by you, Malik, and two perspectives on European integration and education will be provided by Mina, and the Vice President of Turkey. The other agenda items are unchanged. At the end of day 1 we will either move to the base of the Christ statue as planned for the customary group photo, or we will change the location at short notice to Sugarloaf or Ipanema beach. Any questions on these issues?'

Habbib asked, 'Wouldn't it be safer to just agree to change it now but keep that to ourselves? I mean any attack is certainly going to be at the statue, for its obvious symbolism. Why make it easier for Al-antaqam to strike?'

There was agreement via nodding heads and comments, but Kalil raised his voice and said 'No! If we do move it then we are showing weakness. Any change must be due to known risks, not potential ones. The security level is already at its highest and the number of checks and controls are much greater than people will realise. We already have the ability for short notice changes to walking routes and the location of the live broadcast. The real risk is to me. I welcome it.'

'What!' Habbib exclaimed. 'What to you mean, Sabal?'

Kalil put his hands up for calm and the others went quiet. 'Let me explain. What I am about to say, you might totally disagree with, or you might think I am crazy, or stupid, or that my ego is out of control. Maybe this is true,' he paused, smiling. 'My friends, when I made my comments to Salina about there being no need for pious behaviour now, and that I believed that Allah wanted us to get on with life and to expand our thinking and behaviour for the betterment of mankind, or whatever I said back then, that was what I meant. It was not an unconsidered statement. I had been thinking this way for a long time. I could say that I had seen into the heart of Allah, the Beneficent, the Merciful, as that would be supreme arrogance, but I believe that I have come to understand Him, and everything that has occurred since Revelation Day points to this too. Consider these clues, which we have all either witnessed directly or heard about or seen coverage of since the Muslim world was left alone on Earth.

'One. The Sunni-Shia war between the Saudi Caliphate and Iran-Iraq resulted in the destruction of almost all its combatants. Not a fighting man was left alive after that conflict, nor any usable military equipment. And it wrought the almost complete destruction of Mecca and Medina. With few exceptions, the region was left with a largely female population apart from men under the age of 18. The peace that then followed led to a disarmed, enlightened, female governed plutocracy with no adherence to the harshest or skewed interpretations of the Quran, Hadith and Sunna, which had preceded the war.

'Two. Across the Middle East and North Africa in particular, practices by men responsible for carrying out Sharia that was most harsh against women, or sought to violently limit their rights and freedoms, saw those men struck down in the act of their violence. Some reports say that hundreds, possibly thousands of men died within a matter of weeks, halting all further actions against women.

The practices ended out of fear, no doubt, but they have never been resurrected.

'Three. There were mass male deaths within the leadership of countries dominated by religious zealots like the Taliban in Afghanistan that led to women taking control of government decisions and services. This had never happened before. We now have a totally female dominated government and bureaucracy in Afghanistan, as well as in seventeen other countries, across central Asia and Africa, and these demographic upheavals are continuing.

'And lastly... forgive me this... when I made my comments to Salina, and the world, I was not struck down by Allah.' Kalil sighed heavily and sat back in his chair and waited for counter arguments.

Mina Ahmed was the first to stand and put her hands up for silence, which occurred quickly. 'Gentlemen, if I might respond first?' she requested, but continued immediately, 'Kalil has again made the points which we have each debated many times, and none of them are in dispute as far as the facts are concerned. Some are anecdotal, but Salina and Michael, my personal reporters,' she laughed, 'have been to many of the places referenced by Sabal and have told me that the male to female ratios and ages they have seen there do support all the statements and reports that we've seen or read over recent years.

'But whilst I sincerely wish Sabal's conclusion to be correct, In Sha Allah, then why are we still seeing growing areas of fundamentalist behaviour, especially across Africa?'

Malik Shah put up his hand and said, 'I have a theory on that.' He looked around the table and saw that the others waited for him to continue. 'I think, if Sabal is correct, that this might be a final test. So, I do understand your faith, Sabal. But, to test Allah's will in this way might be seen as a supreme act of hubris. But, then again, you were not struck down last time, so maybe you are right. But it is a risk nevertheless.'

'If you are wrong, Sabal,' Asif challenged, 'then our entire world might erupt in a new war between fundamentalism and liberalism. Are you prepared to risk this?'

Kalil looked stern, 'Yes, I am. But will you all back my judgement in this?'

'Do we really have a choice?' Habbib asked, laughing without humour.

'We do,' Shah answered, 'but the choice is somewhat cowardly, although some of you might disagree with that assessment. If we leave Sabal to take the initiative alone, even though we have each supported his position so far, then we would be running from the fight. I do believe it is a fight, between fundamentalism and a more open society.'

Kalil interrupted just before Habbib began to speak, saying, 'Perhaps I need to acknowledge though that my position is unlikely to have been portrayed accurately in areas of the world in which the Pakindesh family of nations has limited impact. We should remember the way that the world was pre-RD, and how the Americans were lambasted as the great Satan by Iran and a growing number of Islamic nations. Or perhaps more accurately by their disenfranchised minorities, which were easy to manipulate and see their problems as caused by an outside power rather than their own corrupt governments.'

'And your point is?' Ahmed asked.

Kalil smiled, 'Thank you, Mina, for bringing me back down to earth,' he laughed, the others joining in. 'Yes, okay. I am saying that we have failed to see the expected living improvements in several nations across Africa and the Middle East. Less so in Asia. Whilst there are no shortages of houses and resources and food now, with only a few limited and short-lived exceptions, true representative government remains a failure across too many countries. We have not seen the end of fundamentalist beliefs that we expected, or I expected.'

'That is true, Sabal,' Habbib agreed. 'What disappoints me the most is that the North African migrants to Europe don't seem to have left behind their uneducated, or simplistic, beliefs. Why?'

'Tribal rivalry!' Asif exclaimed. 'Look at France. It remains a place with intense rivalries between Nigerians, Algerians, Turks, Somalians, and others. Rather than take on the European identity and history that surrounds them, they seem incapable of advancement.'

In the brief silence that followed, Kalil nodded his head slowly, thinking. 'Maybe this is the real test for us?' he suggested. 'Left the way things are, whilst seemingly at peace with each other, the countries that are leading a more enlightened, or liberal, lifestyle, are being threatened. Yet we have ignored this, assuming greater wealth, education and sophistication will improve and bring us all together. Perhaps we are wrong, and there is a need for another lesson. Don't misunderstand me, but perhaps Allah is calling us to deliver this? All of us, not just me.'

Habbib coughed, 'Sabal, I respect you immensely, as you know. I truly believe that you have done more for the benefit of mankind since RD than almost anyone else, but with the support and equal vision of Ghulam too, of course. There should be no support from any government anywhere for warfare, or terrorist activity, or for a return of harsher interpretations of the Quran. I do not understand why people would be drawn towards that position. It is not as if there is a common foe, or arguments to rid the world of non-Islamic people, because all of us were saved.'

'Gentlemen,' Ahmed said, taking a deep breath, 'with all due respect to you all, I have a different view, as a woman, and as a person without any political background. So, perhaps my view might be more relevant here. All of you have political backgrounds pre-RD, but I do not. It seems to me that whilst we have made great strides in all areas of humankind's development, we perhaps cannot take undue credit for the world that we were left with.

'We inherited a world of endless bounty; in food, housing, industrial capacity, energy, technology, and a vastly improved environment, which of course benefited from a much smaller population. The population decrease alone provided the greatest benefits. Add to that a single belief system, regardless of devoutness differences, and we were also bequeathed, at least theoretically, a world without the desire or need for warfare based on conquest for land, food, access to the sea, or the subjugation of other races. And yet, within weeks, we experienced Sunni versus Shia warfare, without any consideration that our new world had been created with a unified purpose...' she paused, taking a deep breath.

Habbib interrupted her flow, 'Your point, Mina?' he urged her, laughing.

'Okay, Paul, yes I was going on there a bit, sorry. My point, gentlemen, is that the outcome of all the incidents since RD that challenged the ideal of our new world, were isolated and came to a bad end, some extremely harshly. No regime that challenged the collective peace survived. No person that tried to subjugate another survived. To date, nothing serious has been allowed to divert our world onto a violent or fundamentalist path. I do not believe that Allah will allow this to happen now, either. Sabal Kalil has shown us the way forward. I think he is being guided by Allah Himself.'

AARON FADEL

Letting out a deep breath of relief as he threw himself onto his bunk, he marvelled at just how far sheer nerve could take you. He remained extremely tense but nevertheless pleased with the way in which his task had been made easier by Hussein treating him as a lackey. Nothing like being treated with disdain to lessen the chance of suspicion. He had a half hour before the wargame briefing that Hussein was to deliver to the senior and key junior officers in the wardroom. He'd been tasked with taking notes, keeping quiet, and observing. That was entirely to his liking.

His limited spare time was soon up, and he made his way to the wardroom and was stood at the back as Hussein entered, Admiral Pereira walking behind him. The men that were seated immediately stood to attention, were put at ease by Hussein, and the Admiral sat to one side, saying, 'The floor is yours, Commander.'

'Thank you, Sir,' Hussein acknowledged, and then quickly addressed the room, 'Gentlemen, as you are aware, we are to embark upon a different kind of wargame over the next 24 to 36 hours, compared to what you have been used to in the past. I will now explain the scenario.'

He opened an A4 folder and began to read the outline. 'Situation: Military tensions have been rising between a number of anti-Pakindesh groups, backed by Indonesia-Malaysia, some elements of North African coastal nations, and minor terrorist activity that is assumed to be linked to Turkish and French fundamentalist groups backed by their governments. Over the past 48 hours, Pakindesh patrol boats in the Indian Ocean off Myanmar and a frigate off the coast of Somalia have been engaged by land-based missiles, causing casualties and significant damage. In addition, drone attacks have engaged Pakindesh fishing vessels south of Sri Lanka. High level emergency communication with Indonesia-Malaysia, and Somalia have been met with expected denials, but PSS intelligence suggests that these nations are indeed responsible, although evidence is limited, and insufficient to take retaliatory action at present. The Pakindesh Airforce has increased patrols over coastal regions of Somalia and Malaysia, plus Sri Lanka.

'Concurrently, PSS intelligence suggests that a terrorist attack is most likely from Turkish or French supported groups, but no timetable or additional information is forthcoming. High level meetings between Presidents Kalil, Asif, Habbib and Ahmed are taking place in London at present and their personal bodyguards and security detail have been increased.

'Gentlemen, each of you has been provided with sealed envelopes with timestamps on them, one for each 2-hour period from 1800 Zulu time. Other updates will be provided by me in between these times, so do not get lazy. Please open these envelopes only at their appointed time and act upon the escalating scenario as you see fit. The game will begin in 30 minutes time, at 1400 Zulu. Good luck, gentlemen. Please take your posts.'

There was immediate activity as the officers exited the room, leaving Hussein with the admiral, and Cadet Officer Fadel.

Pereira smiled, 'Well done, Hussein. I think that set the right tone. I will be very interested to see how they react in half-an-hours' time,' he chuckled. 'Your scenario is ingenious. Watch and learn, Fadel. You are lucky to be able to be involved in a wargame like this so early in your career.'

'Yes, Sir, thank you. I am hoping to learn a lot,' Fadel said.

'Stick to me like glue, Fadel,' Hussein ordered. 'Let's head to the bridge now,' he said and led the way, Pereira following.

SALINA

As her flight approached the coast of Brazil, the sight of the beaches lifted Salina's heart, as breathtaking scenery always did. She never tired of seeing beautiful places, whether beaches, forests, mountains, desolate landscapes, or even bleak and icy realms. She loved it all. Descending into Rio brought her mind into focus. This trip was going to be a very different one, without Michael, left at home at his own request. His love life was taking precedence. Hers was non-existent, she sadly acknowledged. Sabal Kalil had granted her another meeting, a whole half day having been set aside, without cameras or publicity. It was as if he needed to talk openly as much as she needed to delve deeper into his thoughts.

On the way to her hotel, she soaked up the atmosphere. Happy people, strolling, swimming, playing soccer on the beach, shopping, walking hand in hand, enjoying the sunshine, cafes overflowing with diners, the smell of the ocean, a light breeze blowing, sun glinting on waves. Once checked in she sat on her balcony, after sending a few emails and text messages home to put her family at ease. There was a fruit platter in her room, and she was nibbling at strawberries and eating slivers of sliced mango with a fork, drinking a long glass of sparkling mineral water with lemon, and being rejuvenated by the ocean's hypnotic calming influence. She had almost 24 hours before meeting with Kalil, but she was tired. A nap was needed.

Two hours later, after a shower to wake herself up, she ventured out for dinner rather than getting room service. Eating alone in public didn't phase her. She enjoyed people watching and getting into conversations with locals. She had booked into one of her favourite hotels, the Rio Othon Palace, its name having survived RD, as had most of the hotels, tourist spots, restaurants, street names and icons of the country. That was one of the things she found most interesting about the world now; people, for the most part, had kept the historical names of places, even when their origins could have been criticised by fundamentalists as being un-Islamic. But that didn't happen, apart from in a minor way in parts of the Middle East.

Dressing simply, in a sleeveless knee length lemon dress with a white, thin leather belt, and flat comfortable shoes, she wandered out onto the street, turning right and then right again to lead her to the beach front. Being on Ria Aires Saldanha, one street back from the beachfront Avenida Atlantica, the hotel location was convenient as well as beautiful, and there were innumerable good restaurants within walking distance. She rarely ate in hotels apart from breakfasts, unless feeling exhausted, which usually meant ordering room service rather than using the restaurant. Within ten minutes she picked a Thai restaurant opposite the beach and took an outside table.

Saying she wasn't overly hungry, the waiter talked her into a series of small entrée dishes to provide a better sample of their menu, rather than a larger main course. She concurred, smiled, and perused her fellow diners as she waited for the food. It was a young set, mainly in their twenties and thirties, with a few older couples mixed in. The conversations were lively, some seemingly intimate and seductive in nature, all relaxed, happy. The thought struck her abruptly. Yes, they were happy. Most people were happy these days. Once you excluded those involved in politics or stressful occupations, the overwhelming emotion, compared to the pre-RD world, was of happiness, and peace of mind. True, people were clearly far more affluent, or perhaps less saddled now with the struggle for survival, or the bone-weary necessity of constantly seeking a better life in a world of horrible injustices and disparities in wealth.

But possibly because in the Pakindesh aligned countries at least, and mimicked elsewhere, all income, and access to services, was equal and provided, whether for a heart surgeon or a streetcleaner. Job satisfaction and intellectual stimulus had become the driving force of personal fulfilment. Health care was free, as was education to university levels. Housing was literally there for the taking, although environmental overlays provided limitations against excessive or wasteful behaviour. Struggle for survival had been replaced by the attainment of wisdom and enlightenment. But people were wary not to equate that openly with Buddhist philosophies of the past.

Salina played her guessing game, assessing the other diners with their possible professions or pastimes. The young lovers in the corner, mid-twenties, were clearly in the throes of pre-seduction. He couldn't take his eyes off her, and she was being cleverly coy and demure, yet flirting brilliantly. I give it no more than another month before they are in bed together, she thought, smiling. The couple in their fifties, maybe early sixties, were long married, still chatty yet comfortable in their own space, conversation not necessary but finding common ground for topics. Four young men eating healthily were on the prowl for girls, but more interested in the football on the beach, now dying down as the sun set. Any attractive woman passing by was appraised, carefully but still obviously. The two women in their thirties behind them were old friends, she decided. One had a ring on her finger, so married. The other was more attuned to single men, so seeking a mate. As for the two men in their late forties at the bar, they were more of a conundrum. Impeccably dressed, fastidious even, and close friends. Or lovers? Possibly. Homosexuality was no longer dangerous to admit to, especially in Pakindesh countries, a big change since RD. These two were either professional colleagues, maybe even politicians, or were a couple. Or both. Without being able to hear their conversation she could not decide, yet.

Once the first two courses of entrees arrived, she ceased her people watching and concentrated on the food. Forty minutes later, well fed, satisfied, and drinking a long black coffee, despite it potentially keeping her awake later, she took out a notebook and started to make an entry in it, writing questions or topics that she wished to bring up with Kalil the next day. Whilst doing so, she noticed that the two women were saying their goodbyes, and then the unmarried one left after they hugged. The married woman gathered up her few belongings and walked towards Salina's table, stopping just short of it, and making eye contact.

'Please excuse me, but are you Salina Ahmed by any chance?'

Used to being recognised in many places, the question did not phase Salina. 'Yes, I am.'

'I thought so. You are very famous here these days, as I'm sure you know. Could I talk to you for a moment?'

'Of course. Please sit down.'

'Thankyou. Are you here to do another interview with our President?'

'No, not this time,' Salina said, being accurate rather than more candid.

The woman looked suddenly perturbed, 'Oh, do excuse me, how ill-mannered of me. My name is Shalima,' she said extending her hand, which Salina shook lightly.

'Pleased to meet you, Shalima. You live in Rio then?'

'Yes, I was a teenager when my family migrated here from Chennai.'

'Really? What was that like for you?'

Shalima considered the question a moment. 'I am not used to being asked that these days, even by other migrants, as so many of us had similar experiences that we just accept that they are not worth discussing,' she laughed. 'But I suppose that's not always true really. For me it was exciting, but a little scary too. I had to leave my school friends behind, but it was an adventure, and my parents were so happy to have passed the tests for migration. I have two younger brothers, and they were thrilled to be going on a long plane journey. My father was a doctor, so he was in the category of necessary migrants, along with engineers, fishermen, teachers, mechanics, power station operators and so on.'

'What is your happiest or most fun early memory of getting here?' Salina asked.

'Getting our house allocated. We lived here on this avenue. I couldn't believe the beach here and how clean it was, and the standard of the houses and apartments. We were given a huge five-bedroom apartment on the tenth floor of a building that looked completely new to me. It was heaven. And the school experience was good too. New friends, everyone excited to be here, all our parents so happy that it rubbed off on all the kids. It was a wonderful time.'

'I see you are married,' Salina said, pointing to Shalima's hand.

'Aha, an observant journalist, of course,' she laughed. 'Yes, happily married to a doctor too, and we have two girls.'

'I got the impression that your friend is still single?'

Shalima arched her eyebrows in surprise. 'Wow, very observant then!'

'Comes with the territory I'm afraid, appraising people before I get to know them, sorry.'

Shalima laughed, 'No need to apologise. Yes, Ludmilla, not the name she was born with, is searching for mister right, as they say. Her options tend to be too old, too immature, too needy, too stupid, or not attractive enough. She's had many offers, but as she says, the offers tend to be to bed her rather than to marry her.'

'I see. The perennial problem of womankind,' Salina chuckled.

'Surely not you too?'

Salina shrugged. 'Being a travelling journalist, I tend not to be in one place long enough to settle down.'

'Yes, I can see that would be the case for you and being famous would he hard for many men to accept I suppose.'

'Very astute of you. Yes.'

'So, what are you going to do about it?'

'I am not sure. There is a man I like, although he'd be surprised to hear it, I think. But I am having trouble seeing us together. Very different worlds,' Salina said, surprising herself at her candour.

'Sounds like you have your man but just need to capture him in the right way.'

'What is the right way?'

'Aha. That my dear is the million-dollar question. They are all different. But if he is right for you, it will all become clear. My only advice, especially in this new world we inhabit, is not to worry about career differences. Those things are far less important now. Happiness is all around us. Grab it when you can and let the rest just happen. You are young. Life is good. Allah will provide.' On that advice, Shalima stood up, took out a card from her handbag and handed it across the table. 'Any time you need someone to talk to in this foreign city, I am available, if you wish. It has a been a pleasure to meet you, Salina.'

Salina stood and uncharacteristically hugged her new friend. 'Thank you, Shalima.' She quickly found a business card too and handed it over.

As she turned to leave, Shalima added, 'Love will happen for you, Salina, In Sha' Allah. Goodbye.'

Salina sat down again, began to finish her coffee, disliked its now more bitter taste so left it, paid her bill, and walked back to the hotel. Once there she made a few notes and went to bed, not thinking much about the following day's meeting with Kalil. She slept deeply.

The sun was streaming through the window when she awoke at 7am. 'Wow, ten hours sleep. You must have needed that, girl.' She showered and dressed, deciding not to go for an early morning run, and ordered room service breakfast, which she ate on the balcony a half hour later, soaking in the views once more. After that she made a quick call home to Michael to discuss a few things and then went for a leisurely stroll along the beach front for an hour. Her meeting with Kalil was set for 11am. Fifteen minutes beforehand she booked a self-drive taxi on her phone App and was driven to the Palace.

Entry formalities were minimal, her arrival scheduled. She was led this time to an inner courtyard area with two reclining chairs sitting each side of a marble topped table, the surrounds filled by citrus trees in large pots. Asked by a member of staff what she would like to drink, she requested a lemon drink with ice and waited for Kalil to arrive. A few moments later he walked into the courtyard, smiling, and she stood. He surprised her with a hug and a kiss on each cheek.

'Welcome back, Salina. You are well I Hope?'

'Very well, Mister President. Are you?'

'Always. Your mother sends her love. I was with her yesterday. A formidable lady. Clearly it is in your family's genes,' he laughed.

'Our family are monopolising you, it would seem,' she laughed.

'Or is it I that am monopolising you?' he quipped in return.

Just then her drink was delivered and there was also a plate with a selection of small biscuits and pastries on it. Kalil was served coffee and a similar plate of food. Once settled and having taken a sip each, Salina asked, 'Is it okay if I record our discussion on my phone, just for my own sake, not for publication or anything?'

'Of course, if you wish. And I wish you to call me Sabal today, no formalities, agreed?'

She was not surprised. 'Of course, if you wish, I would be honoured.'

'Don't be,' he laughed. 'You did me a favour last time, giving me the catalyst to say what I thought and ignore the consequences. I am not sure how else I would have reached that position without your interview.'

She nodded in acknowledgement. 'I thought I was lucky to… well… get you to open up. But I think you had rehearsed that interview in your head and fine-tuned it long before I asked to meet with you and record the discussion.'

'Not quite. Yes, I wanted to go public with my opinions, but I had not committed to it until it occurred. I had probably gone over my views in my head many times, debating with myself whether it made sense, looking at the evidence, but always pulling back. I was worried for a long time whether it was a mistake to say what I did. But in the end, I was convinced of my view, and I needed to say it. Since then, I suppose there has been a whirlwind of opinions, and a lot of criticism too. Time will tell how it all plays out.'

'In what way?'

'I have stirred a hornet's nest, Salina. Some people don't like that. Am I going to get stung?'

'Are you afraid of being attacked?'

'All politicians fear the possibility of extremists seeking to assassinate them, or just harm them, or the public turning against them. It is not the change in levels of support, but rather the missed opportunities that would occur if we were thrown out of office. In the old days I suppose it was more the loss of position and money and reputation. For some it was the real fear of being killed if they were in less democratic places, with more volatile mobs beyond the gates.'

He paused and she allowed the silence to grow for a while as she took another drink and nibbled on an apricot-filled croissant piece. He refilled his coffee from the adjacent pot. She watched him, trying to decern his real mood. She couldn't.

'Well, I suppose I should explain why I requested this meeting, Sabal,' she began, taking his nod as a sign to continue. 'After the last time we met, there has clearly been an enormous amount of discussion, everywhere, about whether you are right, or whether you should be…'

'Executed for blasphemy, hubris, whatever. That an example needed to be made of me to appease Allah, as if He would need appeasing anyway. Yes, I am aware of the polarisation of views that I started. But leaving the public aside, what did you think? Maybe not immediately, but after due consideration?'

'Does it matter what I think, Sabal?'

'Of course. You are accepted by millions of people as the voice of reason in a complicated world. You have become the eyes and ears of political armchair strategists and travellers. Your wrap-up analyses are listened to by millions, and you can change minds.'

'Is that why you agreed to see me again? You want my endorsement?'

Kalil laughed. 'No, not really. It would be useful perhaps, but no, if I am in trouble then I am afraid that your support, no matter how widely it might spread, would not save me. I am not worried, Salina. I truly believe that my view is backed by evidence and that it makes sense. My heart tells me this also. But this will not save me from those that are easily led. Like before Revelation Day, there will still be those that can be manipulated by unscrupulous leaders, and not all of them can be dismissed as uneducated, or the poor lacking hope, especially now. We rightly fear such things less now. After all, we do not have poverty anymore, in theory at least. You have been to most parts of the world. Do you still see poverty and injustice?'

She thought about his question for a moment. 'Yes. There is still poverty, or perhaps, let's say there are still places where the rich-poor gap remains significant. But there is a difference, I think. I have been to places where there is overcrowding and where the sanitation systems could be better or the houses better. But unlike before, the people are generally happy, and nobody is seeking a handout. They remain in these places out of nostalgia, or family history. It is like there is a need for continuity with the past. People liked their communities. They didn't like to struggle for food, money, or access to services, but those things are provided almost everywhere now. So, whilst there is no need to crowd together in substandard housing, and clearly millions of people have moved to modern apartments or better living options in other places, especially in empty cities, and their children can go to school, and hospitals are available, and services are free. But... I think there is loneliness too. People, some of them, fear the losses.'

'What do you mean by that?' Kalil asked, frowning.

'I have never voiced this before,' Salina began, 'but I think some people fear that there might be another mass removal one day.'

'Why would they think that?'

'Why not?'

'But the lives of everyone have been immeasurable improved since Revelation Day. Surely, they accept that?'

Salina considered that, accessing her memories of places and people. 'Maybe. Maybe not.'

'Explain yourself, please?'

She frowned, getting her thoughts in order, so as not to blurt out a stream of unintelligible angst that had been collecting in her head for years. Taking a deep breath, she began, 'Okay. Let me give you my own perspective. First off, I miss my friends that died. I refuse to say they were removed, whether accurate or not. They are gone and just the same as if they had died or were killed. We didn't get to go to funerals or hold memorial services for them. One day they were with us, then they were dead, then they disappeared. We can sugar coat it as much as we want but they were murdered, if the definition of murder is taking someone's life against their wish...' She paused. Kalil slowly nodded his head, agreeing without stemming her flow of thoughts.

'Okay, so we, all of us, lost hundreds of friends and acquaintances, and for some people, family too, like President Habbib's wife for instance. We lost links to what we took for granted, the continuation of normal life, which was enhanced and improved by cultural diversity whether we accepted that or fought against it, playing the racist card when it suited us. We lost most of the world's musicians, sports teams, movie stars, comedians, inspirational leaders in many fields, like scientists, adventurers, inventors, entrepreneurs, you name it. And then we looked around and we were left within a very finite group of people, more alike but still mostly scared and bewildered, but some jubilant I realise.

'In the next phase, many of us, especially those from westernised democratic countries, soon woke up to the fact that we couldn't run our world. Not immediately anyway. In places where we were originally a clear minority, like the U.K., U.S., and most European countries, we didn't have the skills to run the basics, power, water, infrastructure, hospitals, transport. The list was endless. So, we had to migrate to a small number of cities where there would be enough of us to make a go of what we then saw as the post apocalypse. I notice that those early descriptions were very soon replaced and sanitised by the more devout amongst us. It became Revelation Day, didn't it? That suited the fundamentalists very well. Allah had delivered them to the new world and had destroyed the infidels.

'I didn't feel that way. I was scared shitless, Sabal; I mean it. Every day was a day of fear. Fear of being discovered as a fraud, a misfit, an unbeliever, or heretic pretending to be a good Muslim. Like so many of us in the U.K., the majority were not active Mosque attendees. Most of us, especially the kids, couldn't understand any Arabic, could just read passages in the Quran, it wasn't a living language for most of us. Yes, we knew the main prayers by rote, drummed into us from an early age, but that waned. So, when we went back to school it was another time of intense fear of being discovered wanting.

'But we survived that period, at least in England anyway, but only because enough of the adults fought against the growing fundamentalism in the schools and we were lucky enough to get things working again, quickly enough to avoid the hardliners accusing us, the less devout, of causing the problems. We were very lucky.

'Meanwhile, the Middle East had reverted to type and started killing each other once more. But this time there was no scapegoat to blame like the Americans or Israeli's or westerners or Christians. It was harder to play the victim card this time. No-one else had caused their new problems. And the old enmities of Shia versus Sunni again boiled over.

'When that left Mecca destroyed, and Medina badly damaged, and Tehran of course, one would have thought that enough was enough. For most, it was. But we still have those fundamentalist idiots around, don't we? I'm sorry, I'm rambling now. Forgive me. I think I needed to get that off my chest, Sabal.'

Kalil had a look of pity on his face, but quickly changed his expression to one of wonder, with a supportive smile. 'That took courage, Salina.'

'I don't think so, Sabal.'

Kalil shrugged, 'Okay then, so what about now, after 11 years or so? Have your thoughts changed?'

'Hmm. I suppose so. Yes, in some ways. We've all made new lives, haven't we? We had no choice. And don't throw the old observations at me, please. Yes, without RD my mum would never have become the Prime Minister, and maybe Michael and I would not have become journalists with the following we have, and maybe Charlie wouldn't have become a doctor, although he had more chance of attaining that dream than the rest of us. And I can agree that the world has avoided a climate change catastrophe, which maybe could not have happened without the loss of six billion people and their polluting footprints and associated destruction of resources.

'So, the animals and the oceans thank Allah for RD. As do the forests and the ice caps. And the poor that survived and inherited better lives, which their various politicians or leaders failed to achieve for them before. But was the price paid worth it, Sabal?'

'I ask you that, Salina. Was it worth it?'

'If I say no, are you going to be terribly disappointed in me?'

He considered the question, for almost 30 seconds, and she waited. Finally, he said, 'No. I would not be disappointed, Salina. I understand your position, and your grief. It is different for me, or my generation. I only saw a continuation of the same issues for the rest of my life. Disappointing politicians, diplomacy games that turned to warfare and conflict when they failed or bought us some more times of peace when they didn't. The status quo would ever remain so. China would have become a growing problem, and conflict would have occurred, although not major nuclear conflict. I don't know whether we would have avoided climate change increasing the temperature beyond the tipping point or not. As for most of history though, except for times of warfare or pandemics, people's lives would have continued to improve, decade on decade, life expectancy would have continued to rise, which brings its own issues, but medical science would keep pushing amazing boundaries, new technologies would continue to change our lives, mostly for the better.

'The growth in totalitarianism might have slowed again and democracies hopefully would have once more started to expand, once people like Putin, Xi, Kim Jong Il, and other unsavoury egomaniacs died off, or were killed. Or, maybe not, perhaps those worst examples would have flourished and continued to threaten world peace. Maybe that was foreseen by Allah, and He decided enough was enough? Who knows?'

Salina snorted in disbelief, 'Surely not! You are not crediting Allah with seeing that pessimistic future and deciding to short-circuit it are you? Isn't that a cop out?'

'Ha! Yes, I suppose it is somewhat of a cop out. I suppose if Allah saw that kind of future there would have been many ways for

Him to change it. If I was all powerful, knowing and seeing, I would probably have done things differently. But then, I am mortal, just a man without power, so how dare I second guess Allah?'

Salina shook her head. 'Sabal, you have neatly brought us back to the core issue, being your second guessing of Allah's intentions. Was that meant or is it a coincidence?'

'I don't know, Salina. Perhaps 'All Roads Lead to Rome' and this issue is the elephant in the room, as they say, isn't it?'

'Don't confuse the issue for me. What do you think will happen after tomorrow's symposium? Are you going to be lauded as a new Prophet, or will some lunatic try to kill you?'

Kalil instantly frowned. 'Do you have a premonition on this?'

'No, of course not, but...' she paused, seeing his facial expression and change in mood. 'What is it, Sabal? I didn't mean anything by it. Are you worried?'

He quickly recovered his composure. 'My apologies, Salina. Always there is doubt in my mind. This is natural. I came to my conclusion about Allah's intentions, and ever since, although I still believe my instinct, I might be guilty of unbelievable arrogance, and perhaps I will die a terrible death in front of the crowd, as a lesson to all. In Sha' Allah.'

'You are frightening me, Sabal. Are you worried?'

He pursed his lips, then shook his head. 'No. No, I am not worried. I am convinced of my... analysis. It makes sense. Do you think I am mad?'

'No, not at all. When you first stated your position, I was astounded. Not by your conclusion but by the courage it took to say it. The backlash was to be expected, especially from the fundamentalists, or those that would clearly lose their own powerbases. Clearly nobody whose existence is tied to religion or adherence to Islamic doctrine as the core meaning in their lives will support your conclusion. How could they? And you were hated by many of them because you didn't immediately die, by Allah striking you down. That must have angered them even more.'

'Of course,' Kalil agreed, 'but now those people have a second chance to see me publicly sacrificed for my hubris. I think I read that premonition somewhere recently. It has a nice ring to it, doesn't it? If I don't survive tomorrow, Salina, it has been a real pleasure getting to know you.'

'Please don't do that. Don't joke like that. You must survive. I want your view to be endorsed, more than anything. Don't do anything rash, Sabal.'

'I don't intend to, and as many precautions have been taken as possible, from a security point of view. But...' he paused, raising his hands, palms out.

'It is in the Lap of the Gods, then, as I think Homer once said,' Salina stated.

'Indeed. And that being the case, it is time for lunch and different discussions.' He stood up and almost instantly there was activity in the room, and they were led inside to a small dining room, already set for lunch. The next hour was very different, a much lighter conversation, and by the end of it, Salina was happier, optimistic, and ready to see what the next day would bring. She left with some sadness but was also glad to be seeing her mother for dinner. Kalil kissed her on both cheeks as she left him and she wished him well for the next day's events.

MINA

'I can't believe we ate that much food, Salina!' Mina exclaimed, looking at the dishes on the table between them.

'What can I say, Mum, we're pigs!' Salina laughed. 'But I was really looking forward to trying this place. I think they were right when it was described as the best Indian and Kashmiri restaurant in Rio.'

'It has been lovely to catch up like this, somewhere exotic. I don't think we've ever been able to do that before,' Mina said.

'Well, we don't exactly have careers that allow it, do we? Especially you. I like the look of your bodyguard.'

'Yes, I thought I saw you checking him out,' Mina laughed. 'He's a nice young man, well respected by the security team. Don't distract him, his job is hard enough and they are all on edge now, because of the threat to Kalil tomorrow, and so the rest of us are potential targets too.'

'I didn't know that! You didn't say, Mum!'

'What is there to say? I'm the PM of a Pakindesh-allied nation. Obviously, I'd be a possible target if some lunatic wishes to make a statement against Kalil and his supporters.'

Salina thought about that for a moment. 'Yes, of course. Stupid of me. I just assumed that it was only Kalil that would be the prime target of protesters.'

'Let's not mince words, Salina. Kalil is likely to be the target of an assassin rather than a protester. Hopefully that won't be the case, but the security teams are taking no chances with any of us.'

'Of course. I'm surprised then that they let you come out, rather than eat in the hotel?'

'Well, they didn't like this, but I insisted. I'd be the least threatened, compared to Asif or Habbib or Shah.'

'You've got me worried now, Mum. Let's get back to the hotel, should we?'

'Calm down, Salina. Yes, we can go, but don't get spooked. It's not like you. What's up? Tell me.'

'Not here, not now. When we get back to the hotel, okay?'

'Alright, let's go then.' They paid the bill and left, and were driven back to Mina's hotel, and went up to her suite. Once there, Salina relaxed a little and they made peppermint tea. Settled on the couch, Mina went back to the issue on her mind. 'Now, tell me, what's the matter?'

Salina contemplated the answer to such a short but complex question. 'I think Kalil is more worried than he lets on. I think he sees tomorrow as a test of his conviction, and whether he lives, or dies, will be in Allah's hands.'

'Hmm, well, there's nothing new in that, Salina. That was pretty much the situation immediately after your bombshell interview with him, wasn't it?'

'Maybe, but it feels different. He seems different. He's still firm in his... conclusions, but maybe less so of his own mortality,' Salina suggested.

'He said that?'

'No, not at all. Or not in so many words. But reading between the lines, that was how I took it, later when I replayed the recording in my room. He is not worried for himself, but I think he is very worried for Pakindesh if things become violent.'

'Understandable. Look, Salina, you know I cannot tell you things. You must respect that. You're a journalist, you know how these things work. Need to know basis, all that sort of stuff. All I can say is that whatever precautions have been deemed necessary have been taken. Between us, you know that I am far from being devout.

Yet I am here, in this position, against all odds. That must mean something. Either that or it's a quirk of fate. Either way I need to trust in... either Allah's guidance, or who knows what positive forces are out there, looking after our family. Worry about what we can affect, forget the rest. Take precautions, trust in Allah. Okay?'

'Okay, Mum. I need to go now, I'm very tired. I won't see you tomorrow, will I?'

'Well, you might see me, but we won't get a chance to talk or be together, no. But I will see you at home next week. Take care my darling,' Mina said as she hugged her daughter and kissed her, then watched with some trepidation as Salina left.

KALIL

The next day, the crowd at the Maracanã Stadium was not at its 78,840-seat capacity, partly due to having been deliberately decreased for crowd management purposes, and to allow for a cleared area behind the stage, set up for the various speakers on the day. There were areas in front of the main stage, on the playing pitch, for dignitaries to be provided with seating befitting their status. The other reason for the reduced capacity was simply because the event was boring to most of the city's inhabitants, and so the guests tended to be those with links to the political and social agenda of the day. It was being televised around the world because it was a major event held every two years in one of the countries within the greater Pakindesh sphere of influence, or of the Commonwealth of Pakindesh Nations, as they were officially known, being a hangover from the days of the British Commonwealth.

Sabal Kalil looked across at the crowd before him and approached the microphone on the dais of the stage, smiling at the polite and spontaneous applause. His charisma was unblemished. He had decided to open proceedings by reciting the most well-known prayer of thanks to Allah; the Du'a from the Quran. He was aware that this was going to be unexpected, as there had rarely been a prayer to open what was essentially a political symposium.

In addition, his decision was also to partly confuse some in the audience, who would not know how to reconcile his devotional prayer to Allah with his radical statement about it being time for the world to live less devoutly, and that this was, in Kalil's view, Allah's intention for them all now. He had always enjoyed messing with the minds of his friends, detractors, and enemies alike.

He was as familiar with the prayer as any devout Muslim, having recited it since he was a young boy. There had been times when his devotion had wavered, especially when he was in his 20's for a spell, more interested in his social life than his religion. Then, later, during his military studies, when he was especially careful not to antagonise his fellow cadets of Hindu and Sikh beliefs, he had chosen to show a far less devout persona to those around him. Pragmatism was a necessary stage of his education into human nature and keeping a low profile as an officer cadet was paramount for all students of minority religions in India if they wanted to advance. He brought his thoughts back to the present.

He took a deep breath, relaxed, held his hands in front of his body palms out, closed his eyes and began to recite the prayer in English, being the official Pakindesh language. His voice was deep, resonant, and confident.

> *'Worship Allah, and be of those who give thanks.*
> *Blessed be the name of thy Lord, full of Majesty, Bounty, and Honor.*
> *So celebrate with praises the name of thy Lord, the Supreme.*
> *Praise be to Allah, who has guided us to this.*
> *Never could we have found guidance, had it not been for the guidance of Allah.*
> *And He is Allah, there is no god but He. To Him be praise, at the first and at the last. For Him is the command, and to Him shall you be brought back.*
> *Then Praise be to Allah, Lord of the heavens and Lord of the earth. Lord and Cherisher of all the worlds! To Him be Glory throughout the heavens and the earth, And He is Exalted in Power, Full of Wisdom!*

The crowd was largely silent, awed, smiling, welcoming of their President, but within a few seconds of his prayer recital, there was a huge roar of approval.

HUSSAIN

The war games had been going well. Hussein was in control, and the evolving scenario written on 'The Greens' was steadily increasing the pressure on the junior officers as the situation 'on the ground' deteriorated, making it necessary to react in ways that some of them had never contemplated before.

The mock scenario worsened when it was explained that a night terrorist act at sea crippled two of the aircraft carrier's escort ships, a destroyer, and a frigate, via the planting of limpet mines against their hulls during the night. The ships were deemed to have been sunk and they were out of the 'game'. In secondary actions there was sporadic intelligence coming through that the British Houses of Parliament were under attack from a French marine company that had landed by helicopters and fast attack boats north of London and on the Essex coast, then advanced to the city. Most bridges leading to the Parliament buildings were now blocked and guarded by armed troops, keeping the British police and other armed response units away from them. The French Air Force had achieved air superiority and 30% of the Pakindesh aircraft carrier's fighters were deemed lost in aerial combat over the first few hours of the morning, making it necessary for the carrier to steam north to be further out of air attack range.

The wardroom was full when Commander Hussein took the next 'Green' sheet from his file and read it to the assembled men.

'At 1400 Zulu time a message was sent from the Houses of Parliament to inform the world that the French Turkish Islamic Alliance was now in control of the building and the government, that the building was booby-trapped with explosives and that 62 Members of Parliament were imprisoned in the basement. An ultimatum stated that one MP will be executed each half-hour from 1800 hours unless the country surrenders to French Turkish control. Secondly, a Turkish regular army contingent of brigade strength has landed in Hull and is heading south to London. French and Turkish air attacks through the night have rendered British Air Force capability destroyed on the ground, as well as inflicting significant damage to army bases within 200 kilometres of London. French and Turkish forces now have air superiority over the UK and its sea lanes. It is assumed that regular French and Turkish forces will control the area around the Houses of

Parliament by 1500 Zulu. Questions of fact or correlation, gentlemen?'

A lieutenant raised his hand, and a nod was received from Hussein for him to speak. He coughed, clearly nervous, 'Sir, do we have any military assets coming from Pakindesh to assist us within the next 2 hours?'

'No. Next question?'

A lieutenant commander asked, 'Can we assume that the British Government will not surrender and therefore that the hostages are expendable, Sir?'

'A good question, commander, but not one that we can expect to be privy to in the timeframe. However, as a Pakindesh ally, one can assume that Britain will be urged not to surrender. Next?'

'Can Pakindesh satellite intel show us where the Turkish forces are so that we can coordinate an air attack against them, Sir?' asked a sub-lieutenant?'

'Now that is an intelligent question, lieutenant. Yes, our satellite intel can track the Turkish brigade. So, what do you intend to do about that?'

'Hit the Turks on the road at a place advantageous to our air assets but as far as possible from the French Air Force, which will be concentrating on London and on attacking us,' the same officer answered.

'Clearly a good plan, no matter what our potential inferiority in the air might be. But I would like you to think outside of the square, gentlemen. What is the worst outcome for Pakindesh, not just militarily but politically?' Hussain asked, looking from face to face as he did so.

The junior officers were hesitant to express an opinion now, so the previously outspoken lieutenant commander did so, 'Loss of London, and the government, which would symbolise a victory for the French Turkish Alliance in the eyes of the rest of the world, Sir?'

'It would, commander. But would elimination of the French forces, even if it meant sacrificing the Parliament and the hostages, be seen as a British victory, politically?' Hussain asked, leading the group to his predetermined solution.

'I believe it would, Sir, and it would also galvanise Britain into retaliatory action, supported by us of course,' the sub-lieutenant stated.

'It seems to me that you are contemplating an attack on the Turkish brigade, and to eliminate the French units in London, even if you need to sacrifice the Houses of Parliament, whilst we still have some naval air capability left. Am I reading the room correctly?' Hussein asked, trying to remain facially impassive.

There was a consensus in the wardroom.

'In that case, gentlemen, I suggest you put a plan together within the next 30 minutes and assemble the assets needed. To let you know what has previously been sanctioned by Britain for this wargame, we can fly unhindered for the next 5 hours, and blank and smoke rounds from naval gunfire are available to mimic actual targeting on London. The rounds have purple paint markings on them to identify them as being primed for self-destruction after 2 kilometres of flight from firing, although otherwise they look like normal live rounds. The gunners should therefore treat them as for normal rounds when calibrating, so accurate gunnery is important to achieve. The same for the air to ground missiles on the fighters when attacking the designated position of the Turkish forces, which, whilst looking real, are mock vehicles. Any questions?' Hussain finally asked. There were none. 'Then to your planning tasks, gentlemen. Go and defeat the French Turkish Alliance,' he laughed, as they streamed out of the wardroom to put the agreed plan into action.

FADEL

Aaron Fadel, having intensely observed this charade, now knew what was really at play, and it scared the hell out of him. Before he had a chance to think some more, Commander Hussain sent him off to shadow the naval gunnery commander, whilst he and the Admiral went to his quarters for a discussion.

Fadel watched as Pereira and Hussain walked off, not liking being away from his adversary, or too far from Pereira either. Think, man. What is happening here, he considered, as he slowly made his way to the bridge. What is Hussain trying to achieve? It's not as if there really are any French and Turkish forces attacking London, so what is his plan? London is safe, and the Prime Minister is in Rio at the Pakindesh symposium anyway, as are all the key Pakindesh leaders. That is where the action is, potentially. There's nothing happening here. Anyone could walk into London and take it if they wanted, probably, whilst all eyes are on Rio, and... oh good God! He stopped dead, willing his brain to work it out. The only real live threat to London wasn't some terrorist madman, or foreign forces. This carrier group was the main threat. It could decimate London if it wished to, being so close and with so much firepower! But that wasn't possible, surely? It was ridiculous. They wouldn't be attacking non-existent forces, what would be the point? Unless...

PEREIRA

In the Admiral's quarters, Pereira praised his Commander, 'It's going well, Hussain. Very well put together, I think. I like the scenarios. It is always good to test the officers' thinking about the politics behind military issues, I think. I like the way you've put this together. Do you think their plan will be to destroy the Houses of Parliament then?' he laughed.

'I hope so, Sir, otherwise I'll have to prod them in that direction. I'm not sure whether they will split the remaining strike aircraft between the Turkish brigade and the French assets around Big Ben though,' Hussain stated, as he fingered the pistol tucked into his pants at the small of his back.

Pereira frowned. 'No need to use the fighters against the French ground forces really, the gunnery on our remaining ships is more than enough to destroy the Houses of Parliament, being this close to shore. For me though I'd have moved the group much further north, out of French fighter range. We are still vulnerable here, within the current scenario, don't you think?'

'Yes, definitely, but I wanted us to remain within striking range of central London, Sir.'

'Why? It's not realistic. We could be destroyed by the French Air Force here. They would outnumber us ten to one in the air, and we could never survive multiple missile attacks now that we've been deemed to have lost one destroyer and one frigate.'

'That's true, of course, but then how could I arrange to actually destroy central London?' Hussain asked, a slight smile appearing on his face.

Pereira looked bewildered, 'What do you mean? The scenario could play out with our fighters from further north rather than using gunnery from here.'

'You really are a fucking idiot, aren't you, Pereira?' Hussain scoffed, as his superior officer jumped up and tried to formulate a response. By the time he was upright, Hussain had pulled his pistol out and aimed it at Pereira's chest, its silencer adding to the clear threat.

'What... what are you doing Hussain?'

'My God, you're slow, Admiral. What am I doing? I am orchestrating a real attack on London of course. We are about to destroy the Houses of Parliament, after which French terrorist units will infiltrate the capital and take control of TV and radio stations and confirm that Britain has surrendered to the French Turkish Alliance. Hopefully Kalil and the rest of the false Islamists will be eliminated in Rio within the hour as well.'

'You're a lunatic, Hussain! You can't possibly get away with this. It's impossible, you will –.'

Two silenced shots killed Pereira before he could finish, and he was thrown back into the chair behind him, dead within seconds.

Hussain replaced the pistol to its hidden position and left the room, locking the door behind him, and made his way back up to the bridge.

RIO DE JANEIRO

In his planning, Al-antaqam decided that he needed to make a statement. Killing Kalil in the football stadium was one thing, but to do it as the world leaders posed for their customary group photo, this time at the base of the Christ the Redeemer statue would be poetic justice and have far more impact. It would be a clear message from Allah not to interpret His will, and once seen in vivid colour, Kalil's death witnessed for all to see, the world would realise that Allah's will, and his teachings must be obeyed. That message would confirm to the people that they must return their lives to intense devotion to Islam, and Sharia would expand everywhere with the strictest interpretations. These new infidels must be purged from the Earth. He was confident that he could eliminate not only Kalil, but hopefully the others as well. His plan was to eliminate Muhammed Asif, Malik Shah, Paul Habbib and Mina Ahmed. The British Prime Minister was irrelevant. She would be relegated to a low-level whorehouse if he had his way. He was not attracted to her, but if the opportunity arose to capture her and rape her that would be a bonus. He smiled at the thought, then castigated himself for his lack of focus.

The Pakindesh leaders would be ferried to the Redeemer Statue by helicopter, he was sure, but that meant that the timings were fluid, and he would need to be hiding in wait long beforehand. The location was clearly isolated, at the 700-metre-high peak of the Corcovado Mountain, and most visitors took the funicular railway to get there. There would probably be a cursory security detail examination of the area before the dignitaries were taken there, but these days it was unlikely to be thorough. Probably they would just close the area to the railway terminal and café areas, to allow Kalil and the others free access to helicopter to the pathway leading up to the foot of the statue.

It was a relatively open area, so concealment was very difficult. There were thicker trees and scrub to the right of the statue as one looked at it, but those were too far back and the wrong angle to get a clear shot. Along the pathways up to the foot of the statue was open ground with minimal cover, or grassy areas, and the slopes did not allow for a decent field of fire. Kalil would be at the front of the statue for the photos. Any approach, say at a run, from the rear right side towards Kalil would be seen and thwarted easily. He could hide in the thicker trees about halfway along the approach route on the right, but it was a poor option. It allowed a chance to hit their helicopter but that was all.

No, there was a better way, one that allowed a much greater chance of escape. He knew what was necessary. His fallback option would be used. When he'd thought of it a week beforehand, he dismissed it as too complicated, but really that wasn't the case. A simple kidnap, some subterfuge, a small amount of violence; no problem.

KALIL

'Fellow citizens of the Commonwealth of Pakindesh Nations, I would like to expand on my comments some months ago regarding what I believe to be the direction that Allah is pointing us towards,' Kalil began as he looked around the stadium at the crowd, now instantly going silent, the low murmuring of the past few minutes quickly diminishing.

'I know that my comments annoyed many people around the world, especially in Indonesia-Malaysia and in the Middle East. My views questioned what everyone assumed was the reason for our salvation by Allah, the Beneficent, the Merciful, after Revelation Day. I do not profess to know Allah's will. How could I, or any of us? I do not apologise for my analysis of the world we now are lucky enough to live in, whether within the Pakindesh family or elsewhere. Let me be candid, and ask you to be honest, in showing your opinions to a series of questions I wish to put to you all.

'By a show of raised hands, please tell me, how many of you feel that you are showing sufficient and acceptable adherence to the Quran?'

Slowly at first, then within a half-minute there were more raised hands, until approximately 70% of the crowd endorsed their own practices.

Kalil nodded his head and smiled. 'Now, and please, again, be honest, with me and with Allah, how many of you attend a mosque less often each year over, say, the past five years?'

This time there were hands raised, then dropped, then raised again, as people looked around for similar acknowledgements around them. Eventually, after waiting for a minute and a half for the crowd to be content with their choice, Kalil announced, 'More than seventy percent, again,' he pronounced, clapping, 'Thank you for your honesty my friends.

'Now, given that most of you, and I, attend a mosque far less often than 5 or more years ago, yet we believe that our level of devotion to Allah is sufficient, how many of you are happy with your lives and the world in general?'

This time, arms were raised rapidly, and it was hard to see anyone being negative. Kalil smiled broadly. 'I am so very happy, that you are all happy. I am not arrogant enough...' he paused, laughing lightly, 'well, perhaps still a little too much,' he added, and the crowd laughed with him, 'to say that your happiness is due to the good governance within the Pakindesh Commonwealth of Nations. However, in most of the world there has been good governance, assisted massively by the benevolence and plenty that we were blessed with after Revelation Day. The profound changes in circumstances and in the way that we live our lives now, and to choose how we live and in what paths we take, means that we enjoy a freedom of choice unprecedented in history.

'This could not have occurred without us being chosen to survive the loss of six billion other souls. I do not believe that they were sent to hell as infidels, as some radical elements state. I believe that Allah saw the need to change the world's direction and rebalance the planet's health by such an awful yet necessary culling of lives. Perhaps like a culture in a petri dish, we were outrunning the resources to maintain ourselves and were polluting ourselves to death. I hope and believe that those lost to the world are in heaven and being looked after and are wishing us to succeed better than we were able to do when there were so many of us struggling for a better life.

'I wish to share with you, in some cases repeating, the evidence that has convinced me of Allah's intentions for humankind. I do not, and will not, ever, claim to be a prophet, like Muhammad, praise be His name. I am a mortal man, and I have never been privileged to hear directly from Allah, or the Prophet. I will keep this simple.

'One. Those religious leaders that were overly zealous or hard line, or women haters, or were involved in Sunni versus Shia warfare, or the most savage interpreters and practitioners of Sharia, are all dead. Countries where the religious leaders tried to follow a harsh path, did not survive.

'Two. Mosque attendance has steadily declined over the past ten years and adherence to Islam, apart from during Ramadan and Eid in particular, is probably at the lowest level ever in Islamic history... without consequences.

'Three. Where people's lives follow a good path, with consideration, courtesy, love, compassion, and practice assistance to others, they have flourished.

'So, I wish to recommit myself to the analysis and conclusions I came to over a month ago. I believe that Allah, in his ultimate wisdom, is satisfied with our behaviour and progress. I believe that He has left us to our own fate now, free of indoctrination, or the need to adhere strictly to the Quran, Hadith or Sunna in our daily lives, unless we wish to.

'I believe that Allah is now gifting us His freedom, to thrive and advance and be good custodians of the world. If you wish to follow religious doctrine, that is your choice. If not, that will not be a bad mark against you. We have been freed from our ritualistic ties to Allah, peace and praise be upon Him. It is now up to us, all of us, to make this world a better place, to care for it, protect it, cleanse it, and to make all our lives better, and to advance humanity in ways yet unknown.

'May peace and prosperity and love follow all of you throughout your remaining lives. And enjoy the gift of the world which Allah has bestowed upon us, without conditions. Enjoy your lives,' Kalil concluded.

There was a sudden and enormous outpouring of noise; cheering, crying, arm waving, screaming, people falling or sitting down, hugging each other, kissing family members and friends, and this went on for a long time, beyond Kalil's exit from the stage and into the underground passages of the stadium, where he was met by security and staff.

HUSSAIN

The plan was reaching its most difficult phase now. Either the ship's crews would simply accept the scenario laid out, and the statement he'd made that they would be able to fire salvos of purple-painted self-destructing munitions towards selected targets, by the fleet's significant gunnery capacity, and aircraft-fired missiles, or someone would question this. He had some allies on board, and especially within the gunnery and armaments sections of the aircraft carrier and its three destroyers. But any questioning of the simulated attack on London, would need to be countered strongly.

The final test was the next phase of the wargame, and the core group of officers under review were quickly assembled on the bridge for the final scenario update, and for their operational plans.

'Quiet, gentlemen!' Hussain ordered, looking around the group for their expressions. All looked excited, some nervous of their decisions being ridiculed under review, as he read from the last green sheet of paper in his hand. 'Forty minutes ago, the Turkish brigade attacked one of the UK's main military bases in Colchester, northeast of London and overwhelmed it. That base now is assumed to be in foreign hands and needs to be retaken or destroyed. Two MP's have been publicly executed by the terrorist group in control of the Houses of Parliament. The British Prime Minister, currently in Brazil as part of a meeting of the Commonwealth of Pakindesh Nations symposium, has authorised attacks as necessary to retake the nation's seat of government, even at the expense of infrastructure damage and the deaths of hostages. We have been advised by British historians that the basement levels of the Houses of Parliament would survive damage to the main building and that a hostage rescue would be successful even if the main building was destroyed. The Pakindesh Security Service has reason to believe that France and Turkey plan to issue formal notice of the British Government's surrender to their forces in a press conference within 90 minutes. Gentlemen, you have fifteen minutes to finalise your plans.' Hussain then walked to the rear of the bridge and smiled, as the group began their assessment of options, their urgent chatter rising in tempo.

Aaron Fadel was part of the group, having been seconded to the NGLO, the Naval Gunfire Liaison Officer, to learn from him. This officer coordinated the awesome firepower of the supporting ships within the carrier group, some of their guns having a range of up to 24 kilometres.

Partially listening to the intense chatter and ideas being bandied across the group, he knew that his conclusion was correct. This team was about to endorse an attack on the Houses of Parliament and Colchester army base, and they were fully engrossed in the task and their ability to win this wargame against the French-Turkish forces. It sounded as if the plan was to deploy the three guided missile destroyers, PNS Mysore, Delhi, and Mumbai to within striking range of the Houses of Parliament and bombard the building, to kill the phantom terrorist group holding the hostages.

Even as a wargame, the plan seemed ridiculously excessive and hasty to Fadel, but it was clear that the team was engrossed in the exercise. Nothing he could say would be taken seriously. He had to listen and learn and then decide how to act. Hopefully he was wrong.

He looked across at Hussain. The man was calm, in control. Where was Admiral Pereira? Why wasn't he also evaluating his officers? Hussein couldn't be acting alone, surely?

Fadel approached the NGLO, 'Sir, is it common to conduct live fire exercises like this?'

'This won't be a live fire exercise, Fadel. We will be using self-destructive rounds. Only the gunnery actions, of target setting, loading, and firing will mimic real battle conditions. The rounds will self-destruct within two kilometres of their flight path.'

Really? 'I have never heard of such... useful live fire exercises before, Sir. Is this new technology, the self-destructive rounds I mean?'

The NGLO, Commander Hukkeri, looked slightly phased by the question. 'Er, yes, they are. I haven't conducted a live fire exercise using them before. It was Commander Hussain that arranged for the ammunition and designed this exercise to test the ships' companies. Apparently, he has run an exercise like this before, off the coast of India.'

'I see, Sir. And have the fighter pilots also used these dummy rockets and munitions too?'

'I am not sure; presumably. The air crew are not within my remit. But the pilots have always had the ability to abort their rockets in flight, although this time, if they are sent on a dummy mission, they will be able to fire and forget their AIM Sidewinder missiles, as the armament will also have a minimal flight range before self-destruction. Any other questions, Fadel?'

'Er, no, Sir. I'll just use the head whilst there's time, Sir,' he said and quickly made his way off the bridge before permission was given. He had to find Pereira. Despite the admiral being kept out of the loop, it was time to tell him what was going on.

He almost lost his way in the confusing network of passageways, but then realised where he was, changed direction and found the Admiral's cabin. He knocked on the door. No answer. Maybe Pereira was elsewhere on the ship, looking over other activity? Surely not. He knocked again and tried the handle. The door was locked. Damn! No time for timidness. He placed his back against the wall behind him, raised his leg and slammed his foot into the door above the handle. There was a loud sound of splitting wood, but the door remained firm. A second and then a third kick did the trick, and the door gave way, and he quickly entered the room. It was empty. Damn, where was Pereira? He was about to leave when he noticed some red stains on the carpet near the desk. Blood? There was an adjoining door, presumably to a shower room. He opened it and found Pereira crumpled in a heap on the floor, pale, blood-stained, and clearly dead, although he checked for a pulse to make sure. No mistake. There were two bullet wounds in his chest.

Time to take down Hussain. The thought was interrupted by the door opening and the figure of a large Chief Petty Officer entered. 'Thank God…' Fadel began, but he was instantly hit in the face and stomach, doubled over and then was knocked unconscious.

RIO DE JANEIRO

Al-antaqam had a fallback plan for getting to Corcovado. He had always favoured the mountain for the execution of Kalil, and he assumed that the Pakindesh leaders would not just be taking a simple group photograph but would want a reasonable amount of TV media coverage too. He left the stadium and drove to a small private airfield where he had previously arranged for the hire of a helicopter and pilot. He had shown some official-looking media credentials as a photographer and cameraman for a local network and had left a sturdy aluminium camera case to be loaded aboard earlier in the day. He kept his shoulder bag with him, a sniper rifle inside dismantled into its five components. The owner greeted him warmly on arrival and escorted him to the aircraft, its rotors already spinning, the pilot doing some last-minute adjustment to instruments. The side doors had large, magnetised logos on them of the local TV network, which he'd provided earlier. He jumped into one of the rear seats of the Bell 206 and was relieved that his request for the two rear side windows be removed for camera access had been done. He put the rear seat headphones on so that he could converse with the pilot.

'Head for Corcovado. I want to be nearby when President Kalil and the others arrive there for their group photographs. But stay 500 metres to the rear of the statue and maybe 150 metres above its head. That way we can approach slowly once the President's group have done all their preparations and are ready to be photographed.'

'No problem. We will be there in 7 minutes, Sir,' the pilot advised.

Using the lid of the aluminium camera case to obscure any possible view of its contents by the pilot, Al-antaqam checked the Glock pistol in the case, and each of the 6 hand grenades he'd smuggled into the country. He then took out a camera he'd purchased and clamped it to the window frame via its 20-centimetre tripod bracket. He arranged the camera angle so that it partially blocked the pilot's view of what he was doing. When the time came, it was going to be easier to drop grenades on top of Kalil's group now than take rifle shots. Otherwise, the pilot might decide to sacrifice himself rather than allow his passenger to shoot the President, no matter what kind of threat could be made against him.

As they approached the Christ the Redeemer statue, its immense size and what it stood for made him shiver. It was an abomination that should have been destroyed. Allah's vengeance against Kalil today would be the symbol for an uprising against those that failed to adhere to a life ordained by the Prophet Mohammad, praise be His name. These apostates would soon be destroyed.

The presidential helicopter was a modified Blackhawk, painted with Pakindesh colours and the flags of each of its allied nations in a circular pattern. It was hovering just above the middle tier of the approaches to the statue and then gently put down, and a group of 8 people alighted from it and began a slow bent over jog away from its rotors and towards the base of the next set of stairs leading up to the statue. Kalil was easily recognised, as was Mina Ahmed. Habbib was the tallest man in the group, Malik Shah the shortest, and Muhammed Asif the youngest looking. Of the other 3 people, two looked like photographers, one male with a professional-looking movie camera, a female with a digital SLR with a long lens, and the last man was clearly security.

The Blackhawk took off slowly and flew out of noise and downdraft range, taking up a position approximately 800 metres to the east so as not to be within the view towards Sugarloaf Mountain to the north. It then hovered in place whilst the official party arranged their photo session.

'Where would you like me to take up position, Sir?' the pilot of the Bell 206 asked.

'Let's wait for them to arrange themselves for the photos at the foot of the statue first, then slowly approach from the southeast. I'd like to get some shots with Sugarloaf in the background as well as the statue as we pan around, but stay maybe 200 metres from the statue, at about its head height. I don't want to be distracted, or to annoy them, so if their official helicopter pilot or security people questions you just say we have authority to film for tonight's news broadcasts, okay?'

'Yes, Sir, no problem,' the pilot replied and began to manoeuvre as instructed.

On the ground, Kalil was walking up to the statue at a leisurely pace, the others following behind, Mina dropping back a little and breathing harder. It was not a difficult climb up the few sets of stairs at the end of each level. When they arrived at the base, Kalil said, 'Is it not magnificent? No matter what religion it honoured, the sculpture and the design are sublime, and it most definitely enhances this amazing city.'

'I have to agree,' Mina said. 'It is beautiful, Sabal.'

'No matter how often I visit Rio, the statue always impresses me,' Habbib agreed.

Asif smiled, 'Okay, Sabal, you've convinced me, this is a great location for our group photo. I just hope it doesn't send the wrong message around the world.'

'Such as?' Kalil asked.

'Well, not so much across Pakindesh nations, but the Middle Eastern states aren't going to like the symbolism, are they?'

Kalil smiled, 'Maybe the beauty of the location and the views will soften their hearts, Asif,' he laughed. 'The TV chopper should get some good shots of it all anyway,' he said, raising his arm to it and waving. 'All PR is good PR,' he added.

The group then arranged themselves in a small semicircle and their photographer started to take some photos.

Kalil's bodyguard, Sarim, made a call on his radio back to his superior at the palace as the photos were occurring. 'Base, this is Kilo Bravo one, can you confirm how many aerial TV choppers are authorised for Corcovado and for how long?'

'Wait one, Kilo Bravo,' was the response as his question was being relayed back at the palace. About 30 seconds later his radio crackled, 'Kilo Bravo One this is base, over.'

'Kilo Bravo One, go ahead, over.'

'There are no authorised TV choppers for the photo shoot, over.'

'Kilo Bravo One, there is a small chopper overhead with a cameraman taking footage from about 200 metres away, over.'

'This is base, wait, out.'

After another 30 seconds, the base operative asked, 'This is base, what TV station markings does the chopper have, if any, over?'

'Whiskey Zulu Nine studio logos, over.'

'This is base. Let me call the station and check it out, over.'

'What a beautiful location, Sabal,' Mina said, shielding her eyes from the sun's glare. 'It would have been a terrible loss of an icon if this statue had been destroyed. For its time, it was clearly a masterpiece.'

'I agree. One doesn't have to be linked in any way to Christianity to appreciate its beauty,' Kalil said. He looked at his watch, glanced quickly around at the group, all of whom seemed ready to depart after having taken their own photos on their phones, and motioned for them to move back to the helicopter again. They walked leisurely down the series of stepped walkways, away from the statue.

The WZ9 News chopper had moved further away, probably to film their take off, Kalil assumed. Once back at the presidential Blackhawk, the group started to get back aboard into the rear compartment seats, the co-pilot assisting them, all apart from the cameraman who was staying behind to film their departure, after which he would return to the city via the funicular railway.

Kalil's security detail were catching up when one of them took a call on his radio.

The noise of the rotors made it difficult for him to hear. 'This is Kilo Bravo One, say again, over.'

'This is Base. The Whiskey Zulu 9 studio says that they don't have a news crew scheduled to film at Corcovado today, and all their journalists are accounted for, over.'

'Kilo Bravo One, are they sure about that, over?'

'Base. Yes, I had them double check. If your chopper has their markings on it, then it must be a freelance film crew, over.'

'Thanks, base, Kilo Bravo One out.' *This feels wrong*, he thought, jogging over to the Blackhawk to talk to the co-pilot. He pressed his face close to the co-pilot's ear and shouted, 'I don't like that news chopper being here. Can you call them to back way off?'

The co-pilot nodded, and the pilot, also hearing the request put his thumb up to acknowledge the order. All the passengers were aboard now, and Sarim wondered whether to remain on the ground, but there was no point to that, so he climbed in too.

The pilot radioed on his open local channel, 'Whiskey Zulu Nine news crew, this is Presidential One, withdraw away from Corcovado, acknowledge.'

Above and well to the rear of Presidential One, the pilot of the Bell 206 turned to his passenger, who had also heard the radio exchange, and said, 'I am being ordered to leave this airspace.'

Al-antaqam said curtly, 'I heard. Let me just get a final shot. Tell them we are leaving but hover above them for a few seconds whilst I get a departing still photo.'

'I don't know, they won't like it.'

'A few seconds above them, I'll be quick, I promise. Just tell them we're leaving but go slow in that direction and hover briefly. I'll tell you when I have the shot, okay?'

The pilot looked unhappy but nodded, 'Okay.' He then radioed, 'Presidential One, we are leaving your airspace, departing above you, and then to the northeast, over.'

'Assholes,' the Presidential One pilot muttered to himself, then said on his intercom, for the security head, 'They are leaving. I'll wait for them to be clear before moving.'

The sliding door was still open and Sarim jumped back down to the ground and walked away far enough to watch the News chopper, which was now slowly moving towards them at about 50 metres higher altitude, the cameraman clearly visible. Sarim's sixth sense was making his heartbeat race. He put his hand inside his jacket and around the grip of his Glock.

Now was when it would all come together, In Sha' Allah. He opened the lid of the aluminium camera case. Inside were his six American-made M26 hand grenades, tied together. For five of them the pins had already been removed and the lever handles secured to their grenade bodies by sturdy elastic bands. All six were tied together, so only the one with its pull ring in place, securing its safety pin, needed to be pulled out. As each grenade weighed 454 grams, the bundle of six represented almost three kilos, but could be dropped out of the open window easily when the camera was pulled back, and then the first explosion in just under 5 seconds would destroy the elastic bands, triggering the other five to explode, if that didn't happen immediately with the first blast. No-one in the Blackhawk could survive the explosions of grenades and subsequent jet fuel fire.

He held the intact grenade in his left hand, put his right index finger in the pull ring and expended the necessary force to remove it, then pushed the whole bundle out of the window, shouting, 'Got it, go, quickly.'

On the ground below, Sarim watched as something was dropped from the News chopper above. Without hesitation, he withdrew his firearm and fired eight shots at the departing aircraft within two seconds, the rounds aimed at the side window cameraman.

FADEL

He couldn't have been unconscious for long but felt groggy and had been tethered to the desk leg by a white plastic cable tie around his right wrist, with other ties securing his ankles together. He tried shouting for help, but knew in advance that it was probably useless, with the entire crew involved in the wargame and there being no-one posted near the admiral's cabin. It was a miracle he hadn't been killed too. He needed to cut these ties off but how? Looking around the room gave no immediate comfort. The cabin was shipshape, neat, tidy, and minimalist in décor. He could reach the desk drawer with his free left hand though and hoped that it would have something that could assist his escape. He pulled it out and rummaged through it. No scissors, knife, or even a letter opener. The desk leg was metal, but the corners weren't sharp enough to cut through plastic cable ties. The bathroom would have something useful, perhaps, but it was too far away.

'You stupid idiot, Fadel!' he shouted aloud. His ankles were tethered but he could feel the impact of his ankle holster above the ties. Surely not? He grabbed at the leg of his pants and couldn't believe his luck. The gun was still there. The CPO was obviously in a hurry, to have missed his holster. Allah be praised. He placed the gun against his ties, making as much space between his ankles as possible, and then fired a shot through the ties and away from himself. They shredded and his feet were free. He then did the same with his hand tie, placed the muzzle against it and fired a shot towards the bed. Success!

He was about to leave the room, then stopped to consider how he was going to put a stop to Hussain. The man clearly had allies on board and presumably more than just the Chief Petty Officer with the strong right arm. Is the NGLO, Commander Hukkeri, part of this? It would make sense to have the person in command of coordinating the significant naval gunfire armaments involved, but Hussain would have to be working with a very small number of people or the security of his plan would be more difficult to maintain. Clearly, arranging for the purple paint and identification markings to be put on what had to be huge amounts of gunnery rounds would have needed help. But that might have occurred months ago, even been a contingency plan waiting for the right timing to occur.

Think. What would you have done, and where are the flaws in all of this? The scenario Hussain has portrayed is extremely fanciful. And no British Government would sanction attacking the Houses of Parliament to kill the terrorists, based on the idea that the hostages would survive that action, rather than enter negotiations. It was ridiculous. But it was being accepted because this was just a war game, made to make the junior officers think outside the square, so in that way, it was pure genius. And the ploy of the self-destructing rounds was a bonus for the crews, to practice live firing without risk. What about the aircraft though? There were no French or Turkish invasion forces. Was an attack on Colchester army base of any strategic or political value? Or would the aircraft be re-tasked to attack another London target? Maybe add to the naval gunfire salvos? No, they would have to precede that action, or the pilots would see that the rounds were real and would abort and call off the naval action too. Similarly, they couldn't fire first without also realising that their rounds were real. Same result. So, what was their purpose? Unless... Of course! The Sidewinder missiles were real, but not altered to disintegrate in flight, but upon being fired, to destroy the fighters themselves. What better way to neutralise an aircraft carrier than to destroy its aircraft? Without them it was just a floating landing pad, and a huge target.

Cutting off his train of thought, the cabin door flew open, and the figure of his assailant filled the doorframe, his face surprised to see his prisoner free, and armed.

'Hands up, Chief!' Fadel ordered, but the man sprang forward, attempting to deflect the gun and take the initiative. He died instantly, with a bullet in his brain. Fadel was no stranger to violent death or taking immediate action. But he'd lost the only source of further information he might have had. 'Oh well, time to take Hussain down,' he said, placing the gun in his belt at the small of his back and hurrying along the corridor towards the bridge.

SALINA

Salina had declined Kalil's invitation to attend the Commonwealth of Pakindesh Nations' opening address at the stadium. She'd heard it all before, 'straight from the horse's mouth' she told herself, and the opportunity to take a very long walk along the beach front was far more inviting. Dressed in pink and black mottle-patterned exercise pants, a bright pink sleeveless top and running shoes, she'd already alternated between a five-kilometre run, a two-kilometre cool down slow walk, and then wandered into a grassed area with a running track perimeter and conducted five sets of flat out sprinting for thirty seconds followed by a minute's break. At the end of her regimen, she looked for an inviting café and ordered a mango smoothie and a Caesar salad.

There was a TV on the wall inside the café, with the volume turned down, showing some highlights of Kalil's address and then the leadership group leaving the stadium, getting into the Presidential helicopter, and taking off for Corcovado. She hoped her mum was enjoying the sightseeing. She said she was looking forward to seeing the statue and the views of Rio from there. The nearby sights and sounds of beach games, and strolling pedestrians, and the gentle waves of the sea relaxed her. I could live here, she suddenly decided. With the right man. But could I leave my parents, and Charlie and Michael? Not easily. But... Michael might come too. They could base themselves here as well as anywhere. It's not as if we are home all that much anyway. I can't live in England anymore. I feel the losses too intensely. I am often sad there. Other places, especially vibrant and different ones, hold no bad memories for me. I wonder if mum and dad could leave too, after mum is sick of politics? Charlie could be a doctor anywhere.

A sudden scream from inside the café shattered Salina's thoughts. She looked around in fright. Inside there was the screaming woman, and others, pointing at the TV screen, which showed indistinct images of a helicopter, then the statue and then the sound of explosions.

RIO DE JANEIRO

As the eighth bullet left his Glock pistol, Sarim was knocked on to his back by a fiercely strong wind gust. The Blackhawk had lifted off the ground at the same time and the wind buffeted the aircraft slightly on to its port side and its tail fin spun the aircraft 180 degrees. Above Sarim, the hand grenade cluster was falling from the rear window panel of the News helicopter, but he knew that some of his shots had hit the rear passenger area where the objects had been thrown from. His brain identified the threat as hand grenades less than a second later. The grenades were only a few metres above the Blackhawk when its stability altered, and as it tipped sideways, the non-rotor port side of the tail, slammed into the falling bundle of grenades, knocking them over Sarim's head and over the steep bank behind him.

As the Bell 206 pilot had initially sought to gain altitude, he saw the Blackhawk buffeted by the wind and its tail slew around, so he had instinctively banked his own aircraft over and away from it, and down the mountain's slope to the south, just as the grenades exploded.

As the main grenade was triggered, it was followed immediately by the other five, adding to the size of the combined explosion, and shrapnel was thrown in all directions, some piercing the fuel tank of the Bell 206.

Kalil's cameraman, less than 80 metres from the Blackhawk, was capturing the event as it unfolded but the typhoon-like wind had knocked him off his feet, along with the camera tripod, and the live feed from the camera ended up pointing at the statue but captured the noise of the explosions.

On board the Bell 206, as the grenades were dropped from the window, Al-antaqam was hit by three bullets from Sarim's gun, one in his left shoulder, one grazing his temple and the third hitting him near his heart. Moments later the helicopter was flying over the mountain side when there was a terrible noise, and the aircraft suffered multiple impacts from flying grenade shrapnel.

Less than five seconds later the helicopter's fuel, leaking from its damaged tank, ignited, blowing the rear part of the aircraft apart, incinerating its rear passenger, but throwing the pilot out of the cockpit and away from the doomed machine, where he fell into the dense tree foliage of the hillside.

The Blackhawk pilot managed to regain control as the wind gusts died down and he flew the aircraft to the next highest level where he could land it, closer to the statue, and ordered the passengers not to move. His co-pilot exited and ran down the pathway stairs towards Sarim and the cameraman. He could see on arrival that they were both miraculously uninjured, and he helped them back to the Blackhawk.

It was imperative to get the Presidential party to safety and the helicopter flew away with all its passengers towards the Presidential Palace.

SALINA

The live TV coverage of the incident on Corcovado had everyone in the café screaming, shouting, crying and in shock. But all they could see and hear was distorted. There had been scenes of the Presidential helicopter on the ground, with another smaller helicopter above it, and something falling from that one towards the larger craft whilst a man with a handgun fired at the smaller aircraft. Then the larger aircraft was violently blown sideways and around by the wind and the armed man fell backwards. At that point the camera lost its stable pictures, replaced by blurry images of sky, trees, and the ground, and noises from the rotors, the wind, and an explosion, followed moments later by a second blast.

'Oh God! Mum, please be alright, please,' Salina murmured to herself, hugging her own body, tears streaming down her face. The noise of conversations and statements was overwhelming her. She needed to get out, get back to the hotel and find out what had happened, quickly. She ran out of the café and sprinted away, back towards her hotel, but she lacked the energy. She tried to arrange for a ride on her phone App but there didn't seem to be any available. Looking around it was as if everyone had seen the incident, or at least they had been brought up to date quickly by other people.

She sat down on a park bench and cried. It was perhaps ten minutes before she calmed herself down again. Think. No, don't think. Ignore the worst possibilities. Get back. She stood again and felt fitter. Do this. Get back. Find Mum. She started to run.

FADEL

He thought as he ran. This is one hell of a gamble. If Hussain has others backing him, I could be in real shit here. But if he was well supported, by even a dozen men, then surely, he needn't have killed Pereira? Why do that? Maybe he was challenged? Who can I count on? Hukkeri? Maybe, but if I was planning this, I would have tried to place a supporter in the role of NGLO. That's a key role. But not as key as the guys that load the armaments onto the fighters. The gun crews probably wouldn't think twice about what they shove up the gun, one artillery shell is much like another. They wouldn't realise that they were real until the damage was done. But the fighter pilots, what about them? Wouldn't they check their Sidewinder missiles?

No, probably not. Not their job. They'd leave it to the armourers. His thinking stopped as he neared the last passageway to the bridge and could hear voices. Calm yourself. Act normal. Think.

As he entered the bridge, he saw Hussain listening to the plans of the junior officers.

'It is risky, Sir, but if the British Government has stated that it is better to destroy the terrorists and lose the Houses of Parliament rather than give in to their demands, then who are we to question that?' asked a sub-lieutenant.

'That is a valid statement, lieutenant,' Hussain acknowledged. 'I get the impression that this is your combined view. Am I correct in this?'

There was a murmur of agreement and nodding of heads. 'And what of the Turkish brigade at Colchester Army Barracks?' Hussein asked.

'An easy target, Sir,' a lieutenant commander said, 'we can send a fighter squadron to attack them. They won't have air cover and won't be expecting an attack on them at all. We should be able to do significant damage to them and definitely thwart their advance towards London.'

'I agree,' Hussain said. 'So, if I understand your plans completely, we are to fire a concentrated naval gunfire assault on the Houses of Parliament from the three destroyers now within range, the Mysore, Delhi, and Mumbai, in twenty minutes time, and to have a squadron assault on the Colchester base at the same time. Is that correct?'

There were yesses and nods.

Fadel said, 'May I ask a question, Sir?' he asked Hussain.

Hussain looked shocked to see him there but covered it well. 'Of course, Fadel. Go ahead.'

'Well, Sir, I am not at all familiar with how this kind of live fire drill works. How can we be certain that the rounds have all been altered correctly to explode within a kilometre of being fired? And the same for the fighter aircraft missiles. When and how were these armaments tested, Sir? I mean, any mistake and we could lose aircraft, as well as potentially destroy the mock target.'

'Your question is a little impertinent, Fadel. Do you think that the NGLO, Admiral Pereira and I would take such a risk without adequate testing beforehand?'

'No, of course not, Sir, but I was just with Admiral Pereira, and he sent me back to you to ask you to demonstrate to the officers the naval gunfire in action on a target within sight, so that they could observe the self-destruction of the rounds, and the same for one of the fighters with a missile firing display too.'

Hussain looked shocked, but recovered brilliantly, and smiled, saying, 'I hardly think, Fadel, that the Admiral would have sent you up here to ask this. If you are concerned yourself, I am sure that the NGLO can put your mind at ease.'

'No, Sir, I wasn't concerned at all. I did think that this idea of self-destructive rounds sounded unusual. Well, that was until I went to see Admiral Pereira, and he stated he also had concerns, and asked me to have you provide a demonstration for us all.'

'You're lying, Fadel. I have been worried about you for some time. I was advised that you have a history of mental illness and that I needed to keep an eye on you. I think it best if you reported to the sickbay, now.'

'Why would you think I am lying, Sir? Is it because you know that Admiral Pereira is dead, shot by you in his quarters?' There were gasps around the room.

Hussein smiled. 'Fadel, you are having an episode,' he turned to an able seaman by the door and added, 'Take Fadel to sickbay, please.'

Fadel drew his weapon and aimed it at Hussein's head. 'Everyone please remain where you are, and I will explain myself more fully to you.' He looked around the group of men and none seemed willing to act precipitously, and a few were clearly intrigued.

'Remain calm, everyone. I am not a cadet officer. I work for the Pakindesh Security Service and was sent here to investigate Commander Hussain. The PSS has had intelligence on him for a while and became aware that he was working with Turkey and France to overthrow the British Government. Those so-called harmless naval gunfire artillery rounds are live. The missiles allocated for the fighter planes are likely to have been tampered with to explode on firing to destroy the aircraft. Once the aircraft are destroyed in the air, and the Houses of Parliament destroyed by our gunfire, real French and Turkish forces will be able to act. I do not expect you all to accept at face value what I am saying. But please send some men to the Admiral's quarters. You will find him dead, and you will also find the

Chief Petty Officer dead. I shot the Chief. Ballistics will show that a different gun was used to kill Pereira.'

Hussain shouted, 'This man is clearly a lunatic! He must have killed the Admiral as well as the Chief. He needs to be taken into custody and restrained.'

Fadel remained calm, his pistol unwavering, as he said, 'Commander Hukkeri, please send two men to check on the Admiral and report back with their findings. Once that has occurred, and given that this exercise is just that, an unimportant exercise, without any need to take chances, If I am telling the truth, then I suggest you arrange a firing test for the supposed safe rounds. I don't know how to check the aircraft missiles though. We can't fire one from a fighter in case it destroys the plane and kills the pilot. Any suggestions, gentlemen?' Fadel asked, having altered the tempo in the room, much to Hussain's clear anger.

'This man is a lunatic, I tell you!' Hussain shouted. 'Do not engage with him in this... this idiocy.'

Hukkeri took the initiative. 'If Fadel is telling the truth, then we must take precautions and check out his accusations. He is right to say that there is no urgency in this. I can arrange a test of the ammunition that has been prepared for the live fire. I am sure that one of aircraft armourers can assist to check that the missiles have not been tampered with to explode on firing. Or if not, then to somehow test them. Given the situation we find ourselves in, I am taking temporary command from Commander Hussein, just until this is sorted out. It is surely safer this way. If, Fadel here is having a mental episode, surely it is better to go along with these quite simple tests he suggests?'

Hussain shouted, 'Do not be drawn into this! It might be you, Hukkeri, who is the culprit for the Admiral's death, if he is dead.'

Hukkeri shrugged his shoulders, not in the least perturbed by Hussain's accusation. 'Perhaps that is true. There is no point in me denying it. All denials should be tested. I am quite open to being investigated or questioned. But for now, I suggest that everyone in this room sits down on chairs or the floor and places their hands on their heads. I will perform an examination of each person here to ensure that no-one is armed, apart from you that is, Fadel. Will that satisfy you for now?'

'Certainly Commander. I appreciate it. Thank you. But I will keep my pistol trained on Commander Hussain if you don't mind?'

'Not at all. Now, gentlemen, please carefully and slowly sit down and place your hands on your heads to allow Mr Fadel here to be put at ease as we wait for the report on the Admiral?'

The group agreed by their deeds rather than words. Sufficient doubt had been raised in their minds, and Hussain delayed too, trying to find a reason not to comply. Fadel retained the upper hand. He too sat down on the chair behind him.

Some moments later the two crew members that had been sent to the Admiral's quarters returned. 'It's true, the Admiral is dead and the Chief as well. It looks like different calibre shots for each victim, and there are marks and bits of plastic hand ties to confirm that someone had been tied up to the desk.'

Hussain regained his voice, 'So it looks like Fadel tied up Admiral Pereira, and then...'

'Then what?' Fadel interrupted, 'Why kill the man if he was restrained? And with what weapon? Anyway, look at my wrist marks,' he added, showing his left hand without changing the steady aim of the pistol in his right hand.

'He does have abrasions from a possible plastic tie,' Hukkeri agreed.

'That proves nothing, you idiots!' Hussein shouted, 'He's a lunatic. He killed Pereira and the Chief and now he's trying to fool you all.'

'To what end, Commander?' Hukkeri asked. 'It seems to me that Fadel's suggestion of checking the ammunition and test firing some will cost us nothing but time and a possible delay of the exercise.' Turning to Fadel, he added, 'If we test fire some rounds from the Mysore's guns, and check the aircraft missiles with the armourers to determine if they have been tampered with, will you be willing to give up your weapon if your assertions are proved false?'

'Yes, I will, Commander. If test firing does show that the rounds self-destruct within a short range and the armourers can attest to the missiles being safely fired but self-destruct within a kilometre or whatever range Commander Hussain stated, then I will stand down. In the meantime, I will provide a number for you to call and check my credentials with the PSS, if you will also restrain Commander Hussain for the duration.'

'I will agree to that. Do you, Commander?' Hukkeri asked.

Hussein grabbed a nearby coffee mug and threw it at Fadel, causing him to instinctively move out of its way and stumble, and as he brought his right hand back around to re-aim his weapon, Hussein grabbed a chair and used it to ram into Fadel, who lost his balance, and as he fell to the floor, Hussein kicked the gun out of his hand and made a lunge for it. The two men fought on the floor as others tried to intervene, but Hussein managed to take the gun and jump over Fadel's prone body. He backed up and held the gun aimed at Fadel.

'Give me the gun, Commander,' Hukkeri ordered.

'I don't think so, Hukkeri. As far as I know, perhaps you and Fadel here are in this together. Maybe you killed Pereira and the two of you are seeking to take control of the ship.'

'Don't be ridiculous,' Hukkeri responded, 'none of that makes any sense at all. Fadel's analysis seems the most likely, especially now. Whatever you were trying to achieve, it's over, Commander. Surely you can see that?'

'All I can see is a possible mutiny on board this ship, with dangerous consequences,' Hussain said, looking around towards a junior sub-lieutenant, 'You, lieutenant, I need you to get some armed men to take these two into custody. Then we will continue the exercise.'

'Don't move, lieutenant!' Hukkeri ordered. 'Commander Hussain has no jurisdiction here now. Call the Captains of the destroyers and advise them of the current situation and tell them that the exercise is called off. Ask that one of them flies over here to take command of this ship.'

'Belay that order, lieutenant, unless you want to be responsible for the deaths of these two traitors,' Hussain countered.

Fadel was angry at himself and decided to play a long shot. 'May I ask a question, Commander Hussain?' he asked politely.

Hussain frowned, looking uncertain. 'What now, Fadel?'

'Well, in the spirit of this exercise, why would the destruction of the Houses of Parliament, and all this ship's fighter aircraft, lead to a French-Turkish takeover of the UK? I mean there's no way that Pakindesh would allow that, and I doubt that the British would either. So, the whole plan seems doomed from the start. Just like some pre-RD terrorist megalomania.' *Come on you bastard, debate me. You know you want to. Let your ego come out to play.*

'Is that the best you can do, Fadel. If you are really a PSS agent, then you don't have much intelligence about the strength of the French and Turkish forces and the feeling across Europe for a more conservative way of life.'

'Conservative? You mean fundamentalist, barbaric, Sharia-inspired, anti-female indoctrination, ruled by undemocratic clergy and power-hungry old men? No thanks, Hussain, I think all of us on this ship would reject that way of life compared to the enlightenment that the Commonwealth of Pakindesh Nations has brought about in the world.'

Hussain was starting to get angry but was trying to avoid the trap. 'Turkey and France control most of Europe, Fadel. But our carrier group keeps them at bay, should they desire to invade Britain. It is a minor Pakindesh affiliate, and not worth fighting over. You are the one that contests that France and Turkey desire to take over the U.K., Fadel, not me.'

'Really, Hussain? It is your war game scenario, not mine, so you must have thought it feasible, even if the rest of us considered it ridiculous from the start.'

Hussain regained control of his emotions, smiling, 'Try harder, Fadel. War games are designed to stretch officers and introduce them to radical thinking and the solving of problems that might be new to them. They don't have to be realistic.'

'That's true, I agree. But there's a difference between realism and outright nonsensical rubbish that only a junior NCO would concoct, surely?'

Whilst their verbal battle was going on, Hukkeri had carefully moved closer to the door behind him. He knew that Fadel was aware of this and hopefully understood the importance of playing for time. The rest of the men remained in their places, not moving, watching the contest of minds before them.

'If you are trying to bait me, Fadel, it isn't going to work,' Hussain said, recomposed, smiling.

Fadel sighed audibly, 'No, I suppose not, Hussain. There's little point in a rational man arguing with an idiot in public, is there? Those watching can't tell who's who,' he laughed. 'Although these officers will soon learn the truth,' he added, pointing to the window to his left, 'Looks like a helicopter from one of the destroyers coming in to land.'

Hussain looked sharply left and Hukkeri took the opportunity to run out of the door behind him, just evading Hussain's instinctive shot, as he realised Fadel's bluff too late.

'It's over, Commander,' Fadel said calmly. 'Surely you can see that. Why continue with this farce?'

'Nothing is over, Fadel. Whilst we have been playing this game here, no matter its outcome, we will soon learn of the deaths of the entire Pakindesh hierarchy in Rio. With all those liberal anti-Muslim apostates now dead, the world will return to a more devout path again, as was Allah's will on Revelation Day. All the rest of you,' he continued, 'if you wish to demonstrate your true faith, throw this fool overboard. Let us see if he can swim to shore without Allah's blessing. It's only twenty kilometres or so, Fadel. If you survive the fall you can pray to Allah for forgiveness as you swim in that cold water.'

'You're bluffing, about Rio,' Fadel challenged.

'Well, let's see. You there,' he indicated to a man near a large monitor screen, 'Turn that on and bring up a news channel.'

It took some adjusting but after a minute or so a news channel appeared on screen. There was some jumpy footage of a Pakindesh helicopter on a hilltop, then the image became a mass of sky and tree shots as the camera lost its stability, but the sound was that of more than one explosion.

'Ha, goodbye President Kalil,' Hussain laughed.

Then the picture returned to a studio shot and the presenter said, "*It was surely a miracle that none of the Pakindesh leaders were killed or seriously injured as the failed attempt on their lives was made by a lone-wolf assassin on the slopes of Corcovado earlier today. The assailant is thought to be known as Al-antaqam and has been linked to the President of Somalia, according to an official press statement just released by President Kalil's office. Messages of relief and support have been received from around the world. More will be provided on this story as details come to hand.*"

'No! No, that cannot be!' Hussain screamed. 'It is not possible. Allah's will is clear!'

'Thank God,' Fadel said quietly. He looked at Hussain. 'Give me the gun, Commander. Your plan has failed. It's over,' he said, putting out his hand for the weapon.

Hussain looked conflicted, shaking his head. Then he put the gun in his mouth and fired a round upwards. Blood and brain matter spurted from his head as his body fell to the floor, the gun clattering away from his dead hand. A few men screamed in disbelief or horror, some attempting to wipe blood off their uniforms. Fadel picked up the gun, applied the safety and placed it in his trouser pocket.

SALINA

They seemed to be hugging a lot lately, Salina showing more affection for her mother than in years. Mina had delayed her scheduled return to the U.K. for a few days whilst the aftermath of the assassination attempt died down and the intelligence elements of the PSS homed in on the perpetrators. The news of the botched attempt to attack London was glossed over, with the analysis playing up the amateurish elements of the plan, rather than how close it could have come to working.

Diplomatic games were also occurring between Pakindesh and France, Turkey, Nigeria, Somalia, and Indonesia-Malaysia.

'How much is there in this link to President Dhulbahante, Mum?'

'More than I first thought. It seems that the PSS were on top of their game, as far as the initial information was concerned. But we were very lucky in the end. I still shiver when I realise how close we all came to being killed. Very lucky.'

'Lucky or was there divine intervention?' Salina suggested.

'Since when have you been into divine intervention, Salsa?'

'Since your miraculous escape, Mum. You must wonder, surely? I mean, the way that freak typhoon hit the helicopters and those grenades were knocked out of the way. And the innocent pilot of the News chopper was uninjured, but the assassin was shot and killed by Kalil's bodyguard. I mean that was... well... I don't know; an act of God?'

'Quite possibly, Salsa. Kalil says that this is another sign, from Allah, that it is his will for the Pakindesh leaders to spearhead a simpler path to understanding and wisdom. And, the world is not disagreeing this time, is it? And none of the other countries are complaining about Kalil's interpretation this time. What does that mean, Salsa?'

'That they are scared, I think. Or playing politics and seeing how people react,' she suggested.

'Yes, it could be pragmatism. Or it could be that far more people are now on board with Kalil's hypothesis, and other leaders are afraid to challenge it.'

'Hmm, possibly,' Salsa agreed. 'Kalil wants to see me again, tomorrow. Did you know?'

'No. He didn't mention it to me,' Mina replied. 'Why?'

'I have no idea.'

'Let's change the subject, Salsa.'

'Yes?'

'When are you going to tell Freddy that you love him?'

'What! What are you talking about, Mum? Freddy?'

'Don't play dumb, daughter dear, I know you too well, and I know that you have feelings for Freddy.'

'How?' Salsa asked, quietly, coyly, looking down and not making eye contact.

'Salsa,' Mina smiled, 'You are my daughter. I know all your moods, most of your feelings, your likes, dislikes, ploys, games, insecurities and worries. I love you. I know you better than you know yourself, most of the time. I have seen the way that you look at Freddy, and more to the point the way that he drools over you. The man is besotted. If you don't put him out of his misery, one way or the other, well, it is just being cruel. Love him and take him to bed or let him down as gently as possible. But don't keep the poor man hanging around. It's not fair.'

'Is it that obvious?'

'Then you admit it, Salsa?'

Her face began to light up, her smile widening, 'Yes,' she said quietly, then more loudly, 'Yes, I do. But it is like trying to remember a dream when you wake up, something out of reach that you're not sure if you remembered it correctly. Oh, I must sound crazy, I don't know what I meant by that.'

'Maybe not, Salsa, but I do. It is the realisation of a love denied for so long that you doubt yourself or start to put up barriers and reasons why it can't work, and then before you know it, you've moved on and lost an opportunity to be happy. Is that it?'

'Hell, Mum, when did you become so wise?' she laughed.

'I was always wise, daughter,' she laughed, 'Never doubt it. Your father sometimes does and then gets that look on his face that says, of course she knows, and he just goes quiet for a while to digest it.'

'It is so weird, Mum. It's like the sun rising and lighting everything up. How could I have denied it for so long?'

'Well, you've been busy, you travel all the time, when you are home, you are never static, always planning the next adventure or series of interviews. The bigger question is why Freddy hasn't found someone else, I think, although Amaya's death did hit him hard, and it's only been six or seven months.'

'And?'

Mina smiled, 'And he can't replace you, Salsa. Once smitten, always doomed. He might not be your intellectual equal, but that doesn't matter. He's a good man, and he's fun to be around.'

'I know that. And he is not a fool, or uneducated either. He knows a lot of stuff, and his opinions are always valid, and...' she stopped talking, gaping in surprise at herself.

'A spring wedding then, or summer?' Mina asked.

FREDDY

'Charlie, I just got a text from Salina, inviting me for a coffee at 11am. What's that about?'

'I have no idea. I haven't seen much of her since she got back from Rio. It was an emotional trip, as you can imagine. Michael's been pining for her ever since she left to go there and they've been thick as thieves ever since, going off for long walks and stuff.'

'What's happening with Michael and Tasmeena? Are they an item now?'

'Definitely together, at last. It's weird seeing them hand in hand though,' Charlie said.

'Why?'

'I don't really know. On the one hand I see Tasmeena as this amazingly accomplished Member of Parliament, up to date on everything going on and writing policy, all that stuff. But then I see her giggling like a little girl on the couch with Michael as they watch old romantic comedies and snatch the odd kiss.'

'Sounds nice to me, mate.'

'Oh, I'm not unhappy about it. It has just shown me a different side to Michael, more in control, more mature I suppose. And Tasmeena seems happy to let him be the decision maker on what they do and where they go.'

'Maybe she likes the break from making all the decisions in her daily life. I mean, he's very organised too, like Salina. So, maybe Tasmeena likes to be managed, up to a point,' Freddy suggested.

Charlie nodded, 'Maybe that's it, Freddy. There's eight years age difference though. But Tasmeena never even jokes about Michael being younger. It's a non-issue for them.

'Bit of an old-fashioned attitude there, Doc,' Freddy challenged.

'I know. I can't help it sometimes. Anyway, they are very good together and I hope it works out for them.' Charlie looked at his watch, frowned and said, 'I have rounds to do, Freddy, got to go. See you later,' he said as he ran off to the wards.

At 11am, at Café Zabe on the high street not far from the hospital's main entrance, Freddy was sitting at a table for two and watched as Salina approached. He stood as she arrived, and they hugged, and he kissed her on the cheek.

'You look nice and relaxed after such an eventful trip,' Freddy said as she sat down, adding 'I've ordered you a mug of latte. I hope that's still your preference?'

'It is when I'm home, Freddy, thank you. You're looking well too. Did you see Charlie this morning?'

'Yeah, he dropped by before doing his rounds. Good doctor that lad, everyone likes him.'

'I know. I'm so proud of him,' Salina said.

'Well, I'm proud of all of you. What a bunch of achievers the Ahmed family is. Unprecedented, I'd say. A Prime Minister, an engineer, a doctor, and a world-famous journalistic documentary duo. Hard to keep up with you all,' Freddy laughed.

'Do you mean that, Freddy? I mean that we are hard to keep up with?' Salina asked seriously.

'You've gone all serious on me, what's up?'

'Do you think Michael and Tasmeena will work out, Freddy? I mean with the age gap, the different lives and careers, Michael's travel, all that?'

Freddy was quiet for a moment. 'What's going on with you all? Charlie sort of wondered about that this morning too. Is anything wrong?'

'No,' Salina smiled. 'Actually, everything is right. I hope. I need to ask you a question, Freddy and I'd like you to answer truthfully and unhesitatingly too. Can you do that?'

'Sounds bloody ominous. You're making me nervous now. But yes, I can do that, if you want.'

'Okay then, I have three questions for you, Freddy. Ready?' He nodded, and she took a deep breath. 'Question one. Do you love me?'

Freddy also took a deep breath. 'Yes, I do love you, Salsa.'

She nodded in acknowledgement. 'Question two. Could you see yourself following me around the world if I asked you to?'

'Yes, I could do that too.'

'Question three. Will you marry me, Freddy?'

'Oh my God! Will I marry you? Will I?' Freddy exclaimed, jumping up, knocking the table as he did so and spilling some of their coffees. 'Salsa, I will marry you, love you, travel with you, have babies with you, worship the ground you walk on, be your supporter, bodyguard, husband, father to our children, everything,' he started to cry.

'Salina was hugging him now, kissing his face, running her hands through his hair, and he started to reciprocate. They were necking like teenagers and the other café patrons were clapping and cheering, guessing that something momentous had occurred.

Freddy stopped kissing her and looked around, then shouted, 'We're getting married!' There were cheers and shouts and people came up to shake hands and wish them luck.

'Let's get out of here,' Freddy said, and they walked off into a nearby park.

'Would you have ever asked me to marry you, Freddy?'

He shrugged. 'Once I got up the courage I would, I think. Charlie was urging me on, but I never thought you saw me that way, Salsa. I've been a fool.'

'No, you haven't. Just old fashioned. And that's nice too.'

Freddy stopped, looked into her eyes, then asked, 'So, for how long have you felt this way about me?'

'Longer than I realised. I don't know exactly. But the events in Rio brought it all home to me. I want to settle down. With you that is.'

'But I don't want you to give up what you love doing, Salsa. It's a part of you, and it's important work too.

'Would you like to be part of it with me?'

'You mean travel around and stuff, be your minder?'

'Be whatever you want. But I could use a manager for arranging things. Michael does most of that, but he might be busier soon, with Tasmeena I mean. I don't know. We can sort it out.'

'I can be whatever you want. But yes, I'd like to be with you rather than waiting for you to return home.'

'Okay then. I was thinking of a double wedding next month, if Michael asks Tasmeena and she agrees too. Would that suit you?'

'You'll never stop surprising me, Salsa, and I like that. It's all good, my darling girl,' he said, and they kissed again.

TASMEENA

'You know I can't rush off around the world with you and Michael, Salina. I can't take that much time away from my constituents,' Tasmeena said.

'Actually, you could. I asked mum, and she said that there are no pressing parliamentary issues pending and you haven't taken a real break for years, and that there is nothing to stop you. You have email and IslamNet access almost everywhere, so that's an excuse, Tasmeena. What's going on?'

She sighed, looked seriously at Salina, and shook her head, 'You'll say I'm crazy and dismiss my concerns.'

Salina was surprised at the tone and thought for a moment before saying, 'Are you jealous of my relationship with Michael? Is it our twin connection that worries you? If it is, I understand. I do, truly. Others have told us this as well. I know that we can be all consuming when we're together in a crowd. But we're not like that professionally, when we're away on an assignment. Honestly. It is all professional and about the job or the interviews. So, tell me, what is it, specifically?'

Tasmeena sighed deeply, pausing, considering how to make herself understood without hurting Salina's feelings. 'Okay, yes, it is the twin thing, I suppose, but hear me out...' she sighed again. 'I do understand that the relationship you have is unique, or special. It makes me feel... not excluded, that's not the issue... inferior might be closer to the mark.'

'Inferior?' Salina frowned.

'Sort of. Like, I could never be that intuitive with Michael, and so, he might become disappointed in me, if I don't get him, instantly. He could start to compare me with you and what you have together and then maybe resent me. Oh, look, I know this sounds idiotic. A wife should never be jealous of a brother-sister relationship, but... well, crazy or not, it's real to me, I'm sorry.'

Salina nodded, thinking. 'Yes, I understand what you mean. Look, I want Michael to teach Freddy to be able to do my filming and sound work, so that he and I can go off alone, and Michael can edit what we send him from here, at home with you.'

'And Michael is OK with that?'

'More than that. He wants to pull back and spend most of his time here. He's sick of the travel and the suitcase routines and... well, although you might not believe me, he's sick of being with me all of the time too,' Salina laughed.

'Truly?'

'Yes. Look don't get me wrong. I love Michael and we will never have our bond broken. But we both need to put our efforts into you and Freddy, rather than rely on each other so much. It has been fantastic working as a duo. We get more done because we don't need to second guess each other. There's an intuitiveness that we just have together, obviously. But we also need to grow, and Michael has felt stifled lately. He needs to do his own thing, and... sow his seeds.'

'Are you... do you mean... is that a euphemism, Salina?'

Smiling broadly, giggling a little, Salina said, 'Let me just say that I am looking forward to becoming an aunty long before I'm a mother. So, don't bother buying any more contraceptives.'

WEDDINGS

In keeping with the growing mood change towards lower levels of Quranic adherence and less emphasis on 'the old ways', the twins' joint wedding, held in a local park, was officiated by a civil celebrant. Adhering to Muslim tradition, both couples included a meher, the bridal wealth obligation, requiring a prompt and a deferred amount for the bride. The rings given to the brides represented 'the prompt', and the deferred amount given to the brides, for their security and guarantee of freedom within the marriage, were represented by the official Titles of Abode, the City of London Council's guarantee of property usage in perpetuity, which had been brought into being as the city's population grew, to avoid conflict over housing and to protect historical places. By presenting these property documents, Freddy and Michael were publicly showing that their wives would be independently secure if the marriages broke down.

Both couples declined a recitation of the Fatihah, the first chapter of the Quran, and associated blessings, but they made traditional vows.

'I Salina, offer you myself in marriage in accordance with the instructions of the Holy Quran and the Holy Prophet, peace and blessing be upon Him. I pledge, in honesty and with sincerity, to be for you an obedient and faithful wife.'

Freddy followed, saying, 'I pledge, in honesty and sincerity, to be for you a faithful and helpful husband.'

The celebrant then turned to Tasmeena and Michael, and they repeated the same words.

The marriage contracts were signed in a nikah ceremony. Freddy was the first to propose to Salina. His witnesses were Charlie and Mina, and he stated the details of his meher. Freddy and Salina then demonstrated their free will by repeating the word 'qabul' three times, meaning 'I accept' in Arabic.

Michael and Tasmeena took their turn next, repeating the process, and after the two couples and two male witnesses signed the contracts, the marriages were deemed to be legal according to civil and religious law. Each couple then ate and shared a sweet date.

Following the ceremonies, the Walima wedding feast began, and there was a mountain of food for the guests, which numbered over three hundred people. Traditional symbols of fertility and plenty were included, like fish, chicken, rice, and candy-covered almonds, but the feast itself was less abundant than some traditional weddings, as both couples expressed a desire to not overdo the formalities. Charlie and Mina understood and only Tasmeena's parents seemed slightly aggrieved about the less flamboyant arrangements.

About five hours later the festivities began to peter out and both couples went through a semi-traditional send off into their new lives. In their cases, each couple retired to their new homes, which they'd been living in for some weeks, unofficially. Neither bride was worried about her wedding night as both couples had been sexually active for a while. Although each of the twins had lost their virginity to their new spouses, Freddy and Tasmeena could not say the same. Whilst Tasmeena's experience was limited, Freddy had enjoyed a more interesting past.

HABBIB

'You did well, Fadel. It must have been a difficult role to play,' Paul Habbib said, and beside him in the Oval Office, Malik Shah concurred, nodding his head.

'There were certainly surprises and challenges, Mr President,' Fadel replied, and I was lucky that my instinct on Commander Hukkeri here,' he nodded in the other guest's direction, 'was sound, or I would have been in real trouble.'

'Did you ever suspect Hussain, Commander?' Shah asked.

'I wish I could say yes, Prime Minister, but whilst I thought the scenarios were a little odd, I was fooled into assuming they were intended that way to stretch the younger officers' thinking. And as for the ploy of the amended rounds and missiles, I totally failed to check into those and I feel a fool that I never insisted on a live fire demo, at least for the sake of the participants in the exercise.'

'We can all be wise after the event,' General Cummins said. 'One of the failings of rank structure is that we assume our superiors know more, and automatically give them the respect of the rank or position. We therefore can be fooled for longer than perhaps would be the case in a civilian situation.'

Habbib said, 'A great pity about Admiral Pereira. You were lucky not to have been killed too, Fadel.'

'I keep playing the whole situation over in my head, trying to see if there could have been a different way to play it. But I don't think there was. And I agree with you, Mr President, that luck had a large part to play in the outcome,' Fadel stated.

Cummins shrugged, 'That's always the case in our professions, luck, instinct, timing, initiative. If any of it went wrong, we wouldn't be here to discuss it. I have read the intel reports. Seems that the Chief you shot had been radicalised by a Turkish operative, since identified and dealt with. We have gone through the crew and another four men were implicated, all armourers. So, Hussain kept the operation tightly controlled.'

'But we still don't know who was pulling the strings higher up, or whether there remains a threat to the Pakindesh Nations,' Habbib added. 'However, Turkey and France have been warned, in less than diplomatic language, that they are on notice.'

'What about the African summit group?' Fadel asked.

Habbib and Shah exchanged glances. Habbib said, 'All I can say is that the people actively involved seem to have been recruited individually, and were not acting on behalf of their governments, apart from President Dhulbahante. He's gone underground for now, but we are looking for him. The others have been detained and are being questioned. I am convinced that Indonesia-Malaysia was not an active participant. It made little strategic sense and high-level discussions tend to confirm that they were an assumed later player if the plans had worked out. The whole idea was somewhat fantastic. But if you are convinced that Allah is on your side and wishes for a more devout world, you can make the plan seem sane. If we Pakindesh leaders had been killed in Rio, and the attack on London had been successful, followed up by a French-Turkish takeover of the U.K., then the symbolism would have perhaps been enough to support a stricter religious view. Thanks be to Allah that it never happened.'

Fadel looked around the group, saw Cummins nod to him, and said, 'Am I the only one here that sees all these events as having a degree of divine intervention? I know, as an operative, that this might make me seem crazy, but especially the failed assassination, that whole escape just stretches belief, doesn't it?'

'We've all thought the same thing,' Shah replied. 'We can't possibly know, can we?'

'May I ask what President Kalil's view is on it?' Fadel pushed.

Habbib laughed, 'I think we all know what Sabal Kalil's views are on this, don't we? And the events add further weight to his hypothesis being supported. What amazes me more is that Kalil has in no way allowed himself to become self-congratulatory. He is calm and secure in his views of the future. More than most of us. Most men would have started to see themselves as some sort of prophet, but Kalil gets extremely angry whenever that is said, even as a joke. He is an amazing man.'

The meeting broke up a little later and Fadel went back to work at the PSS building, which had once been the CIA headquarters at Langley. Commander Hukkeri had been asked to a meeting at Annapolis, where he was thrilled and surprised to be promoted to Captain and given command of the Mysore guided missile destroyer. Cummins flew to the U.K. to meet with their senior military group and increase its defence preparedness.

SOMALIA

President Dhulbahante was angry. He'd felt this way for a month. His personal bodyguard of a dozen hand-picked men kept his hideaway safe from prying eyes or unexpected wanderers, assisted by a screen of more than a hundred men ten kilometres from the camp. Two wives kept his urges under control and allowed him to assuage his anger in any way he wished. Nobody interfered if they heard the odd scream in the night, coming from his elaborate tent. He had arranged this camp about 100km from Hargeisa, the capital city of Somaliland, on the Ethiopian border, partly to get away and think, and partly to be away from Addis Ababa, having learned that the Pakindesh Secret Service was looking for him.

How Al-antaqam had failed in his mission to kill the Pakindesh hierarchy still rankled. He felt impotent, and the previous night that issue arose again, or rather didn't. He had resorted to beating his second wife with a leather belt, instead of raping her. Even punishing her failed to arouse him sufficiently and he kicked her out into the cold.

At about 3am, as the wind was building up, he dozed, aided by a sedative placed in his drink by one his guards, someone that supported Pakindesh. Out of the darkness a slightly built figure appeared on the periphery of the campsite. He'd been walking for four hours, using a tracker to bring him straight to the campsite. Near the perimeter screen of men guarding their President, there was a concentrated hum of snoring and snuffling. They had all been sedated, including the perpetrator. The PSS agent walked slowly towards Dhulbahante's tent, cut the rear panel with a razor-sharp knife, and slipped inside. His target was sleeping on his side. He approached him and took out a gag from his pocket and some cable ties. The ties were carefully placed around his ankles and slowly tightened, enough to limit movement. The same was then done to his hands, which were conveniently lying one upon the other. The gag was then positioned over his mouth and its ties intertwined around his neck. When he next opened his mouth to take a deeper breath, the gag was thrust into it and the ties pulled tightly, waking him immediately, albeit still groggy. He tried to kick out at the man on top of him, but the ties stifled that attempt. A hard punch into his nose quietened his escape attempts.

'I have a message for you, from Sabal Kalil. Do you wish to hear it?' the assailant asked.

Dhulbahante's eyes showed fear, but he nodded.

'Good. Sensible. You are about to die. No don't struggle, it is not worth the effort. Your actions in trying to kill the Pakindesh leaders was foolish. Hiring that assassin was very undiplomatic. You are a backward thinking and barbaric man, and you are not worthy of this new paradise that Allah has provided for us all. President Kalil wants you to know that he has discussed your fate with Allah himself...' Dhulbahante's eyes grew wide, whether in shock or disbelief or anger, it was hard to tell.

'Yes, Kalil is the new Prophet, and the new world will be free of religious thought and adherence, replaced instead by openness, love, equality and joy. Your days are done, and you will perhaps be received in hell, In Sha' Allah. But first I must remove your manhood as a symbol of justice for your mistreatment of women,' he added, ripping open his victim's pants, grabbing his penis and cutting it off with a single slice of his blade. He then removed the gag for a moment and thrust the bloodied penis into the President's mouth and then retied the gag, watching as he slowly choked to death. Stating that Kalil was the new Prophet was something he made up on the spot, just to add a last element of vengeance, so that Dhulbahante would believe in his last moments that he was going to hell, not paradise.

When the deed was completed, he left the tent, retracing his long walk away from the area. Three hours later there was the sound of an aircraft, and a searchlight shone from the air onto a prearranged rendezvous point. The PSS agent shone a pencil-like torch with a green filter and flashed a prearranged signal to guide the helicopter down. It hovered a few feet above the ground, and he climbed aboard into the back seat. The trip out to sea and onto a Pakindesh ship in the Gulf of Aden took an hour or so. Once on board he reported to his superiors and then went to a cabin to sleep, which he did, soundly and for eleven hours.

'She was Samantha's favourite designer. Not such a different rationale. Get with the trend, Riaz. Have you looked at the top ten list of British baby names recently?'

'Can't say I've perused that,' Riaz quipped.

'Well, I did. Just for a laugh, sort of. It included Beyonce, Taylor, Pink would you believe, Adele, William, Harry, Charles, George, and Elizabeth. I forget the others.'

'Lots of nostalgia in the male list, especially for the royal family and singers, clearly.'

'Yes, but more interesting was that Muhammed is down to number 74 now,' Mina said, making an interesting facial expression.

'The tide has definitely turned then?' Riaz noted.

'Seems that way.'

Over lunch, after all the pregnancy congratulations had been exchanged, and the grandchildren played nearby, and the adults chatted of domestic issues, Mina and Riaz sat a little further back from the table, hand in hand, smiling. He looked across at her and whispered, 'I love you to the moon and back.'

She smiled too, snuck a surreptitious kiss on his mouth, and said 'I thank Allah every day for you, Riaz, and for all of this.' She then became a little more serious. 'But I also pray that all of those innocents that were removed are being well looked after, somewhere.'

www.ingramcontent.com/pod-product-compliance
Lightning Source LLC
Chambersburg PA
CBHW060348080526
44583CB00012B/225